MW00622580

Advance Praise for

VALLEY THUNDER

The Battle of New Market and the Opening of the Shenandoah Campaign, May 1864

"*Valley Thunder* surely takes its place now among the dozen finest and most complete accounts of any Civil War action, and it would be hard to name any account of a secondary fight of this size that has been better treated. Knight's study is a contribution not just to Virginia or Confederate literature, but a book that will serve the entire Civil War community for generations to come, and probably much longer than my thirty-six years. The only way we will get a better account is if Breckinridge and the others come to life and give it to us from their own lips."

> — William C. Davis, former editor of *Civil War Times, Illustrated*,
> the author of *The Battle of New Market* (1975),
> and the award-winning author of *Jefferson Davis: The Man and His Hour*

"The Battle of New Market has long been neglected. It's been decades since the last book-length treatment of this interesting battle. Charles Knight has now changed that with *Valley Thunder*, a book on this important engagement destined to become the standard reference on the battle. Based on an intimate knowledge of the battlefield, deep and insightful research into newly-found sources, and with a keen eye toward the interplay between terrain and tactics, Knight's book sheds new light on the significance of this battle."

> — Eric Wittenberg, noted Civil War cavalry historian and the author of many
> books, including (with J. David Petruzzi) *Plenty of Blame to Go Around:
> Jeb Stuart's Controversial Ride to Gettysburg* (Savas Beatie, 2006)

"Charles Knight has provided an insightful and well-researched addition to the catalogue of works on the Battle of New Market. The Battlefield Park staff applaud this effort by one of our former co-workers!"

— Scott H. Harris, Director,
New Market Battlefield State Historical Park

"Charles Knight's book *Valley Thunder* offers an excellent re-appraisal of the battle, using unpublished documents and a fresh assessment of the historical record. He offers a new critique of the classic battle and just in time for the Sesquicentennial of the Civil War."

— Troy D. Marshall, Supervisor of Historical Interpretation,
New Market Battlefield State Historical Park

"Mr. Knight has mined fresh material in an attempt to raise the fog of the battlefield. His use of firsthand accounts provide a fresh look at troop positions and movements. *Valley Thunder* is the first major study in forty years of one of the most important secondary actions of the war. It is an important addition to the library of the war in the Shenandoah Valley."

— Col. Keith E. Gibson,
Director, VMI Museum Operations

VALLEY THUNDER

The Battle of New Market
and the Opening of the
Shenandoah Valley Campaign, May 1864

For Carl Bowler
Best regards
[signature]

Charles R. Knight

New Market, Va
5 - 14 - 11

SB

Savas Beatie
New York and California

© 2010 by Charles R. Knight

All rights reserved. No part of this publication may be reproduced, stored in a retrieval system, or transmitted, in any form or by any means, electronic, mechanical, photocopying, recording, or otherwise, without the prior written permission of the publisher. Printed in the United States of America.

Cataloging-in-Publication Data is available from the Library of Congress.

ISBN 978-1-932714-80-7

05 04 03 02 01   5 4 3 2 1
First edition, first printing

SB

Published by
Savas Beatie LLC
521 Fifth Avenue, Suite 1700
New York, NY 10175

Editorial Offices:

Savas Beatie LLC
P.O. Box 4527
El Dorado Hills, CA 95762
Phone: 916-941-6896
(E-mail) editorial@savasbeatie.com

Savas Beatie titles are available at special discounts for bulk purchases in the United States by corporations, institutions, and other organizations. For more details, please contact Special Sales, P.O. Box 4527, El Dorado Hills, CA 95762, or you may e-mail us at sales@savasbeatie.com, or visit our website at www.savasbeatie.com for additional information.

For my Dad,
who sparked my interest in the Civil War

Benjamin West Clinedinst's painting of the charge of
the VMI Cadets at New Market. *VMI*

Contents

Contents (continued)

Contents (continued)

Maps

Illustrations appear throughout the book
for the convenience of the reader

Veterans and townspeople alike gathered on May 15, 1926, for the dedication of a roadside marker about the battle. An elderly Eliza Crim, who with Moses Ezekiel had cared for the dying Cadet Thomas G. Jefferson, is leaning against the monument left of center. Elon Henkel, one of the owners of Henkel Printing (which printed the town newspaper), stands in foreground at the far left with hat and papers in hand. Noted Valley historian John W. Wayland is behind and right of Henkel, with glasses and light gray suit. This monument originally stood on terrain occupied by the 62nd Virginia, but was moved in 1986 to the battlefield park picnic area. *VMI Archives*

Foreword

I t seems a bit strange to be writing a Foreword to a book that in effect supersedes one's own, but that nevertheless is the case here, and it is a pleasure. In 1975, I published *The Battle of New Market*, my second book. For the ensuing thirty-six years it was generally regarded as the definitive work on the battle. The Virginia Military Institute even printed its own edition and issued copies of it to its cadets in the 1970s. The research was great fun tracking down descendants of most of the officers on both sides, and spending many days in the archives at the Institute and elsewhere. Indeed, the research extended as far as Alaska and even a Hungary still behind the old Iron Curtain.

No one finds everything, of course, and it is an axiom of history that new sources start coming to light almost as soon as a book is in print and it becomes too late to use them. Over the years I kept an eye on new findings relating to New Market, but never really thought about the accumulating weight of them. Fortunately someone else did. Charles Knight, who spent several years working at the New Market Battlefield Park in Virginia, devoted years of study to the same sources I found, and uncovered a host of new ones. The result is that his marvelous new book *Valley Thunder* does not rewrite the entire story of the battle and the men who fought it, but it does rewrite significant portions of it and closes many a gap that I was unable to fill.

Valley Thunder is simply the last word we are ever likely to have or need on this crucial small action in 1864. Even handed and non-partisan, Knight gives credit where credit is due, and in the process brings to the fore the actions of some units hitherto slighted, especially on the Confederate side. No one understands the topography of the battlefield better, and Knight's maps reveal a grasp of the nuances of the ground that—when integrated with the movements of the combatants—show better than ever before how this action played out. I am happy to see that he accords General John C. Breckinridge full marks for the ability he displayed in winning the battle against heavy odds, and also lesser commanders like Gabriel Wharton and John Echols. If the Union commander Franz Sigel does not rise much in general estimation, still the ability of his subordinates like Henry Du Pont, Joseph Thoburn, and others reveal why a defeat did not turn into an utter disaster.

Valley Thunder surely takes its place now among the dozen finest and most complete accounts of any Civil War action, and it would be hard to name any account of a secondary fight of this size that has been better treated. *Valley Thunder* is a contribution not just to Virginia or Confederate literature, but a book that will serve the entire Civil War community for generations to come, and probably much longer than my thirty-six years. The only way we will get a better account is if Breckinridge and the others come to life and give it to us from their own lips.

— William C. Davis

Introduction

There has been no shortage of published accounts about the May 15, 1864, Battle of New Market, a relatively small engagement made famous by the participation of the Cadet Corps from the Virginia Military Institute. The fighting even inspired a popular children's book (in which one of the slain cadets returns to the battlefield in ghostly form to look for his lost watch) and at least one novel focusing on the cadets. "This is not a new story. It has been related and written many times," explained an early historian of the battle. "Furthermore, it could be told briefly."[1]

Then why tell it again?

Although small in scope by Civil War standards with only about 10,000 total troops involved, the spring combat marked the beginning of the 1864 campaign in the Shenandoah Valley. New Market pitted Major General John C. Breckinridge, a former vice president of the United States, against Major General Franz Sigel, a former German revolutionary who owed his position more to political influence than military merit. The campaign and battle included running cavalry fights, fascinating interactions with Valley civilians, forced marches, bold infantry attacks during a heavy rain storm, flanking operations, and a chaotic retreat that nearly cost the Federals the loss of a small but important army. But it was the participation of the young men from VMI

---

1 William Couper, *Virginia Military Institute and the Battle of New Market* (np, nd), 1.

that catapulted the battle into the popular imagination of the public at large and has given New Market a stature in Southern folklore that arguably exceeds its military significance. This romanticizing of the battle began not long after the guns fell silent on that stormy day in May 1864.

One writer in the early 20th century described the historiography of the battle this way:

> The amount of literature of the Battle of New Market is unusual. In the North and in the South, following the official reports, came the published letters of many participants. Then came addresses by accomplished and eloquent men, histories of regiments and histories of the campaign. And with this growing literature came divergencies [sic], contradictions, and some rhetorical over-statement.[2]

If one believed popular myth, some 250 teenage boys almost single-handedly whipped a much larger Yankee army and captured several pieces of artillery in the process. In reality, thousands of Confederate troops fought at New Market, but seared into the popular consciousness is the idea that they played only a supporting role while the cadets carried the day. A Virginia Department of Historic Resources highway marker placed alongside the old Valley Pike decades ago to commemorate the battle did nothing to dispel this popular notion. In fact, it had the opposite effect:

> On the hills to the north took place the Battle of New Market, May 15, 1864. The Union Army, under General Franz Sigel, faced southwest. John C. Breckinridge, once Vice-President of the United States, commanded the Confederates. Colonel Scott Shipp[3] [sic] commanded the Cadet Corps of the Virginia Military Institute, which distinguished itself, capturing a battery. The battle ended in Sigel's retreat northward.

Even the entry for the battlefield in the *Virginia Landmarks Register* contains faulty information: "The VMI cadets . . . distinguished themselves with the

---

2 James Power Smith, "The New Market Campaign," *Southern Historical Society Papers*, vol. 41, (1916), 155-6. A veteran of the Rockbridge Artillery, Smith is best known as an officer on the staff of Lieutenant General Thomas J. "Stonewall" Jackson. A Presbyterian minister after the war, Smith was one of the most prolific writers of Stonewall Jackson's inner circle and was very active in veterans organizations in the years after the war.

3 "Shipp" is the postwar spelling of his surname. At the time of the Battle of New Market, he spelled it with only one "p." The wartime spelling is used throughout the book.

capture of a battery and an enemy flag."[4] The Cadets captured one gun, not "a battery," and they did not capture any enemy flags.

In reply to an earlier publication in the *Army and Navy Journal*, VMI historian Jennings C. Wise penned an impassioned synopsis in 1912 about the battle's place in history:

> The facts of an event of such importance to the Southland, so cherished in the annals of war, so unsurpassed in point of gallantry even in the story of medieval chivalry, should not be mis-stated in any respect. The record of this event is no longer one prized solely by the people of Virginia and the South. The glory of the deed is a common heritage of the English-speaking race.[5]

Noted early 20th century Shenandoah Valley historian John Wayland explained *why* the cadets' role had been so oft-repeated and embellished:

> The importance of the charge of the cadet battalion in this battle has no doubt been over-emphasized; but it was striking and thrilling and effective; and because of the youth of the cadets, their steady discipline, and their splendid heroism, their unexpected participation in this battle has been given the widest renown in martial song, on flaming canvas, and in cherished story. It was a thing to stir the blood and to grow vividly upon the memory from generation to generation.[6]

Accounts of the battle appeared in print within days because town residents had the good fortune of having a local newspaper editor present on the field

---

4 Calder Loth, ed., *The Virginia Landmarks Register* (Charlottesville, VA, 1986, Third Edition), 424. Added to the *Register* in 1970, the complete entry reads: "Gen. John C. Breckenridge's [sic] Confederate brigades, joined by the 247-man cadet corps of the Virginia Military Institute, repulsed the Union forces at New Market on May 15, 1964 [sic], thus preserving the supply and communication lines between the Army of Northern Virginia and the Shenandoah Valley. This victory permitted General Lee to concentrate his full efforts toward halting the Union advance on Richmond. In their only engagement of the war, the VMI cadets, the eldest of them under eighteen, distinguished themselves with a gallant charge and the capture of a battery and an enemy flag. The 160-acre battlefield, just west of the town of New Market, is owned by the Commonwealth and exhibited as a historical park and a memorial to the cadets who fought and died there. On the eastern edge of the battlefield is the restored Bushong House, used by both sides as a hospital."

5 Jennings C. Wise, "A Letter Concerning a Noble Tradition," *A Scrapbook of Papers*, (Richmond, VA, 1912), 11.

6 John W. Wayland, *Battle of New Market*, (New Market, VA, 1926), 10. Wayland is considered the preeminent historian of the Shenandoah Valley and wrote more than thirty published works about Valley life and Valley history.

during the battle. Writers were quick to point out the gallant role played by the cadets of VMI. After all, were not the finest youth of the Confederacy enrolled in the so-called "West Point of the South?" And were not also these same young men destined to be the leaders of a future Confederate Army? Their baptism of fire *had* to be reported.

Unfortunately for history and for the other Southern troops on the field, little else was mentioned and the tactical details of the battle began to fall by the wayside. The only Southern battle report after the war to find its way into the *Official Records* was written by Lieutenant Colonel Scott Ship (the commander of the VMI Cadets). This lone account served to exacerbate the already skewed view held by the public at large. The only known copy of a report of the New Market campaign, which is housed at VMI, is an unfinished draft written by one of Breckinridge's aides and published here for the first time in Appendix 2.[7] General Sigel's complete report also failed to find its way into the *Official Records*. This important document, housed in the Sigel Papers at Western Reserve Historical Society, is also published for the first time in the same appendix.

In the years following the war, accounts of the engagement began to appear in larger quantities. Most of the cadets left some memoir of that day, be it a published account or a letter to a former comrade-in-arms. Nearly to a man, the cadets believed that May 15, 1864, was a turning point in their lives. And indeed it was and rightly should have been. What was overlooked was that for most of the other men in both blue and in gray, May 15th was simply another date in a list of bloody dates. Around the turn of the century articles on the battle—some of them quite acidic in tone—appeared in *Confederate Veteran*. As with most postwar accounts, the writers disagreed about many things, including which regiment could rightly lay claim to captured artillery, which regiment broke first under fire, and in some instances even where a particular unit was on the field (in some cases this latter issue remains cloudy even today).[8]

---

7   The largest and most historically valuable collection of New Market-related material is held at the Virginia Military Institute Archives. In addition to Breckinridge's unfinished official report (see Appendix 2), the archives includes memoirs of dozens of cadets who participated in the battle, as well as correspondence between cadets and other veterans of the battle and Edward R. Turner, the first "non-partisan" historian of the battle, during the research for his book *The New Market Campaign*.

8   For example, the location of, and role played by, the 30th Virginia Battalion during the battle has plagued historians for decades, as has the small company of Confederate engineers attached to Breckinridge's command. More perplexing is the status of the 23rd Virginia Cavalry. Some accounts have these men fighting dismounted with the infantry, while others

Even the senior officers at New Market disagreed about how the various pieces of the battle puzzle fit together. George H. Smith, commander of the 62nd Virginia Mounted Infantry, and George M. Edgar, commander of the 26th Virginia Battalion, spent years compiling material on the battle. In writing to Edgar more than four decades after the fight, Smith confessed, "I thought I knew something about the battle of New Market at its conclusion, but have been so much mystified by the various accounts given of the affair that I have come to realize that I know nothing of it."[9]

Each commander (Smith and Edgar) was convinced that his respective regiment—and his regiment alone—was responsible for the outcome of the fight at New Market. Both were determined to prove their point, differing opinions be damned. One wonders what each man thought of the other's accounts of the battle during their long years of correspondence. Edgar's notes offer a clue. When Smith claimed for his own regiment honors that Edgar rightfully thought belonged to his own men, Edgar wrote in the margins of Smith's account, "This is enormously absurd. . . . It pains me to read this."[10]

The first academic book-length study of New Market did not appear until 1912, nearly five decades after the battle. Edward R. Turner's *The New Market Campaign* (Richmond, VA: Whittet & Sheperson, 1912) was the inaugural effort by a non-participant to understand the action and share his findings with general readers. Turner believed that his work would be "a final statement" on the battle.[11]

Unfortunately, Turner's effort has a clearly Southern bias because his sources were nearly all Confederate veterans of the engagement. He drew heavily from Colonels Smith and Edgar's collections, which are invaluable to any study of the battle (although Smith's perceptions and opinions on the fighting changed frequently and can be very confusing). Although some of Turner's conclusions are questionable, the book is of considerable value to

---

have them mounted with the rest of the Southern cavalry. Harder still (in fact a nearly impossible task) is trying to pinpoint the location of the various regiments and battalions comprising the Federal cavalry on the field on May 15. In all cases the confusion arises, at least in part, because of the lack of primary source material from those units.

9   George H. Smith to George M. Edgar, March 16, 1906, G. M. Edgar Papers, University of North Carolina, Chapel Hill. The Edgar Papers is another invaluable collection of New Market material. Edgar may have been working on a book of his own about the battle until he essentially became Edward Turner's assistant for Turner's own book on the fighting.

10   George H. Smith to George M. Edgar, April 22, 1908, Edgar Papers.

11   Edward R. Turner, *The New Market Campaign* (Richmond, VA, 1912), viii.

historians of the battle and is almost a primary source in and of itself because several key Confederate officers guided Turner through his research and writing. It is not an exaggeration to say that the book was written, in places, by George Edgar. As with most of the early scholarship on the war, Turner had the benefit of talking with veterans. Although Turner specifically stated that his intention was to put in perspective the role played by the various units, he (apparently unwittingly) helped to perpetuate the cadet legend. Some veterans charged that Turner attempted to please everyone, and in the end pleased no one. VMI's early historian, Jennings Wise, relied heavily on Turner's book in his own 1915 history of the institute, but labeled Turner's conclusions "pitiful," adding that "Turner is hopelessly lost in the fog which he has done more to create than any previous historian of the battle."[12]

Other works of varying importance appeared over the ensuing decades, but it was not until 1975 that an impartial and accurate study of the battle appeared in William C. Davis' *The Battle of New Market*. Davis' study has stood for decades as the definitive account of the battle. In the thirty-five years since it first appeared, however, several new and important sources have come to light that alter our understanding of the fighting. The official report of Union casualties, lost for decades, recently resurfaced at the National Archives. Its discovery changes which regiment has the distinction of suffering the highest casualty rate at New Market. Also, the role some of the units played on the field, which could not be conclusively determined by Davis, can now be addressed with more certainty. Other newly discovered sources have changed our view of the role played by the VMI cadets. As it turns out, they were not the only underage soldiers present during the campaign. A company of teenage boys from Rockingham County comprised one of the "local reserve" units and earned its own laurels in a cavalry action several days prior to the main battle. The myth that New Market was the only time a military school's cadet corps was engaged in battle was put to rest by the appearance in 1997 of James Lee Conrad's *The Young Lions: Confederate Cadets at War*. As Conrad explained, the South Carolina Military Academy (today's Citadel), the Georgia Military Institute, Florida Military Institute, and the University of Alabama all had cadets who came under enemy fire in the Western Theater and along the Atlantic coast.[13]

12 Jennings C. Wise, *Virginia Military Institute: Military History* (Lynchburg, VA, 1915), 324.

13 William C. Davis, *The Battle of New Market* (Baton Rouge, LA, 1975); James Lee Conrad, *The Young Lions: Confederate Cadets at War* (Mechanicsburg, PA, 1997). Conrad is a VMI graduate.

"How men do differ as to what occurred at New Market," proclaimed a former Northern artilleryman to his comrades at a veteran's reunion in 1912. He continued:

> I have two or three accounts written by comrades, and they do not seem to agree very well. We all do not see alike. There is one thing I do know about the Battle of New Market, and that is this: Breckenridge [sic] gave us a beautiful whipping that day. We ought to have won the battle and we would have won it had we been properly handled. . . . We had marched about forty-five miles, fought a battle, and it was all done in about twenty-four hours.[14]

Of the outcome of the battle, there can be no disagreement.

*   *   *

I have tried, as far as possible, to allow the participants to speak for themselves. Modern writers cannot capture the same tone and emotion as one who was actually there. As a former tour guide and historical interpreter at New Market Battlefield State Historical Park, I have told this story many times. Unfortunately, many of the best *new* sources about the battle came to my attention after leaving New Market, so I was unable to weave them into my tours. Many are presented here, in the context of the New Market campaign, for the first time.

14 Charles H. Senseny, *Address Delivered by C.H. Senseny to his Comrades at the Fiftieth Anniversary of the Enlistment of Battery D, 1st W.Va. Light Artillery* (Wheeling, W.Va., 1912).

Acknowledgments

There are many people I would like to thank for their invaluable assistance in seeing this project to completion.

Civil War author Eric Wittenberg responded to an out-of-the-blue inquiry from a perfect stranger seeking assistance in publishing a manuscript. Eric not only replied, but answered many questions from this first-time author and read the early versions of this manuscript. Historian and author William C. Davis likewise read and commented on this work, answered many of my questions about some of the sources he used in his study of this battle, and graciously provided the Foreword. The late John Heatwole of Bridgewater, Virginia, provided several valuable source materials, photographs, and maps, and also agreed to review the manuscript. Without John's constant support, I likely would have given up on this project many years ago.

Thanks also to the wonderful staff at New Market Battlefield State Historical Park, and especially Judy Drury, Whitney Stroop, and Gary Cunningham for their continued support, and Scott Harris and Troy Marshall for their valuable assistance in providing feedback, images, and new source material. Colonel Keith Gibson at Virginia Military Institute also answered several nagging questions and likewise was quick to answer calls for more material.

I would also like to thank my co-workers at the MacArthur Memorial for their continued support and feedback. It was deeply appreciated.

A huge "thanks" is due everyone at Savas Beatie, and in particular Managing Director Thedore P. Savas for taking on a new author, and Market Director Sarah Keeney for all of her marketing expertise. George Skoch provided the excellent maps for this study, which he interpreted from the drawings of "an ambidextrous squirrel." Lee Merideth put the final touches onto the book with his index.

Other individuals and institutions who deserve recognition for their assistance, in no particular order, include: Maj. Diane Jacob and Mary Laura Kludy, VMI Archives; Michelle McClintick, Virginia Historical Society; Ruth Ann Coski, Museum of the Confederacy; Sheila Biles, U.S. Military Academy; John Hoffman and Robert Owens, Illinois Historical Survey; Ted Hutchinson, Massachusetts Historical Society; John Jackson, Virginia Tech Archives; John Howard and Ted Alexander, Antietam National Battlefield Park; LeAnn Fawver, U.S. Army Military History Institute; Mort Kunstler and Lissette Portillo, Kunster Enterprises; Marge McNinch, Hagley Museum & Library;

Mary Boccaccio, East Carolina University; Sue Greenhagen, Morrisville College; Dwayne Cox, Auburn University; Polly Armstrong and Roberto Trujillo, Stanford University; Vicki Weiss, New York State Library; Joan Ferry, Rice University; Anne Skilton, University of North Carolina, Chapel Hill; Anne Salsich and Connie Hammond, Western Reserve Historical Society; Chris Kolbe and Paige Buckbinder, Virginia State Library; Jan Grenci and Patrick Kerwin, Library of Congress; Lisa McCown and Vaughn Stanley, Washington & Lee University; Christy Venham, West Virginia University; Skip Theberge, NOAA; Jack Masters, Gallatin, Tn.; Joseph Whitehorne, Middletown, Va.; Jerry Holsworth, Winchester, Va.; Terry Lowry, Charleston, W.Va.; Robert Moore, Star, Id.; Andrew De Cusati, Gettysburg, Pa.; Joanne Kartak, Queen Valley, Az; Charles Harris, Ooltewah, Tn; John Glazebrook, Ashland, Va.; Casey Billhimer, Elkton, Va.; Richard Bazelow, Walden, NY; Janet Greentree, Burke, Va.; Bonnie Chumley, Winchester, Va.; Megan Chumley and E. Howard Goodwin, Charlottesville, Va.; Carole Morris Creasman, Sinks Grove, W.Va.; Larry Strayer, Kettering, Oh.; Nancy Armstrong, Endwell, NY; Brian Mathias, U.S. Army; Don Polly, Leesburg, Fl.; Wilda Hogbin, Petersburg, W.Va.; Mark Dudrow, Winchester, Va.; John Crim, New Market, Va.; Virginia Toney, Houston, Tx.; Elizabeth Swiger, Freeport, Fl.; Kristie Poehler of Battlefield Journal.

Finally, a big "thank you" to my wife Sara for tolerating this long project.

Chapter 1

The Breadbasket of the Confederacy

Ⅰ n late April 1864, Kit Hanger of Augusta County, Virginia, wrote a letter to
her cousin in North Carolina. "We are expecting a large fight to come of[f]
in the Valley," she explained, "and I dread it very mutch [sic]."[1] Her fears
proved well founded. On the day that she wrote her cousin, a Union army was
moving into the northern end of the Shenandoah Valley. Its objective was the
town of Staunton, the center of Hanger's picturesque southern Shenandoah
region.

In the spring of 1864, the Shenandoah Valley was still a vibrant farming
community. Although the area had already felt the hard hand of war, and
thousands of its sons were in the ranks of the Southern army, its farms still
produced supplies for the war effort. As long as Confederate troops occupied
the region, those supplies would continue to flow. And as long as those troops
were there in some strength, they were a threat to launch a raid into
Pennsylvania, Maryland, or West Virginia, or to harass the right (western) flank
of the Union Army of the Potomac operating across the Blue Ridge Mountains
in north-central Virginia.

The onset of 1864 brought a new general to Washington, with a new
strategy designed to break the back of the Confederacy and end the war for
good. It would be for future historians to debate exactly when and where it had

---

1 Kit Hanger to Julia Houser, April 28, 1864, John F. Houser Papers, Perkins Library, Duke
University.

occurred, but for many in the South it was becoming apparent by the beginning of 1864 that the winds of war had shifted and no longer favored the Confederacy. "Our affairs look gloomy, very gloomy," concluded a pessimistic Augusta County resident.[2]

The Shenandoah Valley is nestled between the Blue Ridge Mountains to the east and the Alleghenies to the west. Approximately 125 miles in length, the Valley is one of the most productive agricultural regions in the South. Drained by and named for the Shenandoah River, which rises between Staunton and Lexington and flows northward to its confluence with the Potomac River at Harpers Ferry, the geography of the region is the source for some peculiar local terminology. Because the river flows from south to north, the northern end is referred to as the "lower" Valley, and the southern end as the "upper" Valley. Thus, moving north is to go "down" the Valley, and traveling south is moving "up" the Valley.

Neatly bisecting the central Valley is the massive Massanutten Mountain. While its name implies a single peak, it is in reality a series of ridges nearly 50 miles long, stretching from Harrisonburg in the south to Front Royal at its northern end. The area to the west of the Massanutten is known as the Shenandoah Valley proper, and through which flows the river's North Fork. (The North and South Fork of the Shenandoah combine near Front Royal.) The Valley east of the Massanutten is somewhat narrower and is drained by the South Fork of the Shenandoah. This section of the valley is known as the Page or Luray Valley. The mountain is passable only at its center, where a turnpike connects New Market on the west to Luray on the east through New Market Gap. A smaller depression in the Massanutten itself, known as Fort Valley, extends northward from the gap. Samuel Kercheval, author of the first history of the Shenandoah Valley, described Massanutten as "something of the shape of the letter Y, or perhaps more the shape of the houns and tongue of a wagon."[3] A small tollhouse stood at the crest of New Market Gap, explained one historian of the region, "from which each of the valleys of the North and South [Forks of the Shenandoah] present to the delighted vision of the traveler a most enchanting view of the country for a vast distance. The little thrifty

2   Joseph A. Waddell diary, January 1, 1864, Albert & Shirley Small Special Collections Library, University of Virginia.

3   Samuel Kercheval, *A History of the Valley of Virginia* (Strasburg, VA, 1925), 306.

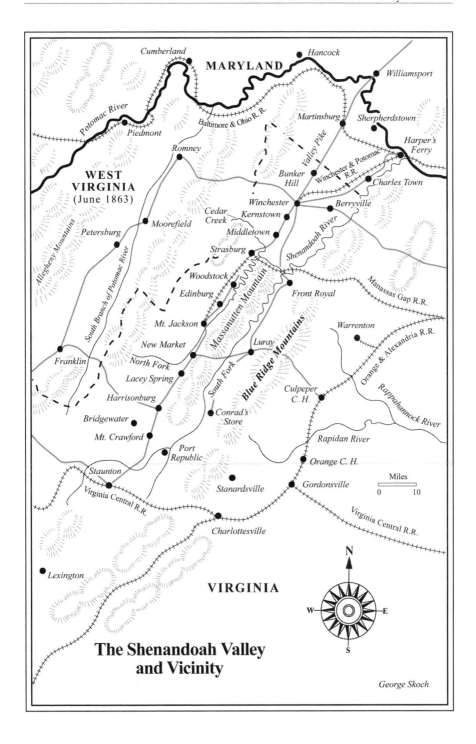

The Shenandoah Valley and Vicinity

George Skoch

village of New Market, with a great number of farms . . . are seen in full relief" at the western base.[4]

The Valley had perhaps one of the best roads in the entire country at the time of the Civil War. The Valley Pike, one of only a handful of hard-surface roads in Virginia, connected Staunton with Martinsburg. The Pike, with its macadamized (mainly gravel) surface, was completed about 1840 and could be traversed in virtually all weather, when rains turned other dirt roads into almost impassable quagmires. Toll booths were situated along the Pike every five miles.[5]

Several railroads connected the Valley with eastern Virginia. The Virginia Central Railroad had its terminus just west of Staunton and served as the major supply link with the Confederate capital of Richmond. The Virginia & Tennessee Railroad, though not in the Shenandoah Valley itself, passed through the mountains of southwestern Virginia, connecting its two namesake states. In the lower Valley, the Baltimore & Ohio Railroad followed the Potomac, connecting Washington and Baltimore with points west. For most of its length, the railroad was on the Maryland side of the river, but it crossed to the southern shore at Harpers Ferry and continued on to Martinsburg and into what is now West Virginia. A spur of the B&O ran south into Winchester. Also paralleling the Potomac was the Chesapeake & Ohio Canal, another vital east-west link. The Manassas Gap Railroad crossed into the Valley east of Front Royal and stretched as far south as Mount Jackson. While these railroads and the canal provided several reliable east-west routes, no continuous north-south railroad existed in the Valley. The Valley Pike, along with several lesser roads, provided the only means of travel up and down the scenic region.

The Valley was as fertile as it was beautiful in the early 1860s. It was those qualities that had first drawn settlers to the region a century earlier. Most of the original settlers—many of them German or Scotch-Irish—migrated south from Pennsylvania, following the greater valley system of which the Shenandoah is but a part. By the 1860s, large farms, not plantations as in the deep South but sizeable nonetheless, populated the area. So plentiful were the harvests that the Valley would be known during the Civil War years as the "Breadbasket of the Confederacy." The region also had several small iron

---

4 *Ibid.*, 306. New Market was originally known as "Crossroads." The town was settled in the mid-18th century, although the present town of New Market was officially created in 1785.

5 Arthur Hildreth, *A Brief History of New Market and Vicinity* (New Market, VA, 1964), 9.

furnaces, which provided the raw materials used by the railroads before the war, and artillery and other articles of war after 1861. Beyond the southern extremities of the Valley in southwest Virginia were lead and salt mines, which would produce most of the Confederacy's supply of these important materials. An early historian of the Valley described it as "Beautiful to look upon, and so fertile that it was styled the granary of Virginia, rich in its well-filled barns, its cattle, its busy mills, the Valley furnished from its abundant crops much of the subsistence of Lee's army."[6]

The Valley was mostly anti-secessionist in sentiment in 1861, though for the most part its citizens remained loyal to Confederate interests once Virginia seceded. (The northwestern counties of Virginia, by way of contrast, separated to form the state of West Virginia in 1863.) While there were some slaves in the region, the numbers did not approach those of Tidewater Virginia. Valley farms were largely worked by the families themselves, and the supplies they furnished the Confederacy fed the Army of Northern Virginia.

The military significance of the Shenandoah Valley was readily apparent in 1861 to authorities in both Richmond and Washington. Confederate forces, initially commanded by Thomas J. "Stonewall" Jackson, had been concentrated at Harpers Ferry to resist any Federal incursion. As an invasion route, the Valley favored the Confederacy. Running southwest to northeast, it pointed directly into the heart of Pennsylvania and Maryland—with the northern (lower) end of the Valley spilling out north of Washington, D.C—with the opposite end deflecting any Union advance up the Valley away from Richmond. The several gaps in the mountains that allowed access to the Valley could be defended by small numbers of troops, which could screen the movements of a larger body of men operating in the Valley proper.

In the spring of 1862, Jackson frustrated attempts by three separate Union columns to capture the region. In the process, he raised alarm in the Northern capital in general, and with President Abraham Lincoln in particular. The Union commander-in-chief was worried that Jackson might attempt a direct attack upon the capital. As a result, Lincoln decided to shift large numbers of troops to the city's defenses instead of to the front where they were originally intended to be employed.

Later in 1863, Robert E. Lee led his Army of Northern Virginia through the Valley to begin his invasion of the North. His movements and intentions were

---

6   George E. Pond, *The Shenandoah Valley in 1864* (Wilmington, NC, 1989), 2.

well masked until he overwhelmed a Union garrison at Winchester in mid-June. After the defeat at Gettysburg, Lee retired into the Valley to rest and resupply his army, as he had done after his first invasion into Maryland had been turned back at Sharpsburg the previous year.

The vast amount of territory and the disproportionate number of troops assigned to it made the region a nightmare for Union commanders and a haven for guerrillas and bushwhackers. Cavalry raids routinely targeted the railroads, especially the B&O line. Residents of the lower Valley would sometimes wake up to discover their homes well within the lines of one army, and by nightfall be occupied by the other side, only to find change again the following day. Winchester, the road hub of the lower Valley, changed hands during the war an estimated 72 times—more than any other town in American history.[7]

During the winter of 1863-64, Ulysses S. Grant was named General in Chief of the Union armies. Grant had amassed an impressive war record. His capture of Forts Henry and Donelson in Tennessee in early 1862 provided the North with its first major field victories. Two months later, Grant absorbed a stunning Confederate surprise attack at Shiloh on April 6 that nearly pushed his army into the Tennessee River, reorganized his men, and drove the enemy from the field the following day. Although many in and out of the army questioned his fitness to command because of his reputed fondness for the bottle, Grant had become a favorite of President Lincoln because of his aggressive nature in the field. From late 1862 through the summer of 1863, Grant worked tirelessly to capture Vicksburg, the last Confederate stronghold on the Mississippi River. His daring plan to cross the river below the city, move inland, and attack it from the east was successful, and the city (and its defending army) surrendered on July 4, 1863. Later that fall in October and November, Grant assumed command in Tennessee. After careful preparation he attacked, knocking the Confederate Army of Tennessee into northern Georgia and lifting the siege of Chattanooga. This impressive string of victories convinced Lincoln that Grant was the man who could draw up and execute the blueprint for final victory.

When word of Grant's appointment reached Richmond, most of the fighting men in gray were not impressed. Lieutenant Colonel Walter H. Taylor, an officer on Lee's staff, expressed a view shared by many: "I do not think he

---

7   Richard R. Duncan, *Beleaguered Winchester: A Virginia Community at War, 1861-1865* (Baton Rouge, LA, 2007), ix. There is some debate as to the number of times Winchester changed hands. I have selected Duncan's figure of 72 because his is the most current as of this writing.

[Grant] is to be feared. He has been much overrated and in my opinion . . . owes more of his reputation to . . . bad management [by his opponents] than to his own sagacity and ability." Taylor predicted that Grant "will shortly come to grief" because of the different caliber of commanders he would be facing in the east.[8]

Grant did not assume new responsibilities unprepared. To date, there had been no overall strategy employed by the Union high command. Instead, each army had operated more or less independently in its respective theater, with little or no cooperation from other forces. This policy, or lack thereof, had allowed the Confederates to shift troops from one threatened area to another. Like the man, Grant's plan was relatively simple: a simultaneous advance by all Union armies, with the destruction of their rival Confederate forces as their main goal, rather than the mere occupation of territory. Territorial conquest and occupation would be a by-product of crippling Confederate forces.

The actual execution of Grant's plan would be three-fold. Major General William T. Sherman would advance into Georgia against the Army of Tennessee. Major General Nathaniel Banks would lead a movement into Louisiana and southern Arkansas to finish off Confederate resistance west of the Mississippi River. In Virginia, Grant would oversee the operations of Major General George G. Meade's Army of the Potomac against its old adversary, Robert E. Lee and the Army of Northern Virginia, traveling with the army rather than remaining in the capital.

To support Meade's advance, Grant planned for two smaller armies to operate on his flanks to further threaten Lee and divert enemy troops away from Meade. To the east, the newly formed Army of the James would advance up the Virginia peninsula between the James and York rivers. This army, commanded by Major General Benjamin F. Butler, was tasked with threatening Richmond or Petersburg (the latter a major supply center and transportation hub) in an effort to compel Lee to divide his army. To the west in the mountains of western Virginia, a smaller command would tie down Confederates to prevent them from moving to reinforce Lee and also sever rail connections and deny Lee supplies coming from the Valley and southwestern Virginia.

In February 1864, the Federal Department of West Virginia was commanded by Brigadier General Benjamin F. Kelley, a former colonel of the

---

8   R. Lockwood Tower, Ed., *Lee's Adjutant: The Wartime Letters of Colonel Walter Herron Taylor, 1862-1865* (Columbia, SC, 1995), 139.

1st Virginia Infantry, one of the three-month regiments that flocked to the Union Army in 1861. After the enlistments expired, Kelley was given more responsibility. His new command included all of West Virginia as well as portions of Maryland and Virginia, including the lower (northern) Shenandoah Valley. It was a sizeable area, with somewhat fluid borders, encompassing whatever was occupied and could be held by Union forces. Through Kelley's new command passed the B&O Railroad and the C&O Canal, and his garrison was responsible for guarding against incursions into Pennsylvania, in addition to protecting key points within the department. However, the number of troops under his command was totally inadequate for the task. Confederate cavalry as well as bands of guerillas raided railroads often with impunity, damaging the track, bridges, support facilities, and the trains themselves, in addition to cutting telegraph wires and intercepting wagon trains and capturing their guards. Because of the limited resources at his disposal, Kelley was hard pressed to do anything but react to the raids as they occurred. In describing how Union efforts had fared in the Valley, one historian observed they "had yielded so many captures of Union garrisons and so many disasters in the field, as to be called the Valley of Humiliation."[9] West Virginia was anything but a desirable command.

During one raid in early February, Confederate cavalry managed to capture Brigadier General Eliakim Scammon, one of Kelley's subordinates, along with several of his staff and a small escort. Days later the West Virginia legislature passed a resolution denouncing Kelley for his inability to stop the raids and called upon Washington to replace him.[10] While Kelley contemplated his uncertain future, the Richmond *Examiner* proudly reported that "Major-General Scammon [sic] and staff . . . succeeded in their 'on to Richmond,' on Thursday, and are lodged and fed at Government expense at the hotel de Libby [Libby Prison]."[11]

While the raid and the action by the legislature probably hastened a change in command, the search for a replacement was already underway. A number of high-ranking, and in some cases politically well-connected, generals were

---

9   Pond, *The Shenandoah Valley in 1864*, 4.

10 Cecil D. Eby, Jr., ed., *A Virginia Yankee in the Civil War: The Diaries of David Hunter Strother* (Chapel Hill, NC, 1961), 212. Strother's writings are by no means friendly to Franz Sigel.

11 Richmond *Examiner*, Feb. 20, 1864. Libby Prison was a notorious prison in the Confederate capital that housed Union officers in a converted three-story brick warehouse.

without a command. Some in Washington had already come to realize that West Virginia was not a command suited to a brigadier general—especially with so many major generals awaiting assignment. Despite his best efforts and intentions, Kelley's tenure as commander in West Virginia was rapidly drawing to a close.

Two generals emerged as the leading candidates to replace Kelley. One was Robert H. Milroy, who had commanded in the region earlier in the war. He had earned the outright hatred of the pro-Southern population of the lower Valley by establishing strict guidelines regarding anyone so much as suspected of having Southern ties. One order executed above his signature required the residents of Winchester to sign an oath of allegiance to the United States or be prohibited from buying food and firewood. Some of the more staunchly pro-Southern residents were sent into exile at Milroy's command.[12] The general generated so much hatred among the populace that the Virginia government offered a reward of $1,000 for his capture.[13] His heavy-handed tactics were sandwiched between two battlefield fiascos. Stonewall Jackson had defeated him in a small engagement at McDowell in May 1862. The second and more crushing loss in June 1863, suffered at the very doorstep of the Winchester citizens he had tormented, was inflicted by the lead elements of Lee's army as it marched north toward Pennsylvania. Despite his relations with the local civilians, or perhaps because of his policies, many of the troops relished the return of their former commander. "No one could have been assigned to our command that would have given more general satisfaction to the troops," wrote an officer of the 116th Ohio.[14]

The other leading candidate to replace Kelley was Major General Franz Sigel. Sigel was born in 1824 in Baden, a province of what is today Germany. He was educated at Karlsruhe Military Academy and had been a prominent figure in the failed 1848 European revolutions. By the time Sigel immigrated to the United States in the early 1850s, he had developed a solid reputation as a soldier among his countrymen. He settled first in New York City and became involved with the Republican Party, then in its infancy, before eventually making his way

12 Roger U. Delauter, Jr., *Winchester in the Civil War* (Lynchburg, VA, 1992), 48.

13 Chester G. Hearn, *Six Years of Hell: Harpers Ferry during the Civil War* (Chapel Hill, NC, 1961), 212.

14 Thomas F. Wildes, *Record of the One Hundred and Sixteenth Regiment Ohio Infantry Volunteers in the War of the Rebellion* (Sandusky, OH, 1884), 79.

Major General Franz Sigel

Library of Congress

to St. Louis, Missouri, where he became superintendent of public schools. Prior to the outbreak of war in 1861, the Midwest, particularly the area around St. Louis, boasted a large population of German immigrants. By one count more than one million Germans immigrated to America between 1840 to 1860.[15] Sigel and several others established themselves as the community leaders of this German population. In the 1860 presidential election, Sigel actively supported Republican candidate Abraham Lincoln, and was credited with bringing the votes of the German-American community into the Lincoln camp.

When war erupted, Sigel was quickly named colonel of a Missouri regiment comprised mostly of German-Americans. Despite his reputation as a soldier, Sigel got off to a poor start in the field. He suffered a humiliating defeat in Missouri in the small running fight at Carthage on July 5, 1861, and again a month later at Wilson's Creek when his command was attacked in the rear and routed. Despite his field failures, Sigel received a commission as brigadier general that August to date from May 17, making him one of the war's early and prominent political generals. In March 1862, he was given a second star and was second-in-command of the Union forces at the Battle of Pea Ridge, Arkansas. Sigel's star brightened considerably when his handling of Northern artillery helped defeat a sizeable Confederate army on March 8.

Sigel's rapid promotion was not unique. Political ties in the early days of the war led to commissions for many men who would sooner or later prove they were better suited to politics than the battlefield. Despite his high standing among his countrymen, fellow officers held a low opinion of Sigel's abilities as a soldier. His former commander in Missouri, Major General Henry W. Halleck, made no secret of his dislike of Sigel, declaring the German to be "unfit for the rank he now holds."[16] As the war continued, Halleck, who later became Chief of Staff of the Army, would emerge as Sigel's most vocal critic.

During the summer of 1862, Sigel was transferred east to serve under Major General John Pope in Virginia. He was given command of Pope's I Corps, which was then stationed in the lower Shenandoah Valley. A rigid disciplinarian who expected perfection from his troops both in battle and on

---

15 Jorg Duppler, ed., *Evolution of a Friendship: Selected Documents on German-American Relations* (Potsdam, Germany, 2002), 23.

16 *The War of the Rebellion: A Compilation of the Official Records of the Union and Confederate Armies*, 128 vols. (Washington, D.C., 1881), Series I, Vol. 3, 94 (hereafter cited as *OR*). All references are to Series I unless otherwise noted.

the parade ground, Sigel soon found that his soldiers did not measure up to his high standards. He quickly set about reorganizing and re-equipping them, something that proved to be one of his strong suits.[17] Despite his best efforts, the men did not care much for their new commander, partly because of his strict demeanor and partly because of his lack of success in the field. Although he remained in the Valley but a short time, Sigel's heavy-handed actions—like Milroy's before him—earned the enmity of the citizens of Winchester.[18] He confiscated furniture from private homes, without compensation, for use in his personal headquarters. He also allowed his artillerymen to train by firing wooden practice rounds over the town, a tactic that triggered considerable alarm amongst the residents, particularly after an errant shot struck a house on Main Street.[19] Not every Winchester resident found fault with Sigel. During the Federal occupation in early 1862, Cornelia McDonald had one of her horses seized by the Federal quartermaster. When she gained an audience with Sigel to discuss the return of the animal, Cornelia found the general to be "quite elegant in manner, very polite and seemed to wish to oblige me."[20] Following a brief stint in command of the largely-German XI Corps in the Army of the Potomac, Sigel was relieved in early 1863 and relegated to a minor command in Pennsylvania.

Politics once again intervened to help the German immigrant, this time in the form of the upcoming 1864 elections. Sigel's supporters knew that the beleaguered President Lincoln needed the German vote, and used that knowledge to pressure Washington for Sigel's return to an active field command. Sigel did little to stop the effort, and in some ways encouraged it. During the winter of 1863-64, Lincoln was entering the last year of his term. He realized that the flagging war effort was sapping morale and that he could very well lose his bid for re-election. As a result, Lincoln began urging the war department to appoint Sigel to some sort of field command, knowing that the move would gain political favors for the administration. General Kelley's failures in West Virginia offered Sigel an opportunity for redemption.

17 Peter Cozzens and Robert I. Girardi, eds., *The Military Memoirs of General John Pope* (Chapel Hill, NC, 1998), 128.

18 Delauter, *Winchester*, 6.

19 Duncan, *Beleaguered Winchester*, 115.

20 Cornelia McDonald, *A Diary with Reminiscences of the War and Refugee Life in the Shenandoah Valley, 1860-1865*, annotated by Hunter McDonald (Nashville, TN, 1934), 49.

In January 1864, Sigel began corresponding with West Virginia Congressman Kellian V. Whaley regarding Kelley's replacement. On the 28th, Sigel wrote the congressman that while he "did not wish to interfere with the position of General Kelley . . . I would be glad if the matter could be decided upon in one or the other way, because if a change will be made it should be made now, immediately, so that the necessary preparations for next spring could be made."[21]

Several days later Sigel picked up his pen and wrote another letter. "It is strange that the Government hesitates so long in this matter," he wrote, "but you know perhaps that I have some good enemies in Washington who have not shrunk from furnishing the President with all sorts of stories about me."[22] The insinuation that General Halleck was responsible for the delay was readily apparent. "I have been made the bug-bear of all that was thought wrong in the German element, and have suffered much on account of it," he complained.[23]

Colonel David H. Strother, one of Kelley's staff officers but better known by his pen name "Porte Crayon" that he used for *Harpers Weekly*, noted in his diary in mid-February that Kelley was resigned to his pending fate. The change in command would come not as a result of

Colonel
David H. Strother

Library of Congress

21 Franz Sigel to Kellian V. Whaley, January 28, 1864, Kellian Van Whaley Papers, Virginia Historical Society. Whaley was a political appointee during the war and served as major in the 9th West Virginia Infantry. He was also a very strong supporter of Abraham Lincoln.

22 Sigel to Whaley, February 2, 1864, Whaley Papers.

23 *Ibid.*

the actions taken by the state legislature, suggested Kelley, "but from outside political influences."[24] By the end of the month the rumor was widespread that Sigel would be given the command in West Virginia. "If the report . . . of my being assigned to the command of the Department of W.Va. [sic] will prove a fact," he wrote his benefactor Congressman Whaley, "I am under great obligations to you, who has done so much to accomplish this end."[25]

On March 10 the rumor became official: Franz Sigel was appointed to command of the Department of West Virginia.[26] While en route to departmental headquarters at Cumberland, Maryland, Sigel received a letter from John M. Phelps of the West Virginia legislature assuring the German general that "there will be no dissatisfaction among the troops when you take command; on the contrary, your appointment will be received with joy by them . . . [and] with universal joy by the loyal people of our state."[27]

Perhaps the legislature forgot to inform the troops of their "universal joy" before news of Sigel's appointment reached their ears. Colonel Strother was anything but enthralled about his new commander, realizing it for what it was when he wrote, "The Dutch vote must be secured at all hazards for the Government and the sacrifice of West Virginia is a small matter." [28] A soldier in the 12th West Virginia had a somewhat less bitter but similar reaction: "We will pass from under the fatherly care of Genl. Kelley, [sic] who has always treated us kindly, to 'fight mit Sigel' and his lager beer and sour crouk satellites [sic]." Concerns also spread that the troops in the department would be transferred elsewhere and replaced by "Sagen beer Dutchmen."[29] While Sigel did not disguise his favoritism for foreigners in his command, these fears were unfounded. Others welcomed the change of command. "I have great confidence in Genl [sic] Sigel," wrote the colonel of the 21st New York Cavalry.[30] Charles Moulton of the 34th Massachusetts quipped that "West

24 Eby, *A Virginia Yankee in the Civil War*, 213.

25 Sigel to Whaley, February 29, 1864, Whaley Papers.

26 Stephen D. Engle, *Yankee Dutchman: The Life of Franz Sigel* (Fayetteville, AK, 1993), 169-170.

27 John Phelps to Sigel, March 3, 1864, Franz Sigel Papers, Western Reserve Historical Society.

28 Eby, *A Virginia Yankee in the Civil War*, 213.

29 Richard R. Duncan, ed. *Alexander Neil and the Last Shenandoah Valley Campaign* (Shippensburg, PA, 1996), 10-11.

30 William Tibbits to "Dear Dudley," May 12, 1864, Author's Collection.

Virginia has been under the superintendence [sic] of the Irish quite long enough and now we are ready to fight 'mit Sigel.' I like the change very well."[31] Not long after his appointment, the officers of the 133rd Pennsylvania staged a ball at Harpers Ferry, with Sigel as guest of honor.[32]

Sigel arrived in person at Cumberland on March 11 and officially took command the following day. Kelley was relegated to a rather nebulous "reserve division" consisting primarily of the troops assigned to garrison duty along the Baltimore & Ohio. Colonel Strother's first meeting with his new chief was anything but reassuring. He thought Sigel to be the antithesis of what a general should be. The unimpressive German, explained Strother, was "small in stature and ungraceful." To Strother's dismay, he spoke broken English.[33] Sigel owed much to his political friends, especially those in West Virginia. Now it was his turn to show that their trust and support was warranted—and to earn the trust of officers like David Strother.

The Federals were not the only ones making changes to their command structure during the winter months. During the winter of 1863-64, Major General Samuel Jones served as the commander of the Confederate Department of Western Virginia.[34] Jones had been appointed in southwest Virginia in December 1862, partly as a result of his lack of talent for field command. His department suffered from many of the same problems that plagued his Union counterpart at the northern end of the Shenandoah Valley: too large an area that contained vital resources with too few troops to effectively defend it. The Virginia & Tennessee Railroad—the vital link with the Western Theater—and the lead and salt mines near Wytheville all came under Jones' jurisdiction. Union cavalry had ridden out of West Virginia on several occasions to strike the railroad, the most recent being in November-December 1863. That raid, combined with Jones' unpopularity, sent authorities in Richmond scurrying for a solution. General Robert E. Lee complained to President

31 Lee C. Drickamer and Karen D. Drickamer, eds. *Fort Lyon to Harpers Ferry: On the Border of North and South with "Rambling Jour"* (Shippensburg, PA, 1987), 172.

32 Thomas J. Reed, *Tibbits' Boys: A History of the 21st New York Cavalry* (New York, 1997), 81.

33 Eby, *A Virginia Yankee in the Civil War*, 213.

34 Jones was one of the most well-traveled officers in the Confederate service, having served in Virginia at the beginning of the war before spending the next two years with brief stints in command in Florida, Alabama, and with the Army of Tennessee prior to assuming command in southwest Virginia.

Jefferson Davis that something had to be done to rectify the deteriorating situation. "I have been disappointed in my expectations of the service of General Sam. Jones' command," explained Lee. "I think a reorganization . . . necessary, and a change of commanders desirable. The department requires a man of judgment and energy, whose discretion can be depended upon without always awaiting orders." The search for Jones' replacement eventually settled upon a general who had made his career entirely in the Western Theater.[35]

John Cabell Breckinridge was perhaps one of the most recognized names in the 1860s. Born in 1821 in Kentucky, Breckinridge practiced law in his native state and emerged as a leading figure in the Democratic Party. During the war with Mexico in 1846, he served as major of the 3rd Kentucky but did not see any fighting. He was elected to the state legislature in 1849, and two years later was elected to Congress. Tapped by the Democrats to be James Buchanan's running mate in the 1856 presidential election, at age 35 Breckinridge became the youngest vice president in American history. By the latter half of the 1850s Breckinridge was overshadowed within his party by only Stephen Douglas. When the party split along regional lines because of the inability to select a candidate for the 1860 election, Breckinridge received the nomination of the Southern Democrats for president. At the same time, he was elected to a seat in the Senate, to take effect immediately upon the end of his term as vice-president.

The Kentuckian carried the Deep South in the 1860 presidential election, beating his former rival Douglas who had been nominated by the Northern Democrats. Still, Breckinridge finished a distant second to Abraham Lincoln in the four-way race. Harboring fears that Lincoln's election would lead to war, Breckinridge took his seat in the Senate as the Southern states, one by one, seceded from the Union. When his native state adopted an awkward stance of neutrality, Breckinridge attempted to follow her lead in the Senate by opposing Lincoln's war efforts or, as Breckinridge termed it, "that series of usurpations which has now left nothing of the Federal Constitution."[36] However, as Kentucky itself would soon find out, neutrality was not something easy to maintain in the electrically charged climate. By the fall of 1861, Breckinridge, one of but a mere handful of representatives from Southern and lower border

---

35 *OR* 33, 1,086.

36 "Address of John C. Breckinridge to the People of Kentucky," October 8, 1861, in Frank Moore, *The Rebellion Record* (New York, 1864), III, Documents, 254.

Major General John C. Breckinridge

Library of Congress

states to remain in Congress, found his loyalty to the Union being called into question. While he had committed no act against the United States, because of his Southern sympathies he found himself faced with arrest and imprisonment if he remained in Washington. As he saw it, the only alternative to arrest was to cast his lot with the Confederacy. "I resign because there is no place left where a Southern Senator may sit in council with the Senators of the North," the former vice president explained to his constituents.[37]

Upon his arrival in the South, Breckinridge was commissioned a brigadier general and given command of a brigade of Kentucky troops, the so-called "Orphan Brigade." His first major action came at Shiloh in April 1862, where he led the reserve corps and third line of attack.[38] Unlike other political generals, Breckinridge performed admirably on the battlefield, winning the respect of his men and his fellow officers. Although Shiloh ended as a sharp defeat for the South, Breckinridge's actions earned him a promotion to major general. "As a hard and desperate fighter," one of his officers later remembered, "he had few, if any, superiors in either army."[39] After Shiloh, Breckinridge and his division were shuttled between the defense of Vicksburg and field service with Braxton Bragg's Army of Tennessee. His service with the Tennessee army would both solidify his reputation as a capable field commander and launch one of the most celebrated Confederate feuds.

The Battle of Stones River near Murfreesboro, Tennessee, straddled the New Year from December 31, 1862 to January 2, 1863. Breckinridge was posted on the extreme right flank of the army in a very disadvantageous position, separated from the rest of the army by Stones River. His commander, General Braxton Bragg, ordered Breckinridge to assault the Union forces opposite him with his division and several supporting units. Breckinridge protested that the Union position was too strong to carry with his small force, and even if he did carry it, he would not be able to hold it because it would be exposed to Union artillery fire. Bragg was adamant that the attack be made as directed, and Breckinridge carried out his orders. As he predicted, his men were unable to secure more than a temporary foothold before being driven back with heavy losses. By all accounts Bragg was an irascible man. He was unable to see his own shortcomings, but was more than willing to point out failings in others and seek scapegoats to cover his own battlefield failures. When the Army of Tennessee withdrew from the field following Breckinridge's repulse, Bragg laid the blame for the defeat at the feet of the Kentuckian. Allegations between the

---

37 *Ibid.*

38 A "corps" in name only, for it was nothing more than a small division.

39 John Echols, *Address on the Life and Character of Gen. John C. Breckinridge* (New Market, VA, 1877), 11.

two officers flew fast and thick, opening up a rift that threatened to tear apart the army's command structure until Breckinridge was separated from the army and sent to reinforce Vicksburg, Mississippi. Whatever respect Breckinridge had for Bragg was lost, and his transfer left unsettled a feud that would continue to simmer. Relations between the two men were never the same again.

By late summer 1863 Vicksburg had fallen and Breckinridge, who did not reach the beleaguered city in time to be trapped with its garrison, was again serving with Bragg's Army of Tennessee. Once again positioned on the right side of the battle line, Breckinridge's division found itself in the thick of the fighting at Chickamauga that September. On the second day of the battle Bragg's men broke through the enemy lines and drove the Federal Army of the Cumberland off the field and into Chattanooga, scoring what would be the Tennessee army's only major victory of the war. When Bragg failed to follow up his victory and push the Federals out of Chattanooga, a near-mutiny erupted within the army's high command. A petition signed by most of the army's generals—though notably not by Breckinridge—was sent to Richmond calling for Bragg's removal. Matters had reached a critical—and dangerous—stage. When President Davis refused to remove Bragg, the general took matters into his own hands by ridding himself of his most troublesome subordinates with transfers out of the army. Breckinridge remained, and by virtue of his senior rank was given temporary command of a corps as Bragg's army sat in a semi-siege of Chattanooga.

And it was at Chattanooga that Breckinridge turned in his worst performance of the war. When Union forces under U. S. Grant attacked in late November, Breckinridge's lines on the heights above the city on Lookout Mountain and Missionary Ridge were overrun. The result was a catastrophic Confederate defeat that drove the broken army into North Georgia and ended Bragg's tenure as its commander. Some, Bragg foremost among them, alleged that Breckinridge was inebriated during the battle. Although "it cannot positively be denied that Breckinridge was drunk," explained the Kentuckian's biographer William C. Davis, "Bragg's charge is hardly sufficient to warrant the assumption that the Kentuckian was under such influence."[40] Drunk or not, his dispositions for battle were clearly inadequate to repel an assault, and many in the South blamed Breckinridge for the debacle. His military career was at its nadir when orders arrived for him to report to Richmond.

---

40 William C. Davis, *Breckinridge: Statesman, Soldier, Symbol* (Baton Rouge, LA, 1992), 396.

On February 15, 1864, Breckinridge's service with the Army of Tennessee officially came to an end. Despite his performance at Chattanooga, many officers in Lee's Army of Northern Virginia held the Kentuckian in high regard, though most knew him only by reputation. Rumors swirled that the Kentuckian was in Richmond to accept a command in the Virginia army. Lee's staff was prepared to receive him. Walter Taylor, one of Lee's closest aides, wrote home that "we were notified on yesterday that Genl [sic] Breckinridge . . . would today visit General Lee but he did not arrive." Luxuries were scarce in camp, prompting Taylor to add, "I hope he can be comfortable with little for we have not much to induce visiting to our Head Qrs [sic] camp."[41]

The rumors were dispelled ten days later when Breckinridge received orders to report to Dublin Depot, headquarters of the Department of Southwest Virginia. He arrived there on March 4, relieving Samuel Jones of his command. As Breckinridge would soon discover, the department "was no plum."[42] It included southwest Virginia up to the southern end of the Shenandoah Valley, together with parts of Kentucky and West Virginia—and sometimes eastern Tennessee as well. In all, Breckinridge's new assignment covered some 18,000 square miles of generally mountainous territory. On paper he had only 7,000 poorly armed and ill-equipped men to defend this sprawling area, hardly enough to mount a successful defense, let alone launch any sort of effective offensive. Major J. Stoddard Johnston of Breckinridge's staff wrote after the war that the department's "great extent of exposed front, with the small force for its protection, had always rendered it a precarious command, and it had proved disastrous to several of [Breckinridge's] predecessors."[43]

Federal activity in the area had been increasing of late, and it seemed likely that Breckinridge would soon be faced with a serious threat. One soldier of the 51st Virginia wrote about the change in command in early February and his belief that the next fight would hit close to home: "My opinion is that right here in this country will be the next fighting in the spring."[44]

---

41 Tower, *Lee's Adjutant*, 111.

42 Davis, *Breckinridge*, 406-7.

43 J. Stoddard Johnston, "Sketches of Operations of General John C. Breckinridge," *Southern Historical Society Papers*, June 1879, 257-8. Johnston's "Sketches" very closely mimics (and in places is almost verbatim) General Breckinridge's official but unfinished and previously unpublished New Market campaign report, which Johnston drafted. See Appendix 2.

44 Thomas W. Fisher to "Parents," February 8, 1864, Dianne McGinley Gardner Collection.

Just beyond the northern reaches of Breckinridge's domain was the Shenandoah Valley. The man immediately responsible for its defense was Brigadier General John D. Imboden. A native of Staunton, Imboden was intricately familiar with the area. He worked as a lawyer before the war and was a staunch secessionist—politics not exactly popular in that region. Imboden raised an artillery company in 1861 and was elected its captain. He performed admirably under Stonewall Jackson and later received permission to recruit a cavalry battalion, formed primarily of men recruited from behind Union lines, for the purpose of harassing Union efforts in West Virginia. The response to this recruiting effort was better than expected, and the battalion quickly grew into a brigade. The larger organization brought with it promotion to brigadier general for Imboden. Imboden spent much of 1863 giving Milroy and Kelley a collective headache, conducting raids against the B&O and disrupting communications and supply lines. Imboden's finest hour came during the retreat from Gettysburg, when he was given command of the "Wagon Train of Wounded" and successfully defended Williamsport against overwhelming odds, protecting the army's crossing point on the Potomac River. Formally given command of the Valley District in late July 1863, Imboden made the most of the meager forces at his disposal, which rarely numbered more than 2,000 men of all arms under his direct command. With them Imboden kept watch over the Valley, protecting Lee's strategic left flank against Federal threats.

Command of the Valley was not something Imboden had actively sought or wanted. In fact, it was quite the opposite. He made no secret of the fact that he did not desire promotion or independent command. "As to my promotion," Imboden confided to a friend, "I do not desire it. I asked the President . . . [to] relieve me of the command and remit me to the simple command of my brigade." He continued with a refreshingly honest self-appraisal: "I do not want a major general's commission. . . . I feel that I have as high military rank as I am qualified for."[45] Some of his contemporaries agreed with him. According to Historian Robert K. Krick, "Many superiors and colleagues held Imboden up as the symbol of Valley cavalry incompetence."[46] During the larger 1864

---

45 John D. Imboden to "Major," April 25, 1864, John D. Imboden Papers, King Library, University of Kentucky.

46 Robert K. Krick, "The Cause of All My Disasters: Jubal A. Early and the Undisciplined Valley Cavalry," in *Struggle for the Shenandoah: Essays on the 1864 Valley Campaign*, ed. by Gary W. Gallagher (Kent, OH, 1991), 88.

A postwar image of Brigadier General John D. Imboden

Library of Congress

Shenandoah Valley Campaign under Jubal Early, the Confederate cavalry would perform poorly on several notable occasions. Even though he had little regard for mounted troops to begin with, Early had a special contempt reserved for Imboden. Regardless of his competency, the decision had been made: the Valley belonged to Imboden.

As the spring campaigning season approached, Breckinridge and Imboden knew they would be tested. What remained to be seen was what would be thrown against them. If the Yankees mounted a major offensive in the Valley, Breckinridge knew his response would depend upon Imboden being able to keep the Federals occupied long enough for reinforcements to arrive. Similarly, if Breckinridge was threatened, it would probably fall to Imboden to expeditiously come to his aid. Viewed from the opposite side of the lines, Franz Sigel knew that with Grant in overall command, action would not be long in coming. Both generals would have agreed with the sentiments of one of Breckinridge's soldiers who wrote, "I hope and believe that with the end of 1864 will come the end of this unholy war."[47]

47 T. W. Fisher to "Parents," February 8, 1864, Gardner Collection.

Brigadier General Benjamin F. Kelley, who commanded the
Department of West Virginia before being replaced by Franz Sigel. *Library of Congress*

Chapter 2

Fighting Mit Sigel

Winter months were normally a time of relative inactivity for Civil War armies. Because of the poor state of roads and fickle means of transportation, few major campaigns were undertaken in the dead of winter. Troops built semi-permanent camps and devoted their time to resting, letter writing, and sometimes furloughs to visit their homes. The generals used the time to reflect on their previous campaigns and to plan for the upcoming spring offensives. In West Virginia during the winter of 1863-1864, however, there was little rest for the troops on either side. One of Imboden's men confided to his wife, "I doubt very much whether we shall see any winter quarters this winter as we have a very extensive country to protect. In fact I think it is more than General Imboden can do. We ought to have more troops."[1]

There had indeed been more activity than usual that winter. In what turned out to be Benjamin Kelley's last major operation as commander in West Virginia, that December he ordered a cavalry raid through the mountains west of Staunton and into southwest Virginia against the Virginia & Tennessee Railroad. A smaller second column under Colonel George D. Wells was dispatched to create a diversion in the Valley by threatening a move on Staunton. With only his small brigade to oppose the move, Imboden requested

---

1 Isaac White to Jinnie, November 18, 1863, Isaac White papers, Special Collections Department, Virginia Tech Library. White was the assistant surgeon of the 62nd Virginia Mounted Infantry of Imboden's brigade.

reinforcements. General Lee responded by sending Jubal Early with two infantry brigades and a division of cavalry into the Shenandoah. Early arrived too late to stop Brigadier General William W. Averell's cavalry from striking the Virginia & Tennessee line at Salem, but Early and Imboden were in a good position to cut the Federals off on their retreat and possibly capture the entire force. As luck would have it, bad weather combined with faulty information about Averell's whereabouts to frustrate Confederate efforts and the raiders returned more or less unscathed. Early's attempts to damage the column in the Valley were equally futile. With all his cavalry in the mountains chasing Averell, none were left to pursue Wells. Still, the reinforcements from the Army of Northern Virginia had prevented further damage in the Valley. Early was ordered to remain there and forage for provisions in West Virginia. He and his command returned to Lee's army in late February, about the same time changes in command structure were being made on both sides.[2]

Early belittled Averell's accomplishments, writing that the destruction wrought by the Federals was minimal, and that Averell's "raid really amounted to very little except the name of it."[3] A different view was taken on the other side of the Potomac. One Massachusetts newspaper reported that "the expedition penetrated the very heart of the enemy's country, diverted and employed from ten to twenty thousand of Lee's army, in their front and rear, and on their flank, and escaped without the smallest loss."[4] These small operations were just a taste of what was being planned for the spring campaigning season.

Franz Sigel spent most of March familiarizing himself with his new command, making inspections of the various garrisons, and having his staff compile numerous reports on unit strengths and disposition. He could not have been pleased by what he found. He had roughly 23,000 troops at his disposal, but most of them were dispersed to guard the Baltimore & Ohio Railroad. Complicating matters was the fact that roughly half of his troops lacked extensive combat experience, and more still had never functioned for any length of time as part of a larger force. Concentrating his scattered forces for

---

2   Jubal A. Early, *Jubal Early's Memoirs: Autobiographical Sketch and Narrative of the War Between the States* (Baltimore, MD, 1989), 326-340.

3   Early, *Autobiographical Sketch*, 331. Early was no fan of cavalry, regardless of whose side it was on.

4   Worcester *Aegis and Transcript*, January 9, 1864.

offensive operations would leave much of the territory open to attack. In an effort to free up his troops for active field service, Sigel appealed to the West Virginia legislature for state militia to guard the railroad. His request was denied.[5]

In a report to Washington at the end of March, Sigel outlined the myriad problems he faced in West Virginia. "By far the greater part of these troops are in positions which they cannot evacuate without great danger to the Baltimore & Ohio Railroad," he explained. Uncovering the railroad, Sigel continued, would subject it to danger not only from Confederate cavalry, but also "because it would be left in the hands of a population which is for a great part disloyal, and would take opportunity to destroy it as soon as we withdraw." Furthermore, Departmental Headquarters at Cumberland, which Sigel called "the most important city between Baltimore and Wheeling—is totally unprotected." As to the quality of the troops, Sigel found them to be "poor" in both discipline and military ability. "I will do the best I can," he assured Washington.[6]

Sigel's instructions for the upcoming campaign arrived at the end of March. They were delivered by Major General Edward O. C. Ord, a favorite of Grant's from their days together fighting in the Western Theater.[7] The offensive in West Virginia that Grant had in mind for Sigel consisted of a two- pronged assault. One column, under Brigadier General George Crook, would advance from West Virginia against the Virginia & Tennessee Railroad. Crook's thrust was essentially a large-scale replication of Averell's previous winter raid that promised better results. A second column, approximately 10,000 men under Ord, would advance simultaneously with Crook, but operate farther north.[8]

In its original form, Grant's plan left little for Sigel to do beyond organizing and supplying the columns from his headquarters in Cumberland. Grant further minimized Sigel's role as chief quartermaster for Ord's operation by

5   Engle, *Sigel*, 172-173.

6   *OR* 33, 762-765.

7   Ord was a native of Cumberland, Maryland, which was perhaps one of the reasons Grant wanted him in that department. Ord is best known as commander of the Army of the James during the latter months of the war. Elements of his command were instrumental in the final breakthrough at Petersburg and in the last pursuit of the Army of Northern Virginia. Ord was present for the surrender of Lee's Army at Appomattox and purchased the small table upon which the surrender documents were signed.

8   *OR* 33, 765-766.

Major General
Edward O. C. Ord

Library of Congress

specifically stating that Ord's troops were to live off the land. By all appearances Grant recognized Sigel's shortcomings as a field commander, and he was doing everything he could to limit the German officer's direct involvement without provoking a national political firestorm.

After rethinking the logistics involved, however, Grant changed his mind. The general-in-chief informed Sigel to be prepared to move up the Valley from Martinsburg with a large wagon train to meet and re-supply Ord and Crook, with all three columns meeting at Staunton. Years later in his memoirs, Grant wrote that "either the enemy would have to keep a large force to protect their communications, or see them destroyed and a large amount of forage and provision, which they so much needed, fall into our hands."[9] The main focus of the operation was still an attack against the railroad in southwest Virginia; occupying the Shenandoah Valley remained a secondary priority. Grant advised Sigel that the proposed movement from Martinsburg "will not require much more than an escort for the wagon train."[10]

The operations in West Virginia were designed to hamper Confederate operations elsewhere in Virginia. "I don't expect much from Sigel's movement," Grant is said to have remarked, but "if Sigel can't skin himself, he can hold a leg while somebody else skins."[11]

---

9   Ulysses S. Grant, *Personal Memoirs of U.S. Grant*, 2 vols. (New York, 1886), vol. 2, 131.

10 *OR* 33, 858.

11 Horace Porter, *Campaigning with Grant* (New York, 1991), 46.

As is often the case in military operations, a clash of personalities erupted before the operation even got underway. Simply put, Sigel and Ord never really hit it off and relations between the two were considerably strained almost from the outset. On March 30, Ord wrote to his wife that he had met with Grant the previous day. Grant, he explained, "will give me a command [but] I do not yet know how extensive, or whether it will be permanent."[12] Ord was probably Grant's choice for departmental command, but Sigel was forced upon him by the Lincoln administration, leaving Ord in a subordinate role. Sigel seems to have realized this, and may have been jealous of the warm relations—and likely influence—Ord had with Grant. Ord had assumed command of Major General John McClernand's XIII Corps in Grant's army at Vicksburg, and when Grant came east that winter, Ord was one of only three western officers who accompanied him—a sure sign of the confidence Grant had in Ord's abilities. Grant's preference for occasionally dealing with Ord and Crook directly, rather than following proper channels and going through Sigel, is evidence of both his confidence in those officers, and his lack of confidence in Sigel's abilities to manage the situation. The breach of military protocol irked Sigel, who complained that "all dispositions were made in such a manner as if I did not exist at all."[13]

Sigel was not the only one miserable with the current command situation. By the second week of April, Ord was complaining to his wife about his new post. "I . . . have not had a very delightful time 'Mit Sigel' and think I shall get out of this as soon as I can," he wrote on April 9. It was about this same time that Ord learned Grant "did intend a Department for me and that the politicians and elections interfered."[14] Ord may have intended to play a waiting game to see if Sigel would resign or be reassigned, which would allow him to slide into West Virginia departmental command. He also had time to ponder whether he had made a good career decision in coming east with Grant. "I feel that in changing [Major General Nathaniel] Banks for Sigel I have gained a loss," he confided to his wife.[15]

12 E. O. C. Ord to Molly Ord, March 30, 1864, Ord Papers, Special Collections Department, Stanford University Library.

13 Davis, *The Battle of New Market*, 22.

14 Ord to Molly, April 9, 1864, Ord papers.

15 *Ibid.* Ord commanded the XIII Corps under Major General Nathaniel Banks in the Department of the Gulf prior to his assignment to Sigel's department. Like Sigel, Banks was a

How much and how well Ord and Sigel were communicating with one another during this time is open for debate. As Grant had outlined it, Ord was to be in actual field command of one of the two offensives in West Virginia. Even without specific orders, the movement could be expected to get underway around the beginning of May, the traditional jump-off point for the active campaigning season. Ord, however, seemed both unconcerned as that date approached and unsure of why he was there. On April 11, he wrote Molly that there was "nothing special that requires me just here," which prompts the question of the level of the communication flow between Ord and his immediate superior.[16] Ord continued, writing that he had requested that Grant transfer him to Wheeling, a move that would put him about as far away from the front as possible and still be within the confines of Sigel's department. Still, Ord was a good soldier who understood his role in the larger picture of war. "I have tried with the help of Providence to do my duty, through all the changes and in spite of . . . partisans [politicians]," he concluded, "and I shall continue so to try, with a vision to the future good of my whole country."[17]

Four days later Ord wrote his wife again, telling her that he would gladly accept a commission as a major in the engineers if it meant getting out from under Sigel's command. The German general, he complained, "was a clever enough gentleman, but like almost all the foreign officers of rank, feels a hesitation in enforcing his orders" and had difficulty gaining the respect of his officers. Although he had been under Sigel's command but a short time, Ord was enough of a professional to sense that disaster loomed ahead. "I would like to be relieved altogether from any of the responsibility of events to come."[18]

The relationship between the two generals continued to deteriorate. "Sigel is jealous as the devil at my having come here," grumbled Ord.[19] Despite what

political appointee. Banks had been Speaker of the House of Representatives during Franklin Pierce's administration and served as governor of Massachusetts immediately before the war. He was defeated more than once in 1862 by Thomas J. "Stonewall" Jackson. Although a military liability in the field, Banks was too politically important to ignore. Lincoln had to find a home for Banks, and sent him to the Gulf Coast in late 1862. His Red River expedition in early 1864 was a disaster.

16 Ord to Molly, April 11, 1864, Ord Papers.

17 *Ibid.*

18 Ord to Molly, April 15, 1864, Ord Papers.

19 Richard Duncan, *Lee's Endangered Left: The Civil War in Western Virginia, Spring of 1864* (Baton Rouge, LA, 1998), 22.

Sigel termed as "the most energetic measures" to implement Grant's plan, Ord found that the force assembled for him at Beverly was several thousand men shy of the promised 10,000. Sigel blamed this on the weather and the poor condition of the roads,[20] an explanation supported by an officer of the 12th West Virginia who observed that the area's roads were such that "it seems almost impracticable for artillery and wagons to get along."[21] Years later, Sigel claimed that he had concentrated at Beverly "all the troops that could be spared" for Ord's column. Gathering any more for Ord's column would have left "the whole region from Harper's Ferry and Martinsburg to Cumberland and Parkersburg . . . unprotected and exposed to hostile enterprises." In truth, both generals had reason to be miserable with their respective assignments.[22]

In the midst of this growing controversy between the two ranking generals, Grant sent one of his staff to Cumberland with detailed instructions for Sigel's operations in the coming weeks. Why he felt this necessary is unclear, but he may have felt it necessary because of input from Ord and others in the department regarding Sigel's lack of competency. Outlining for the department chief exactly what was expected of him, rather than trusting Sigel to use his own discretion, made it more likely that the operations would resemble what Grant intended. Lieutenant Colonel Orville Babcock arrived at Sigel's headquarters at Cumberland on April 15 with a five paragraph letter of instruction that included one overall very clear message: "You must occupy the attention of a large force, and thereby hold them from re-enforcing elsewhere, or must inflict a blow upon the enemy's resources, which will materially aid us."[23]

Although Grant's message was easily understood, implementing it was becoming more problematic by the day: relations between Ord and Sigel were by this point strained beyond repair. Ord's disgust for Sigel was too much for even that old professional to handle. "The duties as subordinate under political generals are not pleasant or profitable," he wrote his wife. "It is pleasanter to be king among dogs than dog among such kings."[24] On April 17 Edward Ord's

---

20 Franz Sigel, "Sigel in the Shenandoah Valley in 1864," in Robert Johnson and Clarence Buel, eds., *Battles and Leaders of the Civil War*, 4 vols. (Secaucus, NJ, n.d.), vol. 4, 487.

21 Duncan, *Alexander Neil*, 18.

22 Sigel, "Sigel in the Shenandoah Valley in 1864," 487.

23 *OR* 33, 874.

24 Ord to Molly, April 16, 1864, Ord Papers.

request to be relieved of his duties with the Department of West Virginia was granted.

Once out from under Sigel's command, Ord felt more at ease expressing his feelings to his wife about his brief period in West Virginia. Indeed, his personal correspondence in the days immediately following April 17 displays a deep measure of personal relief at having escaped West Virginia with his reputation intact. His letters also bristle with criticisms of Sigel that were more pointed and harsh than during his tenure under that officer. Ord admitted he had been "excessively vexed or rather mortified" at being placed under Sigel's command the previous month. Still, he felt it his duty as a soldier to follow orders despite his personal feelings. In his heart of hearts, however, he also knew he could not faithfully execute his duty "unless supported and trusted by my commander." Instead of support, at least according to Ord, Sigel became "jealous and obstinate," and "if I attempted to play lead horse, [would] have to drag a bigger wheel and break down in the effort." Rather than continue in a difficult situation and risk being made a scapegoat in the event of a defeat in the field, he explained, "I asked to quit." His decision—always a difficult one for a professional soldier, risked having his career put "on the shelf, but . . . better the shelf than what I saw before me."[25]

Part of what Ord saw before him was Sigel assembling a field army in which Ord likely had but little faith. The army was drawn from the various regiments and batteries stationed throughout his command. Whatever his other shortcomings, Franz Sigel—much like George McClellan—was an excellent organizer. Many of the units available to Sigel had not seen much action, having been assigned to garrison or guard duty for much of the war. Those that had seen real fighting had for the most part not been on the winning end of it. Regarding the fighting trim of the troops themselves, very few measured up to Sigel's high standards. "The condition of the troops is poor," he reported to Washington after an inspection tour,

> from the fact that they have been lying still for a long time...They are scattered by squads, companies, and regiments, and not united in brigades or divisions. Brave as the soldiers may be individually, and with the exception of a few well-drilled and well-disciplined regiments, they have become loose and degenerated by inactivity and

---

25 Ord to Molly, April 20, 1864, Ord Papers. Ord was reassigned to the XVIII Corps of the Army of the James (of which he eventually assumed command).

garrison life. They may be made soldiers, but at this moment they are very far from understanding their duties.[26]

The commanding general's honest assessment of his troops was echoed by an officer of the 34th Massachusetts. "The 54th Pennsylvania is fair; the 12th West Virginia pretty good; the rest are barely passable," concluded the 34th's Lieutenant Colonel William Lincoln.[27] The 34th Massachusetts was arguably the best drilled regiment in Sigel's department, and its officers and men firmly believed it. It seems they were unable to hide the disdain they felt for other, less capable, outfits. Lieutenant Colonel Thomas Wildes of the 116th Ohio complained that his and the other western units "were looked upon as a lot of barbarians by these well drilled, well disciplined, highly cultured eastern soldiers."[28]

The 34th Massachusetts did offer a stark contrast to the other Federal regiments in Sigel's department. Having served garrison duty at Washington and Harpers Ferry for most of the war, their uniforms and equipment were still all but pristine. The 116th Ohio's Lieutenant Colonel Wildes took note of that fact when he observed "it was so much more neatly dressed and so completely equipped, compared to our own regiment, that it was a sort of curiosity to our 'rough Ohio fellers,' as its officers and men often spoke of us."[29] The regiment was indeed so "completely equipped" that it included a brass band—a rarity in Sigel's department. "We have a rich store of music on hand in this deluded little corner of America," wrote a member of the regiment.[30] The band was long a fixture with the regiment. On Thanksgiving Day 1863, the officers of the 34th had organized a ball at Harpers Ferry, of which a reporter in attendance wrote, "nothing so recherché has occurred in this line for years in Harpers Ferry."[31]

The battle and field experience of the other units assigned to Sigel's command varied widely. The 18th Connecticut and 123rd Ohio, for example,

---

26 OR 33, 764. Regardless of Sigel's ability as a field commander, his observations were accurate and justified.

27 William S. Lincoln, *Life with the 34th Massachusetts Infantry in the War of the Rebellion* (Worcester, MA, 1879), 261.

28 Wildes, *Record of the One Hundred and Sixteenth Regiment Ohio Infantry Volunteers*, 80.

29 *Ibid.*

30 Drickamer, *Fort Lyon to Harpers Ferry*, 168.

31 Worcester *Aegis and Transcript*, December 19, 1863.

had both been nearly destroyed at Winchester in June 1863 during the opening phase of the Gettysburg campaign. Although many of the enlisted men captured at Winchester had been exchanged and returned to service, many of their veteran officers remained in POW camps. A mostly German regiment, the 28th Ohio had seen hard action at "Burnside's Bridge" at Antietam in September 1862, as had the 23rd Ohio, whose ranks included two future U.S. Presidents (Rutherford B. Hayes and William McKinley). The 54th Pennsylvania had spent its entire career guarding the B&O, only a few of its companies had participated in defending the line against Confederate cavalry, and the regiment as a whole had seldom served as a cohesive unit. Battery B, 1st Maryland Light Artillery, or "Snow's Battery" as it was more commonly called, saw heavy fighting during the Peninsula campaign in the spring and summer of 1862, but little action since. Alternately, the 21st New York Cavalry and 1st New York Veteran Cavalry regiments were new organizations, though comprised mainly of combat veterans.

Most of the troops were being marshaled in the Harpers Ferry-Martinsburg area or at Beverly, deep in the mountains of West Virginia. The men of the 12th West Virginia discovered that getting there was easier said than done. According to Alexander Neil, the 12th's assistant surgeon, the march to Beverly was "over the worst roads and through the deepest mortar I ever saw." Recent rains and melting snow had turned the already primitive roads into ribbons of meandering mud. Neil drove his point home by joking that only the ears of the mules pulling the wagons were visible above the "mortar."[32] Accompanying the West Virginians on that difficult march were 250 head of cattle, herded along to provide sustenance for the troops. William Hewitt, the 12th's historian, remembered this episode years after the war as "the first opportunity the members of the regiment had of playing the part of 'cow boys' [and] they performed the task with the zeal of novices and had a jolly time of it."[33]

Bringing together large numbers of troops required appointing commanders to the newly created brigades and divisions. Major General Julius Stahel was named as chief of cavalry, superseding William Averell. Stahel was a native of Hungary and, like Sigel, was another officer who owed his position

---

32 Duncan, *Alexander Neil*, 16.

33 William Hewitt, *History of the Twelfth Regiment West Virginia Volunteer Infantry* (Steubenville, OH, 1892), 100.

Major General
Julius Stahel

Library of Congress

more to political influence than military talent. He had been colonel of the 8th New York at the war's outset and later led a brigade in the Valley in 1862. He "got his commission when the fury for foreigners was at its height and when the German influence was highest in Washington," claimed Colonel Strother, who went on to describe Stahel as "a very good fancy cavalry officer who has never done anything in the field and never will do anything."[34] Stahel quickly became one of Sigel's favorite officers, and the latter added the position of chief of staff to his subordinate's responsibilities.

Stahel was not the only foreigner Sigel appointed to prominent command. Brigadier General Max Weber, another German and Sigel favorite, was given charge of the Harpers Ferry garrison. Although a relative unknown to the non-German element, the men at Harpers Ferry found Weber capable enough. "He is a German, one of General Sigel's friends and I guess a pretty smart man" a clerk at Weber's headquarters explained, "though I never heard of him before he came here."[35] Just how unknown Weber was to the men in the ranks was apparent when a portion of the pickets guarding the bridge at Harpers Ferry failed to salute the general as he rode by. "I had never seen him, did not know

---

34 Eby, *A Virginia Yankee in the Civil War*, 223. Strother's assessment of Stahel was a bit off, for Stahel would earn the Medal of Honor for his actions at the Battle of Piedmont on June 5, 1864.

35 Arthur M. Stone to "My Dear Mother," April 17, 1864, Draughon Library, Auburn University.

him," a soldier in the 18th Connecticut explained. "Did not see the star denoting his rank until it was too late."[36]

Augustus Moor of the 28th Ohio, one of the senior colonels in the department, was picked by Sigel for brigade command. Moor was born in Leipzig, Saxony, and fled to the United States as a teenager after participating in a failed 1830 revolt. He settled in Philadelphia, where he joined a local militia company. Moor served in the 1st Pennsylvania Dragoons in the Seminole War, rising from lieutenant to lieutenant colonel. He later moved to Cincinnati, where he established a bakery and beer garden that become a popular haunt of the city's German population. Moor served again in uniform during the Mexican War, rising to the rank of colonel. He returned to Cincinnati and his beer garden and in the spring of 1861 helped raise the all-German 9th Ohio and later the 28th Ohio. Moor's regiment, as well as the 30th New York Battery, was composed entirely of German immigrants. While Sigel did not implement the grand substitution of German troops and officers that some had feared would occur, in the words of one of his artillery commanders, Sigel "was always keenly alive to the interests of his fellow Germans which he sought to promote by every means in his power."[37]

Brigadier General Jeremiah Cutler Sullivan's route to infantry command in West Virginia followed an unusual road, even by Civil War standards. An 1848 graduate of the United States Naval Academy, Sullivan served six years in the navy on four different ships before resigning to study law. When the war broke, out, he helped recruit and organize the 6th Indiana Volunteers, was elected captain, and led it in battle at Phillipi, in western Virginia. Commissioned in the Army in 1861 as a colonel, he eventually rose to brigade command and participated in battles in both major theaters of the war until the fall of 1863, when he was relieved of command and returned east. He was assigned to lead an infantry division—a "division" on paper only—in West Virginia in 1863, a prominent position owed more to the fact that his father-in-law was department commander Benjamin Kelley than to any demonstrable field ability. Sullivan was Stahel's counterpart with the infantry, and was one of the senior commanders inherited by Sigel he did not replace.

36 Charles H. Lynch, *The Civil War Diary of Charles H. Lynch, 18th Connecticut Volunteers* (Hartford, CT, 1915), 53.

37 Henry DuPont, *The Battle of New Market, May 15, 1864* (Winterthur, DE, 1923), 6.

The leader of the second prong of the planned assault from West Virginia was career soldier George Crook, who graduated near the bottom of his West Point Class of 1852. His lowly position notwithstanding, Grant hand-selected Crook because the Ohio native was by far one of the best military minds in the department. He would go on to serve with distinction in the Valley for much of the remainder of the war before achieving even greater fame on the Plains fighting Indians.

Sigel spent March and early April familiarizing himself with his troops and the area under his command. During this, he sent a constant barrage of letters to Grant, Halleck, and anyone else he thought could do something, complaining of meddling by Ord and that he lacked the men and materiel to undertake an offensive. His pleas and palpable angst for Washington's ears were balanced with a firm military bearing for local consumption. "Sigel is reorganizing the whole department and is getting very strict about everything," wrote the 12th West Virginia's surgeon Alexander Neil.[38] "It was with a good deal of pomp and circumstance that preparations were made," wrote Lieutenant Colonel Charles Fitz-Simmons of the 21st New York Cavalry. "Sigel . . . displayed great fondness for pageantry and parade [but that] only lasted while the enemy was at a distance."[39] Frank Reader of the 5th West Virginia Cavalry was more optimistic when he wrote, "Sigel will put things all right before he is done."[40] Reader continued: "The Department will be organized at last and then we will have affairs in good style once more. I hope it will soon come to pass."[41]

Clashes with Ord, the implementation of strict discipline, and a checkered record of field service spawned an active anti-Sigel element within the department. In early April, one of Crook's brigadiers reported being approached by an unknown civilian bearing a petition to the War Department for Sigel's removal from command. According to William Averell, who later advised Sigel of the petition's supposed existence, the document bore the signatures of Generals Kelley and Sullivan as well as the commander at Martinsburg, Colonel James A. Mulligan of the 23rd Illinois. When Averell heard that his own signature was said to be upon the document, he questioned

---

38 Duncan, *Alexander Neil*, 15.

39 Charles Fitz-Simmons, "Sigel's Fight at New Market," *Military Order of the Loyal Legion of the United States, Illinois* (Chicago, n.d.), vol. 3, 62.

40 Frank S. Reader diary, April 26, 1864, Washington & Lee University.

41 *Ibid.*, April 27, 1864.

the very existence of the petition and, if it did exist, the authenticity of the signatures upon it. The cavalry leader vehemently denied ever having seen such a document, let alone affixing his name to it.[42]

Just as the Federals were preparing for the spring offensive, so too were the Confederates organizing a defensive plan. With only several thousand troops to defend an immense area vulnerable to attack from several sides, John Breckinridge was faced with what his aide J. Stoddard Johnston rightfully termed "the prospect of a trying ordeal . . . as soon as the spring . . . campaign should open." The former vice president spent much of March on a 400-mile inspection tour of his new command. "Wherever he went," Johnston later wrote, "the officers and men were animated by his presence, and new life was infused into all branches of the service."[43]

When Breckinridge assumed command, he had just more than 5,000 troops of all arms—infantry, cavalry, and artillery—present in two infantry brigades and two cavalry brigades, with but a handful of serviceable artillery pieces. By the end of April, that number would grow to 6,500.[44] He could probably count on John Imboden in the Shenandoah Valley for reinforcement when the time came, but that would only add about 1,000 more men. Complicating matters was the fact that neither the Valley nor southwestern Virginia could be stripped bare of troops to reinforce another point, for leaving either open was to invite a Federal invasion into the vacuum left behind.

While many of Sigel's troops had limited or no combat experience, nearly all of Breckinridge's men had seen vigorous campaigning and fighting. Ironically, several of the Virginia units in Breckinridge's force were recruited from counties that had since seceded from Virginia to form the new pro-Union state of West Virginia. Some of these men would be fighting their former friends and neighbors.

In mid-April, General Lee sent a message to Imboden in the Valley warning him of a probable raid against the Virginia & Tennessee Railroad timed to coincide with the advance of the Army of the Potomac. Lee cautioned the Valley commander that should an advance be made up the Shenandoah, no reinforcements could be spared from the Army of Northern Virginia to assist

42 William Averell to Franz Sigel, May 31, 1864, Sigel Papers.

43 Johnston, "Sketches of Operations," 258.

44 Davis, *Breckinridge*, 409-410.

him. The only help available for Imboden would have to come from Breckinridge in southwestern Virginia.[45]

Imboden wasted no time in looking to the defense of the Valley. He called out the local companies of "reserves," or militia made up of boys too young and men too old to join the Confederate army. Rockingham County, in the central portion of the Valley, contributed six companies of reserves, two of cavalry and four of infantry.[46] Imboden also established a line of communication with Major General Francis H. Smith, superintendent of Virginia Military Institute in Lexington, in the event that the corps of cadets from the school need be pressed into service.

Founded in 1839, VMI had produced many of the officers leading Confederate troops, so many in fact that it often was referred to as the "West Point of the South." Several of its professors were also represented in the field, most notably Lieutenant General Thomas J. "Stonewall" Jackson and Major General Robert Rodes. In 1864, the cadet corps, some 280 strong, included several prominent and promising young warriors, including: George T. Lee, nephew of Robert E. Lee; Samuel Letcher, son of former governor John Letcher; John C. Early, Major General Jubal Early's nephew; William Patton, brother of Colonel George S. Patton (the grandfather of General George S. Patton of World War II fame), commander of the 22nd Virginia Infantry, one

Virginia Military Institute, Lexington, Virginia, 1857. *VMI Archives*

45 Clifford Dowdey and Louis Manarin, eds., *The Wartime Papers of R. E. Lee* (Boston, 1961), 703-704.

46 John L. Heatwole, *Remember Me is All I Ask: Chrisman's Boy Company: A History of the Civil War Service of Company A, 3rd Battalion Virginia Mounted Reserves* (Bridgewater, VA, 2000), 13.

of Breckinridge's regiments; James Morson, nephew of Confederate Secretary of War James Seddon; John S. Wise, son of former governor Brigadier General Henry Wise; Jacob Imboden, John Imboden's brother; and Robert and William Cabell, John Breckinridge's nephews. Another noteworthy member of the corps of cadets was William Charles Hardy of Norfolk, Virginia, whose sister Mary would later marry the former colonel of the 24th Wisconsin Infantry, Arthur MacArthur. Mary and Arthur's youngest son Douglas would become the Supreme Commander of the Allied Powers in the Southwest Pacific during World War II.[47]

When the war first began, the cadets of VMI had been led by Jackson himself to the fields outside Richmond, where they acted as drillmasters for the thousands of new recruits joining the army. They marched with Jackson again to the battle of McDowell in May 1862, but did not see any combat. By the spring of 1864, the boys were longing to fight. Life at VMI could not compare with active campaigning, or at least that was what most of them thought. Nineteen year-old Jacquelin Beverly Stanard, known to his friends as "Bev" or "Jack," captured the feeling of almost all the cadets when he wrote to his mother in late March, "I think you had just as well give your consent at once to my resigning and entering the Army. I want to have some of the glory of . . . the year 64 [sic] attached to my name."[48]

The first classmen (the senior class) at the institute went so far as to petition Superintendent Smith for early graduation so that they might join the army and serve the Southern cause.[49] "Excitement was at fever heat. The fourth class alone felt that it could lick anything in General Grant's army," one "rat" recalled.[50] They were told that Smith had tendered the services of the corps of cadets to General Lee, but that Lee preferred for the boys to stay in the classroom, not wishing to needlessly expose the Confederacy's "seedcorn." Still, Lee concluded, the cadets could be used if the need arose in the western part of the state. Smith advised Breckinridge that the corps that spring

---

47 Cadet biographical sketches are taken from William Couper, *The V.M.I. New Market Cadets* (Charlottesville, VA, 1933). Couper is a very useful source for the young men who comprised the "New Market Cadet Corps."

48 John G. Barrett and Robert K. Turner, eds., *Letters of a New Market Cadet: Beverly Stanard* (Bay Shore, NY, 1961), 47.

49 John F. Hanna diary, April 24, 1864, Virginia Military Institute.

50 Charles J. Anderson, "Recollections of a VMI Rat, 1864," Library of Virginia.

numbered about 250 effectives accompanied by a section of artillery. The cadet corps "is fully equipped . . . we have abundance of ammunition, tents, knapsacks, shovels & picks, and will be prepared to march at a moment's notice," explained VMI's superintendent.[51] The reports arriving at Imboden's and Breckinridge's headquarters suggested that the need might arise for the cadets' service in the field in the coming weeks.

In late April, Breckinridge and Imboden had their limited number of troops positioned to watch for an enemy advance. Their options were limited, for they could not begin to concentrate their men until Sigel revealed his hand. That he would soon be moving seemed obvious; the only question was when and where. "I think we shall leave this place [in] a few days for a long tramp," Isaac White, surgeon of the 62nd Virginia Mounted Infantry of Imboden's command, wrote to his wife from near Harrisonburg on April 30. "I do not know where we are to go."[52]

On May 1, just days before the Army of the Potomac would move against the Army of Northern Virginia, Lee advised Breckinridge to be ready to meet the threat wherever it may appear, and "to destroy him, if possible."[53]

51 Francis H. Smith to John C. Breckinridge, May 2, 1864, F. H. Smith Papers, VMI.

52 Isaac White to Mary Virginia White, April 30, 1864, White Papers.

53 OR 37, pt. 1, 707.

VMI's Superintendent Major General Francis Smith,
seen here in a previously unpublished photograph. *NOAA*

Chapter 3

"We Are in For Business Now"

John Imboden's cavalry actively kept a close eye on Federal movements and preparations in the lower Shenandoah Valley. In early April, portions of Imboden's 23rd Virginia Cavalry were stationed in the area around Winchester, gleaning what information they could about Sigel's intentions for the upcoming campaign. When Federal scouts reported the presence of two companies of the 23rd under Major Fielding Calmese operating on the road between Winchester and Romney, Major Hanson W. Hunter of the 6th West Virginia Cavalry was ordered to dispose of the menace.[1]

Gathering about 150 men from his own regiment as well as from the 7th West Virginia Cavalry and 14th Pennsylvania Cavalry, Hunter rode toward Romney on April 8, only to find his quarry had withdrawn to Winchester. Hunter pushed his mounted column toward the town from the west along the Romney road, arriving just as Calmese and his men were withdrawing up (south) the Shenandoah Valley. The blue horsemen pursued through Winchester and for about a mile or so beyond before calling off the pursuit. Worried that more of Imboden's men were in the immediate vicinity, Hunter returned to Winchester to regroup, leaving about 40 men of the 14th Pennsylvania to watch the Valley Pike. According to one account, Hunter was more interested in conversing with several Winchester ladies than properly

---

1 No two accounts agree on the spelling of Major Fielding Calmese's name. I have used this spelling because the others seem to be phonetic equivalents of it.

deploying his troops in case of a Confederate counter thrust. Whether or not Hunter's attentiveness was misplaced, Southern horsemen appeared on the scene a short time later.[2]

"In a little while the Yankees came back and went down the Martinsburg road; in a few moments they were followed by Calamise [sic] leading his men through the streets," Mrs. Hugh Lee, a resident of Winchester, wrote in her diary. She continued:

> A Yankee officer had the impudence to stop and beckon to our men to come on, that they were ready to fight them, but they soon found out their mistake. . . . In a few moments [I] had the pleasure of seeing our men coming back in small parties bringing prisoners with them. Our men pursued 150 Yankees below Stephenson's Depot, took forty prisoners, killed 7, wounded some and did not lose a single man. . . . It was so refreshing to see those vile Yankees who had been so insolent as they passed through not half an hour before, brought back prisoners. The officer who had dared our men to follow them was brought back, prisoner and wounded."[3]

Hunter's men were driven for three miles north of Winchester, during which they gave up about 27 troopers as prisoners. The small running engagement triggered a bit of controversy within the Union high command. Brigadier General William Averell's report of the affair was damning. In it, Averell described Hunter's actions as careless and lacking common sense. "[T]he Union women who witnessed the affair wept for shame," reported the disgusted general. "The men who were sent out on the expedition would have done better without a commanding officer." Sigel agreed, and ordered Hunter court-martialed for the "disgraceful and dastardly" affair. Hunter left the service several months later, his reputation forever tainted by the April 8 skirmish.[4]

When word of the small cavalry engagement reached General Lee's army, the consensus was that the running victory was a good omen for things to come in 1864. "It was a small affair but still gratifying," explained Walter Taylor, a member of Lee's staff. "All such encourage our men."[5] The Federals earned a

---

2   *OR 33*, 262-265.

3   Mrs. Hugh H. Lee diary, April 8, 1864, Handley Library.

4   *OR 33*, 262-265.

5   Tower, *Lee's Adjutant*, 151.

small measure of revenge the following month when Major Calmese was captured near Strasburg.[6]

In addition to raids by Imboden's cavalry, Sigel's men also faced the prospect of attack by the several groups of guerrillas operating in the vicinity, including those of John H. McNeill, Harry Gilmor, and the much-feared John S. Mosby. The Federals expected regular skirmishes with Imboden's cavalry, and for the Confederate horsemen to adopt standard battle tactics and rules of engagement. However, an encounter with the men riding with McNeill, Gilmor, or Mosby promised to be anything but standard. These guerrillas often attacked in the dead of night, seemingly from out of nowhere, only to disperse back into the darkness, usually with several prisoners and captured horses in tow. These groups, John Mosby's in particular, operated almost exclusively behind Federal lines. They relied on the local populace to house and feed them, although in the case of McNeill's men (many of whom hailed from the lower Valley and panhandle of West Virginia), many returned to their homes when they were not out on a raid. Even at this late stage in the war, Federals had yet to devise an effective plan to counter their unorthodox activities.

Mosby's command (a battalion) numbered several hundred men at its strongest point, but his and other similar irregular organizations functioned best in smaller groups. Operating with a few dozen riders allowed for celerity of movement and made it easier to cover greater distances undetected by enemy patrols. Favorite

Colonel John S. Mosby

Library of Congress

6   Richard Kleese, *23rd Virginia Cavalry* (Lynchburg, VA, 1996), 18-19.

targets included isolated posts, which could be infiltrated at night. Weakly guarded wagon trains offered prime targets once active campaigning began and larger armies were on the move. Any sutler or straggler traveling alone was almost asking to be captured. "This gang caused us no end of trouble," wrote one New York cavalryman.[7] Sigel advised his cavalry chief to undertake every effort to quell these disruptions, but made it clear that no infantry would be available to assist him in this difficult task.[8] Mosby and McNeill would be a growing thorn in the side of the Federals as the weeks passed.

In late March, a detachment of 125 men from the 21st New York Cavalry under Capt. E. B. Gore was sent to scout the area around Winchester. The troopers camped for the night on March 25 at Millwood, a village several miles east of Winchester. Three men from the regiment struck out on their own after dark in search of supper and thought they had found food at a farm house two miles from camp. Instead of finding an evening meal, they "were surprised to find several revolvers suddenly advance into the room" carried by none other than Mosby himself and two of his other officers.[9] While the prisoners and their captors were mounting their horses for the trip to Mosby's camp across the Blue Ridge, one of the New Yorkers took advantage of some turmoil and managed to escape.

The Confederate officers amused themselves on the trip across the mountains by taunting their two remaining prisoners, asking if they had been in any other engagements with Mosby's command. When they reached their destination several hours later, one of the New Yorkers snatched a pistol away from his captors, killed one, and used the confusion to make good his escape with his comrade—one of them mounted on Mosby's own horse.[10]

Apart from light cavalry skirmishes, life for the men along the B&O was routine. Colonel George Wells of the 34th Massachusetts found his duty so boring that he confided to his parents, "I only wish . . . that the regiment could

---

7 Jacob Lester, *Autobiography of Jacob Lester* (Binghamton, NY, 1931), 7, copy courtesy of Nancy Armstrong, Endwell, NY.

8 *OR* 33, 842.

9 When describing encounters with Confederate guerrillas, nearly every Union soldier determined that not only were they Mosby's men, but usually Mosby himself was among them, although he rarely was. However, this seems to be one instance when Mosby himself actually was present. Jeff Wert, in his history *Mosby's Rangers* (New York, 1990), gives this account credence.

10 Boston *Herald*, April 9, 1864.

be with the Army of the Potomac." Wells was the commander of the Martinsburg garrison, a job he did not find to his liking. "I have a nice large room for an office in the best house in town and I sit and say 'no' to weeping women who want passes all day long—but this is not what I joined the army for."[11] Such laments were shared by many of the men in the ranks. "Nothing new today," complained one soldier to his journal. "Military movements are very slow indeed. No signs of a move and we are . . . getting the blues."[12] A visit to Cumberland by Vice-President Hannibal Hamlin on April 9 broke the monotony for the troops there, if only briefly. Beyond Hamlin's visit, however, it remained "all quiet on the Potomac" for the large majority of Sigel's command.[13]

The one place it was not "all quiet" was at Sigel's headquarters. The German general was tasked with implementing his instructions for the upcoming campaign whether General Edward Ord remained with him or not. When relations soured between the two and Ord finally left on April 17, Sigel was forced to revamp the operational plan.

As originally envisioned, George Crook would lead a column to strike at the Virginia & Tennessee Railroad in the vicinity of Dublin and Blacksburg. Supporting Crook would be William Averell with about 2,000 cavalry to raid the salt works at Saltville. With Ord out of the picture, Sigel decided to take the opportunity to leave his desk behind in Cumberland and assume direct command of the column moving up the Valley from Martinsburg. The plan was basically a replication of the Averell-Wells raid of the previous December, though on a grander scale. This strategy would have three separate columns for the Confederates to confront, in an area where they were hard-pressed for enough troops to stop even one invading force. All three columns planned to unite at Staunton in the upper Valley, placing them in a position to either march east against Lee's strategic left flank or capture the Confederate supply center at Lynchburg, Virginia, across the Blue Ridge. The jump-off date for the offensive was set for the first day of May.

Crook's force consisted of 6,100 men, the infantry arranged in three brigades reporting directly to Crook, and two batteries of artillery and one

---

11 George Duncan Wells Letterbook, April 21, 1864, East Carolina University.

12 Reader diary, March 25-26, 1864.

13 Reader diary, April 9, 1864.

cavalry regiment. Averell's Saltville-bound column included about 2,000 horsemen.[14] In a last-minute change, Crook advised Sigel that if they were successful, Averell and Crook would combine their commands and move east independently of Sigel. The German commander was upset at the change, and let Grant know. The new general-in-chief tried to assuage Sigel by telling him that crippling the Virginia & Tennessee was the most important goal of the campaign.[15]

Sigel's own "army" consisted of one infantry division under Jeremiah Sullivan, one cavalry division under Julius Stahel, and five artillery batteries, in all about 9,000 men.[16] Sullivan's infantry was organized into two brigades. The First Infantry Brigade under Colonel Augustus Moor of the 28th Ohio consisted of the 18th Connecticut and 28th, 116th, and 123rd Ohio regiments. The Second Infantry Brigade under Colonel Joseph Thoburn of the 1st West Virginia was comprised of the 1st and 12th West Virginia, 34th Massachusetts, and 54th Pennsylvania regiments. Stahel's cavalry division also was divided into two brigades. The first, consisting of the 1st New York Veteran, 1st New York (Lincoln)[17], 21st New York, and detachments of the 14th Pennsylvania and 1st Maryland Potomac Home Regiment, all under the command of Colonel William Tibbits of the 21st New York. The second brigade consisted of detachments of the 15th New York and 20th and 22nd Pennsylvania, all under Colonel John E. Wynkoop. Rounding out the command were five artillery batteries under Captain Alonzo Snow: Battery B, 1st Maryland Light ("Snow's Battery"); 30th New York ("Von Kleiser's Battery"); Battery D, 1st West Virginia ("Carlin's Battery"); Battery G, 1st West Virginia Light ("Ewing's Battery"), and Battery B, 5th U.S. ("DuPont's Battery").[18]

---

14 Howard R. McManus, *The Battle of Cloyds Mountain: The Virginia and Tennessee Railroad Raid, April 29-May 19, 1864* (Lynchburg, VA, 1989), 8.

15 *Ibid.*, 5.

16 Davis, *Battle of New Market*, 193-5.

17 The existence of two 1st New York Cavalry regiments can be somewhat confusing. The 1st New York (Lincoln) Cavalry is the regiment that was formed early in the war upon the call by President Lincoln for volunteers to put down the rebellion. The 1st New York Veteran Cavalry was formed in November 1863 primarily from veterans of other units whose enlistments had expired. The terminology 1st New York (Lincoln) Cavalry and 1st New York Veteran Cavalry will be used in this narrative to refer to these two units.

18 Letter Capt. Alfred von Kleiser to Capt. Henry A. DuPont of June 13, 1864, in von Kleiser files, New Market Battlefield State Historical Park, states that Alonzo Snow was chief of

Colonel George D. Wells

Library of Congress

Sigel had to do a bit of juggling to get the officers he wanted in command of brigades. George Wells of the 34th Massachusetts was one of his senior colonels and arguably the brightest military mind in Sigel's sphere of subordinates. Sigel, however, wanted his brigades in the hands of men he trusted, so Wells and the 34th were shuffled about to make sure the regiment was grouped with others whose commanders' commissions pre-dated Wells'. Only time would show whether that decision was a wise one.

With the 1st of May only days away, Sigel made his final preparations. "Troops still going and coming and from present indications we will soon be ready for the field," one soldier wrote in his diary.[19] The wholesale movement of men was also observed by another soldier, who noted that "For the last week the forces in this department have all been congregating at Martinsburg."[20] The men were subjected to as much drill as time would allow, and detailed inspections were common. One West Virginia soldier remembered that each inspection "was minute and almost individual in character," with Sigel

artillery during the New Market campaign. According to the obituary of Capt. John Carlin in Wheeling *Register*, March 19, 1887, Carlin held that position. I believe Snow held this position. Snow's own Battery B, 1st Maryland Light Artillery, was under the direct command of one of his junior officers, which lends credence to the presumption that Snow was charged with higher command.

19 Reader diary, April 28, 1964.

20 Arthur Stone to "My Dear Mother," April 29, 1864, author's collection.

seemingly inspecting each man, "looking sharply into their eyes, apparently to see if there was fight there."[21] A soldier in the 1st West Virginia recorded in his diary that he experienced drill or inspection every day from April 24 through 28.[22] The men of Snow's Maryland Battery were subjected to three periods of daily drill. These intense training sessions included experimenting with different types of ordnance at various ranges, though with mixed results. When Captain Snow added an evening dress parade the officers balked. Convinced it was too much, unnecessary, or both, the commander removed it from their schedule.[23]

By this time it was obvious to the lowest private that something was about to begin, and the Army rumor mill began to churn out a host of possibilities. "It is a great mistery [sic] . . . what General Grant is going to do," wrote a Massachusetts soldier. One rumor floating around the camps at Martinsburg was "that Lee was going to send a part of his army up the Valley so as to divide the Army of the Potomac."[24]

Sigel moved his headquarters from Cumberland to Martinsburg on the 25th of April. Two days later he held a grand review of the small army gathered there.[25] The line of troops extended for about five miles, remembered one observer, and the entire affair lasted several hours. It was the first time these organizations had been in line together, and it didn't go very smoothly.[26] "Such a time as we had finding our places in the line was never seen before," remembered Lieutenant Colonel Wildes of the 116th Ohio.[27]

On April 28, tents and excess baggage were shipped under guard for storage at Martinsburg. Orders filtered their way down through the ranks to move out the next morning. As one Connecticut soldier summed it up, "We are in for business now."[28]

---

21 Hewitt, *History of the Twelfth Regiment West Virginia Volunteer Infantry*, 99.

22 Elizabeth Davis Swiger, ed., *Civil War Letters and Diary of Joshua Winters: A Private in the Union Army, Company G, First Western Virginia Volunteer Infantry* (Parsons, WV, 1991), 102-3.

23 Erika L. Quesenbery, *A Snowball's Chance: Battery B, Maryland Light Artillery 1st, Snow's* (Port Deposit, MD, 2003), 182-3.

24 J. Chapin Warner to "Dear Father & Mother," April 20, 1864, Massachusetts Hist. Society.

25 Sigel, "Sigel in the Shenandoah Valley in 1864," 487.

26 Duncan, *Alexander Neil*, 21.

27 Wildes, *Record of the One Hundred and Sixteenth Regiment Ohio Infantry Volunteers*, 82.

28 Lynch, *The Civil War Diary of Charles H. Lynch*, 55.

Brigadier General
Gabriel Wharton

Library of Congress

While Sigel was making his final preparations, John Breckinridge was seeking additional troops. In late April, two more brigades were ordered to report to him. One was a cavalry brigade under Brigadier General John Hunt Morgan. The second was a small infantry command under Brigadier General Gabriel Colvin Wharton.

Wharton was born in 1824 in Virginia. Following in the footsteps of a long line of ancestors who had served in the military, he entered the Virginia Military Institute and graduated second in the Class of 1847. He spent the antebellum years as an engineer in the New Mexico Territory, but when his native Virginia seceded he tossed his lot in with the new Confederacy. He was commissioned a major in the 45th Virginia Infantry. He served with that regiment only briefly before raising the 51st Virginia Infantry, of which he was elected colonel. Wharton fought at Fort Donelson in Tennessee in early 1862 and was one of the officers who escaped prior to the surrender. He spent much of 1862 and 1863 as a brigade commander in eastern Tennessee and southwest Virginia. Together, Morgan's and Wharton's commands boosted Breckinridge's small army by almost 3,000 men. The addition of Wharton provided Breckinridge with three reliable—though still dispersed—infantry brigades, in addition to enough cavalry to credibly meet a Union advance. Wharton's men were headed to Narrows, twenty miles north of Dublin, and his third brigade, led by Colonel John McCausland, was en route to Princeton, West Virginia. Breckinridge's horsemen provided a thin but effective screen along the mountains to provide

Brigadier General
John Echols

Library of Congress

ample warning to allow the infantry to concentrate. The cavalry at the northern end of his line connected with Imboden's men guarding the upper Valley.[29]

General Breckinridge's largest infantry brigade under Brigadier General John Echols was stationed at Lewisburg, West Virginia, about forty miles north of department headquarters at Dublin. Born in 1823 in Lynchburg, Virginia, John Echols was one of the few senior officers in Breckinridge's command who was not a graduate of the Virginia Military Institute. A giant of a man (he stood six foot four inches tall and weighed 260 pounds), Echols graduated from VMI's next-door neighbor Washington College (today's Washington & Lee University) before attending law school at Harvard. He commanded the 27th Virginia of the "Stonewall Brigade" at First Manassas and Kernstown, but a serious wound suffered during the latter battle kept him out of action for several months. He returned to duty in 1863 in southwest Virginia.[30]

With his command so augmented, Breckinridge's main concern was now finding the enemy and deciding how best to defeat him in battle.

29   Ezra Warner, *Generals in Gray* (Baton Rouge, LA, 1983), 331.

30   *Ibid.*, 80.

Chapter 4

Into the Valley of Defeat

During the morning of Friday, April 29, Sigel's main body set out from Martinsburg "for a trip down the Valley," as one soldier termed it.[1] Each man carried five days' rations and 60 rounds of ammunition.[2] Averell left Charleston with his horsemen on May 1; Crook's column moved out the next day from the Kanawha Valley.

The day before Sigel's advance, a contingent of 200 Federal cavalrymen spurred their mounts for Winchester. When a straggler from that party was shot and wounded there, Federal troops—thinking the man had been shot by a civilian—ordered the arrest of three men. They were released after it was determined the soldier was injured by one of Imboden's Rebels.[3] An account several weeks later in the Staunton *Spectator*, provided either by the Confederate shooter himself—probably William R. Jones of the 23rd Virginia Cavalry[4]—or his father went to great lengths to show that the Southern soldier had acted well within the boundaries of accepted military tactics:

1   Arthur Stone to mother, April 29, 1864, author's collection.

2   Jacob M. Campbell diary, April 28, 1864, West Virginia University.

3   John C. Bonnell, Jr., *Sabres in the Shenandoah: The 21st New York Cavalry, 1863-1866* (Shippensburg, PA, 1996), 35.

4   Kleese, *23rd Virginia Cavalry*, 78-9. The *Spectator's* account claims that the "Jones" in question had recently been recruited by a Captain Adams in Winchester. The regimental roster in Kleese contains a "William Robert 'Rammer' Jones," who matches this description.

Sometime after their [Federal cavalry] departure from the town, one of them returned and halted his horse on Main Street, nearly opposite the house occupied by the father of young Jones [the Confederate soldier]. Presently Jones emerged in Confederate uniform and walking across the street directly towards the Yankee, when at a proper distance, accosted him, and demanded his surrender. The Yankee made no reply but moved his hand towards his pistol, which motion Jones perceiving, instantly fired, the ball passing through the left breast of his antagonist. The Yankee fell gently from his horse, and in falling, begged his assailant not to fire again, that he surrendered; whereupon Jones, mounting the horse, ordered him to hand him his saber and pistols, which he did. Jones then, in double-quick, left town by a by-road...safe, fully armed and equipped, and handsomely mounted.[5]

Hopes were high for the campaign, with many of the Federal troops looking for redemption in a theater that had thus far in the war brought nothing but disaster. According to assistant surgeon Neil of the 12th West Virginia, "everybody is in good spirits and confident of a successful campaign."[6] According to another West Virginia soldier, "We were about to start up what had hitherto been . . . the Valley of defeat and humiliation."[7] Arthur Stone of the 34th Massachusetts believed much the same thing. On the morning the army moved out, Stone wrote home, "Before many days pass you will here [sic] of something being done up in this direction."[8]

Sigel's army stretched out for about six miles along the pike, and it took two hours for the entire column to pass a single point.[9] Sigel's headquarters train alone comprised a dozen wagons and ambulances with some twenty-three tents for the headquarters staff.[10] Company F of the 1st New York (Lincoln) Cavalry served as Sigel's personal escort.[11]

The column trudged ten miles that day through some rather unseasonable heat to reach Bunker Hill, a small village halfway between Martinsburg and

5   Staunton *Spectator*, May 24, 1864.

6   Duncan, *Alexander Neil*, 23.

7   Hewitt, *History of the Twelfth Regiment West Virginia Volunteer Infantry*, 104.

8   Arthur Stone to mother, April 29, 1864.

9   Duncan, *Alexander Neil*, 23.

10 Theodore F. Lang to Franz Sigel, May 2, 1864, Sigel Papers.

11 William H. Beach, *The First New York (Lincoln) Cavalry from April 19, 1861 to July 7, 1865* (New York, 1902), 318.

Winchester.[12] The following day was spent in camp there, where Army paymasters paid the troops a welcome visit. A portion of the army was subjected to knapsack inspections, an untimely intrusion that must have caused no small bit of grumbling within the ranks. The rested and paid men were subjected to a heavy rain that evening, which continued throughout the night.[13]

While his army rested at Bunker Hill, Sigel turned his attention toward Crook. Sigel advised the commander at Beverly, Colonel Thomas M. Harris, located in the mountains between his force and Crook's, to "keep up a strong show . . . as much as practicable to create [a] diversion in favor of Genl [sic] Crook."[14] Although Sigel's early effort at cooperation seemed to bode well for Federal success in his department, whatever level of communication that existed between Crook and Sigel virtually ceased a short time after the campaign got underway.

The Federals broke camp Sunday morning and entered Winchester that evening. The ground over which they moved was some of the most beautiful in Virginia, but it was also some of the most contested terrain in the country, having been the scene of almost weekly small-scale engagements. "There was perhaps not a mile along the whole route over which we passed along which there could not be seen a soldier's grave," one West Virginia soldier remembered.[15] Colonel Strother of Sigel's staff had a similar recollection: "The country was a picture of desolation . . . on all sides were seen graves, bones and dead animals."[16] An officer from the 12th West Virginia described Winchester as "one of the most desolate places" he had ever seen.[17]

Sigel's army entered Winchester to a mostly cool reception from the local population. The town was largely pro-Southern in sentiment and had changed hands dozens of times during the war. Previous occupations by Union troops had not always been kind to its citizens. One soldier remembered that many of the townspeople looked upon them coldly, and only one or two United States flags were displayed when the soldiers entered the town. One of Winchester's

12 Lynch, *The Civil War Diary of Charles H. Lynch*, 55-6.

13 Swiger, *Civil War Letters and Diary of Joshua Winters*, 103.

14 Thayer Melvin to Col. J. M. Harris, May 1, 1864, Sigel Papers.

15 Hewitt, *History of the Twelfth Regiment West Virginia Volunteer Infantry*, 104.

16 Eby, *A Virginia Yankee in the Civil War*, 221.

17 Linda C. Fluharty, ed., *Civil War Letters of Lt. Milton B. Campbell* (Baton Rouge, LA, 2004), 97.

ladies was quite alarmed at being under Federal occupation again. "Goodness!" she exclaimed. "The Yanks are again in possession of this time-worn and down-trodden town."[18] "Here we are again in Yankee hands," grumbled another resident.[19] For the town's handful of Unionist residents, however, the appearance of Sigel's men constituted a welcome sight. "We are once again under the protection of the Stars and Stripes," wrote one.[20]

The troops passed through Winchester and encamped near Hollingsworth's Mill about a mile south on the Valley Pike.[21] A portion of the 123rd Ohio was detailed as the city's provost guard.[22] The 18th Connecticut was sent forward almost as far as Kernstown, where the regiment established a ring of pickets around the town's southern outskirts.[23]

Many of the men in the army were seeing Winchester for the first time, and were struck by the effect the war had had on the once-thriving community. "Winchester was once the most beautiful city of Virginia," recorded Dr. Neil, but three years of war had left it largely in ruins.[24] One New Yorker described the town as a "sad wreck."[25] Colonel William Tibbits of the 21st New York Cavalry noted in his diary, "There are many Union families here. People very much run down by the war."[26]

This was not the first time the Buckeyes from the 123rd Ohio had been in Winchester. They, along with the 18th Connecticut, had been cut to pieces at Winchester the previous summer under General Milroy. The return allowed the veterans of that fight to tour the old battlefield. Many of the men who fell in that engagement were still there, buried in the fields surrounding the town. Some

---

18 Duncan, *Beleaguered Winchester*, 185.

19 Michael G. Mahon, *Winchester Divided* (Mechanicsburg, PA, 2002), 142.

20 Duncan, *Beleaguered Winchester*, 185.

21 William C. Walker, *History of the 18th Regiment Connecticut Volunteers in the War for the Union* (Norwich, CT, 1885), 215.

22 Charles M. Keyes, *The Military History of the 123rd Regiment of Ohio Volunteer Infantry* (Sandusky, OH, 1884), 53-4.

23 Lynch, *The Civil War Diary of Charles H. Lynch*, 56. Kernstown today is effectively the southern suburb of Winchester. During the war it was a separate village several miles to the south along the Valley Pike.

24 Duncan, *Alexander Neil*, 25.

25 Lester, *Autobiography of Jacob Lester*, 8.

26 William Tibbits diary, May 3, 1864, New York State Library.

had been buried in such haste that their remains were visible around the camps, "their bones bleaching in the sunshine," remembered one eyewitness.[27] When several men from the 123rd found one of their comrades partially buried adjacent to the 18th Connecticut's camp, the fallen Ohioan was given a proper burial. The chaplain of the 18th officiated.[28]

At first, admitted one resident, Sigel's Federals "were tolerably quiet."[29] The uneventful occupation did not last long. On May 2, Federal troops burned at least one building on Loudon Street. It was never determined whether the structure was destroyed intentionally, but the cavalryman from the 21st New York shot four days earlier fell in that vicinity. Perhaps the building was torched to extract a pound of vengeance.[30] Two other homes on Main Street were also consumed by flames not long after Sigel's men arrived in town.[31] The implementation of a "strict blockade" between Winchester and Martinsburg— a move that promised to greatly benefit the coffers of a handful of sutlers accompanying the army—did not help matters. It was hoped the sutlers would open their stores to the public as well as the troops. "Almost everyone is out of groceries," one resident complained, "and will buy all that is possible."[32] However, orders were issued that prevented the townspeople from visiting the sutlers. "Our only alleviation in having them [Federals] here is denied us," complained Laura Lee.[33]

Word spread quickly throughout the community that the Yankees were back in the Valley in force, news that was not well received by most of the Valley's residents. One resident of Front Royal, several miles southeast of Winchester, noted in her diary the day after Sigel entered Winchester: "Fancied we saw Yankee's campfires on . . . North Mountain. Report says they are at Winchester en route up the Valley."[34]

---

27 Duncan, *Alexander Neil*, 26.

28 Walker, *History of the 18th Regiment Connecticut Volunteers*, 215.

29 Mahon, *Winchester Divided*, 142.

30 Delauter, *Winchester*, 69.

31 Duncan, *Beleaguered Winchester*, 187.

32 Mahon, *Winchester Divided*, 142.

33 *Ibid.*

34 William P. Buck, ed., *Sad Earth, Sweet Heaven: The Diary of Lucy Rebecca Buck During the War Between the States* (Birmingham, AL, 1992), 252.

Sigel's advance had been anticipated. Once word reached him that the Federals were on the move, John Imboden moved north from the vicinity of Harrisonburg on May 2. His force consisted of the 18th and 23rd Virginia Cavalry regiments, the 62nd Virginia Mounted Infantry (which lacked horses at the time and was thus "mounted infantry" in name only), two small battalions of Maryland cavalry, and one battery of artillery, a total of about 1,500 men. Imboden's intent was to "find out as far as possible [Sigel's] strength and designs."[35]

While Imboden moved northward, Breckinridge's scouts were reporting the presence of a large enemy force (Crook) in the Kanawha Valley. Shortly after this, on May 4, a telegram from Richmond arrived at Breckinridge's headquarters "indicating the probable necessity of taking [his] command to the Valley" to link up with Imboden.[36] This information forced Breckinridge to

---

35 John D. Imboden, "The Battle of New Market, VA., May 15th, 1864," in Johnson and Buel, eds., *Battles and Leaders of the Civil War*, vol. 4, 480. Care must be employed when using Imboden's postwar writings because he had a habit of inflating the importance of his own role.

36 J. Stoddard Johnston, "Draft of a report of the Battle of New Market," J. S. Johnston Papers, New Market collection, Virginia Military Institute Archives, hereafter "Breckinridge's Official New Market Report." The *Official Records*, 37, pt. 1, p. 87, lists the "Report of Major General John C. Breckinridge" for the Battle of New Market. This "report" was sent to Richmond at 7:00 p.m. on the evening of the battle, literally as the guns were falling silent on the field. Its brevity suggests that it was intended only as a telegraphic communiqué with the War Department to advise Davis and his officials of his victory over Sigel, rather than as an official report of the engagement. His final (unfinished) campaign report was not included in the *Official Records* and was probably never filed with Richmond. The only known copy is an 8-page draft handwritten by Breckinridge's chief of staff, Major J. Stoddard Johnston, housed in Johnston's Papers in the New Market Collection at VMI. The document appears to have been written by Johnston and passed to Breckinridge for his review, for it is similar in style to Johnston's postwar writings about New Market and includes a note signed by Johnston that it is a "draft of a report of the Battle of New Market, May 15, 1864, between General Breckinridge and General Sigel written by me." In fact, Johnston's 1879 article in the *Southern Historical Society Papers* about New Market (June 1879, 257-62) is nearly verbatim in places, so it is likely Johnston had a copy of this document when he wrote this article. This after-action report, addressed to Lieutenant Colonel Walter Taylor, adjutant to Robert E. Lee, claims to cover the period of May 5, 1864 to June 19, 1864, which would include not only the New Market campaign but also Cold Harbor and Lynchburg. Unfortunately, the report ends abruptly with the conclusion of the fighting at New Market on the evening of May 15. The report is not dated, but likely never made its way to Taylor, and may not have even been written during the war. This is supported by a brief letter to Johnston dated January 1866 found among R. E. Lee's papers at Washington & Lee University regarding "a copy of the narrative of Genl Breckinridge's operations, which you are compiling for him." General Lee was gathering his papers to compile his memoirs and reached out to key subordinates and former staff officers, especially in those instances where no official report had been sent to the War Department (as was the case for New Market). Fearing for his own safety (he had served as James Buchanan's vice-president before the war and was regarded by some in

Major
William McLaughlin
(postwar)

Washington & Lee University

confront the uncomfortable possibility of having to defend two fronts at the same time—and it was too early to determine which thrust was a feint or diversion. "I trust you will drive the enemy back," General Lee telegraphed the Kentuckian. Lee could offer nothing but moral support, for the Army of the Potomac was now across the Rapidan River and mired in heavy fighting in the Wilderness with the Army of Northern Virginia.[37] The following day, Breckinridge reported, Lee ordered him to move "with all my available force" to the Valley to meet Sigel.[38]

Breckinridge's "available force" to make the move consisted of three infantry brigades and one battalion of field artillery comprised of a dozen guns under Major William H. McLaughlin. Left behind to confront Crook and Averell were three small cavalry brigades under Brigadier Gens. Albert Jenkins, William E. Jones, and John Hunt Morgan, together with a handful of

the North as one of the most important "traitors" of the "rebellion") Breckinridge fled the country after the war and eventually settled in Canada before returning to his native Kentucky years later. In early 1866, Breckinridge was unsure whether the Federal government would prosecute him, and so Major Johnston served as his intermediary with Lee, who wrote to Johnston, "I am very glad to learn a mode of communication with Genl Breckinridge [sic] and will take advantage of it." The name by which Lee refers to Johnston's document, "the narrative of Genl Breckinridge's operations," is similar to the title of Johnston's account of New Market published in *Southern Historical Society Papers* four years after Breckinridge's death: "Sketches of Operations of General John C. Breckinridge."

37 *OR* 37, pt. 1, 712.

38 Breckinridge's Official New Market Report.

unassigned units and reserves. Acknowledging that "the situation of affairs in my Department was precarious," Breckinridge later observed that "nothing but the necessity of preserving Staunton as the left of General Lee's . . . line would have justified its temporary abandonment to the occupation of the enemy."[39] As Breckinridge moved out, he sent a message to Jenkins that "The whole country west of New River is uncovered and depends on you."[40]

Breckinridge personally rode out on May 5. He arrived at Staunton three days later in advance of his troops. The infantry brigades under Wharton and Echols began their march north to the Valley on the 6th, while McCausland's foot soldiers remained behind for as long as possible to keep watch on Crook's movements.[41]

Even as Southern forces moved out, there was still uncertainty about Sigel's movements and Federal intentions in the Valley. On May 6, the Staunton *Vindicator* reported that the Federals had occupied Strasburg, with outposts at Woodstock, but "that the movement up the Valley was to cover the movement of Sigel, who is reported to have crossed to Meade's Army [of the Potomac] by way of Front Royal."[42]

Breckinridge continued searching for additional manpower for his patchwork army even after he arrived at Staunton. Imboden had already called out the reserves of Augusta and Rockingham counties three weeks earlier. The bulk of these were boys 16 to 17 years old and men over the age of 45, most of whom reached the gathered Southern force armed with whatever weapons they could find, usually shotguns and other hunting weapons. The reserves, under Colonel William H. Harman, would not be suited for front-line combat, but could be used to guard supply wagons, freeing up other troops to fight. The call for troops also went out to Superintendent Francis Smith in Lexington: VMI's Corps of Cadets was needed.

Jacob Hildebrand, a 45-year-old Mennonite farmer living near Fishersville in Augusta County, was one of those summoned to report for duty with the reserves. "All persons between the ages of 17 & 18 years and also between 45-50 have orders to report to the enrolling officer at Staunton," he scribbled in

---

39 *Ibid.*

40 Jack L. Dickinson, *Jenkins of Greenbottom: A Civil War Saga* (Charleston, WV, 1988), 68.

41 Breckinridge's Official New Market Report.

42 Staunton *Vindicator*, May 6, 1864.

his diary on April 16. Five days later, locals were ordered to bring their horses to Staunton to be impressed into service.[43] For many it was but the first of several times they would be called into service during 1864.

Although the potential situation in the Shenandoah Valley was precarious for Southern arms, Sigel and his commanders gave the Confederates an unexpected gift: the time to organize and prepare to meet them. After taking Winchester, any sense of urgency of mission drained out of Sigel's schedule. The day his forces marched into Winchester, Sigel sent word to Grant that he estimated enemy strength in the lower Valley to be no more than 3,000, but anticipated that Southern reinforcements would arrive soon. "We will . . . push our advance toward Cedar Creek," about twelve miles south of Winchester, he confidently added.[44] His tone suggested that he intended to move as far as possible up the Valley before the Confederates could assemble a sufficient force to resist the thrust. Thus far, communications from Crook suggested his advance was also moving apace. The day after he confidently informed Grant of his intentions to press up the Valley, however, Sigel asked the General in Chief, "I would very much like to know what your expectations are."[45] He could not advance much farther, continued Sigel, without significant reinforcements. In what surely must have surprised Grant, Sigel asked if there were any elements of the Army of the Potomac operating in the Valley. An exasperated Grant reminded his department commander that his troops were the only ones west of the Blue Ridge Mountains. Grant also re-outlined the plan: Sigel would march for Staunton, and if the enemy prevented such a move, he would advance to Cedar Creek and at the very least observe enemy movements in the Valley to prevent a move by the Confederates across the mountains to reinforce Lee's army.[46]

43 John R. Hildebrand, ed., *A Mennonite Journal, 1862-1865* (Shippensburg, PA, 1996), 40. On the 23rd, Hildebrand and all others eligible for service in the reserves were organized into a four-company battalion, with companies commanded by Captains Joseph F. Hottel, John Nunan, Robert W. Stevenson, and James C. Cochran. Hottel, of Company A, was a veteran of the 52nd Virginia Infantry. Two days after the Augusta reserves were formed, Hildebrand petitioned for, and eventually received, an exemption from military service. Hildebrand, *A Mennonite Journal*, 40-2, 82.

44 *OR* 37, pt. 1, 364.

45 *Ibid.*, 368.

46 *Ibid.*, 368-9.

Despite intelligence on enemy weakness and the exchanges with Grant, Sigel failed to comprehend the need for a quick advance. Even though his scouts were inflating Imboden's actual numbers twice over, Sigel still would have a two-to-one advantage in manpower. If he was concerned that additional Confederates were on their way—which indeed they were, though the Federals did not yet know this—it was all the more reason for prompt action. Knowing that Grant was heavily engaged with Lee, and having been told again what was expected of him, Franz Sigel did exactly the opposite of what his superior expected: he established himself and his army in Winchester. "No person but the Gen'l [sic] commanding has the slightest idea what disposition is to be made of the forces here," complained a 12th West Virginia officer.[47]

On May 5, Sigel ordered all the residents of the town into their homes and conducted a massive house-by-house search for contraband items, which resulted in the destruction of a large number of weapons. For two days no one was allowed to enter or leave the town.[48] "Old Sigel is worse than Milroy," one resident confided in her diary. "Not a soul has been permitted to leave town or one citizen to come in. Sigel has arrested every boy and man he can find out in the country and a good many of the townspeople," she continued.[49]

By all appearances, Sigel had abandoned any idea of an advance. The army reverted to the same routine it had followed before departing Martinsburg—drill, inspection, review. "Nothing of special interest occurred," remembered one bored Connecticut soldier. "The troops were drilled, inspected and reviewed nearly every day."[50] Several days before, Sigel had issued orders dictating at least three hours of drill per day, "at least two hours in the morning, and one in the afternoon."[51] One Pennsylvania soldier sarcastically summed up a typical day in camp at Winchester: "Drill, brigade drill, made a gallant charge today."[52]

---

47 Fluharty, *Civil War Letters of Lt. Milton B. Campbell*, 98.

48 Delauter, *Winchester*, 69.

49 Quoted in Garland R. Quarles, *Occupied Winchester 1861-1865* (Winchester, VA, 1991), 93.

50 Walker, *History of the 18th Regiment Connecticut Volunteers*, 215.

51 Julius Stahel circular, April 30, 1864, Augustus Moor Papers, Heinrich Rattermann Collection, Illinois Historical Survey, University of Illinois, Urbana.

52 Jacob Cohn diary, May 2, 1864, original in possession of Charles Harris, Ooltewah, Tennessee.

Private Joshua Winters,
1st West Virginia Infantry

Elizabeth Swiger

When Sigel staged a review or brigade drill, it was no small affair. While the troops stood under an unseasonably warm sun for hours on end, he and his staff rode with great flourish around the sprawling drill field. Sigel's propensity for micromanagement became obvious to nearly everyone when he took it upon himself to observe every drill and exercise his regiments performed. If he spotted any errors in the execution of a maneuver, even by a lone private in the ranks, the general would insert himself into the drill and demonstrate the proper way it was to be done.[53] "He puts them thro' [sic] while he is at it. A terrible noise is kept going by the bands all the while," one soldier remembered.[54] According to Private Joshua Winters of the 1st West Virginia, the fields around Winchester are "a vary [sic] pretty place to drill [but] they keep us at [it] four or five hours a day. I do hate to drill these hot days."[55] On more than one occasion, Sigel was witnessed personally conducting

53 Fluharty, *Civil War Letters of Lt. Milton B. Campbell,* 97-8.

54 Reader diary, May 4, 1864.

55 Swiger, *Civil War Letters and Diary of Joshua Winters,* 105.

knapsack inspections.[56] The army commander was convinced of his unquestionable knowledge of military tactics and drill field maneuvers. When one of his regimental officers questioned an order, Sigel exploded, "I don't want any suggestions from battalion commanders! All I want from them is to listen carefully to the orders, as they are issued, and to repeat them, precisely as they are received."[57]

On May 5, the same day Sigel confined residents to their homes and searched many of them, he held another of his grand reviews of the army. This time, however, he wanted to see how his men would behave in battle. In one of the most comedic episodes of the entire campaign, Sigel staged a mock combat on the hills outside Winchester. An Ohio officer described it as "the funniest farce ever witnessed," and concluded that it would never be forgotten by anyone who took part in it.[58] An officer in Snow's Battery described their part in the mock action: "drill[ing] with a regiment of infantry, skirmishing, charging, resisting infantry and cavalry; advancing, retiring." Although one of the battery's junior officers blundered during one portion of maneuver, Sigel declared the battery to be "the finest he ever saw."[59]

At the beginning of the "engagement" the 34th Massachusetts was deployed as skirmishers while the rest of the army deployed behind them. As the infantry charged and fired with the artillery booming over their heads, the Bay Staters, obedient to their orders, continued to advance as chaos took root behind them. A large part of the confusion that ensued came about because few of Sigel's or Stahel's personal staff spoke English, and almost none of them and only a handful of the field commanders knew brigade or battalion maneuvers. The men of the 116th Ohio were sent from one end of the field to the other before being given the order to charge. To cap off their experience, the regiment's colonel didn't hear the order to withdraw and a staff officer had to be sent after the regiment.[60]

Once the maneuvers ended, Sigel's exhausted and confused army returned to camp. Someone took note that the camp of the 34th Massachusetts was

56 Fluharty, *Civil War Letters of Lt. Milton B. Campbell,* 98.

57 Thomas Lewis, *The Shenandoah in Flames* (Alexandria, VA, 1987), 25.

58 Wildes, *Record of the One Hundred and Sixteenth Regiment Ohio Infantry Volunteers,* 84.

59 Quesenbery, *A Snowball's Chance,* 185.

60 Wildes, *Record of the One Hundred and Sixteenth Regiment Ohio Infantry Volunteers,* 84-85.

empty. In all the confusion, the 34th had been forgotten. The soldiers were still out skirmishing with an imaginary foe. A frustrated Lieutenant Colonel William Lincoln of the 34th Massachusetts summed up the embarrassing affair by writing, "The day's casualties footed up, killed, none; wounded, none; missing, the 34th Massachusetts Infantry."[61] Lieutenant Colonel Wildes of the 116th Ohio was equally appalled by the entire affair, which "bred in everyone the most supreme contempt for General Sigel. . . . Not an officer or man retained a spark of respect for, or confidence in, him."[62] When Sigel decreed that the army undertake a similar exercise the next day, Colonel Wells, commander of the 34th, refused to take the field, saying he would not serve under such "fools."[63] The second day's attempt reportedly produced only slightly better results.

* * *

Imaginary foes were soon replaced by real ones in the form of Confederate guerrillas. Once Sigel moved from Martinsburg to Winchester, he had a supply and communications line vulnerable to attack. The target presented an opportunity that John Mosby and John McNeill were anxious to exploit.

Mosby's 43rd Virginia Cavalry Battalion caused such consternation and havoc in the counties of Northern Virginia and eventually the lower Shenandoah Valley that the area came to be known as "Mosby's Confederacy." His past exploits included snatching a Federal general from his bed in the middle of the night while operating well behind Union lines. "No one could tell when or where to expect Mosby, Gilmore [sic] and McNeill," remembered a New York cavalryman in Sigel's army. "They were quick in their movements and required unceasing vigilance to guard against their sudden attacks."[64] An early biographer agreed. Mosby and his men attacked "relentlessly . . . like bees by day and night hawks by night."[65]

Sigel received a rude introduction to Mosby and his men on May 1 when the "Gray Ghost" personally led a party of about ten men in a raid against the

---

61 Lincoln, *Life with the 34th Massachusetts Infantry*, 264.

62 Wildes, *Record of the One Hundred and Sixteenth Regiment Ohio Infantry Volunteers*, 85.

63 Lincoln, *Life with the 34th Massachusetts Infantry*, 264.

64 Beach, *The First New York (Lincoln) Cavalry*, 319.

65 Virgil C. Jones, *Gray Ghosts and Rebel Raiders* (McLean, VA, 1984), 232.

Union supply line near Bunker Hill, capturing eight wagons, thirty-four horses, and twenty prisoners. Reinforced by another twenty rangers, Mosby entered Martinsburg, surprising its garrison and capturing another fifteen horses and several more prisoners. The missing horses and men were not noticed until the next day. In response, Sigel sent a dispatch to the post commander at Martinsburg directing that any wagons sent to the front be escorted because of the threat posed by Mosby and his rangers.[66] The frequency with which the Gray Ghost raided Union supply lines prompted one Federal cavalryman to write that Mosby "needed neither quartermaster nor commissary" because of the amount of supplies he requisitioned at Federal expense.[67] Eventually Mosby would turn loose two of his four companies in the Valley just to harass Sigel.[68]

In a vain attempt to keep Mosby at bay, Sigel ordered cavalry to constantly patrol the roads around Winchester. While some thought these precautions demonstrated that Sigel was a "vigilant, careful commander," others believed he was squandering his advantage in numbers for no apparent purpose.[69] Colonel Strother thought that sending detachments of cavalry on patrols and after groups of raiders far away from the main body of the army was akin to courting destruction.[70] A New York cavalryman agreed: "Day and night he kept his cavalry in motion . . . sending them out in all directions . . . with no definite instructions or apparent object."[71]

Brigadier General Max Weber, a German officer in charge at Harpers Ferry, employed a somewhat unique tactic to keep Mosby and other Confederate raiders away. Federal engineers had laid pontoon bridges across the Potomac and Shenandoah rivers there, replacing the permanent bridges destroyed earlier in the war. Each night, Weber had fifteen feet of the bridge planking taken up and laid "cross-ways on the bridge [to] form a kind of breastwork of them so that if the rebels should attempt to cross they would make rather a dear job of it."[72]

---

66 OR 37, pt. 1, 2-3, 372.

67 Fitz-Simmons, "Sigel's Fight at New Market," 61.

68 Wert, *Mosby's Rangers*, 161.

69 Fitz-Simmons, "Sigel's Fight at New Market," 105.

70 Eby, *A Virginia Yankee in the Civil War*, 224.

71 Fitz-Simmons, "Sigel's Fight at New Market," 62.

72 Arthur Stone to mother, April 29, 1864.

While John Mosby was terrorizing Sigel's line of supply, John McNeill jumped into action. Early on May 5, rumors began circulating among the Union camps that Confederates had struck the railroad running west out of Martinsburg. If the rumors were true, Sigel could be facing potentially serious logistical problems. West Virginia Governor Arthur Boreman telegraphed Washington that morning: "To my surprise . . . the enemy are on the railroad at New Creek and Piedmont." Later that morning the rumors and Boreman's message were confirmed; the Confederates had extensively damaged the railroad.[73]

During the night of May 3, McNeill with about sixty troopers left camp near Moorefield and struck out for the B&O. At dawn on May 5, the horsemen rode into Bloomington, where they captured an eastbound freight train. After cutting the telegraph wires, McNeill left about a dozen men there to stop any trains coming from the west. With the balance of the command McNeil rode east to Piedmont, no small prize in itself as the B&O had an extensive repair facility there. The raider sent three of his men into the town under flag of truce aboard a captured locomotive to demand the surrender of the small garrison. When the Union commander refused, his mind was quickly changed when McNeill closed in with the rest of his force.[74]

Fearing that Union troops could arrive at any moment, McNeill wasted no time in destroying the extensive railroad facilities in the town. In less than an hour his men burned seven buildings, including the roundhouse and engine shop, and destroyed nine locomotives and nearly eighty freight cars. In an effort to pour salt in the wound, McNeil sent six engines with a full head of steam down the line toward New Creek.[75]

Just before the telegraph wires had been cut that morning, a message had been sent to New Creek warning of McNeill's presence in the area. If there was any initial doubt about the veracity of the report, the huge column of black smoke rising five miles to the west dispelled it. A detachment comprising seventy-five infantry and one cannon was sent from New Creek to intercept McNeill. When the men arrived, they found Piedmont little more than a smoldering ruin. Pressing on, they caught up with the raiders at Bloomington,

73 OR 37, pt. 1, 381. The wartime village of New Creek is modern-day Keyser.

74 Davis, *Battle of New Market*, 36-37.

75 OR 37, pt. 1, 69.

with scarcely enough time to open fire before McNeill beat a hasty retreat into the mountains.[76]

The damage was not limited to just Piedmont, for the detachment McNeill left at Bloomington also met with considerable success. There, the raiders stopped two freight trains and allowed the citizens of the town to take whatever they desired from their contents. The next train they ambushed included two carloads of Union troops on their way to Washington. As the train screeched to a halt, Captain John Peerce, commanding the small detachment of McNeill's men, rode up to a Federal officer riding in one of the cars and demanded the surrender of all 115 men aboard. The surprised officer, with Peerce's pistol aimed point blank at his face, complied with the demand. When McNeill's command reunited, the raider led his Confederates in an effort to destroy the railroad bridge across the Potomac to Cumberland, but the Union troops from New Creek arrived too quickly and the attempt ended in failure.[77]

In the wake of the raid, B&O President John Garrett fired off a series of telegrams to Secretary of War Edwin Stanton in Washington denouncing Sigel for not going to greater lengths to protect his railroad. Only days before the raid, Garrett advised Stanton, he had "advised General Sigel of the great importance of Piedmont, with its extensive shops and machinery, and of the urgent necessity to protect, but a few or no troops were left in that vicinity." Garrett took little comfort in Stanton's assurance that several Ohio militia units were on their way to protect the line. The railroad official bluntly blamed Sigel for the disaster, claiming that McNeill's "success resulted from the entire exposure of so extensive and important a point as Piedmont." To Sigel, Garrett wired, "I need not urge upon you the importance . . . of doing all that is possible in the prompt disposition of forces to protect and preserve from destruction the work and structures" of the railroad.[78]

In his report to Washington Sigel dismissed the raid as "insignificant," but went on to insist that he could not assemble two small armies for service in the field and at the same time adequately protect the railroad from raiding parties.[79] Though he tried to play down the effects of McNeill's raid, other commanders

---

76 *Ibid.*, 68-69.

77 Davis, *Battle of New Market*, 38.

78 OR 37, pt. 1, 382-383.

79 *Ibid.*, 401.

saw the attacks in a different light. "The raid on the road at Piedmont must wake us up," opined Baltimore commander Major General Lew Wallace. "[S]uch a thing must not happen to us."[80] Part of Wallace's concern may have stemmed from the fact that his wife was aboard one of the trains stopped by McNeill's men.[81] One officer who was definitely awakened by the enemy raids was General Kelley, who openly declared the Federals "must kill, capture, or drive McNeill out of the country before we can expect quiet or safety" along the railroad.[82]

Accompanying one of the Ohio militia units being rushed in to help guard the railroad was an Ohio newspaper editor who passed through Piedmont several days after the raid. If he was under any illusions about what life near the front was like, the surrounding terrain dispelled them. "The sight of these ruins aided us to appreciate the fact that we were in the enemy's country," he wrote.[83]

80 *Ibid.*, 392.

81 Jones, *Gray Ghosts and Rebel Raiders*, 236.

82 OR, 37, pt. 1, 415. Kelley had been an official with the B&O before the war.

83 Richard R. Duncan, "The Raid on Piedmont and the Crippling of Franz Sigel in the Shenandoah Valley," *West Virginia History*, vol. 55, 1996. As of this printing, the online version was available here: www.wvculture.org/history/journal—wvh/wvh55-2html.

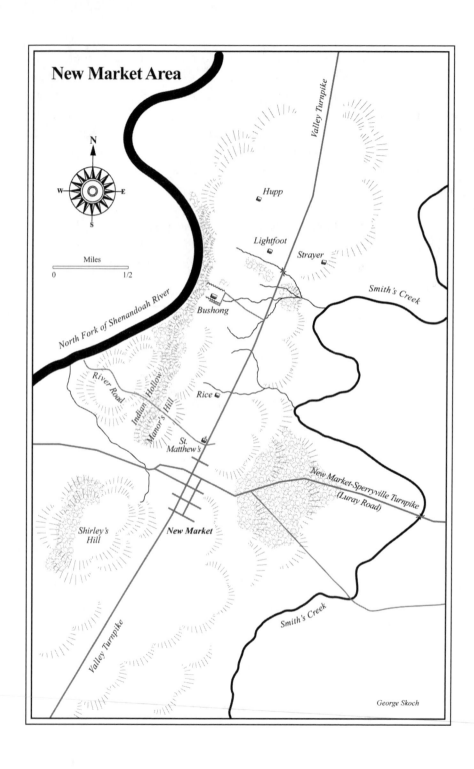

New Market Area

N
W E
S

Miles
0   1/2

Valley Turnpike

Hupp

Lightfoot

Strayer

Smith's Creek

North Fork of Shenandoah River

Bushong

River Road

Indian Hollow

Manor's Hill

Rice

St. Matthew's

New Market-Sperryville Turnpike
(Luray Road)

Shirley's Hill

New Market

Valley Turnpike

Smith's Creek

George Skoch

Chapter 5

"We Will Give them a Warm Reception"

On the evening of May 10, VMI's Corps of Cadets was hastily assembled outside their barracks. "Suddenly the barracks reverberated with the throbbing of drums," recalled Cadet John Wise. "We awoke and recognized the long roll. Lights were up; the stoops resounded with the rush of footsteps seeking their place in the ranks."[1] An officer stood before them, lantern in one hand, paper in the other. He had just received a message from General Breckinridge in Staunton, which "amid breathless silence" he proceeded to read. "Sigel is moving up the Valley," he began,

> was at Strasburg last night. I cannot tell yet whether this is his destination. I would be glad to have your assistance at once with the cadets and the section of artillery. Bring all the forage and rations you can. Have the reserves of Rockbridge ready, and let them send at once for arms and ammunition, if they cannot be supplied at Lexington.[2]

It might have taken a moment for the stunning news to sink in, but when it did the cadets knew their long wait was finally over. They were going to war.

Some 257 strong, the cadets set out for Staunton at 7:00 a.m. the next morning. General Francis Smith, VMI's superintendent, was ill and unable to accompany the cadets. Commanding the four companies in his stead was

---

1   John S. Wise "The West Point of the Confederacy," *Century Magazine* (January 1889), 464.

2   John C. Breckinridge to Francis H. Smith, May 10, 1864, Francis H. Smith Papers, VMI.

Lieutenant Colonel Scott Ship, the commandant of cadets.[3] Ship was not far removed from being a cadet himself, having graduated fourth out of a class of twenty-nine in 1859.[4] He served briefly in the 4th Virginia Cavalry in 1863 and as major of the 21st Virginia Infantry, but had spent most of the war at VMI.

Ship organized the corps for active campaigning. Eight cadets from each company were detailed to serve the institute's two rifled pieces.[5] The section was placed under Cadet Captain Collier H. Minge, the senior cadet officer. The responsibility and trust placed on Minge's shoulders was weighty, for this was

the first time the artillery section was being entrusted solely to a cadet. Usually a professor was placed in command, as was the case with the four infantry companies.[6] Twenty-seven cadets, mostly the youngest and those who were ill, were left behind to guard the post.[7]

The cadets made eighteen miles the first day and reached the small hamlet

Lieutenant Colonel
Scott Ship,
VMI Commandant of Cadets

VMI Archives

---

3 Col. William Gilham also accompanied the cadets. General Smith was ill, so he appointed Gilham "acting superintendent" in his stead. However, exactly what role Gilham played during the campaign and the battle is unknown. He did outrank Ship, but Ship was in command of the Cadet Corps at New Market. Gilham is rarely mentioned in any of the accounts of the march or the battle. It is possible that he may have been serving as an aide of some sort to Breckinridge.

4 Ship biography drawn from Scott Ship Papers, VMI.

5 Couper, *Virginia Military Institute at the Battle of New Market*, 2-4.

6 Wise, *Virginia Military Institute*, 306.

7 Preston Cocke, *The Battle of New Market and the Cadets of the Virginia Military Institute* (Richmond, VA, 1914), 5.

Cadet Captain
Collier Minge

VMI Archives

of Midway, aptly named because it was the midpoint between Lexington and Staunton. Cadet Edward Tutwiler recalled the night spent at Midway: "As we had no tents, we improvised a rude shed built of poles and leaves. . . . There was a fearful thunder storm. . . . We had camped near a Presbyterian Church, so we opened a window and climbed through it into the church, where we found nice cushions in the pews. We soon slept where many a good follower of Calvin had slept before us."[8]

The rain dimmed prospects for the next day's march. "The roads were a perfect loblolly," recalled Cadet Jack Stanard, ". . . and we had to wade through like hogs."[9] The Institute's surgeon R. L. Madison, who had accompanied the cadets on the march, allowed tired and footsore cadets to ride his horse, providing them a brief respite.[10] Despite the rain and the muddy roads, the cadets turned in a credible march and reached Staunton on the afternoon of May 12. Colonel Ship rode ahead of the battalion and reported to Breckinridge, who ordered the cadets to go into camp about a mile south of town.[11]

8   Couper, *The VMI New Market Cadets*, 211.

9   Barrett and Turner, ed., *Letters of a New Market Cadet*, 61.

10 *Shenandoah Valley*, June 23, 1921.

11 *OR* 37, pt. 1, 89.

Cadet J. Beverly Stanard

VMI Archives

The immediate future promised hard and grim work, but the exuberance of youth overrode any thoughts of the realities of war. That evening in Staunton, the boys found entertainment in the form of the several girls' schools. The cadet band played "The Girl I Left Behind Me" as the young cadets filed past one of the institutions of higher learning. "Not one of us were thinking of the girls we left behind us," Cadet John Wise joked. "The girls we saw before us were altogether to our liking."[12] Bev Stanard and several companions stole away into town that night to a friend's house where they found several young ladies.[13] Wise remembered that the cadets' popularity with the young female population caused some resentment among the veteran troops and prompted one regiment to sing "Rock-a-bye, baby" as the cadets passed, mocking their youthful appearance.[14]

In the days before the cadets arrived, the infantry brigades under Echols and Wharton arrived in Staunton, along with McLaughlin's artillery. The last leg of the journey for some of these men was made via the Virginia Central Railroad, west of town.[15] In Staunton they received a welcome period of rest

12 John S. Wise, *The End of an Era* (New York, 1901), 289.

13 Barrett and Turner, ed., *Letters of a New Market Cadet*, 61-2.

14 Wise, *End of an Era*, 290.

15 Rufus J. Woolwine, *Memoirs of a Confederate Soldier: Rufus James Woolwine, Captain, Co. D, 51st Virginia Regiment*, transcribed by Mabel B. Norris, Virginia Historical Society.

while the army consolidated around the town. Several members of the 22nd Virginia, part of Echols' Brigade, attended worship at the Presbyterian Church. The service was presided over by the Rev. Joseph Wilson, father of the future 28th President Woodrow Wilson.[16]

While the Confederate army was gathering around Staunton, unwelcome news arrived from Dublin. The first bit of information Breckinridge learned was that Colonel McCausland's infantry brigade would be delayed. Just as the troops were boarding railroad cars in Dublin on May 7, a courier rode up and announced to McCausland that a large column of Yankees (George Crook's column) was only a day's march away. Brigadier General Albert Jenkins, commanding the Department for the absent Breckinridge, wanted McCausland to remain to aid in the defense of the town.[17] The absence of McCausland was bad enough, and the news was about to get much worse.

Jenkins and McCausland took up a defensive position several miles outside Dublin at the foot of an eminence known locally as "Cloyds Mountain." Breckinridge's wife was evacuated from the town as the troops took up their position. By all accounts the Confederate troops were confident of success. "We will give them a warm reception here," Jenkins wired Breckinridge. "We will not be driven off."[18] As the evening of May 8 wore on, the Confederates could see reflected on the clouds the glow from the campfires of the Federals just across the mountain.[19]

The next morning Crook attacked the heavily outnumbered Confederates. In a brief but costly battle, the Southern line was bombarded by artillery, flanked, and finally collapsed. General Jenkins fell mortally wounded and was captured while Colonel McCausland waged a rearguard action as he fell back from the field. A corporal in the 45th Virginia called this engagement "the hardest fight . . . our Reg [sic] ever was in."[20] One Federal officer recalled that Cloyds Mountain was "a place where the shooting was terrible, and I can't see how I escaped."[21] Now in command of the Confederate force, McCausland had

16 Terry D. Lowry, *22nd Virginia Infantry* (Lynchburg, VA, 1988), 57.

17 McManus, *The Battle of Cloyds Mountain*, 18-9.

18 *OR* 37, pt. 1, 724-5.

19 McManus, *The Battle of Cloyds Mountain*, 19-20.

20 Henry C. Carpenter to "My Dear Sister," May 20, 1864, Virginia Tech.

21 Ironton *Register*, October 13, 1887.

little choice but to retreat and abandon Dublin—and the wealth of supplies stored there—to Crook's victorious Yankees.[22] "We drove them [and] followed them to Dublin Station," recalled a Pennsylvanian.[23]

Among those who fell at Cloyds Mountain was Presbyterian Minister William P. Hickman. According to local lore, Hickman received word of the approaching Yankees that Sunday while delivering a sermon. As the story goes, the Reverend interrupted himself to call his entire congregation to arms. "Seeing an invading army coming into his very neighborhood was more than his courageous spirit could stand," claimed a postwar account, "and shouldering his musket, he went into the very thickest of the fight." This account, published thirty years after the battle by his widow and based upon Hickman's own diaries, however, states that he did indeed travel to the battlefield, but with the humanitarian intention of ministering aid to the wounded.[24]

The defeat of Jenkins and McCausland exposed the nearby bridge over the New River, which also fell into Federal hands after an aborted defensive stand there by McCausland's survivors. Stretching nearly 800 feet long, the covered wooden bridge carried the Virginia & Tennessee across a fifty-five-foot deep canyon through which ran the New River. The Federals set fire to the span, which succumbed to the flames in less than two hours. All that remained were the stone piers.[25]

In addition to the bridge, Crook's troops also put the depot, support structures, and all the commissary supplies in nearby Christiansburg to the torch. Although a number of Federal troops came into the town looking for food and sufficiently frightened many of the ladies there, they were apparently well-behaved. Some of the more "polite" soldiers even offered to pay the Southern women for meals. But despite the fear at having their town falling into the hands of the "unfeeling demon" Yankees, "we got off much better than I anticipated; am thankful it was no worse," wrote one Christiansburg woman.[26]

22 Duncan, *Lee's Endangered Left*, 53-66.

23 Albert A. Wright diary, May 9, 1864, Fluhr Collection, USAMHI.

24 H. William Gabriel, "William P. Hickman in the New River Valley, 1852-64," *The Smithfield Review*, vol. 3, 1999, p. 64.

25 *Ibid.*, 67-8.

26 Jane Wade to "My Dearest Husband," May 15, 1864, Virginia Tech.

As bad as it was, the debacle at Cloyds Mountain and Dublin was somewhat offset by the news that William Averell's cavalry had not been able to reach Saltville and was turned back by General Morgan's troopers at Wytheville. Even better was the news that Crook, despite his crushing victory over Jenkins and McCausland, appeared to be retreating back to West Virginia.

Crook's abrupt turnaround was the result of faulty intelligence captured at Dublin that Lee had defeated the Army of the Potomac. Since he had not heard anything from Sigel since leaving the Kanawha Valley, he was concerned that his small column would become isolated. "Knowing that the safety and success of our enterprise depended on the Army of the Potomac being able to keep the enemy from detaching any part of his command . . . to cut off our retreat . . . I concluded our safety lay in falling back nearer to our base," Crook later recorded.[27]

The news Breckinridge received from the department was bad, but it could have been much worse. After sifting through the intelligence, a silver lining to the rapidly unfolding situation became clear: with Crook and Averell on the retreat, Breckinridge could now focus solely on Sigel and the Valley.

* * *

While Breckinridge was gathering various commands together at Staunton, John Imboden was moving down the Valley to slow Sigel's sloth-like advance. He had left Mount Crawford, south of Harrisonburg, on May 2 with about 1,500 troops. Three days later the bulk of Imboden's command arrived in Woodstock and reported Federal cavalry twelve miles from his position.[28] Satisfied that Sigel was not preparing to advance farther, Imboden proposed to Breckinridge a joint offensive into West Virginia to drive a wedge between the divided forces of Sigel and Crook.[29] John McNeill's raid on the Baltimore & Ohio Railroad at Piedmont, however, served as the catalyst to stir Sigel into action and Imboden's grand offensive was scrapped before being seriously considered.

After learning of McNeill's brief reign of terror at Piedmont, on May 6 Sigel dispatched 500 men from the 15th New York and 22nd Pennsylvania Cavalry

27 George Crook, *General George Crook: His Autobiography* (Norman, OK, 1960), 115-6.

28 Imboden, "The Battle of New Market, VA., May 15th, 1864," 480.

29 *OR* 37, pt. 1, 716-7.

regiments to deal with the threat. The column was placed under the command of Colonel Jacob Higgins of the 22nd. The blue troopers caught up with McNeill on the afternoon of May 8 in Moorefield. The Confederates were resting their horses outside town when Higgins and his vastly superior force approached. Having caught the enemy unaware, an over-eager sergeant in Higgins' command squandered the opportunity for surprise when he mounted a one-man charge against the sole Confederate picket.[30] McNeill hastily formed his command and left town abruptly, leaving behind a rearguard of twelve men under Lieutenant Bernard Dolan, who somehow managed to hold the Federals at bay and discourage them from pursuing.[31] Two or three of McNeill's men were captured in the town, but the remainder made good their escape.[32] When a search the next day failed to locate the Confederates, Higgins prepared to return to Winchester that night.[33]

Imboden's scouts greatly exaggerated the strength of Higgins' column at 1,300 troopers, nearly three times its actual size. Imboden telegraphed Breckinridge on May 9 that "McNeill's safety requires me to dash on his pursuers."[34] Accordingly, he planned to take the 18th and 23rd Virginia Cavalry regiments after Higgins, leaving the 62nd Virginia, several unattached companies, and the reserves with one battery of artillery under Colonel George H. Smith at Woodstock to watch Sigel, who still appeared content to remain at Winchester for the time being.[35] To disguise his true intentions, Imboden later claimed that he allowed the rumor to be spread that he was simply moving the camp of these two regiments into the mountains "in search of better grazing for our horses" when his men departed on the afternoon of the 9th.[36]

Imboden and his men had the advantage of being more familiar with the area than their adversary, since many of the men in the 18th and 23rd regiments were from the surrounding counties. The Southerners rode all night through a treacherous pass in the mountains known locally as "The Devil's Hole" on the

---

30 Duncan, "Piedmont."

31 Roger Delauter, *62nd Virginia Infantry* (Lynchburg, VA, 1988), 28.

32 Samuel C. Farrar, *The Twenty-Second Pennsylvania Cavalry* (Pittsburgh, PA, 1911), 201.

33 Bonnell, *Sabres in the Shenandoah*, 43-44.

34 *OR* 37, pt. 1, 726.

35 *Ibid.*, 726.

36 Imboden, "The Battle of New Market, VA., May 15th, 1864," 481.

road to Moorefield, where they expected to find Higgins. On the morning of May 10 Imboden positioned his two regiments, about 800 men, in Lost River Gap to ambush Higgins. As the head of the Federal column approached, Imboden's pickets fell back into the gap to lure the rest of the Federals into the trap. The ruse worked superbly. The Federals hastily assumed a position on a hill commanding the Moorefield Road and were hit head-on by the 23rd, which carried the position.[37]

With his path to Winchester blocked, Higgins decided to fall back to Romney. When Imboden's men, joined by McNeill's raiders, pursued the blue horsemen, the retreat quickly fell into confusion. "We got them on a stampaid [sic] and run them all day," remembered a trooper with the 18th Virginia.[38] Another of Imboden's men described the pursuit as "a running fight in which only the rear of the enemy, and the advance of the Confederates could use their weapons. . . . The fastest horses of the Confederates, and the slowest of the 'Yanks' are the men who did the fighting."[39]

Higgins' retreat degenerated into a rout, his men throwing away their arms and equipment and anything else that could impede their flight. The wagon train accompanying the column was lost along with all the ammunition and supplies it contained. A final stand was attempted at Romney, but the exhausted Federals were quickly pushed out of the town and continued their flight northward. The sixty-mile pursuit halted at the Potomac River, where Higgins and his men crossed to Old Town, Maryland. Once across, the full extent of the disaster became apparent. Higgins had lost about fifty men, his entire wagon train, his men and horses were thoroughly exhausted, and many of the soldiers were out of ammunition. According to Higgins, his men rode seventy-five miles in thirty-six hours without a halt or chance to feed the horses. General Kelley reported to General Halleck in Washington that Higgins had been "cut to pieces."[40] The upshot was that he and his command would play no further role in the campaign.

*   *   *

37 G. Julian Pratt to "Capt. B. Allison Colonna," Nov. 19, 1910, New Market collection, VMI.

38 Roger U. Delauter, *18th Virginia Cavalry* (Lynchburg, VA, 1985), 17.

39 Pratt to Colonna, November 19, 1910, NM coll., VMI.

40 *OR* 37, pt. 1, 70-71, 421, 427-478.

As soon as Imboden departed from Sigel's front to chase after Higgins, the German general decided to resume his advance. Sigel was spurred in part by the knowledge that fifteen regiments of Ohio militia were en route to his department to guard the railroad. Feeling more secure about his supply lines and communications, on May 8 he advised Grant of his intentions to move south up the Valley to join with General Crook.[41] Morale in Sigel's army improved at least for one Federal, who wrote in his diary, "On to Richmond will be our cry before long and then for a family trip up the Valley which will be good fun."[42]

With the 34th Massachusetts leading the column behind a cavalry screen, the small army departed Winchester on May 9.[43] The Federals made only twelve miles that day, but not before about a half-dozen men went down under an unusually hot sun.[44] "This is rather hot weather for marching," complained one soldier.[45] The troops set up camp north of Cedar Creek between Middletown and Strasburg on the Valley Pike. Sigel established his headquarters at Belle Grove, the beautiful limestone home of the Hite family, one of the original families to settle in the Valley. The house dated to the late 1700s and had stored in its attic a treasure trove of historical documents from Virginia's colonial era, some bearing the signatures of such notables as George Washington and Thomas Jefferson. Many of the troops thought those items would make fine souvenirs, and helped themselves to their own small piece of American history.[46]

The majority of Sigel's men spent May 10 in camp, many performing the obligatory drill and inspection. "Officers seem bound to keep us busy," one soldier grumbled.[47] After drill there was time for some relaxation. Many of the men took advantage of the proximity of Cedar Creek as a way to beat the unseasonable heat. Charles Lynch of the 18th Connecticut had his swim interrupted. "While enjoying a bath and a swim in Cedar Creek, felt something

---

41 *Ibid.*, 406-7.

42 Reader diary, May 7, 1864.

43 Lincoln, *Life with the 34th Massachusetts Infantry*, 273.

44 Reader diary, May 9, 1864.

45 John Davis to Dr. Cyrus B. Smith, May 10, 1864, Fondren Library, Rice University.

46 Eby, *A Virginia Yankee in the Civil War*, 223-224.

47 Lynch, *The Civil War Diary of Charles H. Lynch*, 58.

around my leg under water. It did not take me long to pull the thing off, which proved to be a water snake," he wrote. "With a jump I was soon out of the water."[48]

Just beyond his headquarters at Belle Grove, Sigel found another excuse to delay his advance: Confederates had destroyed the bridge over Cedar Creek. A detachment of engineers used a nearby barn to supply the wood to rebuild the structure. Some 100 men from the 28th and 116th Ohio regiments spent all of May 10 working to repair the span, but when the army moved out the following day the bridge still was unfinished. Many of the troops simply forded the creek.[49]

As the army advanced, the men faced constant reminders that they were in hostile territory. Private Edgar Kendall of the 21st New York Cavalry was shot while a detachment of the unit rested at a crossing of the Shenandoah River near Strasburg. Several other men from the detachment quickly apprehended the culprit, who apparently was a civilian. Sigel ordered the bushwhacker hanged immediately. Kendall died five days later.[50]

For the most part, local residents wanted nothing to do with the Federals. Some women turned out at their doors to taunt the Yankees as they passed.[51] Others stayed out of sight until the invading army moved on. Only a few gave food and water to the men in blue.[52] Even the weather seemed to be of pro-Confederate sentiment, alternating between unseasonably hot one day to pouring rain the next.

Not just civilians were interested in Sigel's move south from Winchester up the Valley. Although John Mosby had moved east across the Blue Ridge to turn his attention to Grant and the Army of the Potomac, he left behind portions of two of his companies in the Valley "to embarrass Sigel as much as possible."[53] One of these, commanded by Capt. A. E. "Dolly" Richards, spent May 9 concealed in the woods near Newtown between Sigel's camp along Cedar Creek

48 *Ibid.*

49 Augustus Moor daybook, May 9, 1864, Moor Papers; Lincoln, *Life with the 34th Massachusetts Infantry*, 274.

50 Bonnell, *Sabres in the Shenandoah*, 52.

51 Charles G. Halpine, *Baked Meats of the Funeral* (New York, 1866), 299.

52 Walker, *History of the 18th Regiment Connecticut Volunteers*, 216.

53 *OR* 37, pt. 1, 3.

and Winchester, capturing stragglers along the pike.[54] After nightfall, Richards and his men rode north toward Winchester. Encountering the advance guard of a wagon train headed for the front, the Rebels identified themselves as a detachment of the 1st New York Cavalry headed for Martinsburg. In the darkness, the guards were none the wiser and allowed the Confederates to approach. It was not until Richards' men were in the act of disarming the guards that the deception was discovered. When firing broke out, Federal reinforcements rapidly approached and the raiders retreated, losing one man wounded but inflicting several casualties on the Federals.

The other detachment of rangers under Capt. Samuel Chapman captured six men and seven horses of the 1st New York Cavalry east of Winchester.[55] Mosby himself made another appearance May 10. He attacked an outpost near Front Royal, captured sixteen men including an officer, and seventy-five horses—all without losing a single man.[56]

On one raid the partisans captured the payroll and sutler of the 21st New York Cavalry.[57] A detachment of Mosby's men struck a wagon train near Strasburg on May 12 guarded by troopers of the 13th Pennsylvania Cavalry, killing two and capturing four.[58] Several small detachments from the Federal Signal Corps left along the Valley Pike to relay communications to the front vanished without a trace; once again, Mosby was the prime suspect.[59] One Federal cavalryman asserted that his comrades would prefer to be ordered onto the "picket line, or into battle, than do patrol duty on the highway between Harpers Ferry, Martinsburg, Winchester and the front" because of the ever-present threat posed by Mosby and his guerillas.[60]

As a result of one such attack near Strasburg in early May, the names of several prominent Confederate sympathizers in the vicinity were turned over to Sigel as being party to the raid. "A very intelligent young colored man" from Strasburg identified an "Isaac Roughner" [Ruffner] as "the leader of this group

54 Newtown is modern-day Stephens City.

55 James J. Williamson, *Mosby's Rangers* (New York, 1896), 165-167.

56 *OR* 37, pt. 1, 3.

57 Bonnell, *Sabres in the Shenandoah*, 51.

58 *OR* 37, pt. 1, 73, 463-4.

59 *Ibid.*, 78.

60 Bonnell, *Sabres in the Shenandoah*, 7.

Colonel
William Tibbits

NY State Library

of assassins," and named about a dozen other locals as "notorious bushwhackers" of this "gang." One of the prominent citizens on the list, according to his accuser, was "a professed Union man, but in daily communication with this infamous gang of Bushwhackers aiding and abetting them all in his power."[61]

Because of the frequency of the raids against his supply lines, Sigel ordered a ban on all out-going mail in an attempt to better conceal his numbers and intentions. This ban even applied to the brigade commanders, but Colonel William Tibbits, commanding the First Cavalry Brigade, wrote on May 12 that he had found a way around it. "The officer in whose tent I now am has charge of the mail and has kindly consented to forward this if placed in an official envelope." Still, Tibbits' friend forbade him from mentioning anything regarding the army's movements.[62]

The pièce de résistance for Confederate guerrillas arrived in the form of an order, supposedly from Sigel's quartermaster, for an unguarded wagon train to be sent to the rear. This was contrary to Sigel's explicit instructions that required sufficient protection for every wagon train. Inexplicably, the wagons began the journey before anyone questioned the lack of a guard or the veracity of the

61 J. B. Salisbury to Franz Sigel, May 18, 1864, Sigel Papers. The veracity of the accusations is suspect given the prominence of many of those named. One of them, George Hupp, had his home in Strasburg taken over by Federal General Nathaniel Banks for use as his headquarters in 1862.

62 Tibbits to Dudley, May 12, 1864, Author's Collection.

order. As it turned out, the quartermaster had issued no such order. The directive was a Southern ruse, and the Confederates were waiting to ambush the rolling stock along on the Valley Pike. The event demonstrated just how far the guerrillas would go in their deadly serious game to disrupt Sigel's all-important supply trains.[63]

Detaching Higgins to West Virginia to chase after McNeill's raiders was only one of several moves Sigel made before resuming the advance. Another cavalry detachment, this one 300 men mostly of the 1st New York (Lincoln) Cavalry under Colonel William Boyd, was dispatched on May 11. Boyd's task was to scout southeastward into the Luray Valley, on the far side of Massanutten Mountain, to assure the safety of Sigel's left flank.[64]

Boyd's column passed through Front Royal, where some of its number set about foraging for food. Seven troopers stopped at the Buck family home. Lucy Buck heard a commotion outside and looked out her window to see one of the Federal cavalrymen trying to scare her father into turning over food for their horses by threatening to have his entire company search the house. Lucy "was angry enough to shoot" the Yankee, but her father convinced the unwanted visitors to leave by giving them sub-par corn destined for chicken feed. Not long after, the Federals left town in a hurry when rumors reached them that Mosby was in the area. The rumor had some truth to it, and several of Mosby's men joined the Buck family for supper that evening.[65]

While Boyd's men were foraging around Front Royal, other elements of Tibbits' cavalry brigade were scouting the front toward Woodstock. An additional 500-man detachment, mostly from the 21st New York Cavalry, was sent out the Back Road, another north-south avenue that paralleled the Valley Pike several miles to the west.[66] It was probably a portion of this detachment that passed by Woodlawn, the home of the Wayland family, several miles from Woodstock. Anna Wayland's diary entry for May 11 reads simply "Yankees about."[67]

63 Wildes, *Record of the One Hundred and Sixteenth Regiment Ohio Infantry Volunteers*, 86.

64 Sigel, "Sigel in the Shenandoah Valley in 1864," 488.

65 Buck, *Sad Earth, Sweet Heaven*, 253.

66 Tibbits diary, May 11, 1864.

67 Anna Kagey Wayland journal, May 11, 1864, Library of Virginia. Anna K. Wayland was the mother of noted Valley historian John W. Wayland.

About 2:00 p.m. on the 11th, Tibbits' horsemen entered Woodstock in a driving rainstorm.[68] The main body of the army arrived shortly thereafter, having broken camp at daybreak that morning. The weather combined with Confederate resistance made for a considerably slow pace. In one of the mounted clashes around Woodstock, Private George W. Baker of the 23rd Virginia Cavalry encountered a lone Federal trooper unexpectedly and at close quarters. Both men drew their revolvers, but neither Baker nor the Northerner felt it necessary to kill his foe. Baker wounded the Yankee in the arm and was himself shot in the hip, where the bullet remained lodged in the bone for the rest of his life.[69]

It was at this point in the campaign that Sigel stumbled upon a bit of good luck. Tibbits' Federals drove Colonel George Smith's Confederates (Imboden had not yet returned) out of Woodstock in such haste that the Rebels left behind several telegrams penned by Breckinridge and intended for Imboden. These invaluable communications revealed that several thousand Confederates were at that moment operating in the upper Valley at Staunton en route to form a junction with Imboden, and that only a portion of Imboden's command was in Sigel's immediate front. Perhaps more importantly, the intelligence revealed that the Confederates were still uncertain of Sigel's destination or purpose. One message dated May 10 stated that Breckinridge had not ruled out the possibility that Sigel may cross the Blue Ridge to reinforce Grant.[70]

Armed with this gift of knowing the enemy's strength and intentions, an energetic commander would likely have immediately set about destroying his opponent in detail. Even the cautious George McClellan, when he found himself in a similar position during the Maryland Campaign two years earlier, was so infused with initiative that he moved forward aggressively, forcing the passes of South Mountain and nearly catching and destroying the Army of Northern Virginia in detail. Franz Sigel did no such thing. Instead, he informed Grant that he had captured reliable and detailed enemy intelligence, but that he would advance no farther than his present position. He would, however, meet

---

68 Tibbits diary, May 11, 1864.

69 Correspondence between the author and Janet Greentree, Burke, Virginia, the great-granddaughter of G. W. Baker. In the regimental history of the 23rd Virginia Cavalry written by Richard Kleese, George W. Baker is listed as being "wounded, May 1864 near Woodstock, Va." This could have occurred in one of the preliminary skirmishes before New Market, or in a skirmish after the battle. Kleese, *23rd Virginia Cavalry*, 61.

70 *OR* 37, pt. 1, 446-7.

Breckinridge "should he advance . . . at some convenient position."[71] Sigel was surrendering the initiative to his enemy by allowing Breckinridge to consolidate his scattered forces and thus dictate the direction and shape of the campaign.

Many years after the war, Sigel claimed the captured intelligence at Woodstock spurred him into action. "The anxiety of Breckinridge to know whether there was any movement in the direction of Grant's army suggested such a movement on our part, while . . . the great struggle between Grant and Lee could not fail to prompt me to energetic action," he wrote.[72] Exactly what he considered to be "energetic action" is unclear, as his unequivocal dispatch from Woodstock dated May 13 stated, "my intention, therefore, is not to advance farther than this place with my main force."[73] His report of the New Market operations, written four days later on May 17, identifies the capture of these telegrams as a turning point in the campaign—and indeed it was, though not in the way Sigel intended or believed. The Federal commander's mind set at the time, at least as evidenced by his report, was that he had already achieved his mission by diverting Confederate attention away from George Crook. "All this information," he wrote, "tended to show that by drawing the enemy into the Valley Genl [sic] Crook might be relieved and thereby be enabled to destroy the Virginia and Tennessee railroad."[74] And so Sigel "energetically" remained at Woodstock for the next several days, doing little more than sending four companies of the 54th Pennsylvania to destroy the iron works at Columbia Furnace southwest of Woodstock on the 13th.[75]

With Sigel's latest spurt of forward movement grinding to a halt, the Confederates (who presumably did not know of the capture of the telegrams at Woodstock) organized themselves at Staunton. When he learned of the small but sharp defeat at Cloyds Mountain, General Lee wired Breckinridge, "It may be necessary for you to return" to southwest Virginia. The final decision, however, was left to Breckinridge's discretion. "You must judge," Lee advised him.[76]

71 *Ibid.*

72 Sigel, "Sigel in the Shenandoah Valley in 1864," 488.

73 *OR* 37, pt. 1, 447.

74 Franz Sigel, Report of New Market, May 17, 1864, Sigel Papers.

75 Campbell diary, May 13, 1864.

76 *OR* 37, pt. 1, 728.

Major Harry Gilmor

Library of Congress

The Kentuckian had another decision to make. Major Harry Gilmor was in Staunton awaiting court martial for an earlier raid on the B&O where his men had helped themselves to the property of the train's civilian passengers just as freely as they had to U.S. government property. Gilmor's 2nd Maryland Cavalry Battalion was as infamous in Southern circles for its lack of discipline as it was feared by the Federals for its tenacious fighting abilities. Because this was not the first such reported incident involving Gilmor's troops, the high command in Richmond recommended that his command be disbanded and his troopers reassigned to other units.[77] No final decision had been reached on either Gilmor's future or the fate of his battalion. The urgency of the situation and Gilmor's familiarity with the Valley, however, all but required the cavalryman's return to service. For Breckinridge, the decision was anything but agonizing. Desperately in need of men and horses, he restored Gilmor to command and sent him to the front to aid in slowing Sigel's advance.[78]

Capt. T. Sturgis Davis' small company was the only other Maryland unit in the Valley, so Gilmor's men had originally been assigned to Davis. At that time Davis was the most advanced Confederate force and serving as Imboden's eyes in the lower Shenandoah. Gilmor's restoration to command created a problem

77 Harry Gilmor, *Four Years in the Saddle* (New York, 1866), 146-7.

78 Special Orders No. 1, May 10, 1864, Harry Gilmor papers, Maryland Historical Society.

since he outranked Davis. In fact, Davis was not even aware that Gilmor had been released from arrest. Military protocol dictated that because of his rank, Gilmor could not serve under Davis, but Gilmor's troops accounted for two-thirds of the men under Davis' command and, in his advanced position, he was reluctant to part with them.[79] Until Imboden returned from West Virginia following his rout of Higgins, Davis and Gilmor's sixty troopers were the only cavalry operating in Sigel's front.[80]

After giving his troops a day to rest and recover from their sixty-mile running battle, Imboden returned to the Valley on May 12. There, he found Colonel Smith with the 62nd Virginia and various attached commands positioned near Mount Jackson, several miles north of New Market. As Imboden soon learned, Sigel's infantry and artillery were still at Woodstock, but his cavalry was becoming increasingly aggressive. Major Gilmor and his Maryland horsemen were immediately sent to the front to counter this threat, with a directive to find a way to get behind the Federals and harass them. Another concern for Imboden was Boyd's Federal column of troopers operating across the Massanutten. If the New Yorkers seized the gap at New Market, they could cut off Imboden's communications with Breckinridge at Staunton.

Late on the afternoon of May 12, while Gilmor was resting his men during a spring thunderstorm and planning a raid, firing erupted from the direction of the picket line near Mount Jackson. A mounted Union patrol was methodically pushing back Confederate pickets. Gilmor saddled up the rest of his command and charged into the oncoming Yankee riders, stemming their advance and allowing his own pickets time to reform. As the Federals wheeled about and headed back down the Valley Pike, Gilmor followed close on their heels, pursuing through Mount Jackson and beyond to Red Banks, a tiny hamlet several miles north of Mount Jackson. There, the Confederates ran into a large detachment of the 21st New York Cavalry under Major Charles Otis. Heavily outnumbered and now under fire, Gilmor wisely found discretion to be the

---

79 OR 37, pt. 1, 729. Davis is sometimes identified as a major, but he signed his correspondence from this time "captain."

80 *Ibid.* This telegram, dated May 11, 1864, from George H. Smith, 62nd Virginia to John C. Breckinridge states that the two Maryland units were the only cavalry with him. However, it is possible that one mounted company of the Rockingham County reserves was assigned to Davis prior to Imboden's departure. See Heatwole, *Chrisman's Boy Company*, 23-24. If this was the case, why Smith did not include them in his count is not known.

better part of valor and headed his command back to Mount Jackson. Gilmor continued retreating until he reached Hawkinstown, two miles north of Mount Jackson.[81]

Once out of immediate danger, Gilmor observed that the pursuing Federals had become strung out along the pike. Wheeling his command, he charged into the advance of the enemy, reversing the tactical situation. Now it was the Yankees' turn to retreat in haste, with Gilmor's Confederates once again in close pursuit. When Otis and his main body of soldiers was again encountered, Gilmor ordered his men to halt. The firing of an enemy volley convinced him to once again retreat. When his troopers reached a point between Hawkinstown and Mount Jackson, Gilmor decided to make a stand. Pausing near a tollgate on the Pike to fire a shot, he spotted a Federal officer drawing a bead right on him. Gilmor turned his horse to ride off, but the bullet struck him in the lower back. Somehow he remained in the saddle and, although in much pain, made it back to Rude's Hill. The Federals broke off their pursuit at Mount Jackson. Gilmor's wound was treated that night at Mount Airy, a large mansion owned by John Meem just north of Rude's Hill. The bullet had lodged itself a mere two inches from his spine, where a doctor proclaimed it more painful than dangerous. Unwilling to miss any action, Gilmor had the wound bandaged and prepared to be back in the saddle the next day.[82]

* * *

Early on the morning of Friday, May 13, General Breckinridge set his small army in motion from Staunton, having "determined not to await [Sigel's] coming, but to march to meet him and give him battle wherever found."[83] Imboden, keeping an eye on Sigel's cavalry movements, determined to make a stand at New Market.[84]

Concerned lest Boyd's troopers in the Page Valley gain his rear via New Market Gap, Imboden sent the wounded Gilmor with his battalion to ascertain the whereabouts of the Federal cavalry. The Marylanders rode into Fort Valley,

---

81 Hawkinstown today is but a small cluster of houses immediately past the northern edge of Mount Jackson.

82 Gilmor, *Four Years in the Saddle*, 147-151.

83 Breckinridge's Official New Market Report.

84 *OR* 37, pt. 1, 783.

a small vale in the Massanutten itself extending north from New Market Gap.[85] Once there, Gilmor learned that a party of about fifty Federals was also in Fort Valley headed to join Boyd. Apparently Sigel had second thoughts and now wanted to recall his scattered forces before another disaster befell them. Thus Lieutenant Norman Meldrum and his troopers of the 21st New York Cavalry had orders to find Boyd and bring him back to the Valley before he was attacked so far from the main body.[86]

Another force consisting of the 12th West Virginia and Carlin's Battery had been dispatched to the vicinity of Edinburg to link up with Boyd as he crossed Massanutten Mountain, and to presumably provide support should Boyd's horsemen be pressed by Imboden.[87]

Gilmor failed to interdict Boyd's column, but he was able to track down Meldrum's smaller party. The Federals were discovered sleeping in a barn during a rainstorm on the night of May 13. Rather than risk an attack in the darkness, Gilmor decided to set an ambush for the unsuspecting enemy. By sheer luck the Yankees happened to take a different road the next morning and so avoided what appeared to be a well-planned trap. For all his troubles Gilmor netted only one Federal straggler. The New Yorker informed him that while seeking shelter from the downpour the previous night, the Yankees had stumbled upon a local still and the entire command had become intoxicated. Gilmor knew exactly what that meant: Meldrum's men were in no condition for a fight.[88]

The news inspired the wounded (and by now certainly exhausted) Gilmor, who mounted his command and rode after the Yankees. He caught up with them trying to cross the South Fork of the Shenandoah River at the foot of the mountain. Recognizing the tough spot he and his men were in, Meldrum turned to his command amd shouted, "We must now fight or go to Libby," a reference

---

85 "Fort Valley" or "Powell's Fort Valley" was named for one of the earliest settlers of the Valley, an Englishman and somewhat of a recluse of dubious character named Powell, who operated several silver mines in the area and was said by the locals to have not allowed outsiders into his "fort." John W. Wayland, *A History of Shenandoah County, Virginia* (Baltimore, MD, 1998), 174.

86 Gilmor, *Four Years in the Saddle*, 151-52.

87 Linda C. Fluharty and Edward L. Phillips, *Carlin's Wheeling Battery* (Baton Rouge, LA, 2005), 49-50.

88 Bonnell, *Sabres in the Shenandoah*, 54.

to Richmond's infamous Libby Prison.[89] In the sharp but brief engagement that followed, Gilmor and his men killed two Federals, captured eleven, and seized thirteen horses. Nine more Federals drowned trying to cross the swollen river, and Lieutenant Meldrum's horse was killed in the fighting. The remainder of the Federals scattered.[90]

Boyd, meanwhile, entered Luray about noon on the 13th, where his men destroyed a large quantity of stockpiled supplies. From there the Federal column turned west for New Market Gap.[91] That afternoon Imboden sent a message to Breckinridge from New Market telling him of Boyd's presence in Page Valley. "A few hours will develop their purposes," advised Imboden. "If he comes on I will fight him here."[92]

Boyd and his roughly 300 troopers rode up the eastern face of Massanutten Mountain in the late afternoon, unsure of exactly what they would encounter on the far side. As they crested the mountain at New Market Gap, the valley in all its beauty and splendor spread out below them in a gorgeous panorama. From their vantage point in the gap they saw a large body of troops deployed just north of New Market. South of these troops was a large wagon train and cattle herd. Boyd called together his officers to discuss the situation. Almost to a man they believed the troops to be Confederates. The one exception was Boyd himself, who thought the men comprised the vanguard of Sigel's army. Exactly how he reached this conclusion is unclear because if these troops were Federals, they were traveling with their wagons and supplies in *advance*, rather than in the *rear*, of the army. In fact, the troops belonged to Imboden, who had fallen back across the North Fork of the Shenandoah to Rude's Hill.[93] In an effort to conclusively determine their identity, Boyd sent a small party under Capt. James Stevenson to the base of the mountain.[94]

Private David Crabill of the 18th Virginia Cavalry was on picket duty on the Luray Road when he reported seeing a small body of cavalry riding through the

89 Reed, *Tibbits' Boys*, 98.

90 Gilmor *Four Years in the Saddle*, 152-5.

91 James H. Stevenson, *Boots and Saddles: A History of the First Volunteer Cavalry of the War Known as the First New York (Lincoln) Cavalry* (Harrisburg, PA, 1879), 264.

92 OR 37, pt. 1, 733.

93 Beach, *The First New York (Lincoln) Cavalry*, 264-5.

94 Stevenson, *Boots and Saddles*, 323-4.

gap.[95] For Imboden, there was no doubt as to the identity of the troops on the mountain. In a telegraph message to Breckinridge from Imboden, the operator attached a short message that the enemy had just been sighted in the gap.[96] When news arrived of the Federals in the gap, Imboden ordered the 23rd Virginia Cavalry under Colonel Robert White and Capt. George Chrisman's company of mounted reserves—the so-called "Boy Company"—to deploy on a low rise overlooking Smith's Creek astride the Luray Road at the base of the mountain.[97] The 18th Virginia Cavalry, under Colonel George Imboden, the general's brother, together with a pair of McClanahan's guns, were ordered to move along a rough little-used farm track south of the main road that would bring them up unobserved on the enemy's southern flank.[98]

On the way toward the gap, Imboden's troopers passed Private James B. Johnson of Company F, 18th Virginia Cavalry. Johnson was serving temporarily as wagon master of Imboden's supply trains. Realizing that an engagement was in the offing, Johnson—whose role as wagon master made him technically a non-combatant—remarked to Allmon Sager, driver of Imboden's headquarters wagon, "I'm going along on that just to see the fun."[99]

Boyd watched as Imboden deployed for action. Rather than wait for his scouting party to return, however, the Federal officer advanced down the mountain with his entire force.[100] Lieutenant Colonel Charles T. O'Ferrall of the 23rd Virginia Cavalry was not prepared for such a bold display. "The movement was a great surprise to us," he wrote. "We could not understand why this regiment should be moving in the very jaws of our brigade. . . . They were making themselves our game and we prepared to bag them."[101]

When Stevenson and his scouts returned with the news that they were indeed facing a sizeable body of the enemy, Boyd decided to continue to the foot of the mountain and then follow Smith's Creek northward in the hope of

95 Heatwole, *Chrisman's Boy Company*, 26.

96   *OR* 37, pt. 1, 733.

97 Heatwole, *Chrisman's Boy Company*, 26.

98   *OR* 37, pt. 1, 733.

99 Robert A. W. Sager, *The Battle of New Market: May 15, 1864* (Petersburg, WV, n.d.) copy at NMBSHP, 4.

100 Stevenson, *Boots and Saddles*, 265.

101 Charles T. O'Ferrall, *Forty Years of Active Service* (New York, 1904), 94.

avoiding a confrontation with Imboden. It was not to be. The Federals were making their way across Smith's Creek when "the bluff above us . . . became alive with horsemen," recalled one of Boyd's officers. "The next instant we heard the well-known 'rebel yell,' accompanied with a shower of bullets and shouts of 'Now we've got the d—d Yankees! Give 'em h—l!'"[102]

As Boyd's men deployed to return fire on the 23rd and Chrisman's company on the ridge above, the 18th Virginia Cavalry thundered up on their flank and rear, joined very shortly by McClanahan's guns, which opened a devastating fire on the Union horsemen.[103] Private John Henton of Chrisman's company had just taken a plug of tobacco out of his haversack when the fight began, and in short order it was shot out of his hand.[104] "It was then too late to retreat," one Federal recalled. "In less than ten minutes two heavy columns of cavalry came charging down on us, one in our front and another in our rear."[105]

Imboden's glory-seeking wagon master Jim Johnson found himself in the middle of the fight. "A Yankee officer, on a beautiful big black horse" suddenly appeared out of the confusion near Johnson. In his rush to see the fight, Johnson realized he had forgotten to buckle on his sword belt and was unarmed except for a small pocketknife. Regardless, Johnson's fighting blood was up so he ran up to the officer demanding, "Hold that horse or I'll blow your D– – – brains out!" The officer quickly complied, turning over his sword and side arms to Johnson, who mounted the horse and escorted his prisoner into town, eventually turning him over to Imboden personally. Duly impressed, the general allowed Johnson to keep the weapons and the horse as trophies.[106]

Struck from different directions, Boyd ordered Stevenson to rally the troopers at the base of the mountain, but in the confusion he could amass but a few. The embattled Federals tried to charge through the ranks of the 18th Virginia to extricate themselves from the trap, but were unable to carry out the difficult maneuver. Organized resistance concluded when the Federals melted into small groups in an effort to scatter into the mountainside. "Our men were seen running in all directions on foot, their horses having given out . . . while

---

102 Stevenson, *Boots and Saddles*, 265.

103 Beach, *The First New York (Lincoln) Cavalry*, 325-6.

104 Heatwole, *Chrisman's Boy Company*, 27.

105 Beach, *The First New York (Lincoln) Cavalry*, 331.

106 Sager, *The Battle of New Market*, 4.

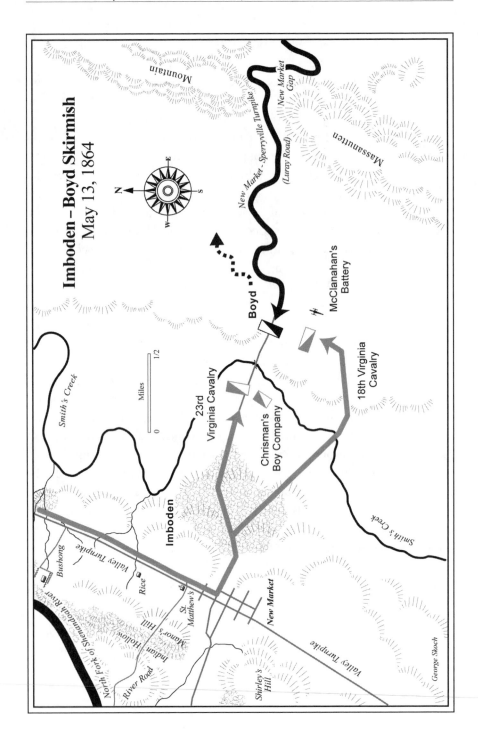

Imboden – Boyd Skirmish
May 13, 1864

some of the horses rushed along wildly, without riders, the saddles under their bellies," Capt. James Stevenson wrote. Both Stevenson and Colonel Boyd narrowly avoided capture, though the former lost his hat to a bullet and had several more pierce the blanket roll on his saddle.[107]

Others were not so lucky. Boyd lost about 125 men, which amounted to nearly half of his force (nearly all of them captured), as well as 200 horses. The remainder were hiding in the woods on the slopes of Massanutten, waiting for darkness before attempting to reach their own lines. That night a torrential downpour broke loose, soaking the hapless Northerners on the mountain but hindering the pursuit of those diligently hunting them.[108] The unnecessary fight had been an unmitigated disaster for Boyd and his men. One Federal cavalryman summed up the combat by writing, "Many a poor fellow bit the dust in this engagement."[109]

John Kiracofe of the 18th Virginia Cavalry, however, estimated that only two or three Federals were killed in the engagement, but 150 or so were captured, along with that many horses. According to Kiracofe, he "captured one prisoner, his horse and all that was on him consisting of one saddle, bridle, halter, two blankets, new gum cloth and number of other things."[110]

"The wonder was that the whole of Boyd's command was not captured," marveled one of the few Federals who made their way back safely to friendly lines.[111] One of those who did escape was Robert Cowan of the 1st New York (Lincoln) Cavalry. Somehow he made his way into Fort Valley and headed northward. He eventually reached Passage Creek, which the recent rains had spilled out of its banks. As Cowan attempted to cross, the swift-moving waters swept him from his horse and he drowned. His riderless horse and corpse were discovered the next morning by a local farmer, who buried Cowan on the edge of his farm in an unmarked grave.[112]

---

107 Stevenson, *Boots and Saddles*, 265-70.

108 *Ibid.*, 267, 270.

109 C. Armour Newcomer, *Cole's Cavalry: Three Years in the Saddle in the Shenandoah Valley* (Baltimore, 1895), 125.

110 John H. Kiracofe to "Dear Wife & Daughter," May 16, 1864, Library of Virginia.

111 Beach, *The First New York (Lincoln) Cavalry*, 329.

112 Bonnell, *Sabres in the Shenandoah*, 201-2. The grave was unmarked until the 1990s, when the present land owner erected a stone.

Sergeant J. J. Snyder of the 1st New York escaped, then was captured, then escaped again. He and several others spent the night wandering the woods of Massanutten Mountain until they stumbled upon a house. Although the others in his party thought it best to steer clear of the residence, Snyder approached anyway. To his surprise there were several Confederates inside (possibly some of Gilmor's men) eating breakfast. Realizing it was too late to get away, Snyder gave himself up simply by joining the Confederates at the table. He convinced his surprised captors that a Federal patrol was rapidly approaching, so they hurriedly made ready to exit. Snyder took advantage of their haste to slip away. He eventually returned to the house to finish his meal, and then forced the owner to take him across the Shenandoah to his own lines.[113]

The trap Imboden laid for Boyd's hapless troopers was so devastating that Alfred Voorhees of the 1st New York Cavalry thought they were up "against 4,000 or 5,000 men." Voorhees was one of the scores of Federals cut off who "took to the mountains." According to the New Yorker, he "stopped there all night [and] slept on a rock on the top of the mountain" in the driving rain storm. Voorhees and many of his comrades were rounded up the next day by Imboden's men. Most of the captives were eventually shipped to Camp Sumter at Andersonville, Georgia. Voorhees would die there that August.[114]

Imboden advised Breckinridge of the victory that evening. The enemy "came upon me from Luray about sunset. We pitched into him, cut him off from the roads, and drove him into the Massanutten Mountain," reported the cavalryman. "Numbers have been captured, together with about half their horses. They are wandering in the mountain to-night cut off. When day breaks I think I will get nearly all of theirs."[115] Horses were rounded up for several days after the combat. Some were found tied to tree saplings, from which the animals had gnawed all the bark.[116]

Imboden was not the only one making a report of the afternoon's engagement. Sensing a major battle in the offing, J. B. Wartmann, editor of the Rockingham *Register*, ventured from his office in Harrisonburg to the front. He was not disappointed. Wartmann arrived in New Market on May 13—just in

---

113 Beach, *The First New York (Lincoln) Cavalry*, 328.

114 Alfred H. Voorhees diary, May 13, 1864, Morrisville State College.

115 *OR* 37, pt. 1, 73.

116 Sager, *The Battle of New Market*, 5.

time for the New Market Gap fight. After the engagement, Wartmann began gathering various accounts of the action. As a local newspaperman he was most interested in the participation of the local units, including Chrisman's company of reserves. In its baptism of fire Chrisman's "Boy Company" performed admirably, capturing about twenty prisoners.[117] Casualties suffered by the company are unknown, but partly as a result of his performance in battle that day, Edwin Kite, who was slightly wounded, was promoted to first sergeant.[118]

For Sigel, the debacle at New Market Gap was the second disaster to befall his cavalry at the hands of Imboden in one week. Colonel Boyd's force, some 300 strong, had been decimated, and his defeat further weakened the army's cavalry wing. Imboden's accomplishments in destroying such a large contingent of enemy cavalry did not go unnoticed and unappreciated. General Lee issued an announcement to his Army of Northern Virginia, partly to bolster its morale, that described the fate of Higgins' force: "A part of the enemy's force threatening the Valley of Virginia has been routed by Genl. Imboden, and driven back to the Potomac, with the loss of their train and a number of prisoners."[119]

That night, Breckinridge with his two brigades of infantry, battalion of artillery, local reserves, and the VMI cadets encamped at Mount Crawford several miles south of Harrisonburg. Imboden remained at New Market, feeling much more secure about his flank with Boyd soundly defeated. By this time Breckinridge and Imboden were separated by only one day's march.

117 Rockingham *Register*, May 20, 1864.

118 H. A. Kite to Edwin Kite, May 24, 1864, NMBSHP.

119 Spencer C. Tucker, *Brigadier General John D. Imboden* (Lexington, KY, 2003), 208.

Union Colonel Augustus Moor,
commander of the First Infantry Brigade. *Larry Strayer*

Chapter 6

"Hold New Market at all Hazards"

While Imboden and Gilmor had their hands full at New Market and Mount Jackson dueling with their Federal counterparts, the main Confederate army was marching to join them.

John Breckinridge set out from Staunton at 6:00 a.m. on Friday, May 13. Gabriel Wharton's brigade took the lead, with John Echols' infantry marching behind it. Trailing Echols were the Virginia Military Institute Cadets, William Harman's reserves, and the artillery under Major William McLaughlin. A long line of wagons rumbled behind the troops, bringing up the army's rear.[1] Three cadets were left behind in Staunton, too ill to make the march.[2]

The troops began the march in yet another rainstorm. Despite the bad weather they made good progress, covering eighteen miles that day before camping at Mount Crawford, about six miles south of Harrisonburg. A thunderstorm soaked the camps that night. Eleven men of the 23rd Virginia Battalion were injured when lightning struck their camp.[3]

Breckinridge had his Confederates on the road again about dawn the next day. Marching through Harrisonburg, the men slogged another full day in the rain. The farther north the column snaked, the more evident it became that the

---

1 General Orders No. 1, May 12, 1864, J. Stoddard Johnston Papers, Museum of the Confederacy.

2 Couper, *Virginia Military Institute and the Battle of New Market*, 2.

3 J. L. Scott, *23rd Battalion Virginia Infantry* (Lynchburg, VA, 1991), 27.

enemy was near. The telltale sign recognized by every private in the ranks was the increasing number of refugees, civilians old and young fleeing from the invading Union army. Besides the refugees, moving this far north in the Valley made it much more likely that a fight was looming on the horizon. By now, rumors and stories of the cavalry fights and proximity of Sigel's army would have been spreading through the tramping column of men. "We were getting sufficiently near to the gentlemen for whom we were seeking to feel reasonably certain we should meet them," VMI's John Wise remembered.[4] The "gentlemen" in blue were near enough to prompt seventeen members of the 23rd Virginia Battalion of Echols' brigade to desert during the march north.[5] An unknown number of the 22nd Virginia, also of Echols' Brigade, quit the army at the same time.[6]

A more ominous and tangible sign of the enemy's approach was the low rumble of artillery fire heard later in the day that Saturday, followed by a trickle of wounded cavalrymen heading to the rear. The army camped for the night at Lacey Spring about eight miles south of New Market. That night the cadets got their first glimpse of the enemy when about 100 prisoners, mostly from Imboden's fight with Boyd the previous day, were escorted into camp. The rain was still falling when the sounds of distant gunfire broke the stillness several times during the night.[7]

What the Confederates in Breckinridge's army heard throughout the 14th of May was the arrival of Sigel's advance guard at New Market. That morning, Sigel had ordered a reconnaissance in force to probe Imboden's position at Rude's Hill.

The main Federal body was still camped around Woodstock on the morning of May 14, with elements operating as far south as Edinburg and a cavalry screen positioned between that point and Mount Jackson. These dispositions courted disaster, the forces widely separated and vulnerable to defeat in detail. The hard lessons taught to Higgins and Boyd over the previous

---

4 Wise, "West Point," 465.

5 Scott, *23rd Battalion Virginia Infantry*, 27.

6 Lowry, *22nd Virginia*, 58. Why Echols' Brigade experienced such a high desertion rate at this time is unknown, but most of the men from his units were from counties that now comprised the new state of West Virginia. It is possible that George Crook's and William Averell's campaign made them concerned for the welfare of their own families and homes.

7 Wise, "West Point," 465.

several days had not yet sunk in. Rather than draw in his command, however, Sigel committed another sizeable portion of his cavalry to probe Imboden's position at Rude's Hill, between Mount Jackson and New Market.

Major Timothy Quinn of the 1st New York Cavalry was dispatched that morning with about 550 men to probe Imboden's line and determine if Breckinridge had reached the field. Quinn and his men set out from Edinburg through a pouring rain. The column reached Mount Jackson without encountering any substantial resistance, but as it reached the bridge spanning the Shenandoah River about a mile south of town, the Confederate position at Rude's Hill came into view. Imboden's men had removed the planks from the bridge, slowing Quinn's advance. After repairing the span, Quinn sent a party of fifty men across to feel out the enemy strength, concealing the bulk of his force behind a ridge north of the bridge.[8]

Rude's Hill was one of the strongest positions in the entire Shenandoah Valley. The Pike approaching it from Mount Jackson crested a small ridge before running into the North Fork of the Shenandoah River. A small bridge spanned the water there, with the Pike continuing for nearly a mile across flat farmland (known as Meem's Bottom), the southern border of which was Rude's Hill. The hill itself stretches from Smith's Creek at the foot of the Massanutten on the east to the Shenandoah River, which makes a 90-degree turn just upstream of the bridge and flows north to south until in the vicinity of New Market, about six miles to the south. Properly manned, the position would be difficult to take by direct assault.

Quinn's skirmishers quickly drove back Imboden's pickets from Meem's Bottom. Reinforced by another sixty troopers, the Federals pressed Rude's Hill directly, driving the thin gray line of defenders from that point as well. According to Quinn, his troopers carried the hill "handsomely."[9] Indeed, they did, but the Confederates were not in force on Rude's Hill. Bringing up the balance of his command, Quinn met and repulsed a light counter thrust and pursued Imboden's horsemen about two miles. After halting briefly to reform his command, Quinn resumed the attack, driving the Confederates to New Market. There, for the first time, Quinn's horsemen encountered stiff

8   OR 37, pt. 1, 73-4.

9   Ibid.

resistance.[10] Major R. B. Douglas and 100 troopers from the 20th Pennsylvania Cavalry charged, driving the Southerners from the town and capturing several of them in the process.[11]

As Imboden's troopers fell back, they passed the McDaniel farm. There, David Kiser, one of several brothers serving in the 62nd Virginia, took advantage of a brief lull in the pursuit to ask two of the McDaniel ladies for some buttermilk they had just made. The women were happy to oblige and were filling his canteen, "but the bullets [began] to fly thick [and] he had no time to thank the ladies and hurried on."[12]

Quinn was engaged for most of the day but lost only four men, a testament to the light opposition he faced and the nature of the fitful fight.[13] Confederate losses are unknown, but appear to have been very light. "[S]kirmish[ing] with enemy all day," wrote one Southern trooper, but there was "very little loss on either side."[14] Light casualties notwithstanding, one Virginian concluded the Federals "gave us a very hard afternoon's work."[15] About 5:00 p.m. Quinn received orders to pull back behind the leading elements of infantry, which were now arriving on the field.[16]

Sigel's infantry had been moving up behind Quinn's horsemen for most of the advance that day. Colonel Augustus Moor, commander of the First Infantry Brigade, had been dispatched from Woodstock at 11:00 a.m. with the 1st West Virginia and 34th Massachusetts, supported by four guns of Capt. Alonzo Snow's battery. It is worth noting that none of these units were part of Moor's own brigade. Although neither Sigel nor Moor explained why Moor was placed in command of troops unfamiliar to him, it is not unreasonable to conclude that it was another example of Sigel's favoritism toward foreigners or that he simply trusted Moor (a fellow German) more than he did Joseph Thoburn, his other

---

10 *Ibid.*, 73-5.

11 Colonel John Wynkcoop report of operations May 14, 1864, Moor Papers.

12 William A. Good, *Shadowed by the Massanutten* (Broadway, VA, 1992), 534. Kiser returned to New Market twenty-three years later, stopped by the McDaniel farm, and offered a belated thank you for their kindness.

13 *OR* 37, pt. 1, 73-5.

14 James C. Hogbin diary, May 14, 1864, Wilda Hogbin, Petersburg, WV.

15 Delauter, *18th Virginia Cavalry*, 19.

16 *OR* 37, pt. 1, 74-5.

Shirley's Hill, looking south from Manor's Hill. *Casey Billhimer*

brigade commander. By the time Moor and his motley force reached Edinburg it had nearly doubled in size, adding the 123rd Ohio as well as 300 cavalry under Colonel John Wynkoop and two more guns. These troops boosted Moor's force to roughly 2,300 men, or fully one-third of Sigel's entire command.[17]

One of the West Virginians advancing behind the horsemen noted that the column "got along very well until our advance of cavalry arrived at Rude's Hill where a slight skirmish ensued."[18] In the vicinity of Edinburg, Moor's men encountered the remains of Boyd's shattered command, most of whom were dismounted and traveling in small groups. Their accounts of the debacle the previous afternoon did little to bolster the confidence of those who listened.[19] Some of Boyd's men, observed a cavalry sergeant, were "pretty near dead."[20]

Colonel Moor's infantry and artillery dribbled onto the field at New Market throughout the afternoon. Moor deployed his infantry into line northwest of the town and unlimbered the guns on a ridge on their right north of town. The artillery settled into a brief but furious duel with Imboden's guns on Shirley's

17 *Ibid.*, 79.

18 Wheeling *Intelligencer*, May 23, 1864.

19 Lincoln, *Life with the 34th Massachusetts Infantry*, 277.

20 William A. McIlhenny diary, May 14, 1864, Mark Dudrow, Winchester, VA.

Colonel George H. Smith,
62nd Virginia Mounted Infantry

NMBSHP

Hill, a commanding eminence immediately southwest of New Market. One section of Snow's battery advanced to the edge of the ravine at the foot of Shirley's Hill. "Shells were flying and we were sent to the left of the Pike to support a battery," recalled Capt. George Thompson of the 34th Massachusetts. "The firing was kept up until dark when it ceased."[21]

Imboden was not present on the field when Quinn was forcing back his troopers. When he learned that Breckinridge was approaching, and feeling confident that Sigel would not attempt anything more than light skirmishing that day, Imboden turned his horse south for a ride to Lacey Spring to confer with the Kentucky general. He left Colonel George Smith of the 62nd Virginia in command at the front. The two generals were sitting down for lunch about noon when a rider galloped up with a message from Smith: Sigel's cavalry, (widely exaggerated at 2,500 men) had carried Rude's Hill and was forcing back the 18th Virginia Cavalry. As if on cue, booming of artillery punctuated the delivery of the message. Smith further reported that he had deployed his own regiment west of New Market to resist the advance. Imboden immediately set out for the front with orders from Breckinridge "to hold New Market at all hazards till dark." Assuming he could do that, after nightfall Imboden would fall back about four miles to join up with Breckinridge's army.[22]

---

21 George W. Thompson diary, May 1, 1864, Library of Virginia.

22 Imboden, "The Battle of New Market, VA., May 15th, 1864," 482.

Imboden arrived at New Market about the time Quinn drove within sight of the town. A quick survey of the unfolding situation provided Imboden with a firm understanding of both the terrain and the initial Southern deployments. Colonel Smith had arranged his regiment in a strong position west of town with McClanahan's six guns in support on Shirley's Hill. His men were in one rank rather than the customary two in order to lengthen his line and give the appearance of a larger force. His mounted cavalry extended the line eastward.[23] One Federal estimated Imboden's strength at more than 5,000 men.[24] The timely bluff convinced Colonel Moor, who was unsure of Imboden's exact strength or intentions, that an attack would be foolhardy. By 5:00 p.m. the light running skirmish had settled into a sharp but relatively harmless artillery duel.[25]

Moor ordered his men to lay on their arms in line of battle during the night and forbade any fires to prevent giving away his exact position.[26] Those two orders guaranteed that the Federals in the fields around New Market would endure a miserable night. "It had been raining all day and continued all night, a cold rain which soaked us to the skin," remembered Edwin Snyder of the 123rd Ohio. "We remained in line all night, sleeping but little on the cold, muddy ground. It was one of the most uncomfortable nights I ever spent."[27]

* * *

In every battle, terrain plays a significant role in how troops are deployed and how the fighting unfolds. The upcoming combat at New Market would be waged in a rough box defined by Shirley's Hill on the south, Bushong's Hill to the north, and the Shenandoah River and Smith's Creek running along the west and east sides, respectively. Understanding the terrain is critical to understanding the battle of New Market.

---

23 *Ibid.*, 482. According to one source (Allmon Sager), Imboden's men crafted three lines of earth and fence rail breastworks, but these are not mentioned in any other accounts.

24 Michael Gardner to Ira Cole, May 16, 1864, Sigel Papers.

25 *OR* 37, pt. 1, 74-5.

26 *Ibid.*, 79-80; Imboden "The Battle of New Market, VA., May 15th, 1864," 482. Although the weather and orders prevented fires in the Federals camps, Imboden wrote many years after the battle that "their [Federal] camp fires disclosed their exact position."

27 Edwin Snyder, *Adventures and Misadventures of a Union Veteran of the Civil War* (Topeka, KS, 1909), 24.

The small crossroads village was a typical settlement along the Valley Pike, sitting at the crossroads of the Pike and a road leading east across Massanutten Mountain at New Market Gap to Luray, and west to Timberville and beyond. The Pike itself, called Congress Street within the town's limits, comprised the town's main thoroughfare. A back road to the east called "Water Street" paralleled the Pike, with several short lanes connecting the two.[28]

Smith's Creek flows northward along the western base of the Massanutten, emptying into the North Fork of the Shenandoah just downstream of the bridge to Mount Jackson. While roughly paralleling the mountain and the Pike for most of its length, Smith's Creek twists in a large double "C"-shaped bend northeast of town, with the bulge protruding west, constricting the narrow land corridor between the Shenandoah River and Massanutten. West of town runs the North Fork of the Shenandoah, which flows east from Timberville before making a 90-degree turn a few hundred yards west of New Market to flow almost due north. Rather than a straight line, the river lazily drifts eastward before turning in a slow "C"-shaped bend opposite the double Smith Creek bulge. The river cuts a high bluff northwest of town before righting itself back on its original northward course. It was the curvature of both streams that created the narrow plateau slightly more than one mile wide north of town, upon which the battle would be fought.

Hilly terrain, in addition to the winding river and creek, would play a key role in the fighting. A series of hills runs roughly parallel to, and west of, the Valley Pike. The most commanding of these is Shirley's Hill, immediately southwest of New Market. It was on and around this high point of ground that Breckinridge would form the bulk of his army. South of that point is a series of interconnected hills, with Williamson's Hill the next in line. North of Shirley's

---

28 Lieutenant Colonel Charles T. O'Ferrall of the 23rd Virginia Cavalry spent so much time during the war in the town, both in camp and also recuperating from wounds, that he referred to it as his "war home." O'Ferrall had fond memories of the town and its residents: "The people of New Market nursed me three different times when wounded. Every house was open to me. I knew everybody and everybody knew me. The whole town was loyal to the core, and sent her full quota to the Army. . . . The Henkels, Zirkels, Shirleys, Neffs, Rices, Wiliamsons, Hoovers, Prices, Moffets, and scores of other families I could mention were as loyal to the cause of the South as were the Patriots of '76 to the cause of the colonies." On one of those occasions when O'Ferrall was wounded in battle elsewhere, he was brought to New Market to recover and put into the care of the Clinedinst family. "I would be false to my own feelings," he wrote, "if I did not mention especially one of the young ladies of the household, Miss Eliza. She was as a ministering angel to me; every wish, whim, or caprice of mine she gratified." O'Ferrall, *Forty Years of Active Service*, 78-9.

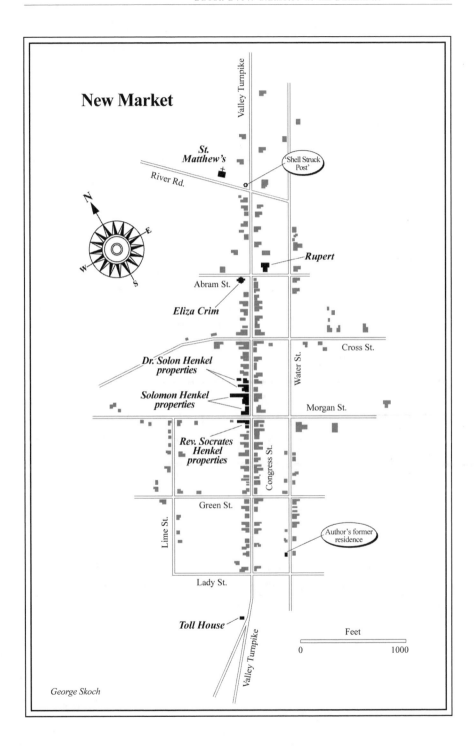

New Market

Valley Turnpike

St. Matthew's

'Shell Struck Post'

River Rd.

N
E
W
S

Rupert

Abram St.

Eliza Crim

Dr. Solon Henkel properties

Water St.

Cross St.

Solomon Henkel properties

Morgan St.

Rev. Socrates Henkel properties

Congress St.

Green St.

Lime St.

Author's former residence

Lady St.

Toll House

Valley Turnpike

Feet

0   1000

George Skoch

Hill is another, slightly lower rise called Manor's Hill. A deep ravine running roughly east to west (through which runs modern-day U.S. 211) separates Shirley's Hill from Manor's Hill. Beyond the latter hill the ground levels out into a softer undulating roll, but the Shenandoah River pushes in from the west, creating an impassable bluff for 19th-century armies. The narrow land corridor, squeezed by the bulges in the Shenandoah River and Smith's Creek as described above, is one mile north of Shirley's Hill. It was there, on the far western point within this constricted land corridor known as Bushong's Hill, that Sigel's army would deploy for battle.

*   *   *

Once darkness settled onto the field and the artillery firing ceased, Colonel Moor formed his infantry into a "U"-shaped line on Manor's Hill.[29] "After taking this position, skirmishers were sent out through the woods to picket the front, when it was discovered that the enemy's pickets occupied the south edge of the woods, about four hundred yards distant," the historian of the 1st West Virginia recorded, "hence there would in all probability be a dispute as to the possession of this particular piece of ground."[30] A "dispute" did indeed develop. "[A]bout 9 p.m.," wrote an officer in the 34th Massachusetts, "the enemy sent forward to drive us from our position. . . . They approached the 1st [West] Va. [sic] but soon fell back having met with a hot fire from them. Then they tried the Ohio boys with like success."[31]

Intentional nighttime engagements were rare during the Civil War, so the Southern probing attacks along Moor's front ranks in the category of the unusual. Combat was difficult enough to control during daylight hours when one could see both enemy and comrades. The reduced visibility brought about by darkness made moving troops especially difficult, and shooting blindly into the night almost as likely to inflict casualties among friends as it was among foes. Although he made no mention of the night probing attack in his article about New Market published after the war in *Century Magazine*, the context and style of the effort dovetails with Imboden and his orders to hold New Market for as long as possible. The general probably concluded that a demonstration of

29 Thompson diary, May 14, 1864.

30 Charles J. Rawling, *History of the First Regiment West Virginia Infantry* (Philadelphia, 1887), 164.

31 Thompson diary, May 14, 1864.

unexpected aggressiveness would give the Federal commander pause before launching any attack of his own, either that night or the next morning.

The marching, bad weather, and fitful Confederate probing conspired to rob the Federals of whatever sleep they might otherwise have enjoyed that night. One aspect of the night probe was recorded by Jasper Harris of the 62nd Virginia, who recalled how he and twenty of his comrades advanced quietly across the fields toward the Federal skirmishers. The dismounted troopers "crawled up close to their line and fired into their faces."[32] Federal Joseph Winters of the 1st West Virginia also left a record of the probe, scribbling in his diary later that night: "Thay advanced on us at dark. The infantry drove them back. All vary tiard [sic]."[33] A Buckeye private in the 123rd Ohio recalled that he and his comrades "laid on our arms all night. Were in a cold rain here skirmishing with some heavy firing every few minutes."[34]

A letter, unsigned but attributed to a member of the 1st West Virginia, appeared in the Wheeling *Intelligencer* several days after the battle. It is the most detailed and accurate account of the nighttime engagement known to exist, its bit of dramatic flair notwithstanding:

We arrived after dark in the midst of a severe shower of rain, and I assure you the prospect before us was dark and gloomy enough. Major E. W. Stephens proceeded forthwith to post pickets in our front, which had gone but two hundred yards from our camp, when they were halted and fired upon by a line of rebel cavalry skirmishers, and after some resistance were driven back to our lines. In a few minutes the rebel line of infantry was seen coming slowly and cautiously towards us, but we were ready for them; every man clutching his rifle, determined to drive the dastard foe. Yet on they came until within sixty yards of our front, when the gallant veterans of the 1st raised on their knees, and poured a deadly volley into the dark line just before them; an answering volley from the enemy was followed by an order from the Major, "fire by file, hold low," and such a fire was poured out from our muskets was irresistible and the enemy broke to the rear. Again were our pickets sent out, and again driven back to the line, followed by the rebel infantry, and again were we forced to drive them back,

32 Jasper W. Harris, "Sixty-Second Virginia at New Market," *Confederate Veteran*, 16, 1908, 461.

33 Swiger, *Civil War Letters and Diary of Joshua Winters*, 107. One postwar account by Allmon Sager, Co. I, 18th Virginia Cavalry, stated that the dismounted troopers got so close to the Federal position they could hear the conversations of the Federal troops and the rattling of cooking utensils. Robert A. W. Sager, *The Battle of New Market*, p. 7.

34 Leander Coe diary, May 14, 1864, Bowling Green State University.

this time, following them through the woods, and establishing a line of skirmishers in our front, and the 4th Virginia Rebel Regiment left us undisputed masters of the field. In this action, as spirited as it was, our loss was but two or three wounded, while the enemy had five killed and a number wounded. After the excitement incident on such occasions had worn off a little, we were permitted to lie down on our arms, in the rain, without fire, minus supper, and ditto dinner; this, too after having marched twenty-four miles, and had a fight of three hours.[35]

One wounded Confederate took what cover he could by propping himself against the back of a fence post. His choice of cover was not the best, for in the light of the muzzle flashes his fence post was mistaken for a human figure—and thus became a conspicuous target for Federal riflemen. The wounded trooper hugged the ground as closely as he could while "the splinters just showered off that big post at every volley."[36]

Another of Imboden's troopers found himself separated from his command and in a precarious position when dawn broke. He had been on the extreme left flank of the line and had not heard the whispered order to fall back, nor had he noticed that his fellow soldiers were no longer by his side. "As it got light enough to see," one of his comrades recalled, "he realized he was out there almost in the enemy camp alone. He crawled back and reached camp safely, but he had been reported killed due to his absence when the roll was called."[37]

The Confederates contented themselves with two light attacks against Moor's position during the night. Before midnight the firing stopped and, reported Moor, "No further annoyance occurred that night."[38] No further annoyance except a lack of camp fires and the incessant rain, which showed no signs of letting up.

* * *

For the rest of Sigel's army camped twenty miles to the rear at Woodstock, conditions were not much better. From that distance the men listened to the

---

35 Wheeling *Intelligencer*, May 23, 1864. The 4th Virginia was part of the famed "Stonewall Brigade" and was not present at New Market. The attacking force was George Smith's 62nd Virginia.

36 Sager, *The Battle of New Market*, 8.

37 *Ibid.*

38 *OR* 37, pt. 1, 79-80.

sounds of gunfire all day and pondered its meaning when it escalated late that afternoon. Even for the rawest recruit in Sigel's army there could be no doubt that the enemy was close. "We are very anxious about the morrow, as we listen to the heavy artillery firing," a soldier in the 18th Connecticut recalled.[39] Some welcomed the prospect of a battle, having been too long on garrison duty on the railroad. Others realized it was easy to be brave when well out of reach of the flying lead and iron. "The cannon shots sound as of old and does a person good to hear the sound when he is 10 miles off," one Federal told his diary that day.[40] The rain continued to fall all night, prompting one West Virginian to recall the misery of trying to rest that night: "[T]hose who tried to sleep found the water collecting in pools around their bodies."[41] Rain or not, for most it was the prospect of a battle near at hand that prevented a sound sleep.

While his men tried to get some rest Sigel was busy issuing marching orders for the remainder of his army at Woodstock. His troops would move at daybreak. According to his postwar recollections, he intended to make a stand at Mount Jackson.[42]

After his second probing attack, Imboden withdrew from New Market. His troops plodded along the Valley Pike toward Lacey Spring, about ten miles to the south, where Breckinridge's troops were camped for the night.

The VMI cadets had taken shelter from the rain in a church. Cadet John Wise was detailed as corporal of the guard, standing watch over the camp while his comrades got what little sleep they could. Looking north through the darkness he could see flickering camp fires in the distance, but was unsure whether they marked the location of friendly forces, or the enemy.[43]

Unexpected or otherwise, war had arrived for the civilians who lived in this part of the Valley. For them, May 14 was a day they would never forget. Armies from both sides had camped in the fields around their picturesque village of New Market before, but this was the first time that fighting of any significance had been fought around their homes. And from all outward appearances, a major battle appeared imminent on the morrow.

39 Lynch, *The Civil War Diary of Charles H. Lynch*, 59.

40 Reader diary, May 14, 1864.

41 Hewitt, *History of the Twelfth Regiment West Virginia Volunteer Infantry*, 106.

42 Sigel, "Sigel in the Shenandoah Valley in 1864," 488.

43 Wise, *End of an Era*, 292.

Jessie Rupert, one of the few Union sympathizers in New Market, remembered the alarm caused by the events of that rainy Saturday.[44] Some of the townspeople packed into wagons whatever possessions they could and headed south, away from the approaching Yankees. Farmers from outlying areas drove their livestock into town, hoping that would prevent them from being carried away by hungry soldiers. Many of the residents who chose to stay busied themselves by burying valuables to prevent looting. By nightfall, Imboden's troops had pulled back from all but the southernmost fringe of the town. "Those who remained of the citizens awaited with closed doors for the entrance of the approaching Yankees," Rupert recalled.[45]

Rupert and her husband had been observing the troop movements from a window of their Main Street home. One of the first Federal cavalrymen to enter the town noticed the couple, reined in his mount, and asked for food, which the Ruperts supplied. Jessie stood by as he ate, answering as best she could his questions about enemy strength, when a bullet struck the road between his horse's feet. A second shot found its mark and the cavalryman fell dead in the street at her feet.[46]

Throughout the night the townspeople listened to the firing as Imboden's troopers probed Moor's line of battle. Rupert also remembered hearing horses and shooting on the streets that night. "It was," she wrote, "a night of horror," and one during which her family—and no doubt many others—"slept with our garments on, ready for flight, if driven in terror from our place between the contending armies."[47]

---

44 Jessie Hainning Rupert was raised in Massachusetts but during a visit to friends in Lexington, Virginia, became acquainted with New Market and the Williamson family. In the late 1850s, one of the Williamsons asked Jessie to teach at a new school she was opening in New Market, an offer Jessie accepted. She soon married Solomon Rupert, who was an ardent Southerner, making an odd couple in the political climate of the time. When the 34th Massachusetts passed through New Market in 1863, Jessie and several of its members became friends when they realized they were from the same part of Massachusetts. Alfred S. Roe, *An Angel of the Shenandoah: A Life Sketch of Mrs. Jessie Hainning Rupert*, (Worcester, MA), 1913.

45 Jessie Rupert, *The Battle of New Market*, Jessie H. Rupert Papers, Hagley Museum & Library.

46 *Ibid.*

47 *Ibid.*

Chapter 7

"We Can Whip Them Here"

Sunday, May 15, dawned on a bad note for Franz Sigel. The German general was unable to find his favorite flask, and soon reached the conclusion that it had been stolen. Everyone who ran across his path that morning was accused of being the thief—even the owner of the property on which the commanding general had set up headquarters. The owner vented to one of Sigel's staff that the general had "wounded my feelings too deeply for healing or apology."[1] By nightfall, the lost flask was probably long forgotten.

Many years after the war Sigel claimed he was fully prepared to offer battle that day. His actions that morning, taken together with most of the accounts left by his soldiers, however, paint a different picture. When daylight reached the Shenandoah Valley that morning, Sigel's army was still strung out for miles along the Valley Pike. The head under Augustus Moor was at New Market, several more regiments were around Edinburg, and Sigel with the main body was leaving Woodstock some twenty miles as the crow flies from the front. In addition, several small detachments of cavalry were stationed along the Pike from New Market all the way back to Martinsburg in a futile effort to protect Sigel's line of communications. Sigel was anything but prepared for battle that day.

In his official campaign report written just two days after the battle, Sigel tried to put the best possible face on why he was drawn into battle at New

---

1 Eby, *A Virginia Yankee in the Civil War*, 224-5.

Market. His surviving communications from the days immediately preceding the battle do not demonstrate any cohesive plan, but his report to his superiors claims he had the town as an objective. "It always appeared to me of importance to occupy New Market," he wrote, "not only because it affords a good position, but because it places one important gap (Brock's) on the west and an important road on the east in our hands which leads to Luray and Thornton Gap." The former he claimed could be utilized to open communications with Crook, while possession of the Luray Road would provide his cavalry an avenue to raid across the Blue Ridge.[2] But this was written after the fact when Sigel had the benefit of hindsight, and at a time when he was facing harsh criticism from his political opponents clamoring for his head.

In a letter written nearly three decades after the battle to a former West Virginia officer who served in his army, Sigel proposed that he intended for battle to be joined at Mount Jackson rather than New Market. "Made aware of the exposed position of the little force of Moor," at New Market, Sigel wrote, "I immediately sent orders for him to return to Mount Jackson, and to General Stahl [sic] to move forward with the main force of our cavalry to cover the retreat of Moor. . . . But this movement was executed so slowly and the distance from Mount Jackson to New Market was comparatively so great, that I resolved to move forward with my whole force."[3]

One of Sigel's aides who observed him on the night of the 14th characterized the general "to be as restless as a chained hyena. His eyes seemed to be piercing every object upon which he cast them, and especially as the dispatches from the front were received."[4] During the evening of the 14th, Sigel ordered Julius Stahel to have the troops at Woodstock prepared to move out by 5:00 a.m. the next morning. Sigel's intention was to concentrate his forces at Mount Jackson and wait there until he received intelligence from Moor regarding enemy strength and intentions around New Market.[5]

This decision would subject Sigel to criticism for failing to both grasp the strategic situation on the eve of battle and realize the significance of the fighting at New Market on the afternoon of May 14. Moor and his temporary brigade

---

2 Sigel, Report, Sigel Papers.

3 Hewitt, *History of Twelfth Regiment West Virginia Volunteer Infantry*, 111.

4 Michael Gardner to Ira Cole, May 17, 1864, Sigel Papers.

5 *OR* 37, pt. 1, 454.

had carried out their orders to the letter. Sigel had asked for a reconnaissance in force to probe Confederate strength around New Market and to seize that point, if possible. Moor accomplished both objectives with almost no loss. And in doing so, he discovered that Imboden was at New Market in considerable strength and did not intend to give up the place without a fight. This news was all Sigel could have asked for from Moor, and should have spurred the army commander into action. At the least he should have coalesced his scattered forces, especially in light of the intelligence captured several days earlier revealing that more Confederate troops were on their way north toward New Market. Instead, Sigel dithered, taking at best halfway measures that left his army open to destruction.

* * *

Several hours before dawn on May 15, Colonel Moor sent mounted patrols forward that determined Imboden was gone from his front.[6] With this information in hand, and taking no chances, Moor made sure his troops were aligned properly in a strong defensive position on Manor's Hill. His front extended from the Shenandoah River on the west into town. Companies B, D, and I of the 34th Massachusetts under Capt. Andrew Potter were thrown forward as skirmishers. The infantry walked slowly through the soggy fields, scaling Shirley's Hill without meeting a single enemy vidette.[7] About 7:00 a.m., Moor received word from one of his forward cavalry patrols that contact had been made with Imboden's force about four miles south of New Market. Instead of withdrawing, however, the Confederates were advancing—and in much stronger force than on the previous day.[8]

While the cavalry was riding south and discovering Confederates moving in their direction, some of the Federal infantry around the town decided to forage. Several Massachusetts men made their way to the Rupert home in search of breakfast. The soldiers were surprised to find that the mistress of the house, Mrs. Jessie Rupert, had been educated in their hometown of Pittsfield, Massachusetts. "How glad and happy they were to meet someone who loved

---

6   *OR* 37, pt. 1, 80.

7   Thompson diary, May 15, 1864.

8   *OR* 37, pt. 1, 80.

the old commonwealth and her people, and the cause for which they were suffering so much," Mrs. Rupert recalled.[9]

Meanwhile, about 4:00 a.m. that morning, Sigel sent Major Theodore Lang of his staff with a dozen couriers to New Market to keep him apprised of the situation there. When Lang arrived, he found Moor posted in a strong position, but one he could not hope to hold for long against superior numbers. Learning from a deserter from Imboden's command the strength and identity of the Confederate forces, Lang dispatched a courier to Sigel advising the commander of Moor's situation.[10] The staff officer was surveying the field when Confederate troops appeared on the hills in the distance.[11]

* * *

John Imboden got very little sleep that night. His men had fought a substantial delaying action against superior numbers the day before, launched a nighttime attack, and finally executed a withdrawal in the middle of the night in the face of a strong enemy. Several hours before dawn on the 15th, Imboden was awakened "by the light of a tin lantern shining in my face." The messenger was none other than General Breckinridge, who informed his subordinate that his men would reach the fields south of New Market about daylight.[12]

Breckinridge knew Sigel was at New Market, but he was not certain of his strength or dispositions. Imboden confirmed the presence of infantry and the army commander had heard the artillery duel late the previous afternoon, so he knew the Federals were present with more than just an advance cavalry force. From intelligence reports he knew that Sigel outnumbered him at least three to two, and possibly by more. What remained to be determined was Sigel's intention. Imboden had not expected the Federal commander to advance on the 14th, but was proved wrong and the Confederate cavalry was forced back to New Market. Was Moor's advance element a reconnaissance in force or an

---

9 Rupert, *The Battle of New Market.*

10 Theodore F. Lang, *Personal Recollections of the Battle of New Market*, NM coll., VMI. This "deserter" is not mentioned anywhere other than in Lang's account. It is possible that Lang was referring to a prisoner captured the day before, or it is also possible that the "deserter" was actually a planted counter-intelligence ploy.

11 Theodore F. Lang, *Loyal West Virginia From 1861 to 1865* (Baltimore, MD, 1895), 113.

12 Imboden, "The Battle of New Market, VA, May 15th, 1864," 482.

effort to secure the crossroads and the gap at New Market preliminary to making a move eastward across the Blue Ridge? Perhaps Sigel was finally advancing on Staunton in earnest? Breckinridge had no way of knowing for certain what the German had in mind. He could not know even whether Sigel was aware of his presence with Imboden. But as Breckinridge sat in his headquarters tent that rainy Saturday night and into Sunday morning, he resolved that whatever Sigel's intent, the Federals would advance no farther than New Market without a fight.

Breckinridge decided to set a trap for Sigel and hope the Federal commander blundered into it. Imboden and his cavalry would feign an attack on the Union position at New Market early in the morning and then fall back, hopefully with the Federals in hot pursuit. By that time Southern infantry and artillery would be dug in on advantageous ground somewhere south of New Market, waiting for Sigel's men to appear. Once the Federals realized their mistake, it would be too late to extricate themselves and Breckinridge's infantry would crush them.

The Confederate main body began marching for New Market, about eight miles distant, shortly after 1:00 a.m.[13] The troops were roused to consciousness after a short rest and formed without drums or bugles so as not to alert the enemy of their presence. Before the cadets moved out, Capt. Frank Preston offered a moving prayer. John Wise remembered that there were few dry eyes in the ranks when he finished.[14] Cadet John Howard recalled that "several cadets near me remarked . . . 'If they are going to pray over us, maybe they think we are going to get into a fight after all.'"[15] On the short march to New Market, the cadets passed men from one of Wharton's regiments who had broken ranks to sit along the edge of the Valley Pike. "They seemed as merry, nonchalant, and indifferent to the coming fight as if it were their daily occupation," remarked Wise.[16]

Several miles south of New Market, Breckinridge halted the column and ordered Imboden to reestablish contact with the Federals still believed to be in the vicinity of New Market. Companies A, F, and H of the 18th Virginia Cavalry

13 Breckinridge's Official New Market Report.

14 Wise, *End of an Era*, 293.

15 John C. Howard, "Recollections of New Market," *Confederate Veteran*, February 1926, p. 57.

16 Wise, *End of an Era*, 293.

rode forward under Lieutenant Julian Pratt and pushed the Federal skirmishers back to New Market.[17]

As the cavalry trotted northward along the Pike, the wagons and ambulance trains were sent to the rear, guarded by Harman's reserves. The infantry was deployed, Wharton's Brigade on the left, Echols's men en echelon on the right behind Wharton, and the cadets in reserve to the left-rear of Echols.[18] About 550 men from the 62nd Virginia of Imboden's command reinforced the infantry. The initial deployments were made in the vicinity of Hardscrabble, the Williamson family home that dated to the time of the American Revolution.[19] The infantry immediately set about strengthening their position with fence rails.[20] These dispositions were completed "shortly after daylight."[21]

Imboden soon made contact with Federal troops south of New Market. It did not take him long to conclude that they had no offensive aspirations that morning. Initially, Federal skirmishers occupied the southern end of New Market and Shirley's Hill, but the 18th Virginia Cavalry drove them back. The main Federal force up that morning—still just the troops under Augustus Moor from the previous day—were in position along the River Road stretching from Manor's Hill into the center of town near St. Matthews Lutheran Church. As soon as this information was relayed to Breckinridge, the Kentuckian abandoned the idea of a defensive trap and began formulating plans for his own offensive.[22]

Once Julian Pratt's battalion of the 18th Virginia Cavalry cleared the Federals off Shirley's Hill, the troopers established a skirmish line stretching from the crest of the high ground east across the Pike, their right flank resting in woods beyond the road. With the Federals swept from the high ground south of town, Breckinridge and Imboden rode to the top of Shirley's Hill and took in the terrain falling off to the north.[23] The position offered a panoramic view of

---

17 Pratt to Colonna, November 19, 1910.

18 J. Stoddard Johnston, *The Battle of New Market*, NM coll., VMI.

19 Good, *Shadowed by the Massanutten*, 371. "Hardscrabble" is one of the oldest homes in that portion of the Valley and remains a private residence today.

20 Woolwine, *Memoir of a Confederate Soldier.*

21 Breckinridge's Official New Market Report.

22 *Ibid.*

23 Pratt letter, November 19, 1910.

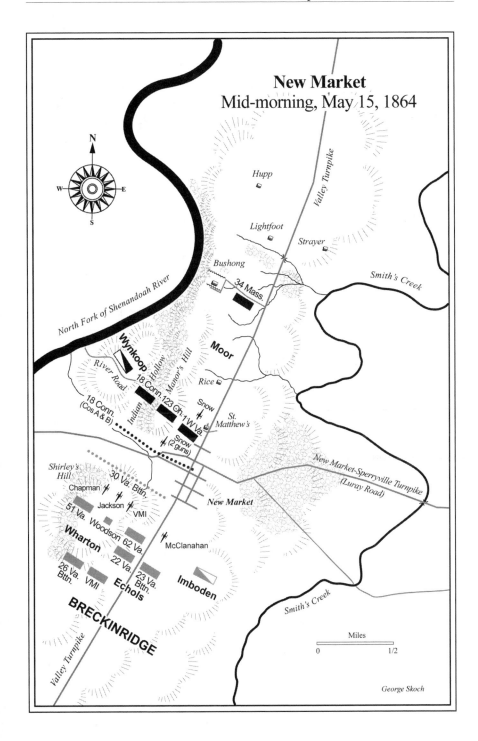

New Market
Mid-morning, May 15, 1864

Valley Turnpike

Hupp

Lightfoot

Strayer

Bushong

Smith's Creek

34 Mass.

North Fork of Shenandoah River

Wynkoop

Moor

River Road

Indian Hollow

Manor's Hill

18 Conn.

18 Conn. 123 Oh. 1 W Va.

18 Conn.
(Cos A & B)

Rice

Snow

St.
Matthew's

Snow
(2 guns)

*New Market-Sperryville Turnpike
(Luray Road)*

*Shirley's
Hill*

30 Va. Bttn.

Chapman

Jackson

51 Va.

Woodson

62 Va.

VMI

Wharton

22 Va.

23 Va.
Bttn.

New Market

McClanahan

26 Va.
Bttn.

VMI

Echols

Imboden

BRECKINRIDGE

Smith's Creek

Valley Turnpike

Miles

0   1/2

George Skoch

the arena that would soon become the field of battle. "[A] few words of explanation from me as to roads, streams, etc," explained Imboden, gave the Confederate commander all the information he needed to formulate his plans.[24]

Breckinridge could see the Manor's Hill position offered the Federals a strong defensive line, but it had its flaws. Although it commanded a clear field of fire on the approach to the ravine west of New Market, it was dominated by the much higher Shirley's Hill, upon which Breckinridge and Imboden stood. Rebel artillery unlimbered atop the southern heights could easily rake the entire area with a devastating fire.

Eager to assume the offensive, the Kentucky general studied the terrain to determine how best to do so. If Breckinridge had any idea of flanking Sigel, natural obstacles and the recent rain put an end to the notion. The Shenandoah River to the west and the high rock bluffs northwest of town would prevent either side from executing a turning movement from that direction. Massanutten Mountain and Smith's Creek created similar barriers to the east. The recent rain, which continued off and on that morning, had raised the Shenandoah River and Smith's Creek well above their usual banks, making both difficult or impossible to ford. A wide turning movement was out of the question.

These limitations, however, also offered opportunity. The terrain would pin the Federals into a narrow peninsula from just north of New Market all the way back to the bridge spanning the Shenandoah between Rude's Hill and Mount Jackson. If the Federal position could be overrun, the possibility existed of capturing much of Sigel's command before it could cross the bridge.

But was an assault against an enemy holding a narrow front with protected flanks feasible? Although very muddy in spots, the terrain falling off across the Southern front was conducive to an advance. Other than a handful of houses, farm buildings, and fences, there were very few obstacles to break up troop formations. About one mile north of New Market, particularly along the Valley Pike, the ground turned rather rocky and was cut by several ravines, but south of that point it consisted mostly of open fields. The flip side, however, was that these open vistas would provide a clear field of fire for Federal troops stationed on Manor's Hill. If an advance became bogged down, attacking Confederates might find themselves sitting ducks for Federal artillery and small arms fire.

---

24 Imboden, "The Battle of New Market, VA, May 15th, 1864," 483.

Determined to strike a blow, Breckinridge turned to Imboden and boldly declared, "We can attack and whip them here, and I'll do it."[25] The infantry and artillery would attack immediately, sweeping along the Valley Pike, explained the army commander. Imboden would take his command, except for the 62nd Virginia, which would join the infantry (strengthened by the addition of some dismounted troopers from the 18th and 23rd Virginia Cavalry regiments), and McClanahan's battery to the right, which would attempt to cross swollen Smith's Creek and harass Sigel as much as possible on his left flank.[26]

With his decision made, Breckinridge formed his troops in three lines on the reverse slope of Shirley's Hill to shield them from view of the Federals. Gabriel Wharton's Brigade formed left of the Valley Pike on the high ground. Lieutenant Colonel John Wolfe's 51st Virginia held the far left of Wharton's line, with the 30th Virginia Battalion (or at least part of it) under Lieutenant Colonel J. Lyle Clark next in line to the right, and Colonel George Smith's 62nd Virginia extending the battle line close to the Pike. Attached to the 62nd was one company of Missourians under Capt. Charles Woodson. The Missourians formed the left-most company of the 62nd, with three companies of men from the 18th and 23rd likely constituting Colonel Smith's right flank elements.

John Echols' Brigade took up a position to the right-rear of Wharton's line. Because Echols was ill, command fell to the brigade's senior officer, Colonel George S. Patton of the 22nd Virginia. Patton was an 1852 graduate of VMI and a cousin of Col. George H. Smith of the 62nd Virginia. Patton's own regiment was posted behind Smith's Virginians. Lieutenant Colonel Clarence Derrick— the only West Pointer in gray on the field that day and a classmate of George Custer's at the academy—deployed his 23rd Virginia Battalion next in line to the right, anchoring the second line firmly on the Pike.[27]

25 Imboden, "The Battle of New Market, VA, May 15th, 1864," 483. Lieutenant Colonel George Edgar, commander of Breckinridge's 26th Virginia Battalion, remembered a slightly different wording: "I have thrown down the gauntlet to Sigel and he declines to accept it, I will attack him." G. M. Edgar to B. A. Colonna, March 25, 1911, NM coll., VMI.

26 Breckinridge's Official New Market Report. There has been some uncertainty and confusion as to the role the 23rd Virginia Cavalry played in the fighting on May 15. It is certain that at least a portion of the regiment fought dismounted, attached to the 62nd Virginia Mounted Infantry (which was also dismounted). See Appendix 5 for a discussion of this issue.

27   Because Colonel Patton was "an old Virginia Military Institute graduate," recalled a captain in the 26th Virginia Battalion, the VMI Cadets referred to his 22nd Virginia as "Patton's Regiment." Carr letter to Edgar, Edgar papers.

Lieutenant Colonel George M. Edgar's 26th Virginia Battalion initially formed in reserve on the right of the Valley Pike behind Echols' 23rd Virginia Battalion, but shortly thereafter was shifted west "on the left of that battalion, and in rear of General [Gabriel] Wharton's Brigade." The VMI Corps of Cadets formed in reserve in the third line with Edgar's 26th Virginia Battalion. Breckinridge told Lieutenant Colonel Scott Ship, commander of the cadet battalion, that "he did not wish to put the cadets in if he could avoid it, but that should occasion require it, he would use them very freely."[28] Capt. William Hart's company of engineers was probably in the third line with the cadets at this time.[29] McLaughlin's two batteries and the pair of cadet guns were posted on the crest of Shirley's Hill. Imboden (with the 18th and 23rd cavalry regiments, Sturgis Davis' company, and McClanahan's battery) was in position east of the Pike.

*   *   *

The growing number of Confederates on the heights south of town drew considerable interest from the officers and men in blue on the other side of the field. From the top of Shirley's Hill, the Southern troops advancing along the Valley Pike were visible to the skirmishers of the 34th Massachusetts. Capt. George Thompson witnessed "the enemy's skirmishers advancing on the low land on each side of the pike. Our cavalry went out & met them. . . . Soon some officers came up on the hill directly in front of us and looked about with a glass. After an hour or two, an infantry regt [sic] was deployed on the hill in front and advanced."[30]

Positioned behind his skirmish line, Augustus Moor watched Lieutenant Pratt's advance and made ready to receive it. He did not know for certain what he was up against, but he surely harbored reservations about going into battle with the small force at his disposal. One of the most important questions weighing on Moor was when Sigel would arrive with the main body of the army.

28 OR 37, pt. 1, 89. Colonel Edgar's official report, Edgar papers, was also reproduced in the *Supplement to the Official Records of the Union and Confederate Armies* (Wilmington, NC, 1996), Pt. 1, vol. 6, 850-852. Unfortunately, in this report and in all other New Market-related materials reproduced in the *Supplement*, the editor mistakenly inserted [John Austin] before references to General Wharton, when in fact it was Gabriel Wharton who served at New Market.

29 It is all but impossible to track the movements of the engineers during the battle.

30 Thompson diary, May 15, 1864.

Captain
George W. Thompson

VA Library

As Moor weighed his very limited options, a Southern soldier absorbed a memory that would linger with him for the rest of his life: "The little town, which a moment before had seemed to sleep so peacefully upon that Sabbath morn, was now wreathed in battle smoke and swarming with troops hurrying to their positions."[31]

Meanwhile, Confederate skirmishers under Lieutenant Pratt continued their methodical advance, driving back the several companies of the 34th Massachusetts positioned on Shirley's Hill. The withdrawing soldiers from New England were absorbed back into their regiment, which was sent some distance to the rear. The 34th would be shifted around several times before being sent back to its original position. The only accomplishment to show for all this frenetic action would be depriving its men the chance of eating a breakfast they had tried several times to cook.[32]

Reinforcements for Moor dribbled in throughout the morning. The first to arrive was the 18th Connecticut, less three of its companies detailed to guard

31 Wise, "West Point of the Confederacy," 467.

32 Lincoln, *Life with the 34th Massachusetts Infantry*, 280.

the supply lines stretching back to Martinsburg.[33] The regiment left its camp at Edinburg, about fifteen miles to the north, in such haste that its pickets—nearly 200 in number—were forgotten and left behind. "We remained on duty, waiting and wondering why the relief did not show up," one of the Connecticut soldiers recalled.[34] Once they discovered the regiment had marched south without them, the commander of the skirmishers, Lieutenant Robert Kerr, ordered his men to make a forced march through the mud and rain to rejoin it. The Connecticut infantry covered a distance of nearly sixteen miles in only a few hours, making the final exhausting two miles in a dead run. "We were near used up," one of the soldiers grumbled when the erstwhile pickets finally caught up with their comrades at New Market. They made it just as the main body of the regiment was being placed in line.[35]

As the strung-out Federal column moved up the Valley Pike, a growing number of wounded and stragglers threaded through their ranks moving in the opposite direction. The number of non-wounded men heading for the rear disgusted one artilleryman, who wrote, "As we went up there was evidence of a heavy fight going on in front. The road was lined with stragglers who kept shouting to us to give it to them, and then getting to the rear as fast as they could."[36]

The arriving reinforcements found Moor's Federal line of battle forming along the River Road extending west away from New Market onto and eventually over Manor's Hill. With the arrival of the Connecticut troops he had under his command three infantry regiments and another in reserve. Both flanks were covered by artillery, and cavalry was massed on the western flank. The 1st West Virginia anchored the line on the Valley Pike at St. Matthew's Church in New Market. To its right was the 123rd Ohio, with the newly arrived 18th Connecticut taking up a position atop the hill with Wynkoop's cavalry on the right extending Moor's front toward the river. Snow's six-gun Maryland battery unlimbered in the graveyard at St. Matthew's Church on the northern fringe of town, with the four guns of Ewing's horse artillery on its right between the 18th Connecticut and the cavalry. Well to the rear by the Bushong farm was

---

33 *OR* 37, pt. 1, 83.

34 Charles Lynch to B.A. Colonna, August 27, 1912, NM coll., VMI.

35 Lynch, *The Civil War Diary of Charles H. Lynch*, 59-60.

36 Unsigned letter of member of Carlin's Battery, Wheeling *Intelligencer*, May 23, 1864.

A retouched early 20th Century view of Manor's Hill. *VMI Archives*

the 34th Massachusetts Infantry, too far away to be of immediate support, but in a good location to provide a rallying point should one become necessary.

It was a strong position, but Moor did not have nearly enough men to hold such a line against a determined enemy attack. The passage of time only increased Moor's unease, for the Confederate line of battle extended far beyond both of his flanks. Theodore Lang and his charge of couriers watched Southern troop movements from atop Manor's Hill, from which position they continued firing off messages to General Sigel, urging him to come to the front with the remainder of the army. After sending off his fifth such message within one hour, Lang and his riders attracted the attention of one of the Confederate gun crews. Several shells were thrown in his direction and one burst overhead, injuring a courier.[37]

The Federal guns under Snow and Ewing were soon joined by another artillery battery from New York under Alfred von Kleiser. Together, the Federal long-arm commenced firing on the Confederates massing about Shirley's Hill. Confederate guns replied in kind. To New Market resident Perry Cook, "the shells sounded like a circular saw running through a dry plank."[38] Imboden later waxed poetic about the exchange, writing that the discharge of

---

37 Lang, *Recollections.*

38 *Shenandoah Valley,* November 17, 1910.

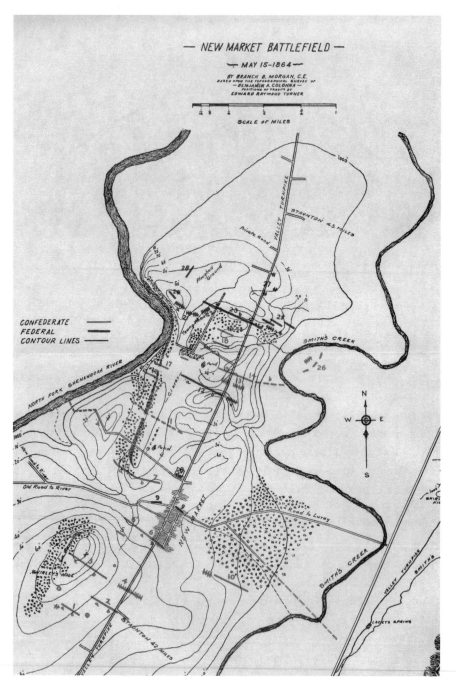

The Colonna Map of the Battle of New Market

Colonna Map (opposite page)

Many of the "VMI New Market Cadets," as they became known, went on to great success in their postwar careers, and many of them left accounts of their experiences on the field at New Market. Many of the known cadet accounts were solicited by Benjamin Azariah Colonna, Class of 1864 and Cadet Captain of Company D during the battle. Colonna, who spent 25 years as an engineer in the U.S. Coast & Geodetic Survey—a forerunner of today's National Oceanic & Atmospheric Administration (NOAA)—took the lead in trying to piece together what had happened on the field at New Market on May 15, 1864. Much of what comprises the New Market Collection in the VMI Archives is Colonna's correspondence with his fellow cadets, as well as other veterans of the battle. One of the results of Colonna's research is a very detailed map of the battlefield that was published in 1914. His time in the USCGS served him well, for the topographic detail on the main field of battle as depicted on the "Colonna map" is remarkably accurate. He was aided in his efforts by some of the Bushong family and other people of New Market. However, because his main focus was the role of the cadets, he ignored the terrain east of Smith's Creek and west of the Shenandoah River. In his quest to be as exact and accurate to history as possible, Colonna included not just troop positions from the battle of May 15, but also what he perceived to be the positions of Imboden and Boyd on May 13, 1864. In addition to the cavalry actions, he also depicted pre-and post-battle campsites and locations of where certain cadets fell, trees, and fence lines that served as landmarks during the battle. The end result is that Colonna compressed so much information onto one map that it becomes cluttered and confusing even with careful study.

Some of Colonna's troop placements—in particular those of Imboden and Boyd on the 13th—are almost certainly incorrect. In his biographical entry for Colonna in *The VMI New Market Cadets*, William Couper writes: "To him more than any other man is due the complete mapping of the battle field at New Market. His expert knowledge of the subject, coupled with his intense interest and love of accuracy, has preserved for all time a picture of that much discussed battle ground."

Colonna's family, originally from the Eastern Shore of Virginia, would establish a large shipyard on the Elizabeth River in Norfolk, Virginia, on land adjacent to the Hardy family estate, where his classmate William Charles Hardy resided. Colonna's Shipyard is still in existence today.

the guns "opened the ball."[39] The cannon fire may have triggered the beginning of serious fighting, but it soon revealed itself to be more noise and flash than substance. The firing, recalled Major Henry Peale, the commander of the 18th Connecticut, "continued with great vigor and . . . great accuracy, although without the infliction of any considerable damage" to the Federals.[40] "The heavens were literally blackened with shells and canister," wrote one Federal.[41] The fitful artillery duel expended large quantities of ammunition as it dragged on through the rest of the morning.

The gunnery display took some Federals by surprise. "[We] were not looking for trouble" that morning, being "in ignorance of the fact of the proximity of Breckinridge's forces," remembered one soldier in blue decades after the fact.[42] The fire interrupted the morning meal for the men of the 123rd Ohio. "We drew a few rations at breakfast," one of the Buckeyes wrote, "and then pitched tents, expecting to remain but no sooner was it done than the enemy opened their cannon on us and we were ordered to strike tents immediately."[43]

Even in the midst of battle soldiers have a way of finding humor in everything. Colonel George Wells, commander of the 34th Massachusetts, had an established reputation as a disciplinarian. Discharging weapons in the regiment's camp, for example, was strictly prohibited. If a musket was fired in camp, Wells routinely dispatched one of his staff officers to investigate. "Orderly go and ascertain who fired that gun and report him to me immediately," were his usual instructions. When small arms fire broke out at New Market that morning, an unidentified Massachusetts soldier was heard to cry out, "Orderly, go and ascertain who fired that gun and report him to me immediately!"[44] It is not known whether Colonel Wells heard the call or if he did, whether he found it humorous.

The artillery fire was underway when a Union officer rode up to the front door of Jessie Rupert's New Market home. "There will be hot work here soon,"

39 Imboden, "The Battle of New Market, VA, May 15th, 1864," 483.

40 *OR* 37, pt. 1, 82.

41 Duncan, *Alexander Neil*, 29.

42 A. J. Gilbert to B. A. Colonna, December 12, 1900, NM Coll., VMI.

43 Coe diary, May 15, 1864.

44 Hewitt, *History of Twelfth Regiment West Virginia Volunteer Infantry*, 116-7.

he announced before advising the Ruperts to move within Federal lines. As if on call, shells began bursting in the streets before the family could leave. "The streets were at once deserted, and cannon balls and shells rolled and exploded in every direction," Mrs. Rupert remembered. The cannonade did not distinguish between civilian and military targets. The concussion from shells bursting in the trees lining the front of their home shook the structure, breaking several glass windows. Understandably afraid to venture outside, the Ruperts found themselves trapped in their own house between the lines. Determined to do what they could to protect their son, they hid their infant under the floorboards.[45]

Several New Market families gathered at the Soxman home south of town in the belief that the residence offered more safety than their own homes in the town proper. Confederate ambulances and medical wagons were posted in front of the Soxman home, and a few errant Federal shells fell in the vicinity. When "one shell came near the Soxman residence, we all went into the cellar," recalled Perry Cook, where the nervous residents and guests "walked the floor, rubbing their hands and did not speak a word. They knew what was taking place."[46]

With the Federal artillery posted around St. Matthew's Church drawing counter-battery fire, errant Southern shells fired back fell randomly about the streets. One young girl whose family lived only two doors up from the church became so frightened by all the explosions erupting around her house that she braved the barrage to run across the street and seek the comfort of a local minister's family.[47]

Julius Stahel and the remainder of the Federal cavalry arrived about the time General Breckinridge's main force reached the the vicinity of Shirley's Hill.[48] Because General Stahel outranked Colonel Moor, Stahel assumed command on the field, which in turn reverted Moor to the command of his own brigade. Like Moor, Stahel also perceived the need for more troops, and

45 Rupert, *The Battle of New Market*.

46 *Shenandoah Valley*, November 17, 1910.

47 Nancy B. Stewart, *Rough Winds: The Battle of New Market*, (Broadway, VA, 1994), 8. In 2006, a 3-inch Confederate Read shell was unearthed in the yard behind the Rupp House on Main Street, adjacent to St. Matthews Cemetery. The shell was likely fired from Confederate guns atop Shirley's Hill. It is now on exhibit at the New Market Battlefield State Historical Park.

48 *OR* 37, pt. 1, 80.

dispatched a message to Sigel to that effect. Stahel was apparently satisfied with Moor's troop dispositions, for the cavalryman made no major changes in that regard.[49]

It was about noon when Franz Sigel "came on the field with a great flourish," observed Major Lang.[50] The commanding general initially dismissed any concerns that he was perhaps courting disaster by committing his forces to battle in their present state, telling Lang that he "was excited" unnecessarily about it.[51] As Confederate skirmishers began to advance on the town itself, Lang, or so he later wrote, inquired of Sigel as to the whereabouts of the rest of the Federal army. When the general nonchalantly replied that "they were coming," Lang claimed to have countered with a caustic, "Yes General, but too late."[52]

* * *

Long after the May 15th combat, Franz Sigel would claim that he decided to offer Breckinridge battle at New Market because of the strategic importance of the crossroads there and also because he thought "that a retreat would have a bad effect on our troops." Therefore, Sigel continued, he "resolved to hold the enemy in check until the arrival of our main forces from Mount Jackson and then accept battle."[53]

In reality, by the time Sigel arrived on the field the decision had already been made for him. Because of his own ignorance of the true conditions at the front and his rather lackadaisical manner in moving his troops, Sigel was now faced with giving battle to an enemy of unknown strength with only a portion of his own army up and in place to wage it. Any chance Sigel had for success that Sunday would depend upon the quick and energetic concentration of his scattered forces into a defensible position, and the cooperation of his enemy.

49 Sigel, "Sigel in the Shenandoah Valley," 488.

50 Lang, *Loyal West Virginia*, 114.

51 *Ibid.*

52 Lang, *Personal Recollections of the Battle of New Market*. If Lang said half the things to Sigel that his postwar writings claim, he would probably have been court-martialed for insubordination. Whether or not he actually said these things, the sentiments conveyed sum up the situation from the Federal point of view.

53 Sigel, "Sigel in the Shenandoah Valley," 488.

Thus far in the campaign, Sigel had not shown any evidence of being able to deliver what the fluid situation at the front now demanded. And John C. Breckinridge had no intention of letting Sigel get comfortable around New Market.

A postwar undated view (early 1900s) of the town of New Market. The town had changed little from its wartime appearance. The only real difference is that the Valley Pike (center) has been widened and telephone poles added. Note the horses & carriages on the unpaved road. *Casey Billhimer*

Chapter 8

"Are They Driving Us?"

W hile he waited for the rest of the Confederate troops to get in position, Gabriel Wharton strode ahead of his line to examine the enemy position and the terrain his men would have to traverse. "I went down in front until I could see the general position of the Federal line—I saw distinctly the battery at . . . the church in the edge of the town and also a battery on a point near some cedars," Wharton later reported. The brigade leader realized that once his men crested Shirley's Hill, they would be exposed to Federal artillery fire—but only as they descended the forward (or northern) slope. Once they reached the foot of the hill they would be shielded from enemy fire in the ravine running west out of town. If his troops could get down the hill fast enough, Wharton reasoned, they might be able to reach the shelter of the ravine before Federal artillerymen could zero in their pieces on his advancing ranks.

The revelation heartened the horseless brigadier. Breckinridge had ordered his field officers to dismount for the attack to make them less conspicuous targets. Unable to relay orders in person, Wharton sent messengers riding with instructions. "[W]hen I give the order to advance," he informed his regimental leaders, "rush down that slope without regard to order." The cadets and the 26th Virginia Battalion, comprising his reserve, would have to follow the example of the front line in order for the attack to be effective, so Wharton ordered them "to conform their movements to mine."[1]

1   Staunton *Spectator & Vindicator*, May 20, 1904.

Breckinridge's infantry on Shirley's Hill was ready to advance sometime between 11:00 am and noon. The six companies of the 30th Virginia Battalion were deployed forward as skirmishers, replacing the screen of troopers from the 18th Virginia Cavalry, who rejoined the rest of the cavalry on the far right side of the Confederate line.[2]

When Breckinridge was satisfied that all was in order, he instructed Major Peter Otey to advance. "Our battalion reached the picket line and was ordered to drive in the enemy's skirmishers, thus bringing on the fight," recalled the major with no little pride.[3] Just before the infantry stepped off, Breckinridge spurred his horse up to the young cadets, who greeted the army commander with a loud cheer. "Young gentlemen," the Kentucky general told them, "I hope there will be no occasion to use you, but if there is, I trust you will do your duty."[4]

Confronting the 30th Battalion were Companies A and B of the 18th Connecticut Infantry under Capt. William Spaulding. The 18th's commander reported that "severe skirmishing shortly ensued" between the opposing lines.[5] As the skirmishing intensified, wounded men began trickling to the rear. One of the injured was the 18th's Joe Abbey, who had been shot in the back between the shoulder blades. A comrade jokingly remarked, "They must have fired from a balloon to hit you like that." The wounded man was in no mood for humor and curtly explained that he had been lying prone on the side of the hill, his back exposed to enemy fire when the bullet found him. His company commander, continued Abbey, "sent me to the rear" to have his wound inspected and dressed. The spreading fight, and likely the pain brought about from his wound, confused the injured Connecticut solder. "Where in Hell is 'the rear'?" he asked his comrade.[6]

---

2   Michael West, *30th Battalion Virginia Sharpshooters* (Lynchburg, VA 1995), 80-1. One account states that only four of the six companies of the 30th were deployed as skirmishers, with the other two held in reserve. The report of Major Henry Peale, commander of the 18th Connecticut, mentions a "double line" of skirmishers, possibly lending some credence to a reserve component.

3   *Response of Hon. Peter J. Otey, at the [VMI] Alumni Banquet, June 1896, to the Toast 'The War Cadets,'* Peter J. Otey Papers, VMI.

4   Howard, "Recollections of New Market," 57.

5   *OR* 37, pt. 1, 82.

6   James Haggerty to B. A. Colonna, June 3, 1914, NM coll., VMI.

The noise and the movement of the troops also agitated a farmer's animals. In addition to Confederate lead, the men of the 18th Connecticut also had to endure an "attack" from a herd of some ten cows being chased by "a large black New Foundland [sic] dog [which] came charging along our line of battle. At first I thought it was a cavalry charge in flank," remembered one Connecticut soldier.[7]

While directing the fight from the skirmish line, Capt. Spaulding fell with a shot to the abdomen. The wound would prove mortal.[8] The regimental chaplain recalled that Spaulding "was brave to a fault" and had been a conspicuous target on the skirmish line, giving encouragement to his men. "Are they driving us?" were the last words he uttered before dying.[9]

The Confederates were indeed driving everything from their front— "sweeping like an avalanche" as one Ohio soldier graphically recalled the initial push.[10] The skirmishers of the 30th Battalion were engaged for only a very short time before Breckinridge ordered his infantry to advance. Within a few short minutes all three Confederate lines emerged over the crest of Shirley's Hill. The manner in which they were deployed impressed the Federals who watched the parade-like advance—and convinced them that the Southern army was much stronger than it was in reality. Any deception on Breckinridge's part was unnecessary, for the flanks of his extended line of battle stretched well beyond the flanks of Moor's Manor's Hill line, making the Federal position instantly untenable. "As soon as the Confederate support came in sight we were ordered to fall back," one Connecticut soldier recalled.[11]

Only at that moment, with three lines of Confederate battle striding toward him and his advance elements falling back, did Franz Sigel realize the mortal danger he faced. "It now became clear to me that all the troops could not reach the position close to New Market. I therefore ordered Colonel Moor to evacuate his position slowly . . . and to fall back into a new position," was how

7 *Ibid.*

8 One member of Spaulding's Company B thought that the fatal shot was fired by a small group of Confederate skirmishers occupying a barn at the base of the hill. C. H. Richmond to B. A. Colonna, December 13, 1910, NM coll., VMI.

9 Walker, *History of the 18th Regiment Connecticut Volunteers*, 220-1.

10 Keyes, *Military History of the 123rd Regiment of Ohio Volunteer Infantry*, 55.

11 Richmond to Colonna, December 13, 1910.

Sigel later spun the event.[12] Moor's line was withdrawn several hundred yards and reformed just south of Jacob Bushong's house and barn, a retreat that abandoned the town of New Market to the advancing Confederates. As Moor fell back, the Federal commander sent orders to Jeremiah Sullivan to hurry forward with the rest of the army.[13]

Moor's new position was held by the 18th Connecticut on the right and the 123rd Ohio on the left, with von Kleiser's battery in support on the Pike. The 1st New York Veteran Cavalry, and likely detachments of other units, were placed in support of von Kleiser's guns. The new line was even shorter than the previous one on Manor's Hill.[14] The other Federal troops on the field were being arrayed in line behind Moor just north of the Bushong farm, leaving Moor's short line to act as a breakwater position to slow the Confederate attack and thus buy time for the main line of resistance to form. By placing his defensive position farther north, Sigel was shortening—albeit slightly—the distance the remainder of the army would have to cover to reach the battlefield.

Writing in *Century* magazine long after the war, Sigel sought to shift some of the blame for making a stand on this ground to the commander of his cavalry escort company. The new line on the Bushong farm was already beginning to take shape, explained Sigel, when "it was reported to me by Captain R. G. Prendergrast [sic], commander of my escort, that all the infantry and artillery of General Sullivan had arrived, the head of the column being in sight, and that they were waiting for orders." In fact, only the 54th Pennsylvania and 12th West Virginia (Colonel Joseph Thoburn's brigade) had reached the field and were moving into position, all the while under a hostile fire. Still absent were the 28th and 116th Ohio (Moor's brigade) and DuPont's battery.[15]

---

12 Sigel, "Sigel in the Shenandoah Valley," 489.

13 Sigel report.

14 Lester, *Autobiography of Jacob Lester*, 9.

15 Sigel, "Sigel in the Shenandoah," 489. One of the main criticisms of Sigel's handling of the fight and even offering battle in the first place was the strung-out condition of his army. His two Ohio regiments (the 28th and 116th, both of Moor's brigade) and DuPont's battery did not arrive until after the battle was largely over, and contributed nothing but cover for the retreat. Sigel's article in *Century* magazine, quoted here, tries to explain that he did not pull back toward Mt. Jackson earlier because he was led to believe by Capt. Pendergrast that General Jeremiah Sullivan and the rest of the army (i.e., the Ohio regiments and DuPont) had reached the field. In reality, those troops were still well to the rear. If there was any substance to the claim that Sigel was misinformed by Pendergrast or anyone else, he would and should have noted it in his report written after the battle ended. He did not. Sigel is either lying to make his decisions look

As the Federal infantry scurried to find their new place in line, the artillery duel—which had fallen away when the Confederate attack stepped off—resumed. Supported by some of Imboden's men on its right, the 30th Virginia Battalion pushed the Federal skirmishers out of New Market, clearing the way for the smooth advance of the main body. "The Rebels were in the town in force," one resident recalled, "and occasionally we saw them lead by a wounded prisoner, or carry into shelter some dying comrade."[16]

Following Gabriel Wharton's instructions, the first waves of Confederate infantry pushed down Shirley's Hill quickly, avoiding much of the hostile fire hastily aimed in their direction. Looking back from his position with the skirmish line, Major Otey described the advance as "rather pell-mell."[17] Wharton was pleased with the swift-moving advance, confident he had not lost a single man from his first line.[18] The Corps of Cadets, however, either did not receive Wharton's order or misinterpreted it. Instead of swiftly moving up and over Shirley's Hill, the cadets tramped forward in perfect formation—presenting a perfect target for the Union guns. Otey, himself an 1860 VMI graduate, described the advance in a postwar speech: "Soon I saw the cadets who were in rear come over the little crest . . . and down they came in as a beautiful and solid a line as I ever saw go across the parade ground."[19] Their disciplined advance impressed even the men in blue who witnessed it. "Nothing could be finer than their advance," agreed Colonel Wells of the 34th Massachusetts.[20]

Visually impressive it was, but the cadets' parade ground tactics proved costly. "The Yankee gunners had gotten the exact range, and their fire began to tell on our line with fearful accuracy," Lieutenant Colonel Scott Ship, commander of the cadet battalion, reported. "Great gaps were made through

---

better in the cold light of history, or the intervening years clouded his memory as to the facts of that day. For an army commander to call out one of his staff officers by name in such a fashion also suggests there maybe have been some lingering personal animosity between the men. Pendergrast was a member of the staff Sigel largely inherited when he assumed command, and some members became rather vocal about Sigel's deficiencies after the debacle at New Market.

16 Rupert, *The Battle of New Market*.

17 Peter Otey to Scott Ship, April 14, 1875, NM coll., VMI.

18 Staunton *Spectator & Vindicator*, May 20, 1904.

19 Otey to Ship, April 14, 1875.

20 *OR* 37, pt. 1, 83.

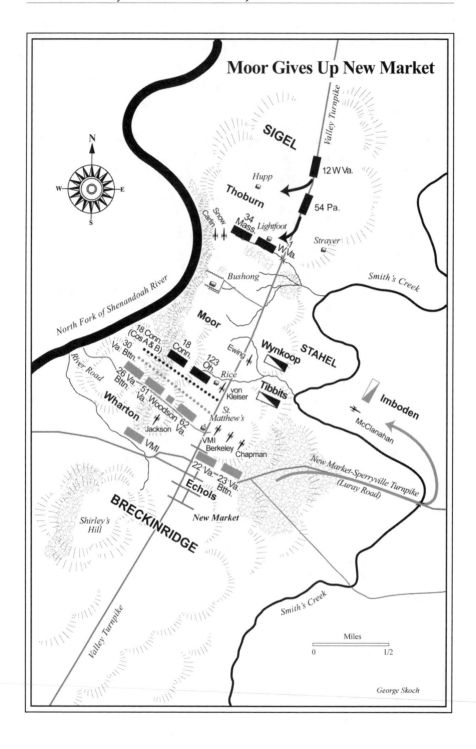

Moor Gives Up New Market

George Skoch

the ranks, but the cadet, true to his discipline, would close in to the center to fill the interval and push steadily forward."[21]

For most of the officers of the VMI cadet battalion, battle was nothing new. Many had served in the Army of Northern Virginia earlier in the war. This was not the case for the cadets. To them, combat was something new and utterly terrifying—far different from the glorious images of the romance of war they had conjured up while hard at their studies in Lexington. "We began to learn, much to our regret, that fighting was not as pleasant as we had anticipated," Cadet John J. Coleman confided (and admitted) to his parents several days after the battle.[22] "I saw wounded men stretched out for the first time," Cadet Nelson B. Noland recalled, "and here for the first time it occurred to me that maybe we were not 'playing soldier' this time."[23] Another cadet, John S. Wise, also quickly discovered just how terrible fighting and warfare really was. "Down the green slope we went," he recalled after the war.

He continued:

> Then came a sound more stunning than thunder, that burst directly in my face; lightning leaped; fire flashed; the earth rocked; the sky whirled round, and I stumbled. My gun pitched forward and I fell upon my knees. Sergeant [William H.] Cabell looked back at me sternly, pityingly, and called out 'Close up, men,' as he passed on. I knew no more. When consciousness returned it was raining in torrents. I was lying on the ground, which all about was torn and plowed with shell."[24]

Wise was one of the first cadets wounded in the battle. About the same time he was struck, Professor Capt. A. G. Hill, commander of Company C, Cadets Charles Read, James L. Merritt, and Pierre Woodlief also fell wounded.[25] Capt. Hill, according to one observer, "fell like a log."[26] Merritt, who was injured by artillery fire, wrote to his father the next day that a shell fragment "knocked me

---

21 *Ibid*, 90.

22 John James Coleman to "Dear Father," in Richmond *Daily Whig*, June 22, 1864.

23 Nelson B. Noland to Charles Read, October 18, 1895, NM coll., VMI.

24 Wise, "West Point," 468.

25 Read's musket was mangled by the explosion of a shell (possibly the same one that struck Wise) and is today on exhibit at New Market Battlefield State Historical Park.

26 Howard, "Recollections of New Market," 57.

Cadet John S. Wise

VMI Archives

about ten feet. . . . I thought the wound was mortal."[27] Another injured cadet stumbled across Woodlief, who had been hit in the leg. The wounded cadet, he wrote with no little disgust, was "whimpering like a child with a cut finger . . . he thought his leg was shot off."[28]

The wounded Corporal Wise was the son of former Virginia Governor Henry Wise, who was now leading a brigade in General Lee's Army of Northern Virginia. The younger Wise had been detailed that morning with three other cadets—including Pierre Woodlief—to guard the institute's baggage. Their orders were unequivocal: remain with the wagon. "When it became evident that a battle was imminent," Wise later wrote, "a single thought took possession of me . . . that I would never be able to look my father in the face again if I sat on a baggage wagon while my command was in its first, perhaps its only, engagement." Having made up his mind to abandon the wagon and join his comrades in battle, Wise gave a short but stirring oration to his fellow guards, advising them that he planned to go to

27 James L. Merritt to W. H. E. Merritt, May 16, 1864, NMBSHP.

28 Porter Johnson to Henry A. Wise, June 8, 1909, NM coll., VMI.

the front. "If I return home and tell my father that I was on the baggage guard when my comrades were fighting I know my fate. He [General Wise] will kill me with worse than bullets—ridicule." When he finished speaking, all four cadets abandoned the wagon and set out for the front, leaving the baggage in the charge and care of its driver.[29] Of the four cadets detailed to guard the wagon, one would be killed and two wounded in a battle they joined by choice.

When they reached the ravine at the foot of Shirley's Hill Breckinridge stopped the advance of his small army, paused to dress ranks, shift positions, and take stock of his situation. Exactly how long the Southern army stayed there is open to conjecture. Lieutenant Colonel George Edgar's 26th Virginia Battalion was shifted from its reserve position near the Valley Pike in the third line to the extreme left of the front line beside the 51st Virginia, anchoring that flank along the Shenandoah River. Although somewhat staggered due to the original echelon formation, the Confederate front now extended from the river on the west to Smith's Creek on the east.

Although the ground covered by the Confederate advance encompasses a relatively small geographic area, it took Breckinridge some time to cover the distance. This was due to a variety of factors, including the presence of Sigel's Federals, the rainy weather (which inhibited visibility), and the muddy terrain, all of which combined to slow the advance. Most Confederate accounts mention this halt in the ravine—the cadet accounts in particular—but the amount of time attributed to it varies widely. Part of the reason for this time discrepancy is the order in which the units arrived in the low ground. The men in Wharton's front line spent longer in the ravine than did the cadets in the third line, for example. Terrain, as it always does, played a key role. Much of Wharton's line passed easily through open fields broken here and there by fences or buildings. Edgar's 26th Virginia Battalion, which shifted from the right to the extreme left, moved through some wooded terrain that slowed its progress. Once these Virginians tried to advance from the ravine, Edgar and the far left of the 51st Virginia found themselves in "Indian Hollow," a wooded and rocky ravine that ascends the western face of Manor's Hill. "Before reaching the crest of the hill," reported Edgar, "I found it necessary (because of the course of the river) to throw my left wing in rear of the right."[30] The rough ground and narrowed front further slowed their progress moving northward. On the right

29 Wise, "West Point," 467-8.

30 Edgar, New Market report, Edgar Papers.

end of the line, Col. George Smith's right-most companies of the 62nd Virginia and Derrick's 23rd Virginia Battalion were in the town itself. Organizing and moving in an urban environment is always problematic.

While the subordinate commanders were redressing their lines and shifting positions, Breckinridge was pondering his next move, adapting his plan to the unfolding circumstances. His official report of the engagement does not specifically mention this halt in the ravine west of New Market, but he does state that it took "several hours . . . until I had occupied the town of New Market" from the time he had deployed south of town near Hardscrabble that morning. What he was now facing to the north was unclear. The first Federal line at the top of Manor's Hill had now fallen back and the location and strength of the next Federal position was, for the most part, unknown. Skirmishers across the entire front had to be pushed ahead. The dearth of sources from the 30th Virginia Battalion, whose men composed the skirmish line, makes it impossible to get a clear picture of just what was going on at this stage of the action from the Confederate point of view. Given all that transpired, the halt probably consumed less than an hour, after which the advance—careful and deliberate—resumed.[31]

Up to this point, only Wharton's troops west of the Valley Pike had run into any real resistance. Imboden recalled that "we on the extreme right were only treated to an occasional random shell thrown through the woods" that masked his position from the enemy. Once the Federals evacuated the town, Imboden rode ahead to his own skirmish line in the woods east of New Market to reconnoiter. "I was rewarded by the discovery of Sigel's entire cavalry force massed in very close order in the fields just beyond the woods," he wrote.[32] The Confederate cavalry leader made a decision that would have serious repercussions several hours later: he moved with his entire mounted command and four guns of McClanahan's Battery to the east side of Smith's Creek intending to enfilade the Federal line. He made this move with the blessing of John Breckinridge. "Tell General Imboden as he knows this ground, and I

---

31 George M. Edgar, "Battle of New Market, May 15, 1864," Edgar Papers. George Edgar was more concerned than most veterans of the battle with pinning down an exact timeline of events. Edgar concluded that the advance resumed sometime around 2:00 pm. The frustration Edward Turner encountered while trying to match up events with a specific time is evident in his book: "It is exceedingly difficult to ascertain the time at which successive events in the battle occurred." Turner, *New Market Campaign*, 39.

32 Imboden, "The Battle of New Market, VA, May 15th, 1864," 483.

don't, to make any movement he thinks advantageous, and I will take all the responsibility," the army leader informed a messenger.[33]

Imboden may not have known it at the time, but the only way across the rain-swollen stream was via the road at the foot of New Market Gap, where he had disposed of Boyd's force two days earlier. The upshot was that Breckinridge would be pressing his attack with an impassable waterway separating his infantry and his cavalry.

* * *

As the battle rolled northward, some of the townspeople emerged from their cellars. Others, such as those who had gathered at the Soxman place south of town, sought a way to return to their own residences. Perry Cook and his cousins decided to take advantage of a lull in the fighting. "We concluded to go home and await results of the battle," Cook explained. Before even reaching the southern outskirts of town, a stray shell burst nearby. "When the smoke showed us our danger, we ran back to the Soxman residence. I do not know if I opened the gate or jumped it." They were soon joined there by several wounded Confederates. When the firing died down again, Cook and his friends tried again. This time several Confederate cavalry interceded, advising against venturing into town. "[B]ut we would not be thwarted in our purpose," continued Cook, "[and] made it home."[34]

As Imboden sought a way across Smith's Creek and New Market civilians sought a way home, Sigel's men worked feverishly to form new lines around the Rice farm on the northern edge of town to meet the renewed Confederate assault.[35] The 18th Connecticut "was hardly in line when the rebels heralded their advance by their peculiar yell," Moor remembered.[36] Major Peale of the 18th was unimpressed with his regiment's new position. His new line was sketched on an eminence several hundred yards south of the Bushong house known as Rice's Hill. The position was a poor one, explained the major, "being in a lane backed by barns and two rows of fences." The heavy rains of the past

33 Turner, *New Market Campaign*, 41.

34 *Shenandoah Valley*, November 17, 1910.

35 Eby, *A Virginia Yankee in the Civil War*, 225.

36 *OR* 37, pt. 1, 80.

week had turned the fields and farm lanes into nearly impassable morasses, and Peale found some of his men "knee-deep in mud."[37]

Companies A and B of the 18th Connecticut were once again deployed forward as skirmishers, where they were soon joined by Company D. This left only about 200 men in the ranks of the regiment.[38] For the second time in the battle, the Connecticut men found themselves in a vulnerable and largely indefensible position, with the Confederate line extending well beyond their right flank. If they stood in the face of a determined attack, Peale and his soldiers risked having their flank turned and the regiment destroyed or captured.

The 123rd Ohio on the 18th Connecticut's left was just as poorly positioned. A large number of Confederates were forming in and around the town, and nearly all of them threatened the Ohioans' vulnerable left flank. One of the Buckeyes described their predicament this way: "As they [Confederates] appeared over the eminence we had lately occupied, they poured in upon us such a storm of shot and shell so thick that the very air seemed alive with bullets."[39]

The renewed attack triggered a groundswell of small arms fire and casualties mounted quickly. Leander Coe of Company D, 123rd Ohio was struck in the arm early in this part of the fighting. "I was wounded while loading the fifth load," Coe wrote his diary, "after which i made my way to the reer as fast as possible."[40] Twin brothers Edwin and Edmund Snyder of Company E, 123rd Ohio, were both hit early in the action. Edmund was reloading his musket after having fired only three rounds before being struck in the groin. "It seemed to me that a red-hot stone, weighing about ten pounds and hurled with mighty force had hit me. It sent me spinning round in the ranks," he recalled years after the battle.[41] Just a few minutes later, his brother Edwin was wounded when a bullet pierced his cap box and lodged in his right side. The leather cap box had slowed the lead bullet just enough to save his life.[42]

---

37 *Ibid.*, 82.

38 *Ibid.*

39 Keyes, *Military History of the 123rd Regiment of Ohio Volunteer Infantry*, 55.

40 Coe diary, May 15, 1864.

41 Edmund P. Snyder, *Autobiography of a Soldier of the Civil War* (Ohio, 1915), 13.

42 Snyder, *Adventures and Misadventures of a Union Veteran*, 24.

As the only Federal guns within range of McLaughlin's Confederate artillery, von Kleiser's six Napoleons firing from the Valley Pike drew considerable attention. One Southern round knocked the wheel off a gun, rendering the gun useless. Faced with this accurate and suppressing artillery fire and the approaching enemy infantry, von Kleiser ordered his gunners to limber their pieces and withdraw, leaving the two infantry regiments and cavalry to cover their retreat.

The damaged gun was sent ahead of the others to join the battery's caissons farther north on the Valley Pike. One wounded soldier from Ohio recalled seeing the crippled gun clatter and scratch its way past him, sparks and "fire roll[ing] from under that broken steel axle as it was dragged over the stones of the pike."[43] The axle eventually lodged itself in the stones. Extra horses were hitched to the piece and passing infantrymen were pressed into service with handspikes to try and pry it loose, but the piece was stuck fast. With Colonel Moor's infantry falling back, the gun had to be abandoned. It eventually fell into enemy hands.[44]

"After a short but resolute struggle," reported the colonel, his line was once again forced to yield to superior numbers.[45] Major Peale reported firing "several volleys" at the attacking enemy lines, but quickly determined that remaining "in that position was worse than useless."[46] With von Kleiser's guns safely withdrawn, the 123rd Ohio began streaming back toward the main line forming well to the north, followed or accompanied very quickly by Peale's 18th Connecticut.

Peale admitted that the terrain and the proximity of the steadily approaching enemy caused "some confusion" in his regiment during the retreat.[47] During the chaotic withdrawal, a Connecticut soldier found himself directly behind Major Peale's large gray horse. "Strange to say," remembered

---

43 *Ibid.*, 13.

44 Von Kleiser to DuPont, June 13, 1864, von Kleiser file, NMBSHP. In the wake of the battle, charges were brought against von Kleiser by a junior officer that von Kleiser should be forced to pay from his own wages for the loss of this gun—a sum of $625. The case progressed all the way to the desk of the secretary of war. Eventually, it was determined that von Kleiser was not at fault for its loss, having taken every possible measure to bring it off the field.

45 *OR* 37, pt. 1, 80.

46 *Ibid.*, 82.

47 *Ibid.*

the infantryman, "[as] I knew the horse, I was more afraid of a kick from the animal than I was of the rain of death that was centered upon that country lane."[48] Another small cluster of New Englanders hurrying to the rear happened upon a religious officer from their regiment who told them that their "only chance for salvation is to kneel down and pray to God to save us," to which one of the more pragmatic soldiers replied, "That's what God gave me legs for, and I'm going to use them while I can."[49]

The more disorganized remnants of Moor's command triggered some confusion in the regiments forming behind them when the havoc-filled collapse of the second position spread the chaos northward. "Men of every regiment were mixed up," confessed one soldier.[50] A Pennsylvania lieutenant "noticed some of our men disposed to go to the rear" along with Moor's broken troops, and his "time was taken up in keeping skulkers in the line." In his company, at least, "all went up and did a soldiers duty" when the battle reached them.[51]

Some portion of the 18th Connecticut reformed behind the main Union line, though exactly how much of the regiment reformed there is unclear. The collapse of the Connecticut regiment angered many, including a member of the 34th Massachusetts who confessed, "There was for a number of years after the war a very bitter feeling in our Regt [sic] . . . against the 18 Conn [sic] for their running away from us at New Market." The few surviving accounts penned by men from the 123rd Ohio suggest that after giving way from their second position, many of the Buckeyes took to their heels and (for the most part) did not stop until they reached Mt. Jackson. As organized regiments, neither the

---

48 James Haggerty to B. A. Colonna, June 13, 1914, NM coll., VMI.

49 C. H. Richmond to B. A. Colonna, February 10, 1911, NM coll., VMI.

50 Haggerty to Colonna, June 13, 1914. Some accounts give the 123rd Ohio little credit for its role during the early stages of the battle, and some seem to blame the regiment for the collapse of the second line. According to William C. Davis, for example, "the 123rd Ohio fired one volley into the oncoming foe and then . . . fell back without orders." Davis, *Battle of New Market*, 108. It is unfair to chastise one of regiments (the 123rd Ohio) for not holding its position without equally blaming the other (18th Connecticut) for the performing in much the same manner. While the Buckeyes did not distinguish themselves during this stage of the battle, the 123rd did sustain seventy-five casualties, or about 10% of its total strength—nearly all of them during the opening phases of the engagement. By comparison, the 18th Connecticut suffered fifty-six losses, but carried only about one-half the number of men into the fight. The 123rd Ohio did not reenter the battle as an organized unit and few of its men left accounts of the battle which, taken together, have conspired to tarnish its role at New Market.

51 George W. Gageby to B. A. Colonna, May 27, 1911, NM coll., VMI.

18th nor the 123rd would play a further role of any significance in the combat yet to come, although some of the Ohioans—individually, in small groups, and a few nearly complete companies—would eventually fall in with other regiments and continue fighting.[52]

While Breckinridge's infantry was driving forward and the Federal second position was collapsing, Julius Stahel's cavalry on Moor's left flank was also coming to grief, courtesy of John Imboden. Using the discretion allocated by Breckinridge, the Southern cavalry leader crossed to the east side of Smith's Creek with his two mounted regiments and a portion of McClanahan's guns. There, Imboden found a knoll that provided an excellent position to rake the Federals he had earlier discovered massed behind the woods. "The position was a magnificent one," Imboden recalled, so well masked that McClanahan's gunners were able to unlimber their pieces without being observed. "Once they opened fire," continued the cavalryman, "the effect was magical. The first discharge of the guns threw [Sigel's] whole body of cavalry into confusion." Unable to cross the flooded stream to drive Imboden and his guns away, the Federal horsemen had no choice but to retreat north out of range. By doing so, however, they uncovered von Kleiser's left flank and the 123rd Ohio, which in turn presented another target for Imboden's gunners.[53]

Even though Moor's advanced line had collapsed, and had done so rather quickly, it did absorb some of the onrushing Confederate wave. Moor's brief stand bought Sigel some additional time to form his main body into a strong defensive position several hundred yards north of the Bushong house.

The new main line was anchored at the top of Bushong's Hill overlooking the Shenandoah River, where Sigel unlimbered the dozen guns from Carlin's and Snow's batteries. Extending his line eastward was the 34th Massachusetts. The 1st West Virginia and the 54th Pennsylvania, which arrived on the field about 2:00 p.m., stretched the front line to the Valley Pike, where the men from the Keystone state anchored their left. The Pennsylvanians and the left companies of the 1st West Virginia were deployed in a grove of young cedar trees, but the remainder of Virginians and men from Massachusetts were left standing on open ground. The 12th West Virginia eventually took up a position in column partly behind Snow's guns and partly behind the Massachusetts

---

52 John W. Adams to Benjamin A. Colonna, February 23, 1911, NM coll., VMI.

53 Imboden, "The Battle of New Market, VA, May 15th, 1864," 483-4.

Captain John Carlin (postwar)

Virginia Toney

infantrymen, except for Companies A and B, which were ordered to the right in direct support of Carlin's battery.[54]

The new line of infantry was under the command of Colonel Joseph Thoburn, the leader of Sigel's Second Brigade. Brigadier General Jeremiah Sullivan, the commander of Sigel's sole division of infantry, seems to have played little if any command role at this stage of the fighting and was probably still far to the rear bringing up the remainder of the army.[55] After he withdrew his remaining five guns from their forward position, von Kleiser took up station on a small rise immediately in front of the 34th Massachusetts.[56] Stahel's cavalry, battered and driven northward by Imboden's gunfire from beyond Smith's Creek, again drew up in position east of the Valley Pike, stepped back

---

54 Hewitt, *History of the Twelfth Regiment West Virginia Volunteer Infantry*, 108.

55 In the detailed battle report of the 34th Massachusetts, Colonel Wells mentions General Sullivan late in the battle as being "conspicuous on the field," but fails to add any detail. If Sullivan was present on the battlefield, which is open to speculation, the existing reports and related documents do not clarify where he was or what he was doing. Sullivan did not file an official report. OR 37, pt. 1, 76 offers what is called Sigel's report, but that is in reality a six-sentence telegraph notifying Washington of the battle. (A copy of Sigel's official report of New Market drafted by one of his aides several days after the battle is among Sigel's Papers at the Western Historical Society. See Appendix 2 for the full report.)

56 The current marked location for von Kleiser at NMBSHP is too far to the rear. His guns were closer to the crest of the small rise in front.

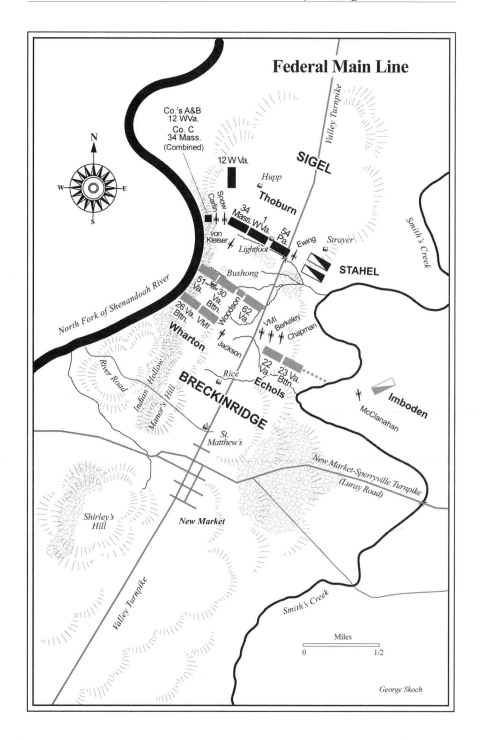

Federal Main Line

George Skoch

from the line assumed by the 54th Pennsylvania. Ewing's guns were unlimbered in support.

Just getting the men to this position had taken hours of effort, and Sigel's army was still not concentrated. Two infantry regiments from Moor's brigade, the 28th and 116th Ohio, as well as DuPont's battery, had yet to reach the field. According to the 54th Pennsylvania's Colonel Jacob Campbell, the Pennsylvania and West Virginia troops reached the field to take up their positions in the main line just as Moor's second position was being overrun. Campbell's men had been on the march from Woodstock since four that morning.[57] The Keystoners covered the last seven miles from Mount Jackson "without halting or rest [and] arrived much fatigued on the field."[58] Rest was not in the foreseeable future. "As soon as we arrived on that ridge . . . we began to fire," remembered a Pennsylvania sergeant.[59]

The West Virginians also reached the field just as the battle was again heating up. "We marched over 20 miles and arrived at or near New Market . . . and had not hardly time to get into line, until we were under one of the hottest fires of the enemy imaginable," wrote Lieutenant Milton Campbell of Company I.[60] "We came up all exhausted & drenched with rain to the skin," remembered Assistant Surgeon Alexander Neil.[61] The West Virginians were given a small reprieve when most of the regiment was placed in reserve on the far right, but wounded men from the front-line regiments began to trickle through their new position, including some friends and relatives in the 1st West Virginia. Breckinridge's front line was not far behind the wounded. "Soon after taking this position we saw a line of gray emerging from the timber perhaps ¼ of a mile in front of us," remembered one of the Federals.[62]

The Confederates nipping at the heels of the retreating wounded were coming on with considerable momentum, having already overrun two Federal positions. However, Imboden's move across Smith's Creek had weakened Breckinridge's main line, leaving the right flank well short of the creek and thus,

---

57 Campbell diary, May 15, 1864.

58 *OR* 37, pt. 1, 86.

59 David R. Bryan to Colonna, March 8, 1911, NM coll., VMI.

60 Fluharty, *Civil War Letters of Lt. Milton Campbell*, 31.

61 Duncan, *Alexander Neil*, 29.

62 J. N. Waddell to Colonna, undated, NM coll., VMI.

in military parlance, "in the air." To correct this, the 23rd Virginia Battalion, now Breckinridge's far right organization, extended its right two companies as skirmishers to cover the distance to the waterway. This tactical disposition, in turn, significantly diluted the battalion's striking strength, but allowed once again for one continuous line stretching from the river to creek.[63] With the line stretched so thin on that flank, and with his few available reserves marching at the other end of the line with Wharton, Breckinridge must have harbored some concern about his weakened right flank.

When the Confederates spotted Sigel's main line, wrote one of Breckinridge's staff officers, "It was evident that the enemy had determined to make his final stand."[64] To bolster his infantry for what promised to be a much more difficult attack, and almost certainly to help discourage a Federal counterattack against his weakened right flank, Breckinridge moved his remaining artillery, less Jackson's Battery (which was deployed just to the southeast of the Bushong House) to a series of small knolls northeast of town. Despite the steady rain, the ground was well suited for such a movement. "[O]f all the regions on this continent there is none that affords such a splendid field for the maneuvering of artillery," declared one of Jackson's officers.[65]

The Confederate army commander accompanied the guns in person, directing their advance as the infantry pressed forward. Rather than remain in a static position, Breckinridge decided the artillery would be more effective if the guns leapfrogged ahead with the infantry. According to a staff officer "as the line of battle advanced, the artillery would limber up, gallop to the front and open fire, making . . . a skirmish line of artillery, frequently in front . . . of the infantry."[66]

Offensive striking power was not the only thing Breckinridge had in mind. By moving the guns aggressively to the front, he also hoped to draw some of the enemy artillery fire away from his advancing infantry. The tactic worked for a time—to the dismay of the Confederate gunners, who found themselves under heavy enemy counterbattery fire. A sergeant serving with Chapman's Battery

63 Breckinridge's Official New Market Report; Derrick quoted in Turner, *New Market Campaign*, 62.

64 Breckinridge's Official New Market Report.

65 Micajah Woods to "My Dear Father," May 16, 1864, NM coll., VMI.

66 Johnston, *The Battle of New Market*.

recalled New Market as "one of the hardest days work I ever did."[67] One of the Yankee guns scored a direct hit on one of Chapman's ammunition caissons, obliterating it and sending its terrified horses fleeing back toward the town.[68] The devastating shot killed one gunner and wounded three more.[69] Cadet Henry Whitehead was serving one of the two cadet guns on the field that day when another Federal round found its mark. "[D]uring one of the many warm times we experienced," he remembered, "I was struck by a piece of shell on my left collar bone. I was knocked several feet from the gun, my uniform torn and I was considerably bruised."[70] Only sheer luck saved other men of that gun crew from serious injury or death, for Whitehead was serving the vent on the piece when the enemy shell struck. Corporal Otis Glazebrook was not more than a yard or two away from Whitehead, with "the handspike in my hand at the time, changing the direction of the piece."[71] Apart from these few episodes, casualties among the artillerymen remained relatively light.

The artillery and small arms fire also took a toll on the town. Shells struck the Central Hotel, at the town's main crossroads, and destroyed a portion of the roof of St. Matthew's Church. Another exploded in a bedroom of the Rice house north of town. Bullets struck many of the structures. Despite the damage and proximity of major fighting, there were no reports of injuries to civilians.[72]

As his troops were moving past the northern edge of town, John Breckinridge and his staff rode along the Valley Pike close to St. Matthew's Church. The ground there is somewhat elevated and perhaps the group drew the attention of one of the Federal artillery commanders. Perhaps a stray shell was hurled in that direction. In any case, Breckinridge was in the act of raising his binoculars to study the Federal position when a shell struck a wooden fence

67 John G. Stevens to George M. Edgar, July 3, 1908, Edgar Papers.

68 D. M. Armstrong to Benjamin A. Colonna, February 17, 1911, NM coll., VMI.

69 Woods to "My Dear Father," May 16, 1864.

70 Couper, *The VMI New Market Cadets*, 230.

71 Otis A. Glazebrook to "My Dear Gen. Nichols," January 15, 1883, NM coll., VMI.

72 Wayland, *History of Shenandoah County*, 317; Catherine Foster, "VMI Cadets at New Market," *United Daughters of the Confederacy Magazine*, July 1957, typescript on file NMBSHP. Some of the surviving wartime structures in New Market still bear scars of the battle. For example, the author's former house, a small white frame home constructed ca. 1798, on what would have been the southern edge of town in 1864—possibly even the southern-most dwelling on that side of the street—has numerous bullet holes in the brick chimney.

post only a few feet away—yet failed to explode. Had it not been for a faulty fuse, the Battle of New Market may well have been altered by a single cannon round. The "shell struck post" became a town landmark, remaining with the shell still embedded in the wood well into the 20th century.[73]

*   *   *

By the time the advance resumed sometime around 1:30 or 2:00 p.m., the previous advantages enjoyed by the Confederates were no longer in play. During their initial move over and down Shirley's Hill, Breckinridge's men outnumbered Colonel Moor's first line of defenders and considerably overlapped his left flank. This time the numbers were about even, but Sigel's main line of Federals held a stronger defensive position.

The Confederate line that stepped off toward Sigel's main line consisted of the 26th Virginia Battalion on the far left, the 51st Virginia to its right, at least a portion of the 30th Virginia Battalion beyond that, and the 62nd Virginia anchoring Wharton's command on the Valley Pike. East of the Pike *en echelon* "100 or 200 yards to the rear" was Echols' small command, the 22nd Virginia with its left on the road and the 23rd Virginia Battalion partly spread in skirmish order on the far right. The VMI cadets remained in reserve behind the center of Wharton's line. Several companies of the 30th Battalion under Major Otey were once again deployed forward as skirmishers, with the remainder of the companies holding Wharton's center.[74] The skirmish line covering Wharton's left front consisted of Company B of the 26th Virginia Battalion.[75]

All went well during the early stages of this third advance, with the Valley Pike serving as a stable guide for the front line. As the Southern infantry moved north, however, the Shenandoah River and the high bluffs on the left narrowed, slowly forcing Wharton's men to shift eastward (to their right). This trick of geography began bunching up and overlapping the formations. As one lieutenant in the 26th Virginia Battalion put it, "we ran against the steep bluffs

---

73 Wayland, *History of Shenandoah County*, 324. Did John C. Breckinridge really come this close to death? Maybe not. The entire "shell struck post" controversy is discussed in greater detail in Appendix 7.

74 *Spectator & Vindicator*, May 20, 1904; Colonel George Smith to George Edgar, March 16, 1906, Edgar Papers.

75 George W. Hines to George M. Edgar, February 24, 1906, Edgar Papers.

of the river and could go no further." Squeezed from the left (he had already moved his left wing behind his right) and unable to adjust because the infantry on the right was using the Pike as a guide, George Edgar ordered his entire 26th Virginia Battalion to shift east. "We flanked to the right until we were clear of the obstructions," remembered Lt. James Washington McDowell, "then faced to the front, directly in [the] rear of the Fifty-first Regiment." Edgar explained that "As the ground would admit of it (in advancing), the companies of the left wing were successively thrown into line." The majority of his battalion, however, appears to have remained in reserve during the rest of the advance.[76]

Unable or unwilling to remain in a central location, Breckinridge guided his mount over much of the field. The Kentuckian was so active that one of his staff officers remarked, "every man in Breckinridge's command was under his eye, while he, with his conspicuous form, was plain to the view of all his troops, who . . . were . . . animated to heroism by his immediate presence."[77] Disobeying his own orders to fight dismounted, Breckinridge spurred his horse forward to join the skirmishers of the 30th Battalion. One of the Virginians recalled "hearing someone say 'Keep cool boys.' Looking around I saw Breckinridge riding within a few steps of me with an eye almost like that of an eagle."[78]

Intent on finding a way to turn the Federal right flank, Gabriel Wharton advanced with the left companies of the 51st Virginia (his former regiment).[79] On the other side of the line, an ill John Echols advanced wearing a black civilian coat over his gray uniform. He exercised little if any direct command.[80] As a result, neither brigade leader offered much direction to the troops occupying the center of the Confederate line.

The ground between the opposing lines now was mostly open, although woods along the ridge overlooking the river provided some cover there, and several shallow ravines near the Pike also offered protection. Because the infantry was advancing en echelon, with Wharton's section of the line a bit ahead of Echols' men, Wharton was once again the first to directly engage the

---

76 Edgar, "Official New Market Report," James Washington McDowell to Edgar, March 24, 1906, Edgar Papers.

77 Johnston, *The Battle of New Market.*

78 West, *30th Battalion Virginia Sharpshooters*, 83.

79 *Spectator & Vindicator*, May 20, 1904.

80 Frank C. Burdett to George M. Edgar, March 12, 1906, Edgar Papers.

Federals. The first direct indication of danger arrived from the concentration of Union guns under Carlin and Snow firing from the high ground behind the Bushong farm. Their shells dropped in and around the Confederate left and center with increasing frequency. Sergeant Major John Schowen of the 30th Virginia Battalion recalled that when "the Yankee battery commenced firing on us . . . I thought I would not live another minute."[81] Breckinridge later noted with pride how his men crossed this largely exposed ground, reporting that they "advanced with great steadiness in the face of a most galling fire."[82]

One of Carlin's gunners agreed. "On they came without wavering," he wrote, "and closing up the gaps that four batteries were cutting through them, and yelling like demons. . . . The order is passed for two-second fuses. The next moment there is a demand along the line for canister, the men work with a will and we pour the canister among them . . . and for about ten minutes we pour canister from twelve guns right into them."[83] The fire ripped large holes in the lines, causing one Confederate staff officer to write of the area immediately around the Bushong house, "Here occurred the heaviest loss of the day."[84]

Only the extreme left of the 51st Virginia escaped the enemy fire during this portion of the advance because it was out of view on the reverse slope of a wooded ridge about 200-250 yards west of the Bushong house. "When we emerged [from the woods] . . . for the first time we saw the enemy's whole force," recalled George W. Dunford of Company B on the far left of the line. "Here we stopped and poured volley after volley into their ranks."[85] Once in the open field, they too found themselves subject to hostile fire. "To stay here meant annihilation for us," Dunford continued. "It was too warm a place for the enemy received us royally."[86]

An officer in the 34th Massachusetts remembered that his men "waited until they were close enough and then rose up and gave it to them. They halted and kept up a hot fire. Three times their colors fell and were raised."[87] A gunner

81 Jack L. Dickinson, *Diary of a Confederate Sharpshooter* (Charleston, WV, 1997), 90.

82 Breckinridge's Official New Market Report.

83 Wheeling *Intelligencer*, May 23, 1864.

84 Johnston, *The Battle of New Market*.

85 G. W. Dunford, "Battle of New Market as seen by G.W. Dunford," NM coll., VMI.

86 G. W. Dunford, "As a Private saw New Market Fight," NM coll., VMI.

87 Thompson diary, May 15, 1864.

in Carlin's battery observed, "We opened on them with canister, and they on us with musketry. . . . It was awful; ten pieces pouring canister into them at one hundred and fifty yards . . . at last they wavered, our boys cheered and gave them double charges."[88]

Colonel Smith's 62nd Virginia advancing in the center just west of the Pike also received a warm reception. Smith—despite his Northern birth—was yet another VMI graduate, Class of 1853. His men were passing just east of the Bushong house across terrain somewhat more rocky than the fields farther west. A small ravine or hollow ran eastward from the front of the Bushong house before the ground rose up to a small ridge upon which rested the lane connecting the Valley Pike to the Bushong farm. When the Virginians mounted this rise, the men of the 54th Pennsylvania and 1st West Virginia, about 300 yards distant, leveled their rifled muskets and delivered a damaging volley. The 62nd soldiered on, closing ranks to drive step by step another 100 yards beyond the Bushong lane. Each yard of ground was dearly bought, as bullets and shell fire tore through the ranks. At some point during this advance Colonel Smith discovered that his left flank was "in the air," meaning it was completely without support. The troops who had been marching there, the 51st Virginia and 30th Virginia Battalion, had been brought to a halt by a fence line north of the Bushong house. Smith's right flank was also without support. The 22nd Virginia and 23rd Virginia Battalion under Echols' command had originally formed *en echelon* behind about 100 to 200 yards behind Smith's right, and so were still trailing some distance behind him. The result of the interposing fence line and original deployment was that George Smith's regiment, for at least several minutes, faced Sigel's entire Federal army alone. During that short span, the 62nd Virginia would lose nearly half its strength.[89]

---

88 Unsigned letter, printed in Wheeling *Daily Register*, May 20, 1864.

89 George H. Smith, "More of the Battle of New Market," *Confederate Veteran*, November 1908, 569. Smith was born in Philadelphia. After the war he married the widow of his cousin, George Patton. According to the driver of Imboden's headquarters wagon, Smith and the 62nd Virginia were given explicit orders to take the guns at the top of Bushong's Hill: "Breckinridge and Imboden and several of their staff were sitting on their horses in the Pike just at the upper edge of town observing the battle. I was standing by and right near both Generals. I personally heard Gen. Breckinridge say to Gen. Imboden: 'General, do you have a regiment that can take that battery over there on that hill, it's playing heavily on our men?' Gen. Imboden replied, 'I have a regiment that will try.' Gen. Imboden said to his courier: 'Tell Col. Smith of the 62nd to report to me at once.' Col. Smith dashed up on his horse and saluted. 'Colonel, take your regiment and take that battery over there on that hill.' . . . As Col. Smith was forming his line,

Captain Charles Woodson
(postwar)

NMBSHP

Attached to the embattled 62nd was one company of Missourians—the only unit from that state to serve in Virginia during the entire war. Company A, 1st Missouri Cavalry, was an ad hoc unit formed in 1863 from a group of exchanged prisoners who had all previously served in Missouri units. Before these men could be sent back to the Western Theater from Virginia, two officers among them— Charles Woodson and E. H. Scott—proposed forming the Missouri men into a single company to serve in Virginia and the War Department agreed. And thus was born Company A, 1st Missouri Cavalry, with Woodson serving as captain and Scott as 1st lieutenant. In late September 1863, Woodson's company was assigned to Smith's 62nd Virginia, another supposedly mounted unit that lacked its complement of horses.[90] In April 1864, the Missourians pledged themselves "in for 40 years or the war," earning the praise of the Harrisonburg press: "There is not . . . in the Confederate service, better soldiers than these Missouri boys."[91]

On May 15, the 1st Missouri fielded sixty-two men and three officers. Woodson was serving as a battalion commander in the 62nd Virginia, so

Gen. Breckinridge said to Gen. Imboden, 'I'm going to put the Cadets in on this.'" Sager, *Battle of New Market*, 10-11.

90 Synopsis of lineage of Woodson's command is from Woodson file, NMBSHP; Thomas F. Curran, "Memory, Myth and Musty Records: Charles Woodson's Missouri Cavalry in the Army of Northern Virginia, Part I," *Missouri Historical Review*, October 1999, pp. 25-41; and Anthony Monachello, "Strange Odyssey of the 1st Missouri," *America's Civil War*, March 1999, 26-33.

91 Rockingham *Register*, April 1, 1864.

Jacob Bushong farm. The orchard is visible on the right. *NMBSHP*

command of Company A fell to Lieutenant Scott. The Missourians were holding the left front of the 62nd, which placed them in the midst of the buildings around the Bushong house. They tramped past the house and into the orchard—almost directly in front of von Kleiser's blazing field pieces.

"My command," Scott wrote in his diary, was "now within close pistol shot of the battery." The Federal gunners spotted Scott's exposed left flank—the 51st Virginia and 30th Virginia Battalion were still negotiating one of the Bushong fence lines and had been slowed by fire from Snow's and Carlin's guns—and concentrated their fire against it with dreadful accuracy as infantry poured in small arms fire. Scott was shooting his revolver at the enemy when Sgt. William Day hobbled up covered in blood from a piece of lead or iron fragment that had completely pierced his body. "Lieutenant, I am almost gone, please help me off," Day pleaded. Before Scott could assist Day, 2nd Lieutenant J. W. Jones, standing next to Scott, was shot in the head and fell "with the brain oozing from his forehead." Scott was escorting the dying Day to the rear when he was struck in the arm by a shell fragment. With one arm effectively crippled, Scott laid Day's lifeless body on the ground as best he could. Another of his men appeared next to him with blood gushing from a neck wound. "Good-bye Lieutenant, I am killed," he uttered. Of the sixty-two men Scott took into battle that morning, only six remained unhurt that evening—by far the highest percentage casualty loss suffered in either army at New Market.[92]

Unsupported on his right and left, and facing a heavy fire that was tearing his command apart, Colonel Smith (and the attached Missourians) had little recourse but to fall back and regroup. "Seeing that the regiment would be annihilated by a few minutes continuance of the fire to which it was exposed," wrote the commander of the 62nd Virginia, "[I] drew it back under cover of the hill south of us." There, using the rising ground as cover, Smith reformed his decimated regiment.[93] The decimation of the 62nd Virginia on their right

92 William T. Price, *Memorials of Edward Herndon Scott, MD* (Wytheville, VA, 1974), 15-6. Six days after the battle, nineteen Missourians answered roll call. William H. Greenwalt to "Miss T. Cromer," May 21, 1864, typescript in George W. Chappelear Papers, Library of Virginia. Many of those reported as "wounded" in Woodson's Company were only very lightly injured.

93 Smith to Edgar, March 16, 1906, Edgar Papers. Smith was not kind in remembering the role the 51st Virginia played in the attack, and he left little doubt where he believed the blame rested for the heavy losses his regiment suffered. "From the halt of the 51st at Bushong's fence resulted the failure of the first line to carry the position of the enemy," recalled Smith, "and there also resulted . . . a loss to the 62nd Regiment of over two hundred men, and, on the left,

cooled the offensive ardor of the 51st Virginia and 30th Virginia Battalion. Both of Wharton's units stopped in their tracks and did their best to hold the ground they had won. The Confederate attack west of the Valley Pike was stymied.

Without the 62nd Virginia and the handful of Missourians left to shoot at, the Federals turned their attention to Wharton's exposed command. The storm unleashed was heavy and deadly. One of the casualties was Major Otey of the 30th Virginia Battalion, who fell injured near the Bushong house. J. Stoddard Johnston of Breckinridge's staff recalled after the war that the decisive moment of the battle was at hand. "The position was critical," he wrote, "and for a time it seemed doubtful as to which [line] would be the first to give way."[94]

Any doubt was soon resolved when the Confederate left-center collapsed shortly after 2:00 p.m.[95] The right half of the 51st Virginia left of the Bushong orchard, and the 30th Virginia Battalion in the orchard itself, gave way under the weight of this concentrated fire. Much of the left side of Breckinridge's line was in full retreat, Woodson's Missourians had been decimated, and the 62nd Virginia was trying to regroup. A gap yawned wide and inviting in the Confederate line. "Just here a cavalry charge would have won the day for the Yankees," admitted the injured Major Otey.[96]

Napoleon, when told of the virtues of a rising officer, is said to have responded, "That's all very well, but is he lucky?" Luck, in the Emperor's eyes, was as much a personal attribute as it was a matter of chance. At New Market, John C. Breckinridge possessed that attribute in spades. The "ugly gap," as one soldier described it, burst open almost directly in front of the Kentuckian's only available reserves: George Edgar's 26th Battalion and the VMI cadets.[97]

Just as the battle reached its crescendo, yet another downpour rolled in, adding its own thunder to the myriad sounds of battle.

---

the loss of the opportunity of capturing the detached battery near the river." George H. Smith, *The Battle of New Market* (Los Angeles, 1908), 22.

94 Johnston, *The Battle of New Market.*

95 Benjamin A. Colonna, "Battle of New Market," *Journal of the Military Service Institution of the United States*, 345-6.

96 Otey to Ship, April 14, 1875, Otey Papers, VMI.

97 Colonna, "Battle of New Market," 347.

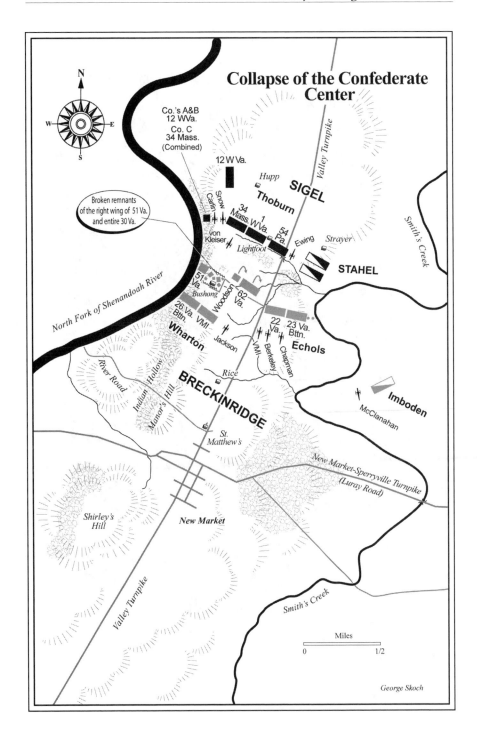

Collapse of the Confederate Center

George Skoch

Private Abraham Dern of Company A, 1st Potomac Home Brigade Cavalry (better known as "Cole's Battalion") in a retouched photograph. Dern was a 25-year-old wagon maker in Frederick, Maryland, before the war. He enlisted in August 1861 and was captured with the Harpers Ferry garrison in September 1862 during the Antietam Campaign, and again in June 1863 during the Gettysburg Campaign. His horse was killed under him during Julius Stahel's disastrous cavalry attack at New Market. *Mark Dudrow*

Chapter 9

"I Felt so Confident of Success"

For the first time on May 15, Franz Sigel determined to go on the offensive. Despite mismanaging much of the campaign and being decisively thrashed in the opening phases of New Market fighting, he now had a golden opportunity to salvage a victory. His main line of resistance was strong, and his well-directed artillery and small arms fire had inflicted serious casualties and driven back much of Breckinridge's attacking infantry. All that was needed to reverse the day's fortune and drive the Rebels from the field was a well-placed and well-led counterattack. To accomplish this feat, Sigel inexplicably turned to his mounted arm. This decision was consistent with his use of cavalry in the weeks leading up to the battle.

Julius Stahel had perhaps as many as 1,000 horsemen massed on the Federal left. Colonel William Tibbits, commander of one of Stahel's pair of cavalry brigades, complained that Stahel had stripped so many detachments from his brigade that Tibbits was left with no one to command. When Stahel suggested Tibbits serve on his staff for the balance of the day, the cavalry colonel claimed he angrily replied, "I [will] be damned if I [will] serve on [your] staff . . . I want [my] brigade."[1]

---

1 Tibbits diary, May 15, 1864. Tibbits' handwriting rivals General Lafayette McLaws' in terms of its illegibility. Documentation regarding the strength of Stahel's cavalry is all but non-existent for the New Market campaign. Stahel's troopers spent much of the day widely dispersed, so it is impossible to know with precision how many were present during the battle. Given the initial strength of his mounted arm, 1,000 cavalry is a reasonable and relatively conservative figure.

Although they had come under fire that morning, the Federal cavalry had thus far had few opportunities to do much shooting of their own. Most of the troopers were now gathered east of the Valley Pike in support of Ewing's battery. Jacob Lester of the 1st New York Veteran Cavalry, part of Tibbits' brigade, recalled that "it was raining hard for the last hour, the ground was soaked, we were on low ground and there were puddles of water everywhere about us."[2]

As the 62nd Virginia and Echols' pair of regiments stepped into range, stray bullets zipped through the ranks of the blue horsemen and wounded infantry passed through their lines. Soon, remembered one participant, "the air was full of whistling bullets." Two men in Lester's Company F, 1st New York Veteran Cavalry, were struck and Captain H. K. Redway's horse was shot out from under him, "But the worst was to come," Lester recalled. "We got orders to 'draw sabre' and I knew we were to charge the oncoming line of rebel infantry." As the Federal horsemen maneuvered into their pre-charge position, "horses got stuck in the mud and fell over each other and in a moment we were mired up like a flock of sheep." When the confusion was finally sorted out, the Union troopers set spurs to their mounts and attacked. Most of the riders drove straight south, east of the Pike, with the right-most element moving onto the road itself.[3]

A worse position from which to launch a mounted attack would have been difficult to find. The ground on Stahel's immediate front sloped down to a ravine and was somewhat broken and thus difficult to traverse. The terrain to his right was even more problematic. There, the Valley Pike, bordered on each side by stone walls, funneled the troopers into a tightly compacted column directly into enemy fire. Waiting to the south was Confederate infantry, and on the open ground just east of the Pike was where Breckinridge had massed most of his artillery. Although the infantry on the Confederate left and center had been driven back, Echols' Brigade on the far right east of the Pike had yet to fire

---

2 Lester, *Autobiography of Jacob Lester*, 9.

3 *Ibid.* The Federal cavalry charge at New Market is one of the least-documented aspects of the battle. The only good account for it is in Lester's *Autobiography of Jacob Lester*, which was published privately decades after the fact, and one barely decipherable original letter and a diary entry penned by Colonel William Tibbits, one of the two Federal cavalry brigade commanders. Ironically, even Tibbits' diary lacks detail regarding this unusual use of cavalry. My interpretation of the direction and manner of the mounted attack is the most reasonable given the extant source material and terrain.

a shot and had suffered few casualties. Stahel's cavalry charge was doomed before it even began.

Breckinridge spotted or was alerted to the fact that Julius Stahel's cavalry was forming opposite his right and immediately took action to repulse the coming attack, calling upon his artillery on that side of the field to throw back the wave about to fall upon them. His pieces there included a pair of VMI guns, a half-dozen pieces of Chapman's Battery, all under Major William McLaughlin's supervision.[4] The Kentucky general "ordered the guns to be double shotted [sic] with canister," explained Breckinridge aide J. Stoddard Johnston in a report of the battle. "It had scarcely been done before they were seen advancing in squadron front, when, coming in range, the artillery opened."[5] "They were ready for us," admitted a sergeant with the 1st Maryland Potomac Home Brigade (Cole's Battalion). "Our battalion marched directly into their artillery fire. Shells were dropping all around us and musket balls were whistling."[6]

The Confederate cadet gunners were aided in their effort by "a low partly demolished rock fence in our front," recalled Collier Minge, the cadet in charge of VMI's two guns. "We got quickly into action with canister against cavalry charging down the road and adjacent fields. When the smoke cleared away the cavalry seemed to have been completely broken up," he continued, "and we

---

4   Most accounts of the battle place Lieutenant Carter Berkeley with two of McClanahan's guns with McLaughlin. However, an account by Berkeley himself states that two of McClanahan's six guns were knocked out of action on May 14, and that the remaining four guns all moved with Imboden east across Smith's Creek. Robert J. Driver, *The Staunton Artillery: McClanahan's Battery* (Lynchburg, VA, 1988), 88.

5   Johnston, "Sketch of Operations," 261. In his unpublished official report for New Market (as penned by staff officer J. Stoddard Johnston), Breckinridge claimed he "advanced six pieces of artillery on the east side of the [Valley] Pike" under Major McLaughlin. This number is too low. Chapman's Battery alone had six pieces, and Chapman was accompanied by the two VMI guns under Lieutenant Collier H. Minge and two of McClanahan's guns from Imboden under Lieutenant Carter Berkeley. See Breckinridge, Official New Market Report. Johnston's unpublished account of the battle in his papers at VMI sets the number at ten, and this is the number Turner used in his book. Turner, *New Market Campaign*, 39. Jackson's Battery was employed west of the Valley Pike and took a position during the climax of the battle southeast of the Bushong House, thus operating separately from the main artillery contingent under McLaughlin's direct command for much of the fighting. Jackson's command suffered only one man wounded (Private Estel Mustard, whose ankle was shattered by a shell fragment). Robert H. Moore, II, *Graham's Petersburg, Jackson's Kanawha, and Lurty's Roanoke Horse Artillery* (Lynchburg, VA, 1996), 67.

6   McIlhenny diary, May 16, 1864.

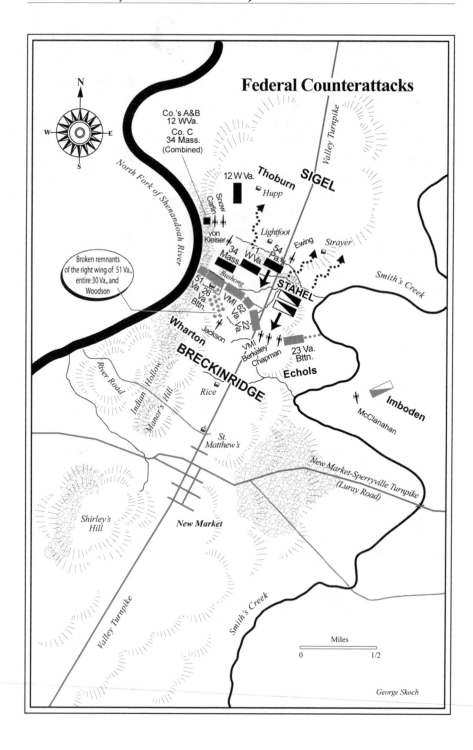

Federal Counterattacks

George Skoch

saw no more of them."[7] One Confederate artillerist wrote that he and his comrades "gave them a blizzard that sent them back hastily to their comrades." Staffer Johnston described the charge as having been "repulsed disastrously." Breckinridge cooly reported that "an attempt was made to charge down the turnpike with cavalry upon my right but a few well directed shells dispersed the squadrons."[8] A Federal sergeant put a fine point on the affair when he wrote, "they mowed us down like grass."[9]

The Federal horsemen were indeed "mowed down like grass," but not just because of the well-aimed Southern artillery. The charge was launched into the mouth of a wide Southern "V", with infantry making up the sides and the ten artillery pieces massed at the point. The left wing of the "V" was comprised of Colonel George S. Patton's 22nd Virginia, which was holding the left side of Echols' infantry formation. When alerted to the pending mounted attack, Patton ordered a partial right wheel so his men would be in a position to fire into the flank of the attackers. On the right side of Echols' line was Lieutenant Colonel Clarence Derrick's 23rd Virginia Battalion, which comprised the right wing of the loose and wide "V" formation. The quick-thinking Derrick called for a formation rarely used in the Civil War: infantry squares. At least a portion of the 23rd Virginia was formed into small squares—an anti-cavalry tactic that would allow the soldiers to fire in all four directions. "I saw for the first time in battle our skirmishers run together and form themselves in fours," remembered John G. Stevens, one of the gunners serving with Chapman's Battery, "placing backs

Colonel
George S. Patton

VMI Archives

7   Collier H. Minge to George M. Edgar, June 5, 1908, Edgar Papers.

8   Driver, *Staunton Artillery*, 88; Johnston, "Sketch of Operations," 261.

9   McIlhenny diary, May 16, 1864.

Lieutenant Colonel Clarence Derrick. *U.S. Military Academy*

together, and with the air of our two guns we drove them back, as we could shoot over our skirmishers."[10] When the "cavalry . . . started to charge us . . . I ordered my men to fire low, and waited for them to debouch out of the heavy smoke," reported Derrick.[11] Captain John K. Thompson of Company A, 22nd Virginia, found his company almost directly in front of the onrushing Union cavalry. Thompson, too, ordered his men to aim low and shoot down the

10 John G. Stevens to Edgar, June 2, 1908, Edgar Papers.

11 Scott, *23rd Battalion Virginia Infantry*, 29; Turner, *New Market Campaign*, 63.

Captain
John P. Donaldson,
Company H, 22nd Virginia
(left)

Lieutenant Noyes Rand,
22nd Virginia (right)

Virginia Tech

horses rather than worry about the men riding them. The result was a tangled mess of dead, wounded, and "panic stricken animals."[12]

One of Patton's Virginians, Noyes Rand, observed a shell burst at the head of the Federal column as it crossed a stone bridge spanning the small ravine, killing several horses and their riders.[13] Jacob Lester, riding with the 1st New York Veteran Cavalry, may have been describing that very shot when he wrote, "A shell from the rebel artillery struck a man at my side carrying away half of his head and spattering his brains, hair and whiskers all over the right side of me. The same shell carried away the left shoulder and arm of a man in front of me and struck another man farther on square in the back, passed through and as he toppled from his horse I saw his whole front torn open and a torrent of blood flowing from it. That one shot," continued Lester, "killed three men right near me and still I was so far unhurt."[14]

With the enemy artillery firing in their faces, and swarms of small arms fire striking men and horses alike, the New Yorkers turned their horses about and

12 Lowry, *22nd Virginia Infantry*, 60.

13 Noyes Rand to B. A. Colonna, January 5, 1911, NM Coll., VMI.

14 Lester, *Autobiography of Jacob Lester*, 9-10.

rode, "without form or order to get to higher ground and to the rear, out of that hell hole of shot and shell." By Rand's account, "only one man, on an unmanageable horse, came through on the Pike." Another Rebel recorded his observations of what may be the same trooper: "One soldier who rode a grey horse could not turn his horse with the rest of them, and he ran through the picket line almost up to our guns," remembered John Stevens, "and when he did succeed in getting him turned, he dashed back through the line to the company—I suppose, unhurt." Capt. Thompson of the 22nd Virginia, however, claimed that three riders made it to his position. According to Breckinridge's report, "some 15 or 20 [reached] my lines as prisoners."[15]

The firing had "partially ceased" by the time these troopers reached the higher ground upon which Ewing's battery, which had been supporting the attack, was unlimbered. A Federal officer there pleaded with men to form a skirmish line to protect the guns, fearful that the Confederates would take advantage of the situation and storm the position. Lester and his comrades regrouped and "advanced about a rod apart toward the enemy again," he remembered. "Our battery fired a charge of grape and canister over our heads, but it exploded too soon and scattered all around me. . . . It is a wonder I was not killed by our own men."[16] The danger of friendly fire, coupled with the storm of lead and iron pouring in from the front and flanks sealed the fate of Sigel's cavalry, which broke madly northward. "This was the end of the cavalry in that fight," summed up one observing Confederate.[17]

Except for killing Joseph Reed, a member of Chapman's Battery, Ewing's artillery achieved little more than spraying the backs of the blue troopers with canister. Now, with the horsemen pounding hard in their direction, Ewing's guns were caught up in the mounted retreat. One of the gunners limbered his piece and was about to ride north when he encountered Franz Sigel, who had spotted the chaos on his left and ridden over to stem the developing collapse. When the general inquired why his gun was limbered up, the sergeant

---

15 Rand to Colonna, January 5, 1911; Thompson quote in Turner, *New Market Campaign*, 64; John G. Stevens to Edgar, June 2, 1908, Edgar Papers; Breckinridge's Official New Market Report. Of those captured, it is interesting to note that one, Private Edward Van Schyver, Company L, 21st New York, eventually swore an oath to the Confederacy and served the remainder of the war in the 10th Tennessee Infantry. Bonnell, *Sabres in the Shenandoah*, 58.

16 Lester, *Autobiography of Jacob Lester*, 9-10.

17 Wise, *End of an Era*, 301.

commanding the piece replied that they had been ordered to leave. "I thinks we fight him a little," Sigel shot back. The artillerymen dropped trail on their piece again and fired off a few rounds before fire from their left forced them to relocate to safer ground.[18]

An officer in the 21st New York was quite frank in his assessment that the cavalry's movements were "uniform in nothing but a general scrambling toward the rear."[19] One of his troopers was equally forthcoming in his admission that he abandoned the field in less than honorable fashion: "I threw off my overcoat and dropped my carbine and skedaddled and didn't stop until I got back to Mount Jackson."[20] "I never knew anything so disgraceful," brigade leader Colonel Tibbits wrote home.[21]

Julius Stahel's rather spectacular repulse was not the only event of import unfolding on the battlefield. While the horsemen in blue were making their disastrous attack, other events on and around the Bushong farm would decide the battle.

*   *   *

The wounded Major Otey of the 30th Battalion was lying in the mud near the Bushong house when he heard cheering. It took him a moment to realize what it represented: his troops and others around them were rallying. "I raise my head from my pillow of mud and see our men still going forward," he wrote. "The rattle of musketry increases, grape and canister is pelting all around me as I lay prostrate."[22]

Although the Confederate center and left had been thrown into confusion near the Bushong house before being driven back in a bloody rebuff, the integrity of the Southern battle line was reestablished fairly quickly. And when it was, it became obvious to both sides that the fence line along the northern edge of the Bushong orchard was a key to this part of the battlefield. Whoever

18 Andrew Kaler to B. A. Colonna, December 1, 1910, NM Coll., VMI; Henderson Reed to George Edgar, June 12, 1908, Edgar Papers. Reed was a member of Chapman's Battery.

19 Fitz-Simmons, "Sigel's Fight at New Market," 64.

20 J. E. Multoon to Benjamin A. Colonna, November 24, 19[illegible], NM Coll., VMI.

21 William B. Tibbits to "My Dear Dad," May 28, 1864, Author's Collection.

22 "Response of Hon. Peter J. Otey at the Alumni Banquet, June 1896."

View from the Bushong orchard fence looking north. *Author*

reached the fence first would control the orchard, and whoever controlled the orchard would dominate the center of the field.

The right half of the 51st Virginia Infantry, fighting at the center of the Confederate line, reformed near the Bushong house around regimental color bearer Sergeant Frank Lindamood, who was standing his ground and madly waving the regimental flag. "In a second a number of his regiment were running to the front and grouping themselves around him . . . I saw them falling like jackstraws, on their backs, faces, sides, and knees," observed one of the VMI cadets. However, Lindamood's actions soon drew the enemy's attention, and he fell wounded. "The flag, which had been perfectly erect in the center of the group, dipped almost to the ground, but some one had it up again in a moment."[23]

As elements of the 51st regrouped, Colonel George Edgar of the 26th Virginia Battalion spotted the yawning tear in the line and yelled for his Virginians to answer the call. "I at once ordered my Battalion forward" to plug the hole, wrote the colonel, "though my line was a good deal broken in passing

23 James A. Davis, *51st Virginia Infantry* (Lynchburg, VA, 1984), 23.

through" the retreating companies of the 51st Virginia.[24] Demonstrating a keen ability in field tactics and nerves of iron, Edgar ordered his company officers to keep the ranks straight at gunpoint, if necessary, telling one of his company commanders, "Captain, do not let these men break through your line; draw your pistol on them and shoot them if they will not halt."[25]

Edgar knew his craft well. He graduated from VMI in 1856 and remained there as a professor. Just as the Cadets had worked as drill instructors for recruits at Richmond at the start of the war, so too did Edgar, who served as drillmaster for the 1st Florida. He joined the 26th Virginia Battalion in August 1861 as a captain and rose through the ranks to command the battalion by the end of 1862. As his men of the 26th Virginia Battalion came on line, the same withering fire that had ripped through the ranks of their comrades in the 51st Virginia only moments earlier struck them. "This was a place to make stout hearts quail," wrote one Virginian.[26] Capt. Thomas Morton of Company F recalled that his men "were falling like broken reeds in a gale." Private Joseph Maddy was standing near Morton when Maddy found that the incessant rain had fouled his rifle. "Captain my gun is choked, I can't get the cartridge down," Maddy called out to his commander. Morton seized the jammed weapon from young Maddy "and tried to ram [the cartridge] down but it stuck fast, then a man fell beside us. I [Morton] picked up his empty gun, found the lock worked right and handed it to [Maddy] . . . [who] hastily loaded the dead man's gun, cocked it, raised it to fire, when at that instant he was struck in the middle of the body . . . and fell at my feet."[27]

24 Edgar, "Battle of New Market," Edgar Papers.

25 Thomas C. Morton to G. M. Edgar, March [date incomplete] 1906, Edgar Papers. A debate raged for years after the war between veterans of the 51st Virginia and the 26th Battalion as to whether the 51st broke in the face of enemy fire, and whether the 26th Virginia Battalion had to forcibly work its way through its disordered ranks to reach the front. The arguments presented in the pages of *Confederate Veteran* magazine and elsewhere were impassioned on both sides, and arguments on both sides had merit. Some elements of the 51st Virginia rallied quicker than others, and the men of Edgar's 26th Virginia Battalion had to, in some instances, advance through broken ranks.

26 Robert K. Krick, *Lee's Colonels: A Biographical Register of the Field Officers of the Army of Northern Virginia* (Dayton, OH, 1996), 127; "Battle of New Market as Seen by G. W. Dunford."

27 Article in *Monroe Watchman* quoted in W. T. Maddy, *A History of Marie Community*, 1925. Maddy's comrades buried his body after the battle in the graveyard at St. Matthew's Church, where his remains rest to this day. There were five men with the surname of "Maddy" serving in the 26th Virginia Battalion, and all were in Company F: Ebner N., Elisha V., Joseph A. (also

Coming up on Edgar's right were Lieutenant Colonel Scott Ship's VMI boys. Although the cadets did not have to make their way through any broken or panicked units to reach the front, they did encounter difficulties of a different variety. "We pushed on amid a shower of musket balls," wrote Cadet John Coleman.[28] The 30th Virginia Battalion, which minutes earlier had been to their front, rallied on the flanks of the cadets, with small clusters of them falling in with other units.

Cadet George Lee recalled how the cadets came to be in the front of an advancing line of battle:

> A short time before we reached the house and orchard, the Confederates who had preceded us . . . were seen in retreat in our front. In fact, they seemed to be much demoralized and were coming back rapidly. I don't know what effect this had on others, but it made me uneasy . . . The battalion began the movement to open ranks [to let the broken troops pass through]. However, the soldiers did not pass through, but turned and went forward again. They did not go in front of us, but in some way got on our flanks . . . mostly to our left.[29]

One of the VMI cadets recalled an officer unnamed to history attempting to rally his broken command near the Bushong house. "I shall never forget his language— 'Rally men and go the front. Here you are running to the rear like a lot of frightened sheep. Look at those children going to the front. Rally and follow those children!'"[30]

The path of advance taken by the cadets carried them past Jackson's Confederate artillery, which was unlimbered and firing from a position just

---

listed as Joseph W. or J. W.), Theodore R., and Thomas C. Most or all were likely relatives because they all hailed from the area around Red Sulphur Springs, Monroe County, West Virginia. All of them except Theodore served in the 166th Regiment, Virginia Militia at the outset of the war, and Joseph, Ebner, Theodore, and Thomas fought at New Market. Elisha was mortally wounded at a skirmish at Lewisburg, West Virginia, in May 1862. Theodore was captured at Cold Harbor several weeks after New Market and was held at Point Lookout, Maryland, and Elmira, New York, before being exchanged in October 1864. Ebner was killed in action at Cedar Creek in mid-October 1864. Almost certainly the author of "A History of Marie Community," from which the account of Joseph Maddy's death is taken, was a descendent of the same family named. See www.wvculture.org/history/agrext/marie.html.

28 Richmond *Whig*, June 22, 1864.

29 G. T. Lee to Henry A. Wise, May 15, 1909, NM Coll., VMI.

30 L. C. Wise to J. R. Anderson, August 27, 1909, NM Coll., VMI.

southeast of the Bushong house.[31] The battery stopped firing when the Cadets tramped up to and around the structure, which split their formation, Companies A and B pouring to the east of the house, and Companies C and D passing to the west.[32] Once past the house, George Lee wrote, "[we] got into the orchard, where canister and other missiles were raining like hail. It seemed impossible for men to pass through such a storm."[33] "I don't believe there could have been faster or more accurate firing than [we were subjected to from the Federal artillery]," wrote Cadet Porter Johnson.[34] "It was about here that the fire was most destructive," remembered Cadet N. B. Noland.[35]

As the cadets moved forward, one of them named John Howard cast an eye skyward. Much like the farmer's dog and cows that had been spooked earlier in the fighting, Howard noticed a flock of sparrows "flying above the battalion, and they were nearly frantic with fright. . . . These did not fly normally. They darted hither and thither without seeming to know what they were doing."[36]

The wildlife was not enjoying the leaden storm, and neither was Scott Ship. Cadet Porter Johnson was directly behind his commanding officer during the advance and noticed the colonel "was pale as he could be. . . . The sweat stood on his face in great drops and it struck me that he was not enjoying himself."[37]

Many of the cadets discovered that marching smartly on the parade ground, where the greatest danger was incurring the ire of the first sergeant, was one thing, but keeping ranks aligned under a heavy enemy fire was something else altogether. "It had been very trying on young and inexperienced nerves to go through such a storm of missiles, doing nothing but marching up against more missiles, keeping in ranks, filling up gaps as the wounded and killed fell out, and being pelted mercilessly, without striking back one single lick," recalled one of

---

31 The guns that currently mark the position of Jackson's Battery are as close as practicable to where they served during the engagement. The actual position of the battery was on land now occupied by Interstate 81.

32 Anderson, "Recollections of a VMI Rat"; Randolph Blain to John B. Castleman, January 15, 1917, NMBSHP.

33 Lee to H. A. Wise, May 15, 1909.

34 Johnson to H. A. Wise, June 8, 1909.

35 Noland to Read, October 18, 1895.

36 Howard, "Recollections of New Market," 58.

37 Johnson to Wise, June 8, 1909.

the surviving cadets.[38] Porter Johnson and his friend John Cocke marched side by side through this "storm of missiles." Cocke kept drifting left, breaking elbow contact with Johnson. "This occurred several times," remembered Johnson, "and I noticing it would call Cocke's attention to it, saying 'Close up, Cocke! Close up!' which he always did promptly, his face flashing hotly but saying nothing. As we drew still near the guns and the shot fell still thicker, I had it seems veered a little off to the right and Cocke noticed it quick as a flash. He said, 'Now Johnson, damn it, you close up yourself! You have been hollering at me all day to 'Close up' now damn it you close!'"[39]

Soon after the chagrined Johnson edged next to his friend a shell exploded only a few feet in front of him. "Here I was turned clean around," he later wrote, "and my gun flew over my head." He continued:

> I never saw it again at least to recognize it as the one I had carried. One piece struck just over the heart, a great rent was torn in my jacket and shirt and the skin cut. I happened to have in the pocket of my jacket two army crackers, some letters and a handkerchief, and I verily believe these broke the blow so as to save my life. But another piece struck me on the arm. My first impression was that my arm was torn off at the shoulder. I felt as if it was gone, as there was no arm there, but when I got over the daze somewhat and examined I found my left arm completely paralyzed and as black as ink from the shoulder to elbow.[40]

Federal guns were extracting a devastating toll from the young cadets, a fact confirmed by Capt. Frank Preston, commander of Company B: "In the advance on this third position, we were subjected to a terrible fire of artillery. When within four hundred yards of their line, three of our boys fell dead from the explosion of one shell, [William H.] Cabell, [Henry J.] Jones, and [Charles G.] Crockett; and fifty yards further on [William H.] McDowell, from my company, fell pierced through the heart with a bullet."[41] A gunner with Chapman's Battery, impressed by the advance of the cadets—which he described as "one of the grandest military movements that I ever saw in my life"—may have witnessed the round that knocked out the trio of cadets recalled by Captain

38 *Ibid.*

39 Lee to Wise, May 15, 1909.

40 Johnson to Wise, June 8, 1909.

41 Couper, *The VMI New Market Cadets*, 52.

Preston. John Stevens was looking "right at them advancing in quick line when a shell exploded about the middle of the company, making a gap, killing some and wounding others, when those next to them instantly picked them up and started to the rear. The company moved right on and did not falter in the least; those on the left made to oblique movement and closed up the gap without ever losing the step."[42]

There were other names Preston could have added to that sad list of injured and dead including Bev Stanard, one of the four VMI students who abandoned their post guarding the supply wagons at the battle's outset. Stanard's leg was broken by an artillery round in the Bushong orchard. One of his comrades stumbled across him lying by a fence. "I found Stannard [sic] badly wounded . . . [his] leg broken by a grape shot, and I tried to make a tourniquet of an old towel and stop the bleeding, and he died a few minutes afterwards while I was with him."[43]

Cadet Edmund Berkeley, Jr., was seriously wounded in the head by an artillery round. Somehow he managed to keep his senses and tend to several of his wounded comrades before pressing on to keep up with the rest of the battalion. He lost so much blood, however, that he grew weak and was unable to keep pace. His wound must have been a ghastly sight. According to Berkeley he encountered General Breckinridge, who took one look at him and ordered one of his staff to give the wounded young man a horse and escort him to a field hospital.[44]

Several other cadets had brushes with death. James B. Preston carried a small copy of the New Testament in his vest pocket. A bullet struck him squarely on that pocket, but the Bible absorbed the impact of the round. James D. Darden was struck in his left thigh. Despite the wound, he kept up with the battalion but was struck again, this time in his left arm, where the missile severed an artery. One of his quick-thinking comrades improvised a tourniquet out of his canteen strap and saved his life.[45]

Charles C. Randolph was one of the handful of cadets who had been in action before as a courier for Thomas J. "Stonewall" Jackson. As the cadets

---

42 *SOR* 6, 870.

43 Couper, *The VMI New Market Cadets*, 23.

44 *Ibid.*, 23.

45 *Ibid.*, 54.

Captain Henry A. Wise,
who took over command of the Cadets.

VMI Archives

advanced, Randolph admonished some of his comrades who were attempting to dodge enemy fire. "There's no use dodging, boys," he told them. "If a ball's going to hit you, it'll hit you anyway." No sooner had the words left his mouth than he fell so seriously wounded that his comrades thought him dead. Randolph would survive, but he lost his hearing in one ear.[46]

Not long after entering the orchard the commander of the cadets, Colonel Ship, was wounded by a shell fragment in the left shoulder. The wound appeared to be mortal, and command passed to Capt. Henry A. Wise of Company A. Seeing their commander fall was a shock to the young cadets. According to Company B commander Frank Preston, "here for the first and only time our line was broken. Even then these brave boys did not retreat, but ran forward 30 yards where in confusion, yet still together, we lay down behind a fence and began for the first time to fire upon the enemy."[47] Preston's recollection was either foggy or he was intentionally masking the fact that some of the cadets, as several recalled, retreated out of the orchard at this time and either fell in with other commands or took themselves out of the fight altogether.[48]

Captain Wise had his own close call about the same time when the tails of his coat were ripped apart. "A shell having shot away all his garments from one

46 *Ibid.*, 164.

47 Quoted in Lynchburg *News*, April 16, 1961. According to Captain John Overton Carr of the 26th Virginia Battalion, Ship "was stunned by a spent ball." However, Carr wrote his account in 1906, more than forty years after the event. Ship, in his official report, simply states he was "disabled for a time." Carr to Edgar, March 25, 1906, Edgar Papers.

48 Lynchburg *News*, April 23, 1961.

particular place, he hunted around desperately for clothes enough to sit on," a cadet recalled with a twist of Victorian humor.[49] Wise had a second brush with eternity a short time later, this one at the hands of one of his own cadets. R. H. Cousins leveled his rifle and pulled the trigger, but the weapon misfired. He was desperately trying to clean the vent, not paying much attention to where the muzzle was pointing, when it discharged only inches from Wise's face while aimed almost directly at him. Cousins was convinced he had fatally shot Wise, and did not breath a sigh of relief until the smoke cleared and he watched in surprise as the officer moved on.[50]

It was now about 2:30 p.m., and matters were about to get much worse for the young cadets of VMI.

*   *   *

About the same time that Julius Stahel's troopers were making their failed assault, and the Confederates were organizing a renewed push onto the Bushong property, Franz Sigel's infantry geared up for an attack of their own. Whether the foot soldiers and horsemen were expected to attack as one coordinated strike is unknown, but coordination was not to be found in abundance in Sigel's army that day.

Colonel George Wells of the 34th Massachusetts was viewing the field from his position on the right of Sigel's main line near the artillery on Bushong's Hill. Next to Wells on the left was the 1st West Virginia under Lieutenant Colonel Jacob Weddle, with the 54th Pennsylvania under Colonel Jacob M. Campbell. The Confederate advance opposite the Bay Staters and West Virginians had stalled and fallen back, but was in the process of rallying. Convinced the tide of battle may have turned in their favor, "Colonel Thoburn, brigade commander, rode along the lines telling the men to 'prepare to charge.' He rode by me," continued Wells, "shouting some order I could not catch, and went to the regiment on my left, which immediately charged. I supposed this to be his order to me, and I commanded to fix bayonets and charge. The men fairly sprang forward."[51] The attack was aimed at the weakened Confederate center, but Wells was not the only subordinate to not fully understand Thoburn's

49 Ibid.

50 Wise to J. R. Anderson, August 27, 1909.

51 OR 37, pt. 1, 84.

shouted command. The result was a staggered, uncoordinated lurch toward Breckinridge's infantry.

The 1st West Virginia in the center of Sigel's line was the first to advance. "The order 'Charge boys!' ran along the line, and then came the shock. We raised up and charged forward, answering the enemy yell for yell, and bullet for bullet," one West Virginian remembered.[52] But the regiment moved forward so quickly that it had no support on either flank. Much like the 62nd Virginia only minutes earlier on the other side of the field, the West Virginians found themselves fighting alone. In a move that must surely have surprised the Federal officers, the Confederates realigned their ranks and revived their attack sooner than expected. Within easy small arms range, the Southerners concentrated their fire on the West Virginians and drove the regiment back.

The West Virginians were falling back when Wells led his 34th Massachusetts, about 450 strong, into the attack. The New Englanders had a number of dogs, the regimental mascots that always took their place at the head of the regiment while on parade. When he realized the regiment was preparing to move, one of them, a "big black bob-tail, who used to distinguish himself by catching pigs and running at my grey horse on brigade drill . . . started ahead of us on our charge, in great glee, but was on his back kicking at empty air with all four feet before he had gone ten paces," wrote Wells.[53]

"As we neared the crest of the hill we met the entire rebel force advancing and firing," reported Wells. To the colonel's dismay, "The regiment on my left, which first met the fire, turned and went back, leaving the Thirty-fourth rushing alone into the enemy's line." Realizing the predicament his men were marching into, Wells tried to get their attention by shouting at them to halt, "but could not make a single man hear or heed me, and it was not until they had climbed an intervening fence, and were rushing ahead on the other side, that I was able to run along the lines, and, seizing the color bearer by the shoulder, hold him fast as the only way of stopping the regiment." The wings of the 34th Massachusetts, however, surged ahead until the men lost sight of the regimental colors and ground to a halt, their formation resembling a large "V" with the open end facing the enemy.[54] By this time the New Englanders had advanced

---

52 Unsigned letter in Wheeling *Intelligencer*, May 23, 1864.

53 G. D. Wells Letterbook, May 21, 1864.

54 *OR* 37, pt. 1, 84.

about halfway to the Confederate line, leaving them some 200 yards from the enemy. By now the regiment was completely exposed and taking a decimating fire in front from the VMI Cadets who had reached the fence line at the northern edge of the orchard, and from the 26th Battalion and 62nd Virginia on both flanks. "We were receiving fire not only from our front but from our left and almost from our rear. In fact we were nearly surrounded," wrote one Massachusetts officer who can be forgiven for some exaggeration.[55] It "beat anything I ever dreamed of in the way of fire," Wells remembered, who knew enough to know it was time to fall back, and quickly.[56]

"The alignment rectified," explained Wells, "we faced about and marched back to our position in common time. I could hear the officers saying to the men, and the men to each other, 'Don't run!' 'Keep your line!'—'Common time!' &c." When the men reached their former position near von Kleiser's guns, Wells ordered the regiment to face about and resume firing. The mistake, though of short duration, was not without cost. "The path of the regiment between our line and the fence was sadly strewn with our fallen," he lamented.[57]

Of the 450 men carried into battle, the 34th lost 215 from all causes—the vast majority of them during this short aborted assault. The New Englanders suffered 43% casualties—the highest number of any Federal unit on the field. Among the killed were all but one of the regimental dogs and Wells' horse "Boston Bar," which had been a gift to him from the Boston Bar Association.[58]

Wells had turned his regiment around and was heading back to the jump-off point when the 54th Pennsylvania was moving to advance. Thoburn's order to attack never reached the 54th's Colonel Jacob Campbell, who like Wells before him may have simply missed the brigade commander's shouted directive. "Observing the regiment on my right [1st West Virginia] making a charge," Campbell reported, "in the absence of orders, presuming it proper to imitate their example, I ordered the 54th also to charge."[59] According to their

---

55 Van Franklin Garrett to Henry A. Wise, April 26, 1909, NM Coll., VMI.

56 G. D. Wells Letterbook, May 21, 1864.

57 OR 37, pt. 1, 84. Company C of the 34th Massachusetts was on skirmish duty on the right side of the Federal line, where it lost half its number captured (including two officers). Wells reached the 450 number he carried into battle by subtracting this company, and "other details." If they are not taken into consideration, losses as a percentage approached 48%.

58 G. D. Wells Letterbook, May 21, 1864.

59 OR 37, pt. 1, 86.

Colonel Jacob Campbell (postwar)

Library of Congress

commander, the men from the Keystone State sprang forward "with alacrity and spirit." Advancing beyond the crest of the hill, Campbell's men leveled their muskets and delivered "a rapid, vigorous, and, as I believe, effective fire . . . for some time . . . on the enemy, and every effort made by them to advance on the front occupied by my regiment was firmly and resolutely resisted and proved abortive." The bold stand was costly, delivered while standing up against "a galling and destructive fire, in which many of my men were killed and wounded." The Pennsylvanians were still standing tall, but another hammer blow was about to fall upon them.

As Wharton's Brigade and the VMI Cadets were advancing west of the Valley Pike, John Echols' two Virginia organizations—the 22nd Virginia and 23rd Virginia Battalion—were advancing east of the Pike. After disposing of Stahel's ill-advised Federal cavalry attack, Echols' Virginians forced the withdrawal of Ewing's battery. Once these guns were gone, only small isolated pockets of the enemy remained in Echols' front. The lack of effective resistance allowed the ill brigade commander to turn his full attention to the embattled Federals still fighting beyond the Pike. And directly on his left-front was the exposed flank of the 54th Pennsylvania.

While Echols was driving northward and preparing to fall upon Campbell's flank, the Pennsylvanians were standing their ground against the assaulting 62nd Virginia. Casualties mounted quickly. "The smoke was so thick I could see nothing in front," observed a Pennsylvania sergeant, who "was kept busy pulling our men back out of the line as [they] were killed or wounded."[60] Henry Helsel of Company I was hit nine times and left for dead but somehow

60 Bryan to Colonna, March 8, 1911.

Looking south from the 54th Pennsylvania's position. *Author*

survived, albeit with the loss of his right arm and a bullet he carried in his leg for decades.[61] The toll in officers was especially high. Lieutenant Colonel John P. Linton was wounded, wrote Campbell, "but remained upon the field rallying and encouraging the men until the final close of the action, rendering most valuable and efficient service."[62] Capt. Edwin Geisinger of Company H was mortally wounded and Lieutenant Killpatrick, of the same company, was seriously injured and carried off the field.[63] Company E's Capt. Patrick Graham suffered a horrendous wound when a bullet struck him in his left eye. He was left for dead on the field.[64]

In addition to Graham, Company E also lost its second lieutenant and first sergeant, leaving the second sergeant to eventually lead the company off the field. Lieutenant Colborn of Company B "fell just as the command commenced to fall back." The officer was carried to a house behind Federal lines, "but finally fell into the hands of the enemy in a dying condition." Another officer, Capt. William B. Bonacker, was seriously wounded while "gallantly encouraging his men" as the Pennsylvanians fell back. "His conduct throughout the whole engagement was most cheering and encouraging to his men," wrote Colonel Campbell, "and his loss is deeply to be regretted. Indeed, the conduct of officers and men throughout was all that I could ask or desire, and entitles them to the highest praise."[65]

The 54th Pennsylvania was being overwhelmed with fire from the front when the 22nd Virginia enveloped them from the east. "The enemy . . . pressed forward his right, which extended some distance beyond our left, and was rapidly flanking me in that direction," Campbell reported.[66] Lieutenant Noyes Rand, adjutant of the 22nd Virginia, recalled that his regiment "led the final charge and came so near flanking the enemy on their left they were forced to give way."[67] Caught up in the excitement, one of the regiment's black cooks,

61 Johnstown *Tribune*, March 15, 1921.

62 *OR* 37, pt. 1, 87.

63 Bryan to Colonna, March 8, 1911.

64 Johnstown *Tribune*, October 2, 1904. Captain Graham's regimental commander believed Graham was killed and noted that fact in his official report. *OR* 37, pt. 1, 87.

65 *Ibid.*, 86-87.

66 *Ibid.*

67 Rand to Colonna, January 5, 1911.

Captain Patrick Graham. Note the injury to his eye. *Brian Matthias*

William Armistead, picked up a rifle off the ground and joined the fight as a combatant.[68]

Unbeknownst to Lieutenant Rand, while Echols' men were turning Campbell's left, other Confederates farther west were enveloping his exposed right. Despite the brave and bloody effort put forth by the Pennsylvania troops, no soldiers on any field could have endured what they did and then survived the flanking of both ends of their line. "Despite the most determined resistance . . . my attention was called to the fact that the regiment [1st West Virginia] on my right (owing to the overwhelming numbers brought against it) had given way, and the enemy was advancing at [an] almost right angle with my line and extending beyond the rear and right of my regiment," reported Campbell. "A few minutes only would be required to completely surround my regiment, and in the absence of any appearance of advancing support I was reluctantly compelled to order my command to retire."[69]

"The order to retreat was sounded," remembered one Keystoner, "not hearing the sound of the bugle I stood behind a small tree loading and firing. When I looked about me I saw the boys retreating, so I gave one tremendous leap to the rear across a ravine, then up the bluff and soon caught up with some of the demoralized regiment. . . . But while in the act of capping my gun a bullet struck my right arm between the elbow and wrist putting me out of commission. A moment later another missile came along striking my left leg between the ankle and knee."[70]

Other members of the 54th Pennsylvania also recorded the final minutes of their fight at New Market. "I could hear cheering on our right but the smoke was so dense I could not see anything," recalled Lieutenant George Gageby. Moving in that direction to investigate, he noticed that the right-most company of his regiment was firing not to the front, but rather almost perpendicular to their line, yet he still could not make out any troops—friendly or otherwise—in that direction. Near the far right of the regimental line Gageby encountered a wounded Massachusetts man and carried him onto the porch of a nearby house, where he "opened the nearest door intending to take him in. As the door swung open I saw through a window opposite it a line of Confederates passing along

68 Lowry, *22nd Virginia Infantry*, 60.

69 *OR* 37, pt. 1, 86.

70 J. C. Yutzy to B. A. Colonna, February 18, 1911, NM Coll., VMI.

the other side of the house. I turned to go back to my regt. and saw them falling back." Deciding that running a gauntlet of Confederate fire was preferable to a stay at Libby Prison, Gageby made for the rear as fast as possible. "Some of them fired at but did not hit me. Then one of them said, 'Look at the Yankee son of a bitch, how he runs!' and they laughed loudly."[71]

Colonel Campbell tried to put the best face possible on the chaotic withdrawal when he reported that the evacuation "was done in as good order as the circumstances would allow, two stands being made by a portion of the command before passing beyond musket-range, and the whole of it finally rallying and forming at a point indicated by the colonel commanding brigade."[72]

The sizeable 54th Pennsylvania marched into battle with 566 officers and men. "Of the noncommissioned officers and privates," reads the official report, "27 are known to be killed, and 42 wounded, all of whom fell into the enemy's hands. We brought off the field 98 [more] wounded. This number does not include some 30 who were so slightly wounded as not to be thought necessary to report. The regiment as a whole sustained 174 total casualties." Campbell's reported casualties approached 31%. If the thirty "slightly wounded" are included, that figure rises to 36%.[73]

By the time the 54th Pennsylvania was being threatened by the approach of John Echols' men from the east, the situation on the western end of the field had made the entire Federal position untenable. Most, and perhaps all, of the artillery in the three Federal batteries had to cease firing in order to avoid hitting their own men, a circumstance that turned the artillerymen from active participants into mere spectators. An optimistic gunner in Carlin's battery watched the unfolding attack, fully expecting that Thoburn's infantry would carry the day:

> Our infantry forms for the charge; they move forward, with the glorious old flag to the front. . . . I felt that the day was ours, for their line was already giving ground. . . . But alas, they do not go more than a hundred yards till they waver and fall back, and we

---

71 Gageby to Colonna, May 27, 1911. Lieutenant Gageby probably carried the wounded soldier to the Lightfoot residence.

72 OR 37, pt. 1, 86.

73 Ibid.; Charles K. Gailey, III, ed., "Federal Casualties at the Battle of New Market, May 15, 1864," copy at NMBSHP. The spot where Captain Edwin Geisinger fell was marked decades later by the 54th Pennsylvania monument.

now felt that it would be a desperate struggle for the battery, for every man knew we were whipped.[74]

While the Federal gunners watched and worried as "the center breaks and retires in a perfect panic," wrote one gunner, Wharton worked several companies of the 51st Virginia and 26th Virginia Battalion along the wooded bluff on the western edge of the field.[75] During the approach, recalled Virginia Captain Edmund Read, "I heard someone call out, 'Charge Read—Charge.' I looked to my left some ten or fifteen steps and saw General Wharton. I did not stop or speak to him." The terrain above the river, coupled with powder smoke, partly shielded Wharton's advancing flankers, who had also taken advantage of the distraction posed by the intense firefight for the possession of the Bushong orchard. "On gaining the top of the hill the enemy's sharpshooters at once fled from their position on the bluff, and I found I had no force in my front but had completely overlapped the enemy's right flank," Captain Read wrote. "I half-wheeled, fired, and we rushed the guns." Other Virginians concentrated their fire against Carlin's and Snow's artillery pieces, which were now sitting silently atop Bushong's Hill.[76]

74 Wheeling *Intelligencer*, May 23, 1864, quoted in Fluharty, *Carlin's Wheeling Battery*, 50.

75 *Ibid.*

76 Read to Edgar, March 29, 1906, Edgar Papers.

(Photo opposite page) View from Union artillery position (Carlin's and Snow's batteries) atop Bushong Hill. These guns wreaked havoc on Wharton's Confederates as they crossed the open fields of Jacob Bushong's farm (center). The roof of the Bushong house is visible left of center above the trees of the orchard. Bushong's barn is right of center. The closest fence line marks Wharton's last position before his final assault. The "Field of Lost Shoes," which briefly slowed the VMI Cadets in their attack on von Kleiser's battery, is the depression left of center in front of the orchard. Partly visible at the far right among the trees is the museum and visitor center of New Market Battlefield State Historical Park (Hall of Valor). Note how the terrain drops off to the west between the barn and the Hall of Valor. The left wings of the 51st Virginia and 26th Virginia Battalion, which were on the western face of this saddle, were sheltered considerably from Federal fire as they advanced, enabling them to turn the Federal flank, capture several guns, and drive off the remainder. *Author*

The Federal gunners leapt to their pieces and replied with canister in an effort to defend themselves and cover the infantry's retreat. By this time it was too late to change the course of the battle. Wharton's Virginians along the bluff were too close, too many, and too determined to be beaten back. "Snow's battery on our left limbers to the rear and retires," one of Carlin's men remembered. "Our guns still throw canister in the very teeth of the foe, but the enemy trains their whole fire upon us, and it seems impossible to save a single gun." Part of the seemingly impossibility was the proximity of Wharton's infantry, part of which under Captain Read of the 26th Virginia Battalion, was making a mad dash for the departing guns.[77]

Given the steady rain, the mud, and the advancing enemy, getting the heavy guns away was no easy task. "The ground was very soft and the recoil of the guns sunk my gun, or the wheels, in the mud nearly to the hub," remembered one of the gunners.[78] Compared to the ordeal Carlin's battery would soon face, Snow managed to get his pieces and men away relatively unscathed, with but five wounded and one horse killed and four others injured.[79]

Carlin initiated his retreat with the withdrawal of his left-most gun. The piece limbered and began rolling, but did not make it ten yards before the driver of the lead team, Rich French, was shot through the head. The gun crew had already left Levi Cassil, "thought to be mortally wounded," on the field, and now another of its crew was dead. When he saw French fall, Curran Mendel, a

77 *Ibid.*

78 Charles H. Senseny to B. A. Colonna, February 23, 1912, NM Coll., VMI.

79 Quesenbery, *A Snowball's Chance*, 189-90.

gunner on that piece, jumped on the team and drove it off.[80] One of Carlin's gunners left a detailed eyewitness account of the chaos that ensued thereafter:

> No. 2 . . . got off without any loss, but both . . . horses were skipped with balls, making the hair fly. No. 3 came next, and before they got their gun limbered three horses are shot, but they get it off the field and then had to leave it, as the horses fell dead in the harness. No. 4, this was the only gun that was left where we fought, and it had five horses out of the gun team killed and disabled, and two men mortally wounded . . . George Bottles was shot through the lungs, Dan S. Morrison through the bowels. The latter was brought off the field, but had to be left at Mount Jackson. No. 5, which was mine and next in line, I had one man struck on the shoulder with a piece of shell. It tore his blouse and bruised his shoulder, his name was Flemming. A shell passed through the hind wheel of my caisson, breaking two spokes, the side rail, the rear cross bar, and one spoke in the fifth wheel. I was off my horse and at the chest when the order was given to retire. I went forward at once and the limber of my gun passed me going to the rear. I ordered them back to fetch off the gun and then came round promptly, but the time lost, by the limber going to the rear was fatal. As they came back there was three horses wounded; the off leader had five balls in him, the off swing was wounded in the leg, and the saddle horse of the wheel team had a leg broken. But the boys kept them up and we took the gun off, the drivers using whip and spur to keep them going . . . passing over plowed ground, our wheels making half way to the axles in the mud . . . No. 6 lost their caisson, and as they retired, Martin Manners, who drove the lead team, was shot through the head. It is believed he is dead. Another man got on at once and they brought the gun off safe . . . William Johnson, gunner on No. 6, was wounded on the foot and John Fennemore, gunner, on the arm."[81]

"Before we reached them [Snow's guns] the enemy abandoned the position [and] retreated," wrote Captain Read, "and when I reached the battery [Carlin's] there were a good many men around the captured guns." Snow brought all six of his guns safely off the field. Carlin, however, stayed too long on Bushong's Hill and lost three guns there—one unable to be removed from its position atop Bushong's Hill for lack of horses and overrun by some of Wharton's infantry, and two more lost when the horses became disabled from wounds during the retreat. According to one eyewitness, William F. Lemons of Company B, 26th Virginia Battalion, shouted out, "I appeal to Captain Read that I was the first

---

80 Wheeling *Intelligencer*, May 23, 1864, quoted in Fluharty, *Carlin's Wheeling Battery*, 50.

81 *Ibid.*, 50-1.

man in the battery!" The officer could not confirm Lemons' claim, "as there was a considerable number of men around them and he could not have been with me, as the guns were captured before we reached them."[82]

Regardless of who got to the guns first, the Federal defensive front was compromised. As Sigel would later admit, "Our whole position now became untenable." His conclusion was fully realized with hindsight. For many of his soldiers still fighting bravely to hold their position, the outcome of the combat was not as obvious.[83]

A Massachusetts captain recalled that after the failed infantry attack, the men of his 34th regiment fell back to their position to support von Kleiser's battery in relatively good order, despite the decimating casualties they had sustained during their brief assault. It was then that he noticed something was amiss: the artillery was no longer firing. "[W]e looked for the batteries on our right," he reported in his diary, but the guns were "flying to the left and but one regiment, the 54th Pennsylvania, was to be seen."[84]

With his regiment staggered but reasonably well in hand, Colonel Wells halted his men, faced them about, and resumed firing into the smoky distance—if not at any visible enemy, then at least in the general direction of Breckinridge's Confederates. Almost immediately a bullet struck Lieutenant Colonel William Lincoln in the shoulder. "The loss of his invaluable services, and the impossibility of making my voice heard in the din," remembered Wells, "rendered it necessary for me to go along the whole line to make the men understand what was wanted." Once his men were aligned to his satisfaction and "well at work, I was able to look about the field, and saw, to my surprise, that the artillery had limbered up and was moving off the field, and that the infantry had gone, save one regiment, which was gallantly holding its ground far to the left."[85]

Franz Sigel was with his troops on the right and came under heavy enemy fire. Several officers and men noted his cool demeanor that afternoon. "General Sigel is a brave man," concluded a lieutenant in the 12th West Virginia. "Sat on his horse during the whole engagement, part of the time in front and part in rear

82 Read to Edgar, March 29, 1906.

83 Sigel, "Sigel in the Shenandoah Valley," 489. Wharton later claimed he captured two guns.

84 Thompson diary, May 15, 1864.

85 OR 37, pt. 1, 84.

of our regiment. He was as cool as if he had been on review."[86] An artilleryman agreed: "Sigel is as cool a man as I ever saw."[87] Another West Virginian remembered an officer reining in his mount next to him. "I looked up and saw General Sigel sitting on his horse, smoking a cigar, and seeming as calm as on parade ground, while I was so excited as to scarcely know what was going on."[88] Colonel Wells remembered seeing the army commander throughout much of the fight. "Sigel was on his horse on the right of our line during most of the engagement, and in the hottest of the fire," Wells wrote in his battle report. "How he escaped is a mystery to me."[89] "Whatever may be said of Sigel's generalship regarding the battle of New Market," wrote one officer with the benefit of hindsight, "it must be said that he acted bravely; was right in the thick of the fight all the time and after the battle began did the best he could to save the day."[90]

Many of Sigel's personal staff did not share in the admiration for their leader. Colonel David Strother recalled that Sigel rode about rather aimlessly, accompanied most of the time by General Stahel and Colonel Moor, "all jabbering in German. In his excitement he [Sigel] seemed to forget his English entirely," Strother criticized, rendering the non-German speaking part of his staff "totally useless to him."[91]

With most of the enemy artillery gone and some of it captured, Wharton found part of his brigade on the flank of the Federal infantry still remaining in line and facing south. "From my position," he wrote, "I could see that I had turned the right flank of the enemy, but that the center and right of my line was hotly engaged and seemed to have been forced back a little or had not kept up its alignment with the left."[92] With his line formed into a wide but shallow U-shaped front, Wharton instructed Capt. William H. Tate to wheel his Company B, 51st Virginia, to the right to enfilade the Federal line. Wharton had

86 Fluharty, *Civil War Letters of Lt. Milton B. Campbell*, 105.

87 Fluharty, *Carlin's Wheeling Battery*, 51.

88 James N. Miller, *The Story of Andersonville and Florence* (des Moines, 1900), on-line version, www.lindapages.com/12wvi/12-andersonville.htm.

89 *OR* 37, pt. 1, 85-6.

90 Hewitt, *History of the Twelfth Regiment West Virginia Volunteer Infantry*, 115.

91 Eby, *A Virginia Yankee in the Civil War*, 226.

92 Staunton *Spectator & Vindicator*, May 20, 1904.

just given the order when the captain was struck by a bullet and killed at Wharton's side.[93]

As the left side of Wharton's line reorganized around the overrun Federal gun position, Captain Read talked with a wounded officer from the 34th Massachusetts. As he was doing so or shortly thereafter, he "observed that the squad who had retreated from the bluff were holding together and trying to rally some of their fleeing stragglers." Instead of attacking the exposed right Federal flank with the rest of Wharton's men, Read gathered members of his company "and pushed after them, when they broke up, running for the riverbank."[94]

Colonel Wells of the 34th Massachusetts described Wharton's approach in his report: "The rebel line advanced until I could see, above the smoke, two battle-flags on the hill in front of the position where the artillery had been posted," Wells wrote. That sight would have been enough to chill the blood of any soldier. With his position compromised the colonel ordered a retreat, "but they either could not hear or would not heed the order." Wells grabbed his color bearer, faced him about, and ordered Color Sergeant John E. Calligan to follow him "in order to get the regiment off the field." It was a near-run thing, remembered Wells, who wrote in his letterbook, "I began to think I should never get the rascals off the field."[95]

At first it was an orderly withdrawal, but the Confederates could taste victory and were in hot pursuit, prompting Wells to tell "the men to run and get out of fire as quickly as possible."[96] One officer found that "a determined charge upon our front, and a withering fire poured into our left flank, and rear, from the now contracting lines of the Rebels was too much."[97] Company C, which earlier had been detached to the far right to provide support for the artillery, was cut off and nearly all captured.[98]

---

93 *Ibid.* Tate was a well-respected officer, who one of his men called "as fine a man and as brave a man as fell during the war. . . . Never . . . lacking in anything where duty called him." G. S. Bralley to C. B. Tate, January 28, 1911, NM Coll., VMI.

94 Read to Edgar, March 29, 1906. Read does not name the officer, but mentioned in a postwar letter that he had since met him in Boston "and talked the fight over with him and some of his officers."

95 *OR* 37, pt. 1, 84; Wells Letterbook, May 21, 1864.

96 *OR* 37, pt. 1, 84.

97 Lincoln, *Life with the 34th Massachusetts Infantry*, 283.

98 Drickamer, *Fort Lyon to Harpers Ferry*, 184.

Colonel Wells himself had several brushes with severe injury or death. "I had three narrow escapes," he wrote in a post-battle letter: "a ball through my hat, grazing the top of my head; one through the sleeve, severely bruising my arm; and one through the sides of my rubber overcoat."[99]

John Adams of Company F had been wounded by a shell fragment early on in the fighting, but had lost consciousness. He came to about the time that the position was being overrun. He crawled as best he could toward the Valley Pike. As he stood, propping himself against a tree stump, he was shot in the right leg, and laid there until litter bearers found him the next night and carried him to the Bushong barn.[100]

By this time in the battle, Wells was developing quite a rapport with his color bearer. Despite the desperate nature of the fighting and the ominous turn of events, the sergeant apparently was in no rush to get the colors off the field. "I had to go back into fire six times to bring the colors off," Wells wrote after the battle, perhaps with a touch of pride. "The bearer would halt wherever anybody told him, but he would not move back except at my direct order."[101] "I felt much relieved on receiving an order from General Sullivan, who was conspicuous on the field, that the line would be formed on the ridge [Rude's Hill] and no stand made before it was reached. I directed the color bearer to march directly there without halting."[102]

On Wharton's left, Private George W. Dunford of Tate's Company B, 51st Virginia, charged toward the withdrawing artillery pieces and the enticing open flank of the infantry line. "With a deep and long drawn out Confederate yell," wrote Dunford, "[we] had covered half the distance to the enemy's guns and about 50 yards from their front when my left leg was paralyzed. A ball had struck me just above the knee. From this point I could see the whole of our line, which but a minute before had seemed to sway in the center as a rope in the wind, had now righted itself and was moving forward in perfect order."[103] Dunford was one of nineteen casualties sustained by his company at New Market.

99 Wells Letterbook, May 17, 1864.

100 John W. Adams to B. A. Colonna, December 3, 1910, NM Coll., VMI.

101 Wells Letterbook, May 21, 1864.

102 *OR* 37, pt. 1, 84-5.

103 "Battle of New Market as Seen by G. W. Dunford."

When his men reached the crest of the hill, Wharton sent a courier to Colonel Edgar of the 26th Virginia Battalion near the center of the line to drive forward as hard as possible.[104] By now it was about 3:00 p.m. Perhaps the Confederates fighting along the line sensed or realized that the Federal fire had slackened. In some places along the line, no doubt, Southern eyes spotted Confederate banners atop Bushong's Hill. Whatever the reasons, the entire line lurched northward in a general advance, with Edgar's 26th Virginia Battalion slightly in advance and likely bolstered by remnants of the 51st Virginia and 30th Virginia Battalion. The VMI Cadets and 62nd Virginia trailed a short distance behind. Echols' infantry on the right was already wheeling into position to enfilade the Federal left flank.

Color Sergeant George A. Woodrum led the 26th in its charge. An observer witnessed Woodrum "standing in the lead of the battle line, waving his flag, firing his pistol and cheering the men through a murderous fire of shot and shell."[105] His cousin, Major Richard Woodrum, also distinguished himself "charg[ing] superior enemy numbers cheering his men with such dash" that the battalion adjutant told Colonel Edgar that "if Woodrum is not promoted I'll resign." Woodrum would remain a major, and the adjutant was killed several weeks later.[106]

Even though the Yankee line was broken and retreating, some units were still offering stout resistance. Pvt. John Midkiff served with Sergeant Woodrum in the 26th Virginia Battalion's color guard. One of Midkiff's comrades saw him fall just as the line reached the top of the hill: "He shouted aloud as he charged with the leading group and was hit by a shot in the mouth. He never knew what hit him as he fell backward stone dead."[107]

---

104 In a postwar letter to Colonel Edgar, Captain Edmund Read of the 26th Virginia Battalion wrote the following about another Wharton order the general claimed to have issued at this time, but apparently did not: "I understand that General Wharton has published a statement saying that I reported 'Edgar cut off by a bluff,' and that he gave me an order instructing 'Edgar to move to the right and join the Fifty-first.' General Wharton is entirely and utterly mistaken. I never reported to him and received no order from him. . . . It is preposterous to suppose that he should have sent me running messages for him when he had a staff and couriers provided for this purpose, especially as I was in command of my company and in action." Read's postwar writings reveal some animosity toward Wharton, though the reason for which is not disclosed. Edmund Read to Edgar, March 29, 1906, Edgar Papers.

105 Terry Lowry, *26th Battalion Virginia Infantry* (Lynchburg, VA, 1991), 39.

106 *Ibid.*

107 Maddy, *History of Marie Community.*

Edgar's 26th Virginia Battalion reached the top of the hill as Carlin's battery was trying to make its escape. At least one gun had already been taken by Wharton's small band of infantry fighting along the rocky bluff. Edgar's 26th Battalion men also claimed the capture of two guns—likely the pair that had to be abandoned after being limbered. "[W]e advanced upon the enemy and put them to flight and took two pieces of artillery," recalled Lieutenant Thomas H. Kirkpatrick of Company E. "This I saw with my own eyes." The first two men to reach them, Kirkpatrick continued, "both belonging to my company," were David C. Jones and the lieutenant's brother, John H. Kirkpatrick.[108]

Another officer of the same battalion, Lieutenant William Worth George, recalled in a postwar letter an even more dramatic event that took place about the same time around the captured guns: "The Twenty-sixth Virginia Battalion moved forward and captured the two pieces of enemy's artillery. . . . This fact is doubly impressed upon the writer's mind because of the following incident, which occurred at that point: the color-bearer of the Twenty-sixth Virginia on the advance fell with the colors about halfway between the crest of the hill and the battery in front. His comrade, well-known to the writer," continued George, "seized the colors and planted them on one of the pieces captured by the Twenty-sixth Virginia Battalion."[109]

The credit for who captured these pieces remained a heated point of contention for years between the men of the 51st Virginia and 26th Virginia Battalion. Each unit claimed that it alone was responsible for seizure of the three guns Carlin ultimately forfeited at New Market. Based on a detailed description of the event that ran in the Wheeling *Intelligencer*, it seems probable that an element of Wharton's 51st Virginia captured Carlin's number four piece—described as "the only gun that was left where we fought." The number three and number five pieces, which initially were able to limber up and roll some distance before being abandoned when their horses fell dead or wounded, are most probably the pieces Edgar's infantry (likely joined by elements of the 51st Virginia and 30th Virginia Battalion) claimed as their own.[110]

---

108 Sworn statement of Thomas H. Kirkpatrick, February 15, 1906, Edgar Papers.

109 William Worth George to Colonel Edgar, May 6, 1906, Edgar Papers.

110 An account written by a teamster in the 18th Virginia Cavalry who assisted carting arms and equipment off the field the following day complicates matters. According to the cavalryman, he encountered a Federal gun on the field that had "Captured by the 62nd Regiment" carved in its barrel. The author does not write precisely where on the field this gun

The postwar debate over who took these guns turned ugly when Capt. Edmund Read of the 26th Virginia Battalion accused General Wharton of cowardice—a specious claim wholly out of character for Wharton, hurled in an effort to discredit the general's claim. According to Read, as his men passed through the broken ranks of the 51st Virginia, "I heard someone call out 'Charge, Read! Charge, for God's sake!' I looked to my left and saw General Wharton crouched behind a tree. . . . I did not stop to speak to him, in fact did not answer him at all, as I had all I could do to attend to my . . . duties. The place was too hot to be stopping for conversation. . . . I did not see him again during the battle." Read also charged that a sergeant in his company, not recognizing Wharton, "called to him, 'Come on and charge with us, damn you!'"[111]

Not far behind Edgar's battalion tramped the VMI Cadets. Because of Lieutenant Colonel Ship's wounding in the Bushong orchard, the young warriors were now led by Capt. Henry Wise. One cadet recalled Wise's order: "Get up from here and give the Yankees hell!"[112] The cadets responded with ardor. "The first thing to do was to climb the fence," Cadet John Howard wrote. "It was an ordinary rail fence probably about four feet high, but as I surmounted the top-most rail I felt at least ten feet up in the air and [the] special object of hostile aim."[113] Directly to their front was the embattled 34th Massachusetts and von Kleiser's guns, which threw several parting rounds at the cadets before limbering up to roll away. Although in an untenable position, Wells' New Englanders were still offering considerable resistance as they began to fall back to avoid being cut off and destroyed. "We pushed on amid a shower of musket balls," recalled one of the VMI cadets. "At one point we were within a few yards of them; and whilst retreating they fell back in remarkably good order, loading and firing on us with much coolness as they retreated." Between the cadets and the Federals was a large depression in the open field, which the steady rain had transformed into a swampy bog. "The mud was nearly knee

---

was found, but he does state that it was a brass cannon, likely making it one from von Kleiser's battery rather than one of Carlin's guns. Sager, *Battle of New Market*, 13-4.

111 Edmund S. Read to G. M. Edgar, February 24, 1906, Edgar Papers. Read's account is the only known claim that Wharton demonstrated cowardice at New Market, and it was written more than four decades after the fact. Few if any participants or students of the battle since have given this claim any credence.

112 Quoted in Couper, *New Market Cadets*, 234.

113 Howard, "Recollections of New Market," 59.

deep," wrote one of the cadets, and "many of us here lost our shoes in the mud."[114]

"The command was given to rise and charge," remembered cadet Edward Tutwiler. "Then it was that we rushed for the battery. We shot down the horses."[115] In describing the final charge against the 34th Massachusetts and von Kleiser's battery, Henry Wise wrote simply, "The order was given to the cadets to advance upon the enemy, and they moved promptly and most spiritedly, driving the enemy in their immediate front from the field, capturing guns and prisoners."[116]

Major Theodore Lang of Franz Sigel's staff was impressed by the bearing of the cadets during the final attack. "I never witnessed a more gallant advance and final charge than was given by these brave boys on that field. They fought like veterans, nor did the dropping of their comrades by the ruthless bullet deter them from their mission."[117]

Federal signal officer Capt. Franklin Town sat on his horse behind von Kleiser's battery observing the final attack. The precision of the VMI Cadets drew both his attention and his admiration. "I think it would have been impossible to eject from six guns [sic] more missiles than these men faced in their wild charge up that hill," concluded the captain. Town was so enthralled by the advance of the cadets that he failed to fully comprehend what the converging flood of gray meant to him, and that von Kleiser's gunners were limbering their pieces and withdrawing. "I . . . was so absorbed in the spectacle that it did not occur to me that I might possibly be included in the capture, until the presence of the enemy between me and the guns brought me to a realization of the circumstances, and I did not then consider it expedient to remain longer where I was."[118]

Once the Confederates saw that the Federals were pulling out, the race was on to seize the artillery. Southern commands overlapped and then merged into masses and groups rather than their formerly well-defined battle lines.

---

114 Richmond *Daily Whig,* June 22, 1864. This gave rise to the area being called "The Field of Lost Shoes."

115 Couper, *The VMI New Market Cadets,* 211.

116 Henry A. Wise, "The Cadets at New Market, VA," *Confederate Veteran,* August 1912, 361.

117 Lang, *Personal Recollections of the Battle of New Market.*

118 Franklin E. Town, "Valor at New Market," *Southern Historical Society Papers* (1916), vol. 41, 181-2.

Cadet Sergeant Oliver P. Evans,
Battalion color bearer

VMI Archives

Conspicuous near the head of the onrushing gray wave was Sergeant Oliver Evans, the VMI color bearer. Four guns from von Kleiser's battery made good their sloppy escape, but one piece—owing to a lack of horses to haul it away—had to be left behind. Evans leapt atop the gun carriage waving his academy's colors.[119]

Cadet Andrew Pizzini reached the now-silent Federal guns before they got safely off the field. He shot at one of the last remaining gunners before the enemy soldier climbed on one of the horses that was still hitched to a caisson. Luckily for the erstwhile Federal target, Pizzini's aim was off and the gunner managed to cut the traces on the animals and ride off to safety.[120]

Amid the deadly confusion of battle, some of the young and inexperienced cadets had a problem identifying targets to shoot. "Up to this time I had not seen a Yankee, to know him, and rushed ahead . . . as fast as I could, looking for something to shoot at," confessed Cadet Nelson Noland. When he reached the edge of a gully with cedar trees sprouting up around it, Noland noticed "a lot of people come swarming out of it who did not look like our folks, and concluded they must be Yankees." With his enemy "bunched" together, Noland leveled

119 It was probably this gun that was found the next day with "Captured by the 62nd Regiment" carved on its barrel. Sager, *Battle of New Market*, 13-4.

120 Andrew Pizzini to B. A. Colonna, June 2, 1911, NM Coll., VMI.

Cadet Andrew Pizzini

VMI Archives

his rifled musket and "shot right into the bosom of them at close quarters and saw one go down."[121]

Somehow amidst all the enemy fire—and despite the order that all officers were to enter into the attack on foot instead of on horseback—mounted Cadet Lucian C. Ricketts emerged from the maelstrom unscathed. He had been detailed as Colonel Ship's personal courier, and as such was given a horse to perform his tasks. Ricketts later rationalized his actions by explaining that Breckinridge's order to enter the fight dismounted was directed to officers, and so as a cadet private it did not pertain to him. Ricketts later claimed he was "the only person on horseback on the firing line of the cadets or elsewhere along the line until General Breckinridge and his staff later appeared."[122]

Ricketts' decision to ignore the order to fight dismounted benefitted Cadet Francis L. Smith. During the final attack against the Federal position, Smith was seriously wounded when a bullet struck him in the chin. The lead projectile shattered Smith's jawbone, traveled deeper into his head, and finally emerged from his neck, narrowly missing his carotid artery. Within a few seconds another bullet struck Smith in the shoulder, breaking his collarbone. When Ricketts spotted his fellow cadet writhing on the ground in agony and realized the nature of his ghastly wounds, he pulled him up on the horse and hauled him

---

121 N. B. Noland to Charles Read, December 18, 1895, NM Coll., VMI.

122 Couper, *The VMI New Market Cadets*, 170.

back to a field hospital in New Market. Ricketts' gallant action saved his fellow cadet's life.[123]

In addition to the lone gun from von Kleiser's battery, the cadets captured many Federals. Company B's Captain Preston estimated that number to be as low as 60 and as high as 100. Cadet Charles Faulkner of Company B alone brought in 23 Yankees.[124]

The most notable and highest ranking prisoner was Lieutenant Colonel William Lincoln of the 34th Massachusetts. Lincoln had been struck in the shoulder during the final assault. Although he was left behind when the rest of the 34th retreated, the wounded officer was determined to make good his own escape. "When he fell, a private and captain came to his assistance," wrote Cadet John Coleman. "One of the cadets rushed upon him whilst attempting to escape. The captain drew his sword and was getting the better of him when another cadet advanced; he then attempted to draw his pistol, when the other cadet ran him through with his bayonet."[125] The two cadets, John Hanna and Henry Garrett, then took Lincoln into custody and later presented the colonel's horse to Scott Ship.[126]

Lincoln was not the only Yankee who did not relish a firsthand view of the interior of Andersonville or Libby Prison. Benjamin Colonna, Cadet Captain of Company D, encountered a Federal officer in the vicinity of von Kleiser's battery. Although surrounded and with no chance of escape or rescue, the obstinate Federal drew his pistol on Colonna and several other cadets. Not wanting to kill him, Colonna ordered one of his men "to shoot him in the legs, but the boy did not take very good aim and shot him higher up."[127]

---

123 *Ibid.*, 170, 190. Cadet Francis Smith was no relation to Superintendent General Francis Smith. The bullet that lodged in Cadet Smith's shoulder was removed and Smith turned it into a watch fob. It is now an exhibit at New Market Battlefield State Historical Park.

124 Lexington *Gazette*, May 25, 1864.

125 Richmond *Daily Whig*, June 22, 1864.

126 Wyndham Kemp to James A. Goggin, March 25, 1888, NM Coll., VMI. Lincoln's wound required the amputation of his arm. As a token of his gratitude, the Massachusetts officer gave his field glasses to General Imboden with the request that he present them to the surgeon who operated on him. Imboden was unable to locate the surgeon, however, and instead presented the glasses to the VMI museum in 1889. They are now on exhibit at NMBSHP.

127 Richard B. Tunstall to Henry A. Wise, March 30, 1909, NM coll., VMI. Although the identity of this Federal officer cannot be confirmed with complete certainty, it can be narrowed down to a few officers from the 34th Massachusetts, which was the only unit on this part of the

Cadet John Hanna,
in a postwar image.

VMI Archives

Although Colonel George H. Smith's numerous accounts of the battle differ often and significantly, he was steadfast in one belief: his 62nd Virginia stepped off on the final attack before the VMI cadets on his left. "[T]hey did not . . . form on the left of the 62nd when that regiment advanced with the 22nd," wrote the regimental leader, "and the result was that the two regiments named led the advance in this part of the field, and continued in advance until the enemy was routed."[128] Given the piecemeal Union withdrawal in front of the advancing 62nd Virginia, Smith's assessment may well be correct. Smith shoved his Virginia regiment into the hole where the 1st West Virginia had been positioned just minutes earlier, a move that placed his men squarely between the 34th Massachusetts on his left, and the 54th Pennsylvania on his right. Smith's bold advance triggered visible chaos amongst

field that had had officers captured. Lieutenant Colonel William Lincoln was one of as few as three (and perhaps as many as five) officers in the 34th who were wounded and taken prisoner. However, Lincoln's own account of his capture seems to exclude him as a possibility. Captains C. R. Chauncey and H. P. Fox, and 2nd Lieutenants Malcolm Ammidown and R. W. Walker were captured and, by some accounts, wounded. According to Lincoln, Walker was wounded somewhere near the Bushong orchard fence, which makes it very unlikely that he was the officer described in Colonna's account. That leaves three officers: Chauncey, Fox, and Ammidown. Both Chauncey and Ammidown of Company C were cut off with their company, which had been detached to the bluffs to guard the right flank of Snow's and Carlin's batteries. The official casualty return given to Sigel's chief medical officer states that Chauncey and Ammidown were wounded and captured. However, Colonel Wells' official report of the battle, Lieutenant Colonel Lincoln's book, and Captain George Thompson's diary all suggest that Chauncey and Ammidown were *not* wounded prior to their capture. That leaves Captain Fox of Company H, who is listed on the casualty list as thrice wounded ("wrist, abdomen and arm") and captured. In fact, Fox was so badly wounded that he was initially listed as killed in action before his capture became known. Given this evidence, the identity of the officer described by Colonna was either Chauncey, Fox, or Ammidown.

128 Smith, *The Battle of New Market*, 23.

the embattled defenders. "I never have seen such havoc," one Virginian wrote.[129]

Realizing that the tide of battle was turning decisively in his favor, John Breckinridge rode up to Edgar and exclaimed, "Colonel, we are driving them." Edgar replied, "Yes General, but we are much broken."[130] Broken they were, but the field and several hundred prisoners and several cannon now belonged to the Confederates. It was about this time, remembered an officer with the 26th Virginia Battalion, that "some sharpshooters on our left front"—likely Company C of the 34th Massachusetts—opened on them with a "very galling fire." Someone, either General Wharton or Breckinridge himself, ordered the captain to "dislodge them and keep a look out for our left flank, which I proceeded to do." In doing so, the officer and a handful of the Virginians "got separated from the main body of our troops for a while." When he returned, he did so "with some prisoners."[131]

As Confederate commands intermingled and pursued the broken Federals, the colors of the 1st West Virginia were very nearly captured. Seeing the flag in danger, Sergeant James M. Burns gathered several men and raced back to save it. Burns was lightly wounded for his effort, but one of his comrades fell with serious injuries. "I was severely wounded, and lying helpless on the field I called for aid," recalled Travilla A. Russell. "[Sergeant Burns] hearing my call, returned in the face of a hot fire from the enemy and assisted me from the field of battle and saved me from capture." Downplaying his role, Burns later wrote that he "was never under a heavier fire." His brave act, however, elicited cheers not just from his comrades but from the enemy as well. In 1896 he was awarded the Medal of Honor.[132]

The chaos brought about by the collapsing Federal line unmasked the 12th West Virginia, Franz Sigel's last remaining fresh regiment still on the field. "The Twelfth was in a bad position," Lieutenant William Hewitt admitted in the regimental history. "We were placed where we could do no good and yet where we suffered seriously, a more trying position on a soldier than where he has a

129 Isaac White to "My Dear Jinnie," May 16, 1864, White Papers.

130 Quoted in Turner, *New Market Campaign*, 140.

131 Carr to Edgar, March 25, 1906. This is almost certainly the same event Captain Edmund S. Read described in a letter written to Colonel Edgar dated March 29, 1906.

132 Darl Stephenson, "1st West Virginia Sergeant Saves Colors, Soldier, Too," *Washington Times*, March 27, 2004.

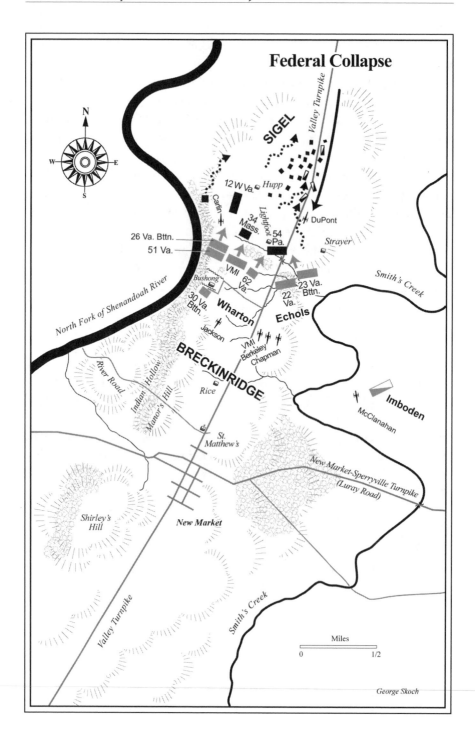

Federal Collapse

SIGEL

Valley Turnpike

N
W   E
S

12 W Va.   Hupp

Carlin

34 Mass.

Lightfoot

54 Pa.

DuPont

26 Va. Bttn.

51 Va.

Strayer

VMI   62 Va.

Smith's Creek

Bushong

23 Va. Bttn.

30 Va. Bttn.

Wharton   22 Va.   **Echols**

North Fork of Shenandoah River

Jackson

VMI
Berkeley
Chapman

BRECKINRIDGE

River Road

Indian Hollow

Manor's Hill

Rice

Imboden

McClanahan

St. Matthew's

New Market-Sperryville Turnpike
(Luray Road)

Shirley's Hill

New Market

Valley Turnpike

Smith's Creek

Miles

0   1/2

George Skoch

chance to return the fire."[133] "Our reg't [sic] was on raised ground and the musket balls of the enemy showered into and around us like hailstones," recalled Lieutenant Milton Campbell. "Can't see how so many of us did escape when the balls flew so thick and fast."[134]

Before a battle begins, some soldiers get a premonition that they will not survive the fight. This happened to a West Virginia soldier named Chrisman. When the regiment assumed its position earlier in the day, Chrisman remarked to a comrade, "I hope I will be killed today." His surprised friend replied "Chrisman, you ought not to talk that way." After a brief discussion the two men changed positions in line, the downtrodden Chrisman now moving into the front rank. "We lay down in line of battle," his companion wrote, "awaiting a charge which the enemy was making upon us. Chrisman lay in front of me . . . Soon I heard a dull sound of something striking and Chrisman stretched himself out at full length, dead from a bullet through the heart."[135] Chrisman has the unfortunate distinction of being the only member of the 12th West Virginia killed in action at New Market.

The fresh West Virginians offered what little resistance they could, but with scores of Federal infantry and rumbling artillery pieces breaking across their front, and masses of enemy infantry moving against them, there was little they could do. "We commenced to fall back," one remembered, "as other Confederate Regts [sic] were about to flank us on our left. Our men still fighting as we fell back."[136]

Companies A and B, 12th West Virginia, had been detached to the bluffs overlooking the river and were quickly cut off by some of Edgar's Virginians sent to dislodge them.[137] Several West Virginians were captured, including James Miller. "Fortunately we fell into the hands of brave captors who treated us kindly," he wrote. "As we walked back over the battlefield the bodies of blue

---

133 Hewitt, *History of the Twelfth Regiment West Virginia Volunteer Infantry*, 108.

134 Fluharty, *Civil War Letters of Milton B. Campbell*, 104.

135 Miller, *Story of Andersonville and Florence*.

136 J. N. Waddell, "Battle of New Market, VA," NM Coll., VMI.

137 Hines to Edgar, February 24, 1906. According to Edgar's battle report, "a portion [of my battalion] was detached to dislodge a flanking party of the enemy that had taken position in the cliffs near the river. To cooperate with and protect the detachment referred to, the battalion was thrown further forward during the pursuit than the rest of the line." Edgar New Market report, Edgar Papers.

and gray were mingled, showing that both armies had suffered severely. My guard permitted me to pick up a blanket, and also a well-filled haversack, and both of these became of good service to me." Indeed they would have been, for Miller was on his way to Georgia and the prison camp at Andersonville.[138]

At least one, and perhaps all three, of Carlin's surviving guns went into battery again about 150 or 200 yards north of their original position. However, they had expended all the canister in their ammunition chests, and the caissons with the reserve ammunition had already reached the Pike. When they realized they were no longer equipped to repulse an enemy attack, the artillerymen wisely limbered up again and joined the ongoing retreat.[139] In the ongoing confusion, a gunner fell wounded and was run over by one of the heavy cannon wheels. Because the ground was so wet, he sank into the soupy mud and sustained no serious injuries before being taken off the field by his comrades.[140]

Another artillery piece, probably one of the two Carlin was forced to abandon because of a lack of horses—or possibly the gun from von Kleiser's battery that was damaged during the opening phase of the battle—became stuck in the mud. Sigel and Carlin assisted the gun crew as they tried unsuccessfully to pry it from the sticky soil. The piece was finally abandoned when Sigel ordered the men to save themselves.[141] "I tried my best to save it, and was nearly made a prisoner by the enemy's skirmishers," the general wrote.[142]

Many of the Federals thought the fastest way to safety was north along the Valley Pike and moved east in an effort to reach it. Others decided that traveling north through the muddy fields on either side of the road was a better option. If the scene around Bushong's Hill was confusion, what was unfolding along the Pike was nothing short of complete chaos. "Our army was literally routed and defeated. . . . I felt so confident of success," observed a West Virginia officer.[143] One artilleryman who gained the Pike was stunned by the confusion he found there. "Our infantry was hurrying to the rear, many of them having thrown

138 Miller, *Story of Andersonville and Florence.*

139 Fluharty, *Carlin's Wheeling Battery*, 51.

140 Wheeling *Daily Register*, May 20, 1864.

141 *Ibid.*

142 Sigel, "Sigel in the Shenandoah Valley," 490.

143 Duncan, *Alexander Neil*, 29.

away their arms—the colors were posted on a knoll, the bugler blowing assembly, officers riding madly over the field with drawn sabres threatening and shouting, a line of cavalry in the rear with drawn sabres, all endeavoring to check them but it was of no use."[144] "[I]t seemed the very gates of pandemonium," recalled a West Virginia officer, "had opened up."[145]

Colonel David Strother and other Sigel staff officers tried to stem the rout and reform the fleeing troops into some semblance of a line. One lieutenant was very liberal in applying the flat of his sword to slow some of the fugitives. When he saw that the tactic seemed to work, Strother was about to try it when the man he targeted was struck by enemy fire and fell before him. The mounted officers quickly drew enemy attention. One officer's horse was shot and killed from under him. An artillery round buried itself at the feet of Strother's mount. He had no more than escaped that brush with death when a spent bullet struck him in the chest. Heeding the warnings, Strother determined it was time to join the retreat.[146]

Throughout the fighting and during the retreat, surgeons worked tirelessly at their trade. Field hospitals close to town were now well behind Confederate lines, and wounded men walked or were carried into houses and farm buildings. Several surgeons found a house of worship (likely Cedar Grove Church), where they "did what we could for the wounded, who were hauled to us in great numbers." The 12th West Virginia's surgeon, Alexander Neil, recalled that there were "about a dozen" surgeons in addition to himself in the building. They had been working there for no more than thirty minutes, he estimated, when an officer arrived to announce that they had to relocate immediately or risk capture. Neil and the 18th Connecticut's surgeon had secured their horses in the vestibule of the church, and so were able to ride away, but not before ordering that those wounded who could be moved should be sent to the rear.[147]

Close by Cedar Grove was a small pond. In their haste to get away, a group of Federal artillerymen were trying to haul a cannon off the field. The work was slow going, and before long they realized that they were risking their own lives in the effort. In an effort to avoid capture, the gunners rolled the piece into the

---

144 Quoted in Fluharty, *Carlin's Wheeling Battery*, 51.

145 Duncan, *Alexander Neil*, 31.

146 Eby, *A Virginia Yankee in the Civil War*, 227.

147 Duncan, *Alexander Neil*, 31.

Captain Henry DuPont,
Battery B, 5th U.S. Artillery

NMBSHP

water, hoping it would fully submerge. The gun was discovered the next day by Confederates scouring the field for weapons and equipment, with just the tip of the barrel visible above the water.[148]

This final Federal line was collapsing and confusion was spreading along the Valley Pike when the head of the rear-most elements of Sigel's army under Brigadier General Jeremiah Sullivan finally arrived. It was about 3:00 p.m. In the van was Capt. Henry DuPont's Battery B, 5th U.S. Artillery. DuPont, as well as the two remaining arriving infantry regiments stretched out behind the guns (the 28th Ohio and the 116th Ohio), had spent most of the day near Mount Jackson listening to the ominous sounds of the battle raging to the south. Sometime after noon, General Sullivan received orders to bring up his infantry as rapidly as possible. For reasons that are difficult to understand, he interpreted the order literally and left DuPont's artillery behind. When Sullivan discovered his mistake, he sent word back for the artillery to come up.[149]

The scene that greeted the artillerymen was anything but encouraging. "The whole Federal line was found to be retreating in the greatest disorder, save a few regiments to the west of the turnpike which were keeping up their formation as they fell back," wrote DuPont after the war. "On the east side of the highway, the Union forces were in total rout and making for the rear in the wildest

---

148 Sager, *Battle of New Market*, 15-6. The battery to which this piece belonged has not been firmly determined, although it may have been the damaged piece from von Kleiser's battery.

149 DuPont, *Battle of New Market*, 15.

confusion—infantry and cavalry mingled with what was left of von Kleiser's battery." Unable to find Sullivan, Sigel, or any other higher ranking officer for that matter, DuPont put his West Point education to work. "I was compelled to act, and did act, upon my own judgment and of course assumed all responsibility."[150]

When he determined there was no organized rearguard, DuPont assumed the role himself. The steady rain severely limited visibility by keeping the battle smoke close to the ground like a heavy blanket of rolling gray fog. The young Delaware officer used this cloak to his advantage. Deploying artillery alone and without infantry support invites the capture of guns. Even though DuPont had no infantry support, he hoped the lingering smoke would hide that fact from the pursuing Confederates. As he put it, "It seemed necessary to risk the loss of some of my guns in order to cover and protect the retreat of the Union troops."[151]

DuPont decided upon an in-depth defense to deploy his six-gun battery. One section (two pieces) were unlimbered on a knoll just west of the Pike behind the 54th Pennsylvania's original position. Another section was deployed about 500 yards farther north, and his last two guns another 500 yards to the north. Technically speaking, he was "retiring by echelon of platoons." In layman's terms, he was leapfrogging his guns backward. The lead platoon, wrote the intrepid officer, "continued to fire with great rapidity and precision until we found ourselves entirely alone, with not a single Federal soldier in sight save the members of our own battery." At that point, DuPont directed the two lead guns to limber and move north to assume a position 500 yards behind the rear-most platoon.[152]

Dupont's clever employment of his guns worked perfectly. As an advancing Confederate observed, "The audacity of this battery caused us to think that it had a strong infantry support, and we paused to form line before advancing further."[153] DuPont's tactical display bought just enough time for Generals Sigel and Sullivan to establish a new position on Rude's Hill several miles north of New Market.

150 *Ibid.*, 16.

151 *Ibid.*, 17.

152 *Ibid.*, 17-8.

153 Colonna, "Battle of New Market," 347.

After forcing its way through the demoralized retreating troops at bayonet point, Sullivan's infantry reached Rude's Hill about 4:00 p.m.[154] "We arrived on the field just in time to witness the falling back of our little army . . . too late to do anything, except to cover the retreat of the broken up and defeated regiments," was how one Ohio officer put it.[155] The 28th Ohio and the 116th Ohio deployed on the southern slope of Rude's Hill near Cedar Grove Church, with Snow's battery unlimbering nearby.

The appearance of DuPont's battery did give the Confederates some reason to pause in their pursuit of Sigel's broken army, but the fact was that Breckinridge's troops were themselves disorganized and exhausted. About 3:15 p.m., he ordered his line halted and re-dressed.[156] "The enemy being routed, the Army move forward some distance and we were halted for reformation," remembered a Virginia lieutenant. "General Breckinridge rode up to Colonel Edgar and addressed him, ' Colonel, the men are a little scattered. I want you to detail an officer and have him take some men with him to the rear and gather up the stragglers, as I think the enemy is reforming on [Rude's] Hill, and we will have to charge them.'" Edgar tasked Lieutenant W. W. George and three or four men to carry out the assignment. George and his squad walked all the way back to town in their effort to gather every able-bodied soldier they could find to continue the pursuit.[157]

For the infantry battalion of VMI cadets the battle was over. During the pause to reorganize, orders arrived for them to resume their reserve position. They were reforming when Breckinridge rode up "splendidly mounted and accompanied by his staff," Cadet Captain Benjamin Colonna remembered. "We hastily formed line and presented arms, whereupon he raised his hat and said, 'Young gentlemen, I have to thank you for the result of today's operation.' Then he turned and rode away, taking with [him] the heart of every one of us."[158] Porter Johnson thought the part played by he and his fellow cadets was "glory enough for one day. . . . I believe ours will last to all Eternity."[159]

---

154 *OR* 37, pt. 1, 80.

155 Wildes, *Record of the One Hundred and Sixteenth Regiment Ohio Infantry Volunteers*, 87.

156 Colonna, "Battle of New Market," 347.

157 W. W. George, "Account of Battle of New Market," March 6, 1906, Edgar Papers.

158 Colonna, "Battle of New Market," 347.

159 Johnson to H. A. Wise, June 8, 1909.

* * *

After reforming broken lines and replenishing empty cartridge boxes, the Confederate pursuit of Sigel's Federals continued. "They were making tracks for the bridge as hard as they could," remembered a Virginia captain.[160] The degree to which Sigel's army had been defeated was evident everywhere: the ground was strewn with weapons and equipment of every variety, all of it abandoned during the chaotic retreat. Many of the victorious Confederates helped themselves to the spoils of war. "The earth for seven miles was spotted with capital blankets and oil cloths, knapsacks, [and] haversacks," observed one satisfied artilleryman.[161] "Most all our boys got oil cloths, overcoats and blankets, boots and so on," explained one Virginian. "I got a splendid gum cloth."[162]

Colonel George Smith of the 62nd Virginia found his cousin George Patton, commander of the 22nd Virginia, and the two colonels walked together behind their advancing regiments. "As we pressed forward in pursuit of the enemy," Smith recalled, "Genl. Breckinridge galloped up and alighted from his horse, insisted that one of us should mount, saying he was ashamed to be on horseback while the men who had borne the brunt of the fight were walking; he then, throwing the reins over his arm, continued with us."[163] By then, however, contact had been lost with the Federals.

When he realized the Federals were fleeing the field, Imboden decided to check in with General Breckinridge and advise the Confederate commander that the cavalry had not been successful in gaining the Federal rear. The flooded waters of Smith's Creek had prevented Imboden's horsemen from crossing into the rear of Sigel's army and cutting off its retreat. In fact, after McClanahan's Battery drove off Stahel's Federal cavalry from its advanced position close to New Market, Imboden accomplished next to nothing. Although the consequence of moving the horsemen east of the creek was not fully realized by either general at the time, the decision deprived Breckinridge of his cavalry when he needed it the most: to pursue and cut apart the fleeing Federals.

160 Staunton *Spectator & Vindicator*, May 20, 1904; Carr to Edgar, March 25, 1906.

161 Woods to "Father," May 16, 1864.

162 Thomas W. Fisher to "Dear Parents," May 18, 1864, Gardner collection.

163 Smith to Edgar, March 16, 1906.

Riding back to the west of Smith's Creek, Imboden found the Kentuckian "on foot and muddy to the waist" near McLaughlin's artillery in an orchard south of Rude's Hill. "Whilst we were talking over the events of the day," Imboden later wrote, "several shells, aimed at McLaughlin, passed over him and exploded in the orchard near us. I expostulated with the general for so unnecessarily exposing himself, when, by moving one hundred yards to the right or left, he would be out of the line of fire. He laughed and said it was too muddy anywhere else than in that orchard . . . and that he would rather risk stray shells than wade in the mud again."[164]

Because his cavalry had nothing left to accomplish on the far side of Smith's Creek, Imboden returned his command to the Pike. McClanahan's guns, which had not pushed as far north as the 18th and 23rd Virginia Cavalry regiments, rejoined the main body first. An officer in the 18th noted that "it was unfortunate . . . that the cavalry had [to] go back over the ground, crossing the bridge and passing over the whole field of battle before they could reach the front, which made it too late to reap the fruits of victory completely."[165]

The rain was still falling when the reformed Confederates stepped within range of the guns on Rude's Hill, which promptly opened fire. Skirmishers advanced to develop Sigel's new position. The last thing Sigel was seeking was another fight—especially with a swollen river immediately at his back and only one bridge to cross it. About 6:00 p.m., what remained of his small army began crossing the bridge to the north bank of the Shenandoah River.[166] Sigel positioned most, if not all, of his remaining artillery—less DuPont's battery, which was still bringing up the rear—on the high ground immediately north of the bridge to cover the crossing of his infantry and cavalry.

Hoping to inflict as much damage on the retreating enemy as possible, Confederate skirmishers pressed on. They were too late. "[O]n reaching the top of the hill the rear of the enemy's column could be seen crossing the bridge," reported Breckinridge.[167] With darkness approaching, Chapman's Battery and the two VMI guns, together with McClanahan's horse artillery, unlimbered on Rude's Hill to harass the retreating Federals as much as possible. "I could see

---

164 Imboden, "The Battle of New Market, VA, May 15, 1864," 484-5.

165 Pratt to Colonna, November 19, 1910.

166 *OR 37*, pt. 1, 76.

167 Breckinridge's Official New Market Report.

the long bottom before us filed with fugitives," wrote one of McClanahan's gunners. "Now we had everything our way; the poor, panic-stricken wretches were flying before us in easy range of our guns and relentlessly we poured shot and shell into them. We continued our deadly fire on them until they crossed the bridge and burned it behind them. We put in our deadly last shots as they were pouring like frightened cattle across the bridge." One of the Federal return shells struck a blow that was visible and audible for a long distance. According to Lieutenant Frederick G. Thrasher, "Charles Dixon was badly burned when [an] ammunition chest blew up. He was at his post cutting forage."[168]

One postwar account claims that Breckinridge rebuked Captain Chapman earlier in the fight for not being as aggressive as the general both wanted and needed him to be. If so, the verbal slap must have stung deeply, and at this late stage in the battle the young officer was trying his best to revive his reputation.[169] According to John G. Stevens of Chapman's Battery, however, Breckinridge never chastised the captain—though he did spend time with the battery, ordering it to cease fire during a duel with enemy guns.

During the firing, one of the cannoneers turned to Stevens and yelled, "The General says to cease firing."

Stevens, who had not heard any order, looked around and spotted General Breckinridge on his horse just behind him. "General, did you say to stop firing?"

Breckinridge affirmed the order. "I don't want you to waste your ammunition."

"General, what do you want us to do?" Stevens asked, unsure what he meant.

"I want you to go closer," answered the army commander.

The reply stunned Stevens, who thought they were already "a little close then, for me." Willing to move any place to get away from where they were, the gunner responded, "General, we will do whatever you say to do."

"Well," replied Breckinridge before riding off, "come on with me, then."

---

168 Frederick G. Thrasher to Edgar, Edgar Papers. Henderson Reed, in a letter to Edgar dated June 12, 1908, *ibid.*, confirmed the explosion (he called it a limber chest), as did John G. Stevens in his June 2, 1908, letter to Edgar, *ibid.*, who wrote, "A shell from a Yankee battery blew up one of our caissons." Driver, *Staunton Artillery*, 89.

169 Minge to Edgar, June 5, 1908; A. S. Johnston, *Captain Beirne Chapman and Chapman's Battery* (Union, WV, 1903), 19-20.

When Stevens realized that Chapman was not with the guns—why is unclear—and no one of rank was present to issue the directive, he took it upon himself to do so. "[A]s I had command of only one gun, I gave the command to both guns to limber up and forward march," explained Stevens.

After the war, Stevens wrote a report of New Market for Colonel Edgar. "I have somewhere read the statement that General Breckinridge said to Captain Chapman that day that he wished he (Chapman) would take his guns where he could hurt somebody," explained the former gunner. "I feel quite sure that General Breckinridge said nothing of the kind, but I know he did say to me just what I have written."[170]

Just as the battle opened with a gunnery duel, so too did it close with one. the fitful firing dying out when the growing darkness put an end to the contest. "We were severely whipt [sic]. . . . The battle was a disgraceful affair at best," wrote an embarrassed surgeon with the 1st New York Veteran Cavalry.[171]

Moving at the end of the withdrawing Federal column, DuPont's artillery reached the bridge about 7:00 p.m. The gunners were preparing to destroy the structure when DuPont noticed a cavalry company lounging nearby south of the span to no particular apparent purpose. He dispatched a courier to inform its commanding officer that if they wished to cross the bridge, now would be the time to do so for it was about to be destroyed. The officer was lingering behind to garner the honor of being the last to cross, and was apparently annoyed that DuPont was about to deprive him of the honor (an honor DuPont would forever after claim for himself).

Once the mounted men were across, DuPont's artillerists consigned the bridge to flames.[172]

---

170 SOR, 6, 870. In his history of Chapman's Battery, Scott uses the oft-quoted "kill somebody" account but does not mention Stevens' version. J. L. Scott, *Lowry's, Bryan's and Chapman's Batteries of Virginia Artillery* (Lynchburg, VA, 1988), 81.

171 L. J. Alleman diary, May 15, 1864, NMBSHP.

172 DuPont, *Battle of New Market*, 18-20. The mounted officer was identified by Franz Sigel as simply "Captain Battersby," who noted his company was "the last to cross the bridge." His full name and unit was J. C. Battersby, 1st New York (Lincoln) Cavalry.

Chapter 10

"Fame!"

As the sound of gunfire died away in the Valley about 7:00 p.m. that Sunday, John Breckinridge sent word of his victory to Richmond:

This morning, two miles above New Market, my command met the enemy, under General Sigel, advancing up the Valley, and defeated him with heavy loss. The action has just closed at Shenandoah River. Enemy fled across North Fork of the Shenandoah, burning the bridge behind him.[1]

The exhausted Confederate troops quickly went into bivouac on Rude's Hill, trying to get what sleep they could in the mud.[2] "When we came off the field we were completely exhausted," recalled one cadet. "I often wished that an artist could have been present, that our little group could have been taken, just as we came off the field of battle, with our faces covered with mud and powder. We presented quite a grotesque and frightful aspect. . . . My pants and jacket . . . were caked over with mud."[3]

---

1   *OR* 37, pt. 1, 87. Although this is listed in the *Official Records* as "Report of Maj. Gen. John C. Breckinridge," it is nothing more than a telegraphic notification of the battle. Breckinridge's official report, as explained earlier in Chapter Four, was written by his staff officer J. Stoddard Johnston, but was not formerly submitted to the Richmond War Department before the end of the conflict.

2   Breckinridge, Official New Market Report.

3   Richmond *Daily Whig,* June 22, 1864.

The cadet was one of the fortunate soldiers who escaped serious injury or death at New Market. Combined, casualties for both sides totaled about 1,350. Federal losses were reported as 97 killed, 440 wounded, and 225 missing, for a total of 762.[4] Confederate losses are much harder to determine because Breckinridge's unpublished report is incomplete, and except for VMI's Lieutenant Colonel S. Ship, no other Southern commanders submitted official reports. Best estimates place Confederate losses from all causes at about 600. One casualty return places Breckinridge's loss at 587.[5]

Other Southerners set out to look for food or for wounded or missing comrades. Some made their way into New Market. "We were very kindly treated by the citizens . . . where ladies took us to their houses and treated us as if we were their brothers," observed one of the cadets.[6] "I entered the town and found it filled with soldiers," John Wise remembered. "In a side street, a great throng of Federal prisoners was corralled. . . . Every type of prisoner was there; some cheerful, some defiant, some careless, some calm and dejected."[7]

Cadet Moses Ezekiel, the first Jewish cadet at VMI and later in life a sculptor of world renown, sought out his wounded roommate, Thomas G. Jefferson, who had fallen with a serious chest wound near the Bushong house. Unable to find Jefferson where he had been wounded, Ezekiel searched a nearby house and located him there. Knowing that Jefferson would not survive without medical attention, Ezekiel sought out one of the ladies of the house for assistance. Together they transported the wounded cadet into town in an ox cart, probably in search of Solon Henkel, the town doctor. Jefferson ended up in a bed in the Clinedinst home. Despite a surgeon's personal attention, the young man's wounds proved mortal. Ezekiel remained with his roommate throughout the night. At Jefferson's request, Ezekiel read from the New Testament. He was still reading when Jefferson took his last breath early on the morning of May 17.[8]

---

4   Gailey, casualty report, NMBSHP. Federal casualties were higher than reported. Colonel Campbell of the 54th Pennsylvania noted that thirty of his men were "lightly wounded" and not included in the 174 total he officially reported. *OR* 37, pt. 1, 87.

5   "Losses of Confederates in the Battle of New Market," Sigel Papers.

6   Richmond *Daily Whig*, June 22, 1864.

7   Wise, *End of an Era*, 304.

8   *Shenandoah Valley*, June 23, 1921.

Cadet Moses Ezekiel, who cared for his dying roommate,
Cadet Thomas G. Jefferson. *VMI Archives*

Another myth of New Market would arise surrounding Jefferson's death. In 1926, an elderly Eliza Crim (who was a much younger Eliza Clinedinst at the time of the battle) wrote her recollections of New Market for *Confederate Veteran* magazine. In it, she recalled going out onto the field to collect a wounded cadet (Jefferson) and, accompanied by Ezekiel, bring him back to her house for medical treatment. After Jefferson died in Ezekiel's arms, she wrote a lengthy letter to Jefferson's mother recounting her son's final hours. Moved by the letter, Jefferson's mother wrote back inviting Eliza to come visit the Jefferson's Amelia County home. She accepted the invitation and took with her Jefferson's

Cadet Thomas G. Jefferson,
one of ten cadets who lost their lives at New Market. *VMI Archives*

coat and the bullet that killed him. According to Eliza, she remained there for nearly a year. When the war came to Amelia Country during the final days of the conflict, Eliza walked home to New Market from Lynchburg, aiding Confederate soldiers along the way.[9]

---

9   Eliza Crim, "Tender Memories of the VMI Cadets," *Confederate Veteran*, June 1926, 213.

Eliza Clinedinst Crim, who took in the dying Cadet Thomas G. Jefferson.
VMI Archives

Her's was a very dramatic tale—but it never happened, at least not the way she described it. When Ezekiel first got wind of the tale more than two decades before it appeared in print, he dismissed the story outright. "It all sounds very beautiful—but there is much more poetry than truth in it," he wrote. "Lydie Clinedinst now Mrs. Crim never was on the bloody battlefield and she never nursed nor attended to Jefferson at all . . . nor did she get his last words. In fact it is all fabrication." Word of Jefferson's death did indeed reach his family, as did his personal effects, but only because of Ezekiel's efforts. Eliza's story was believed by many people and had an aura of truth surrounding it, so much so that she became known as the "Mother of the New Market Cadets."[10] She was also the guest of honor at the dedication of a monument to the fallen cadets at Lexington in 1903, which helped to give her story even more attention.[11] And thus Eliza Clinedinst (Crim) contributed her own chapter to the aura surrounding the cadets at New Market.

Cadet Louis Wise, younger brother of Capt. Henry Wise, sought out medical treatment for himself in town. There, he found several dozen of his comrades in one hospital being tended to by acting superintendent William Gilham. Wise, who thought his wound to be serious, was taken aback when Gilham informed him that it "was only a 'parlor wound' and would entitle me to only a short furlough."[12]

Lieutenant Colonel George Edgar of the 26th Virginia Battalion eventually made his way back to town to check on his own wounded. While there, the adrenaline of the day's activities wore off and he collapsed into one of the hospital beds for some much needed rest. Surrounded by the horrors of the field hospital, with "the surgeons at their ghastly work," however, proved too much even for this veteran officer and after a short time he roused himself and left.[13]

Those who ventured back over the battlefield, particularly around the Bushong farm, were greeted by even worse sights than anything found in the field hospitals. Drawn by curiosity, John Wise and several other cadets ventured back toward the orchard.

"We came upon the dead bodies of three cadets," wrote Wise,

one wearing the chevrons of a first sergeant lay upon his face, stiff and stark, with outstretched arms. His hands had clutched and torn up great tufts of soil and grass. His lips were retracted; his teeth tightly locked; his face as hard as flint, with staring, glassy eyes. It was difficult to recognize that this was all that remained of Cabell, who a few hours before had stood first in his class, second as a soldier, and the peer of any boy in the command in every trait of physical and moral manliness. A short distance removed from the spot where Cabell fell, and nearer to the position of the enemy, lay

10 Moses Ezekiel to Sallie B. Harbaugh, September 3, 1904, NM Coll., VMI.

11 Staunton *Spectator*, June 19, 1903.

12 L. C. Wise to J. R. Anderson, August 27, 1909.

13 Lowry, *26th Battalion Virginia Infantry*, 40.

McDowell.[14] It was a sight to rend one's heart! That little fellow was lying there asleep, more fit indeed for a cradle than a grave. . . . He had torn open his jacket and shirt, and even in death, lay clutching them back, exposing a fair, white breast with its red wound. We had come too late. Stanard had breathed his last but a few moments before. . . . His body was still warm, and his last messages had been words of love to his room-mates. Poor Jack—playmate, room-mate, friend—farewell!"[15]

Stanard's death struck Wise particularly hard, for it was he who had convinced his friend to slip away from the relative safety of guarding the supply wagon and enter the fight. Wise and his fellow cadets gathered the bodies of their dead friends and carried them into town.[16]

Because of Sigel's retreat, many of the Federal wounded had been left on the field. Edmund Snyder, a wounded soldier with the 123rd Ohio, had been left by his comrades at the Cline home, a rather wealthy family by Valley standards whose patriarch was a preacher, the oldest son a physician, and the youngest son a soldier in the Confederate army. He left this account of what he found there:

I shall never forget my first night under the hospitable roof of that quiet old farmhouse. The consecutive nights of arduous picket duty, the two preceding days of hard, fatiguing marching in the mud and rain, the nerve-racking excitement of the battle with its roar and confusion and the disordered rush of the broken and utterly demoralized battalions as they crowded the pike and scattered over the adjacent fields in a senseless, fear-inspired race for the rear and safety, had completely unnerved me, and, lulled to sleep by the soft patter of the steadily falling rain on the rook, I slept the dull, heavy sleep of complete exhaustion. When I awoke the next morning the sun was shining brightly and the birds singing, and it seemed to me that I had alighted in Elysian Fields. Shortly after I awoke the old man came into the room and after inquiring how I felt, said 'Well, sir, your army got across the river and burned the bridge, and now, sir, it will be my duty to take care of you until you are able to be

14 The death of William H. McDowell, one of the slain cadets Wise found on the field, was used by children's author Elaine Alphin as the basis for her book *Ghost Cadet* (New York, 1991). When 17-year-old McDowell's body was discovered, both his gold pocket watch and Bible were missing, neither of which were ever found. It is in search of his lost watch that the ghost of McDowell comes back to haunt the battlefield at New Market. Rebecca McDowell to "My Dear Aunt," July 25, 1864, transcript in VMI Archives.

15 Wise, *End of an Era*, 307.

16 *Ibid.*

moved and then I shall have to turn you over to our folks. Of course,' he added, 'you are our enemy, but just now you are in our lines and it is my duty to take care of you.'[17]

After a stay of ten days with the family, the soldier was taken into town and kept in a vacant store with other wounded Union soldiers. He would spend the remainder of the war in the prison camp at Andersonville. Before he left, however, he gave the Cline daughters a photograph of himself to show to any Federal troops, partly to prove that he had survived his wound, and partly for protection, for it would show that they had taken care of a Federal soldier.[18]

Some of the townspeople scoured the battlefield to administer aid to the wounded. When Southern casualties began to crowd the Rupert home on Main St., Solomon Rupert and a neighbor left armed with bandages, bread, and whiskey, with instructions from Jessie Rupert to aid the wounded Federals still on the field while she tended to their infant son and the wounded soldiers in their home.

Solomon spent all night tending to the maimed, moving many of the unfortunates into a barn near where they fell (presumably on the Bushong property). Sometime after midnight, Jessie received a message from her husband that they needed to find a place to move and treat the wounded Federals. Hoping that General Imboden would help her, Jessie decided to set out and find him. Main Street, she soon discovered, was "crowded with weeping and excited people. There were dead and wounded men, and dead horses and broken down cannon, and many other evidences of the fearful struggle." She eventually found the cavalry officer, who gave her permission to take any vacant space she could find for her purpose. Jessie found an unused warehouse, but the owner refused to open it for her, vowing "that the whole Confederate army was not strong enough to take it for such a purpose." When a company of Confederate troops marched past, Jessie explained the situation to a captain. Irritated by the boorish behavior of the building owner, the officer told his company to "pitch into that door and open it for this lady." Not willing to let her new-found ally go just yet, Jessie convinced the officer to have his men carry straw from a nearby barn to cover the floor of the warehouse.[19] Within a

17 Snyder, *Autobiography of a Soldier of the Civil War*, 14.

18 *Ibid.*,17-9.

19 Rupert, *The Battle of New Market*.

short time the building became the primary location in town for the care of wounded Union soldiers.

One of the wounded Union soldiers who probably owed his life to Jessie Rupert was Corporal Ensign Smith of the 34th Massachusetts. Smith was wounded twice in the battle, once in the foot and again in the chest. The second bullet penetrated his lung and passed completely through him. He was left on the field by his comrades, who assumed he was dead or soon would be. Instead of expiring, Smith crawled to a remote spot on the field and was not found for more than a day. Monday evening he was discovered by a Confederate chaplain. Smith asked the man to seek out Jessie Rupert who, as some of his comrades had discovered just before the battle, was from their hometown of Pittsfield, Massachusetts. When she learned of Smith's plight, Jessie dispatched her husband to find the corporal and bring him to their home. By the time Solomon returned with the wounded Smith the next morning, the soldier was near death. Jessie did all that she could to make him comfortable, but everyone thought his death was imminent. The following morning when they prepared to add Smith to a cart holding soldiers who had died during the night, they discovered he was alive still. Beyond all expectations he began to recover and eventually was well enough to be transported to a hospital in Harrisonburg with other wounded Federal troops. For two months, Smith sucked part of every breath through the gunshot wound in his chest. In early August he escaped from the hospital and spent two weeks making his way north, finally encountering Union lines at New Creek, West Virginia. He married while convalescing at home and returned to duty—without being exchanged—as a courier for General Philip Sheridan. Smith named his first-born son "Rupert" in honor of the family that had saved his life at New Market.[20]

The selfless efforts of the Ruperts saved countless lives. "Mrs. Rupert was very kind to our wounded left upon the battlefield," wrote a Federal officer several weeks later. "Her rare humanity on that occasion, to these sufferers, deserves the best of treatment at the hands of all officers and soldiers in this Department."[21] William Hall, the surgeon of the 54th Pennsylvania, was left in charge of these Federal wounded. He was assisted by local physician Solon Henkel. Dr. Hall later testified to the kind treatment he and his wounded

20 Don Polly, *Corporal Ensign Marshall Smith's Story*, courtesy of Don Polly, Leesburg, Florida.

21 Special orders, June 1, 1864, by order of Major General Hunter, by P. G. Bier, AAG, copy courtesy of Richard Bazelow, Wolden, New York.

charges received not just from the Ruperts, but from several other local families. "We have received the kindest attention and every care possible . . . They have taken our wounded to their houses and have fed them from their private stores. . . . They have sought out our wounded—in barns, outhouses, or where ever the fortunes of war left them—and have labored . . . to ameliorate their sufferings."[22] The tedious and exhausting work left in the hands of the doctors was written up by Dr. Henkel, who said he "assisted in the Federal Hospital three months in attending to wounded. Operated frequently, amputated several limbs, took up femoral artery in two cases. Furnished medicine and other comforts to the sick and wounded."[23]

One of the wounded Federals assisted by local Valley residents was a wounded member of the 21st New York Cavalry. Long after the war, he wrote to the Zerkel family to express his thanks for their care:

> Your family did all that they could for our sick + wounded men and I ask you to convey my heartfelt thanks to them for what they did . . . I can never forget the times that I saw them, young as I was in my 15th year, I had never read, or seen, or heard described anything of that kind of suffering + death. I was twice disable myself on that raid. . . . I saw comrades with portions of the body torn away, many with the limbs shot away close to the body and one who while in the act of firing his musket had been hit with an exploding shell, a portion of it striking his gun at the same time changing it into fragments, another with both lower limbs torn away; the body had so long been exposed to the burning sun that its flesh had come away from the wound having the bone protruding. I could make a drawing of the position of every sufferer in that old building.[24]

Lieutenant Colonel Charles O'Ferrall of the 23rd Virginia Cavalry got a chance to return a favor the night after the battle. His mother lived at Berkeley Springs, West Virginia, an area occupied for a time by the 54th Pennsylvania. In a letter to her son, she mentioned that Colonel Campbell and Capt. William Bonacker of that regiment had been most kind to her and requested that her son look after these two officers should they ever be captured by his command.

22 Sworn statement of Charles G. Allen, William B. Bonacker, William E. Hall, May 28, 1864, copy at NMBSHP.

23 List of items belonging to Solon P. C. Henkel taken by Union forces, undated, Henkel Papers, VMI.

24 Franklin DeBell to Samuel Zerkel, January 23, 1890, copy at NMBSHP.

When he learned that the 54th had been heavily engaged during the battle, O'Ferrall located their position on the field and inquired as to the fate of the two officers. A wounded Pennsylvanian informed the Virginian that Captain Bonacker had fallen wounded on the field. The news sent O'Ferrall hunting for the wounded officer, "the friend and protector of my mother and sisters."

Within less than ten minutes O'Ferrall "found a captain lying in a depression in the field, his knapsack under his head and a canteen of water at his side. Somehow I felt sure he was the man for whom I was searching."

The Confederate bent down over the prostrated enemy officer. "You are Captain Bonacker. Am I not correct?"

Bonacker, probably a tad surprised that a Southerner would be asking him such a question, replied feebly, "Yes, that is my name; why do you ask?"

"Captain, I am Colonel O'Ferrall, and I intend to take care of you."

The wounded officer lifted his hand and O'Ferrall shook it. "You are doing just what your mother told me her son would do if occasion ever arose and he had the opportunity."

O'Ferrall set off in search of an ambulance to carry the wounded Bonacker off the field. A bed was procured at the home of Frederick Zeiler, a friend of the Ruperts. O'Ferrall remained with Bonacker until the next morning.[25]

One of the largest field hospitals was established at the Bushong house and barn, the epicenter of the heaviest fighting on May 15. The house was filled with the wounded and dying of both sides and was the first place many visitors traveled to inquire after friends and loved ones suspected of having fallen in the battle.

Mrs. Allmon Sager, the wife of Imboden's wagon driver, made the trek to New Market the morning after the battle after listening to the rumble of artillery thirty miles away at her home in Mathias, West Virginia. Once she arrived she inquired after her husband (as well as neighbors in his unit) and was directed to the Bushong house. "On reaching the vicinity, sadness appeared to overshadow the area," wrote her son decades later in a lengthy account of her visit. "Work was suspended; farmers were not moving about their premises. Only a few people were seen and they visibly showed their inward grief."

When Mrs. Sager explained her mission, locals directed her to the Bushong House with the words, "Those people will be glad to help you." When she arrived at the yard gate, a teenager walked out to the gate, got her information, and went back inside. A lady hesitant, and visibly perplexed, walked out of the home towards the visitor.

"I'm Mrs. Sager from over the mountains. I'm trying to find my husband; he is with General Imboden. I heard the battle yesterday and I'm so worried as to his safety."

"I'm Mrs. Bushong," she replied. "Please come in with me. I shall be so glad to help you."

Mrs. Sager had no idea she was walking into a field hospital. Once inside, she found the rooms on the first floor jammed with wounded men and, as she would soon learn, the barn as well. "Some were weeping, some were praying and some were cursing," recalled her son. Surgeons had converted one of the lower rooms into an operating room, "cutting and sewing without anesthetics." The moans and screams and prayers and cursing were too much for Mrs. Sager, who eventually broke into tears. As she cried, Mrs. Bushong examined the list of names of all the casualties within her care. Imboden's wagon driver was not among them.

"I will have a note ready for you to take to General Imboden," Mrs. Bushong told her. A short time later she handed a young man a slip of paper. "Rush up to town with all speed and locate the general and give him the note," she instructed.

When Imboden got the message, "the generous and noble general he was, called his courier and ordered him, in all haste to locate Father and tell him to report to the Bushong home immediately." Mrs. Sager ended up remaining with the Bushongs for several days to help care for the wounded.[26]

The Rev. Socrates Henkel was another local resident who tended to the hundreds of unfortunate wounded. During his rounds he encountered General Breckinridge and invited the Southern commander to use his home at the corner of Main St. and Depot St. as his headquarters, an offer the general accepted.[27]

Many of the Union dead were buried, some ratherly sloppily, in mass graves. When Federal troops marched through New Market later in the war, they discovered "in a lime kiln . . . about 30 of our dead, mostly with their faces down and had a slight covering of earth over them but not enough to hide them

26 Sager, *Battle of New Market*, 19-20.

27 Elon O. Henkel to B. A. Colonna, November 27, 1910, NM Coll., VMI; William A. Good, *Grantees of Early New Market Lots* (Broadway, VA, 1997), 16.

from view."[28] Many others were buried in a mass grave in a ravine immediately behind the 54th Pennsylvania's position near the Lightfoot house.[29] Assistant Surgeon L. J. Alleman of the 1st New York Veteran Cavalry discovered that many of the Federal dead had been thrown into crevices between rocks, and that the incessant rains had washed away much of the dirt put over the bodies and "occasionally an arm or leg protruded above the mound."[30]

*   *   *

Even though they now had the Shenandoah River between them and their pursuers, there was little rest for the defeated Federals reorganizing several miles to the north. Sigel maintained a defensive front on the ridges north of the river, but his position could be turned, so he ordered another retreat.[31] About 9:00 p.m., the weary troops headed for Edinburg, with a rearguard composed of five companies from the 116th Ohio, a section of artillery, and a cavalry escort, all under the command of the 116th's Colonel James Washburn.[32]

Many of the Federals had spent much of the day standing in line of battle and fighting in a pouring rain, and in some cases had marched nearly twenty miles just to get into the battle—most with little or nothing to eat. As a result, more marching was simply not possible for many of Sigel's enervated troops. "We were all soaked to the skin from the heavy rain, completely exhausted by the long and most strenuous days work," recalled a New York cavalryman, who left an interesting account of his experience that night after the battle:

> A great fire of fence rails was burning in a field just north of the town [Mount Jackson] and I felt that I would risk losing everything— everything in the world, even life itself, for the drying comfort of that fire. It was then dark and I slipped out of the ranks unnoticed, tied my old mare to a post at the side of the road and ran over to that fire. Oh, how good it felt; my wet clothes began steaming and in five minutes I fell asleep. An officer of our rear guard awoke me and told me to skip along if I didn't want to be captured. I ran over to where I had left my old mare but she was gone and I never saw

28 Quesenberry, *A Snowball's Chance*, 191.

29 Graves, *Around New Market*, 32.

30 Alleman diary, May 30, 1864.

31 *OR* 37, pt. 1, 76.

32 *Ibid.*, 80.

her again . . . I had my carbine, revolver and saber and as I started down the road afoot, I threw the carbine into a large pond of water so had one less thing to carry. For an hour I marched along with the rear guard—an infantry detachment who had half a dozen Confederate prisoners. Every mile or so we stopped to rest for about five minutes, and these prisoners asked to be allowed to sit down, which was denied them. Thinking that I was an officer because I was carrying a sword they appealed to me. I said that I had no objection and then they were allowed to sit down. I stole away in the dark before they discovered that I was not an officer and I climbed over a fence and lay down in some bushes for I felt that must have rest and sleep no matter what the risk.[33]

Two Ohio soldiers set off in search of something to eat and, returning to the Valley Pike, found themselves a good distance ahead of the retreating column "at the heels of Sigel and his generals, making good time." When they had put enough distance between themselves and the Confederates, one of them wrote, "Not the most powerful gun in the Confederacy could have reached Dave, me, or the Generals who led."[34]

The army's demoralization and confusion was apparent to all and admitted to by even its senior commanders. "The manner in which this chaotic mass of wagons, horsemen, artillery, and stragglers moved on (sometimes two or three wagons abreast) was exceedingly fatiguing to the infantry," reported Colonel Augustus Moor, commander of the First Brigade. This was "especially [so] to those regiments that marched out with me on the 14th, they having been continually on their legs for two days and nights without a cup of coffee or even meat rations, numbers of them barefooted."[35]

Throughout the long retreat nearly all the civilians they encountered greeted the soldiers with derision. "The people of this valley are all jubilant over this disaster to our arms," noted a West Virginia officer, "and were tickled almost out of their senses at seeing us on our way back."[36]

When the column rested at Edinburg that night, many of the senior officers of the 1st New York Veteran Cavalry, including L. J. Alleman, the regiment's assistant surgeon, shared accommodations with Generals Sigel and Stahel. Alleman was more than a little bitter about the way the army had been handled,

---

33 Lester, *Autobiography of Jacob Lester*, 10.

34 Gerald Earley, *I Belonged to the 116th* (Bowie, MD, 2004), 72-3.

35 *OR* 37, pt. 1, 81.

36 Duncan, Alexander *Neil*, 32.

and the cavalry in particular, and so was in no mood to put up with the generals. The doctor had just fallen asleep when orders arrived to continue the retreat. Before mounting, Alleman and his comrades "made some coffee and supplied the Gen [Sigel] and staff . . . and Stahl [sic] with the same beverage. I heard General Stahl say that he hoped there would be enough for them," Alleman scribbled in his journal. "I think the old cuss ought to have been satisfied and especially after receiving as solid a whipping as he did."[37]

Many of the Federal wounded were left in the vast Confederate hospital compound on the northern edge of Mount Jackson, where three buildings were filled with as many as 300 wounded soldiers. The medical staff worked throughout the night to save as many men as they could, sending lightly wounded men north after the column. When they finished their first round of work, about 100 were left under the care of Dr. Charles Allen, the assistant surgeon of the 34th Massachusetts.[38]

Sigel's column marched all night. When the leading elements reached Woodstock about 6:00 a.m., the Federals rested in their old camps until the middle of the afternoon. By nightfall the army was once again at its old camp grounds along the northern banks of Cedar Creek between Strasburg and Middletown.[39]

About the same time that Sigel's army reached familiar ground around Belle Grove plantation and Cedar Creek, General Ulysses S. Grant was wondering why he had not heard recently from his commander in the Shenandoah. It had been several days since Sigel last telegraphed the general-in-chief asking for the latest clarification on what, exactly, he was supposed to be doing in the Valley. Two days after the defeat at New Market—apparently Grant had yet to receive word about the defeat, even though Sigel had telegraphed Washington on the night of the battle—Grant inquired of his superiors, "Cannot General Sigel go up the Shenandoah Valley to Staunton? The enemy is evidently drawing supplies largely from that source, and if Sigel can destroy the road there, it will be of vast importance."[40] The reply from General Halleck increased Grant's disgust with Sigel. "Just when I was hoping to hear of good work being done in

---

37 Alleman diary, May 15, 1864.

38 Duncan, *Alexander Neil*, 31.

39 Campbell diary, May 15-6, 1864.

40 *OR* 37, pt. 1, 475.

the Valley, I received instead the following announcement from Halleck: 'Sigel is in full retreat on Strasburg. He will do nothing but run; never did anything else.'"[41] Grant immediately requested that Sigel be relieved of his command, "and someone else put in his place."[42]

Sigel, however, interpreted his defeat as nothing more than a temporary setback, or at least he presented it that way. "We were beaten but not disheartened," he insisted.[43] Regardless of how or for whom he spun it, Sigel had not only lost the confidence of his superiors, but had lost the confidence of most of the officers and men in his defeated army. "How uncertain are my prophesies," lamented a West Virginian just hours after the disastrous battle ended. "Thought this morning that we could whip anything in the Valley and would go right on to Staunton. But how different."[44] "Very few of us wanted to fight any more 'mit Sigel,'" confessed an Ohio officer. "Had he gotten his army well in hand at first, and given battle with it," he concluded, "he might have been victorious."[45]

Artillerist Henry DuPont agreed with these sentiments. The gunner noted Sigel's "habitual carelessness and lack of information in regard to the details of his command."[46] In addition, DuPont continued, "the military administration of his command was very far from working smoothly and efficiently. His spectacular appearances on horseback surrounded by a brilliant but largely incompetent staff and followed by a cavalry escort, did not succeed, as he had apparently hoped would be the case, in inspiring the confidence and good will of those under his command."[47]

These were not isolated instances of disgust for Sigel's ability as a field commander. Other officers were equally repulsed by the performance of Sigel and some of his generals. "There is not an officer of my acquaintance but says that the General Officers did not know what they were about," Colonel William Tibbits wrote to his brother. "The manner in which this army has been

---

41 Grant, *Personal Memoirs of U. S. Grant*, vol. 2, 147.

42 *Ibid.*, 238.

43 Hewitt, *History of the Twelfth Regiment West Virginia Volunteer Infantry*, 113.

44 Reader diary, May 15, 1864.

45 Wildes, *Record of the One Hundred and Sixteenth Regiment Ohio Infantry Volunteers*, 87-88.

46 DuPont, *Battle of New Market*, 20-21.

47 *Ibid.*, 28.

commanded should be investigated."[48] Another officer gave that knife a turn when he penned, "There was no trace of cowardice in General Sigel, just as there certainly was none of generalship."[49] Staffer David Strother spared nothing in his post-battle assessment. "The campaign was conducted miserably by Sigel," he wrote. "[He] is merely a book soldier acquainted with the techniques of the art of war but having no capacity to fight with the troops in the field. . . . We can afford to lose a battle such as New Market to get rid of such a mistake as Major General Sigel."[50]

During the retreat, Sigel received word from General George Crook of his victory at Cloyds Mountain on May 9, 1864. The success and subsequent destruction of part of the railroad prompted staff officer David Strother to remark, "We are doing a good business in this department. Averell is tearing up the Virginia & Tennessee Railroad while Sigel is tearing down the Valley Pike." This remark made the rounds in camp for quite a while. When he heard the joke and traced it to its source, Sigel threatened Strother with a court-martial.[51]

In an effort to regain the reins of army control, the German general resumed drill and inspections. Sigel used the latter to praise his men. During an inspection of the 34th Massachusetts, for example, the commanding general announced, "I for the first time saw the 34th Massachusetts regiment under fire on the 15th, and I am bound to state that it is the best regiment and has the best commanding officer I have ever seen."[52]

Generals Grant and Halleck, however, had already made up their minds. Sigel had lived up to the doubts they had harbored about him before the campaign even began. Grant submitted Major General David Hunter's name as a possible replacement. On the afternoon of May 18, just three days after the defeat, Grant received word from Washington that Hunter was acceptable to the Lincoln administration.[53] Grant's reply demonstrated just how much he wanted Sigel out of the picture: "By all means I would say appoint General

---

48 William Tibbits to Dudley Tibbits, May 28, 1864, Author's Collection.

49 Halpine, *Baked Meats of the Funeral*, 301.

50 Eby, *A Virginia Yankee in the Civil War*, 229-30.

51 *Ibid.*, 229; Halpine, *Baked Meats of the Funeral*, 300-1.

52 Springfield *Daily Republican*, May 27, 1864.

53 *OR* 37, pt. 1, 485.

Hunter, or anyone else, to the command of West Virginia." It was official. Sigel was out.[54]

Not everyone was ready to throw Sigel overboard. When rumors of his replacement began to circulate, some in the ranks were saddened. "I do not like the idea of losing General Sigel," wrote one West Virginian. When word came down that he had indeed been replaced, the same soldier wrote, "The troops are very much dissatisfied at losing General Sigel."[55] One officer wrote to Sigel, "We have no objection to Genl. [sic] Hunter . . . yet we believe great injustice has been done you. . . . Your opposers [sic] have put the worst possible construction on the Battle of New Market."[56] "General Halleck . . . will not allow you to succeed in any department," wrote another.[57] Even Colonel Strother was moved when he turned in his last report. "The tears were standing in [Sigel's] eyes and his lips were quivering," wrote the staff officer. "He said it were better to have died on that battlefield than to have suffered this disgrace. I felt touched by his appearance. He . . . seems utterly cast down by his failure."[58]

On the evening of May 21, David Hunter arrived at Sigel's headquarters at Belle Grove to officially assume command of the department. Mirroring the change of command when Sigel supplanted Benjamin Kelley earlier in the year, with Hunter's assumption of command Sigel—like Kelley before him—was relegated to heading up the department's "Reserve Division."

The new commander's reputation as a general who believed that civilians should be made to feel the hard hand of war was soon put into action. A Massachusetts officer described Hunter as "a stern, unrelenting soldier, who believes in making war of the sternest character wherever he moves in the enemy's country."[59]

Hunter wasted no time regrouping the small army. With hundreds of Ohio militia pouring into the department to guard the Baltimore & Ohio Railroad, thus freeing up other troops, Hunter added the 5th New York Heavy Artillery to his command, offsetting most of the losses suffered at New Market. Before

54 *Ibid.*, 492.

55 Reader diary, May 22, 1864.

56 Samuel Young to Franz Sigel, June 4, 1864, Sigel Papers.

57 Norman Wiard to Franz Sigel, May 31, 1864, Sigel Papers.

58 Eby, *A Virginia Yankee in the Civil War*, 232.

59 Worcester *Aegis and Transcript*, July 9, 1864.

the month expired, Hunter would move south almost all the way back to New Market, en route to Staunton and beyond. He would take with him a new style of war the people of the Valley had yet to fully witness—and one that would earn for him the ire of most of the populace and set the stage for a much larger campaign in the Shenandoah that summer and fall.

* * *

In the Confederate capital at Richmond, news of the victory in the Valley was most welcome indeed. Lee's Army of Northern Virginia had been locked for nearly two weeks in bloody combat with the Army of the Potomac, first in the Wilderness and then at Spotsylvania. Both sides had suffered grievous casualties. Lee lost nearly an entire division captured en masse on the 12th. The day before, cavalry chief Major General Jeb Stuart was mortally wounded at Yellow Tavern while turning back a Federal cavalry raid on the outskirts of Richmond. None of the news from Northern Virginia was good, so word of a battlefield success—any battlefield success—was warmly welcomed by soldiers and civilians alike.

Harrisonburg's Rockingham *Register* ran an extra edition on Monday morning with the headlines: "Fight at New Market! A Great Victory! General Breckinridge in pursuit of the flying General Seigle! [sic]."[60] The *Register* was the first to break the news of the victory because its editor, J. H. Wartmann, was on the field as an observer.

Lee sent his congratulations to Breckinridge on the morning after the battle: "I offer you the thanks of this army for your victory over Genl Sigel. Press him down the valley, & if practicable follow him into Maryland."[61]

Sentiment inside Breckinridge's army was universally ebullient. Breckinridge's report was never finished or published, so his own comments on the conduct of his army in general, or specific officers in particular, are unknown. Lieutenant Colonel George Edgar, commander of the 26th Virginia Battalion, Echols' Brigade, penned a report that August that remained unpublished until 1996. "The officers and men of my battalion, with but few exceptions, fought well throughout the engagement," wrote Edgar, who went on to list by name more than a dozen subordinates. Lt. Micajah Woods of

60 Rockingham *Register*, May 16, 1864.

61 Dowdey, *Wartime Papers of R. E. Lee*, 731.

Jackson's Battery wrote to his father the day after the battle, "Major McLaughlin is in very bright spirits about the action of his battalion and will give us a flattering report."[62]

John Echols, whose small brigade had fought on the right of the cadets during the battle, sent his compliments to Lieutenant Colonel Scott Ship for the conduct of his cadets on and off the field during the campaign. "I cannot refrain . . . from expressing to you my high admiration of the conduct of your noble boys in the fierce conduct of yesterday and my deep sympathy with you all on account of the many casualties which I understand you will have to record," lauded Echols. "I shall always be proud to have had you and your Corps under my command. No man ever led a more gallant band. Nobly have you illustrated the history of your state and the Institution which you have represented."[63]

Breckinridge also paid his respects to the cadets: "Boys, the work you did yesterday will make you famous." One heckler is said to have shot back, "Fame! All right, General, but for God's sake where's your commissary wagon?"[64] The army commander's official commendation conveyed "his thanks for the important services you have rendered . . . [and] his admiration for their meritorious conduct as exhibited in their soldierly bearing on the march and for their distinguished gallantry on the field."[65]

*   *   *

With Sigel on the retreat, any immediate threat to the entire (southern) upper half of the Valley was gone, at least for the time being. How best to further employ Breckinridge's command? Two plausible options presented themselves to Lee. His first instinct was to order the Kentuckian to follow the retreating Federals and try to drive them from the Valley and "into Maryland," which would focus Federal attention to the Valley and thus away from his own army. His other option was to gamble that the Federals would stay put in their camps in the lower Valley, which would allow him to transfer Breckinridge's force eastward to reinforce the embattled Army of Northern Virginia.

---

62 Edgar, New Market Report, Edgar Papers; Woods to Father, May 16, 1864.

63 John Echols to Scott Ship, May 16, 1864, Johnston Papers.

64 Stan Cohen, *Moses Ezekiel: Civil War Soldier, Renowned Sculptor* (Charleston, WV, 2007), 13.

65 J. Stoddard Johnston to Scott Ship, May 16, 1864, Johnston Papers.

Later that same day (on May 16), after rethinking his initial aggressive response to Breckinridge, Lee sent another message to his Valley commander:

> If you [do not deem] it practicable to carry out the suggestion of my dispatch of this morning to drive the enemy from the valley & pursue him into Maryland, you can be of great service with this army. If you can follow Sigel into Maryland, you will do more good than by joining us. If you cannot, & your command is not otherwise needed in the Valley or in your Department, I desire you to prepare to join me.[66]

Breckinridge's men fully expected to follow Sigel. "I suppose we will move down the Valley as soon as we can cross the River," wrote a cavalryman.[67] Capt. William Taylor led a detachment of the 18th Virginia Cavalry across the Shenandoah River on the morning of the 16th. Their horses had to swim the flooded and now treacherous waterway.[68] Major Harry Gilmor and his Marylanders also managed to cross the river which, Gilmor recalled, was almost even with its banks. "The current was terrific," he wrote, "and looked as though a horse could not possibly live in the current." Yet no horses or men were lost in the crossing, although three horses were unable to cross and were swept some distance downstream before emerging back on the southern bank.[69]

Gilmor's men and the 18th Virginia Cavalry were apparently not operating together, for Taylor's detachment reported riding as far north as Woodstock, finding burning wagons and abandoned equipment all along the road. No mention was made of encountering any enemy troops between Mount Jackson and Woodstock.[70] Gilmor, however, claimed to have encountered a flag of truce carried by Major Charles Otis, 21st New York Cavalry, at Mount Jackson. Otis sought to retrieve the body of Capt. William Mitchell of his regiment. Gilmor halted his command and sent the message back to Breckinridge, wasting most of the day until his courier returned near nightfall bearing orders to push down the Valley as rapidly as possible. As Gilmor resumed his pursuit, Major Otis rode with him. As they talked, Otis recognized Gilmor's horse and asked him if he had been wounded a few days previously near where they were

66 Dowdey, *Wartime Papers of R. E. Lee*, 732.

67 Kiracofe to "Dear Wife & Daughter," May 16, 1864.

68 Pratt to Colonna, November 19, 1910.

69 Gilmor, *Four Years in the Saddle*, 158.

70 Pratt to Colonna, November 19, 1910.

now riding. When Gilmor answered yes, Otis told him that he had been the man who shot him. The pair of enemies continued on to Woodstock that night, swimming Stony Creek at Edinburgh, but did not encounter any Yankees. The following morning, Gilmor—still accompanied by Major Otis—pressed on toward Strasburg, where they encountered Federal pickets and a sizeable force at Hupp's Hill just beyond. Otis returned to his lines and Gilmor returned to Woodstock, dispatching a courier with his findings back to New Market.[71]

With Sigel already back in his old position at Cedar Creek and a flooded river between his defeated army and Breckinridge, the Kentucky general decided he could do no further good in the Valley. The Federals were gone from his front, and he had no idea how long it would be before he could get his own army across the Shenandoah to move on Sigel. There were other logistical obstacles as well. The farther north Breckinridge moved, the farther away from his own base of supplies—and friendly troops—he would be. If Sigel continued falling back, however, he would be shortening his supply line. Breckinridge's army was already very small. Another battle, even if a victory, would leave him too weak to mount any offensive across the Potomac. While Lee's suggestion to pursue Sigel into Maryland to draw off Federal forces from Lee's front was strategically sound—he would employ that exact strategy several months later with Jubal Early—the force at Breckinridge's disposal was so small as to constitute nothing more than a minor nuisance, and surely not large enough to warrant the reaction Lee desired. Lee desperately needed troops to offset his Wilderness and Spotsylvania losses, and the Confederacy could not afford to let Breckinridge's men sit idle in western Virginia. There was, of course, a risk involved in withdrawing them from the Valley, but at that time there was no evidence of any pending new Federal offensive there. (This conclusion was incorrect, as subsequent events would prove, but it seemed a safe gamble at the time.)

After spending Monday the 16th in and around New Market, Breckinridge gave orders for his infantry and artillery to return to Staunton on the 17th. From there, they were to travel by rail to join Lee's army north of Richmond. Imboden's cavalry would remain behind to keep an eye on Sigel, but the cavalryman would not have the services of the 62nd Virginia Mounted Infantry for the task. Since the 62nd (mounted in name only) was the lone dismounted unit in Imboden's command, and Lee needed all the foot soldiers he could get,

---

71 Gilmor, *Four Years in the Saddle*, 158-61.

Breckinridge added the 62nd to Wharton's Brigade, which helped offset his New Market losses. Neither would the VMI Cadets be making the trip east to join the Army of Northern Virginia. The young soldiers would spend the two days following the battle caring not just for their own wounded, but assisting in the care of other injured soldiers as well.

Two days after the battle, the cadets buried several of their fallen comrades in the cemetery at St. Matthew's Church. After retrieving the bodies of four of them from a building in town, the Corps of Cadets followed the caissons bearing their caskets north along Main St. to the churchyard. Several townspeople followed the procession. "The large grave for four was dug in the northwestern corner of the old cemetery," recalled one of the New Market residents. "The cadets were filed on north side of grave and extended east from the corner. The burial ceremony was long, and 15 or 20 cadets took part by repeating part of the ceremony. They were buried with honors of war. Three volleys were fired, then the grave was filled."[72]

For the families of the dead and wounded cadets, their fate came as a shock, for most were ignorant of the fact that their sons and brothers were anywhere but in their classrooms in Lexington. "Your letter informing me of the death of my son," replied William H. McDowell's father to a notice from VMI, "came upon me like a clap of thunder in a clear sky as I was not aware the cadets had been called out."[73]

After several days the cadets were heading east—not to join the ranks of the Army of Northern Virginia but to receive the official thanks of President Jefferson Davis and the Confederate Congress in Richmond. The Corps arrived in Staunton on the 21st and was in Richmond two days later.[74]

As word of the victory at New Market spread, and the cadets' participation became more widely known, they found themselves the object of much attention. "When we reached Staunton, one group of young ladies and hundreds of citizens greeted us enthusiastically. One of the girls placed a laurel wreath on our cadet flag," recalled Moses Ezekiel, who kept it as a souvenir.[75] "Every place through which we passed, the ladies were inquiring for the

---

72 New Market *Shenandoah Valley*, November 17, 1910.

73 R. I. McDowell to J.H. Morrison, May 30, 1864, VMI.

74 *OR* 37, pt. 1, 91.

75 Cohen, *Moses Ezekiel*, 17. The wreath now resides in the VMI Museum.

cadets," wrote John Coleman, "not thinking for an instant that we were 'the cadets,' being so dirty and badly dressed. They seemed surprised when we told them we were 'the cadets.'"[76]

The receptions they received in Staunton and along the way to Richmond were nothing compared to what awaited them in the Confederate capital. One of the cadets left an account that ran in a Richmond paper:

> We were received by President Davis and were highly complimented by him and Gov. Smith; Congress too presented us resolutions of thanks through their Speaker. In fact I think they have made entirely too much 'noise' over us. It is true, we fought well, and in the charge our colors were in advance of all the others, but as to the fighting all stood up to it like men, equally as well as ourselves.[77]

When the cadets first arrived in Richmond, they marched directly to the capitol and made camp on the grounds around the building, serenaded there by the Richmond Armory Band. The following day they were reviewed by President Davis and Governor William Smith. Several days later the governor presented the Corps of Cadets with a new state flag, after which a delegation of the Confederate Congress read a resolution thanking the cadets for their service at New Market. This was followed by a formal review of the Corps by General Braxton Bragg.[78] While the cadets were being lauded as heroes, the other infantrymen who had fought at New Market joined the Army of Northern Virginia with little fanfare. They would participate in the desperate fighting at Cold Harbor in early June, and many would lose their lives there.

The cadets' stay in Richmond was cut short on June 6 when they were ordered back to Lexington. Federal general David Hunter had called Lee's bluff and was advancing into the vacuum left behind in the Valley when Breckinridge was pulled out. The cadets arrived in time to witness Hunter destroy everything of value—military or otherwise—at VMI, including the burning of the barracks and the classrooms. Only an empty shell remained. Hunter's men even carried away the large bronze statue of George Washington from the institute's entrance. VMI's Board of Visitors later claimed that Hunter's success was because the cadets were away in Richmond:

76 Richmond *Daily Whig*, June 22, 1864.

77 *Ibid.*

78 Richmond *Sentinel*, May 25 & 28, 1864; Richmond *Examiner*, May 25 and 28, 1864.

Your committee can but regret that the cadets were not sent back to the institute immediately after the battle of New Market. It is now apparent that had this been done, the great majority, if not all the movable public property could have been saved. As they arrived here, on their return, only the day before the entry of the enemy into Lexington, little could be done in this respect. On this account, their detention in Richmond was unfortunate.[79]

With their home destroyed, the cadets remained in the Confederate capital for much of the rest of the war, the city Alms House becoming their new home when they weren't serving in the city's trenches.

Decades after the battle, a U.S. Senator from Delaware introduced a bill in Congress to reimburse Virginia Military Institute for the damages inflicted by Hunter and his men. VMI used the money to construct Jackson Memorial Hall—the home of the VMI Museum. The Delaware Senator had been present on the field at New Market. His name was Henry DuPont.[80]

Not far from Jackson Memorial Hall stands a bronze statue entitled Virginia Mourning Her Dead. It was designed by an artist and former cadet Moses Ezekiel, and unveiled in 1903.[81] Graves at the base of the monument hold the remains of six of the ten cadets killed outright at New Market or who later died of their wounds.

In 1904, the year after Virginia Mourning Her Dead was unveiled, the VMI Alumni Association presented each of the "New Market Cadets" with a bronze medal—the "New Market Cross of Honor."[82]

Every May 15, the Corps of Cadets turns out on the parade ground in front of the imposing bronze statue to honor their comrades who gave their lives at New Market generations before. The names of the ten cadets are called out, to which one of their modern brethren in arms answers, "Died on the field of honor."

The last surviving "New Market Cadet," William M. Wood, returned to Lexington in 1939 to present the Corps of Cadets with a battle streamer emblazoned "New Market" for the battalion colors. Wood answered his final

79 "Report of Committee on the Arsenal," July 1864, VMI.

80 Couper, *Virginia Military Institute and Battle of New Market*, 17. DuPont worked with a former VMI Cadet on this project, Senator Thomas S. Martin.

81 Richmond *Times-Dispatch*, June 24, 1903.

82 Couper, *The VMI New Market Cadets*, 252.

William M. Wood, New Market's last surviving cadet. *VMI Archives*

roll call four years later. With him passed the last veteran of the Battle of New Market.[83]

* * *

New Market, which Gabriel Wharton called "one of the most decisive and important small engagements of the war," has earned a special place in history that exceeds the military importance of the battle.[84] The engagement was the opening salvo of the 1864 Shenandoah Valley Campaign. With the stakes significantly elevated, the larger battles that followed overshadowed the smaller New Market combat. In May of 1864, the Shenandoah Valley had not yet become the second front in Virginia that it would be that summer and fall. In the spring of 1864, the Valley was little more than an afterthought in Federal plans—a leg to be held while the skinning was done across the mountains.

83 Richmond *Times-Dispatch*, May 14, 1939.

84 Staunton *Spectator & Vindicator*, May 20, 1904.

The battle's place in history has been minimized because the fruits of the hard won Confederate victory were short-lived. The aftermath of New Market was one of the few times when General Lee was completely wrong in his judgement of enemy intentions. Following Breckinridge's victory, Lee gambled that the Federals would not attempt another incursion up the Valley for some time. No one could have imagined that a little more than two weeks later the same Federal army, albeit under a different commander, would march past New Market en route to carrying out its original goal of capturing Staunton. By the end of the first week of June, the outcome of the New Market fight was immaterial.

Even though Sigel met with a tactical defeat at New Market, he scored a strategic victory by drawing Breckinridge and most of the infantry and artillery away from southwest Virginia. This diversion opened the door for George Crook's success at Cloyd's Mountain and beyond. However, the grand plan for Federal operations did not succeed under Sigel's tenure. Despite the victory he won at Cloyd's Mountain, Crook retreated back to his base, surrendering the territory he had won. Thus the planned hookup between Crook and Sigel at Staunton, and the subsequent planned march on Lynchburg, never happened.

The battle's memory is kept alive in large part by the legendary image of the boys of VMI bravely charging the enemy and putting them to flight. The cadets have received so much attention for their role at New Market that popular perception has them winning the battle all by themselves. No serious study, of course, presents this view. To do so would be a disservice to the other men in gray who fought there that day. Still, they fought even better than some of them believed possible. "I never thought that we would have fought so bravely," one of them wrote two days after the bloodshed ended.[85] Bravely they did fight, but the undue attention rubbed others like salt stings a wound. "It is a pity that in order to advertise the gallantry of the Cadets, which was most commendable," wrote Captain John O. Carr of the 26th Virginia Battalion more than forty years later, "it should have been deemed necessary to detract from the equally commendable conduct of other commands."[86]

Although some writers have proposed that New Market was the only time an entire corps of cadets from a military school took to the field in open combat, this is not correct. VMI's Corps of Cadets took to the field many times

---

85 Anderson, "Recollections of a VMI Rat."

86 Carr to Edgar, March 25, 1906.

in support of actions in the Valley and the surrounding counties, and served in the trenches around Richmond during the latter months of the war. In fact, they were called out a total of fourteen times.[87] New Market, however, was the only time the Corps engaged directly in real combat as a unit.

Nor were the VMI Cadets the only ones engaged on a battlefield during the Civil War, though they were far more heavily engaged and suffered more severely than did any other cadet corps. On the very day New Market was being fought, cadets from Georgia Military Institute were pressed into service with Joe Johnston's Army of Tennessee to resist the advance of William T. Sherman's army. The GMI cadets participated in the Battle of Resaca but did not sustain any casualties.[88]

The Charleston & Savannah Railroad, linking those two cities along the Atlantic coast, was a constant target of Federal raids during the latter half of the war. Because the South had limited manpower deployed around Charleston, the "Battalion of State Cadets," composed of boys from the Citadel and the state Arsenal, were called out numerous times. These young men found themselves in the midst of a heavy skirmish at Tulifinny Trestle on the C&S in early December 1864.[89]

The West Florida Seminary, more popularly known as Florida Military Institute, also gave up its cadets to turn back Federal invasions of its home state at Olustee in February 1864 and again at Natural Bridge in March the following year. No losses were reported.[90]

The cadet corps of the University of Alabama suffered two casualties defending Montgomery against a Federal cavalry raid in the summer of 1864.[91] They served again in a night fight in the streets of Tuscaloosa in April 1865.[92]

The overriding reason the battle is remembered today—and the battlefield itself survives today—is because of the perpetuation of the New Market legend. Without the participation of the cadets of Virginia Military Institute, the battle

---

87 Conrad, *The Young Lions: Confederate Cadets at War*, 140.

88 *Ibid.*, 90.

89 *Ibid.*, 120-2.

90 *Ibid.*, 134-8. The Florida Military Institute cadets were only allowed to fight at Natural Bridge if they had written permission from their parents.

91 *Ibid.*, 112-3.

92 *Ibid.*, 145-8.

of New Market, like most other engagements of its size, would be little more than a footnote in another book. Such deeds of young valor made for what newspaper folks term "good copy." When considered in that light, the thousands of other men who fought and died at New Market, wherever they may be, are probably thankful the service of the cadets has kept the story of their struggle alive for posterity.

> "He has put off his uniform, but as he marches on he wears on his heart a little bronze cross of a New Market man and the unshaken Cross of a proud but humble follower of an undying faith."
>
> — Epitaph of Charles J. Anderson, VMI 1869

Veterans of the Battle of New Market gathered in the town every May 15 for decades to remember the battle and their fallen comrades. A photographer captured this group of former VMI Cadets at the Confederate Monument in St. Matthew's Cemetery in 1914. They are, from left to right: Preston Cocke (1867), John H. Clarkson (1867), Scott Ship (1859, then a brigadier general and VMI Superintendent), John S. Bagnall (1865), James B. Harvie (1867), Francis T. Lee (1866), Robert G. Cabell (1867, whose brother was killed at New Market), Benjamin A. Colonna (1864), and Henry C. Bowen (1867). *VMI Archives*

Virginia Mourning Her Dead—Virginia Military Institute. *VMI Archives*

Appendix 1

Order of Battle at New Market

Confederate Army: Maj. Gen. John C. Breckinridge

Echols' Brigade: Brig. Gen. John Echols

22nd Virginia: George S. Patton
550 men: 4 k, 32 w, 0 m = 36[1]

23rd Virginia Battalion: Lt. Col. Clarence Derrick
472 men: 2 k, 75 w, 2 m = 79[2]

26th Virginia Battalion: Lt. Col. George M. Edgar
477 men:[3] 0 k, 25 w, 11 m = 36[4]

1   The strength of the infantry units in Wharton's and Echols' brigades is reached using a May 21, 1864, return and adding the losses sustained by each unit at New Market as listed in a copy of the Confederate casualty returns found in Sigel's Papers. The May 21, 1864, figures are contained in Johnston, "Battle of New Market." The actual number present at New Market likely differed from these figures only slightly. Losses in Echols' Brigade, undated, Sigel Papers.

2   *Ibid.* See also, note 4 below.

3   *Ibid.* "Official Report of Lt. Col. George M. Edgar on the part his battalion, the 26th Virginia bore in the Battle of New Market, May 15, 1864," Edgar Papers, places the strength of Edgar's battalion at 425. This report, however, was written several months after the battle. I have used the same formula to reach his strength as for the other infantry units because I believe the May 21, 1864, return yields a figure closer to Edgar's actual number at New Market.

4   *Ibid.* This report must be incorrect, as several deaths are well recorded for Edgar's battalion, including J. W. Maddy, whose final moments are described in the text. Two others from the 26th are listed as killed at New Market on the Confederate monument in St. Matthews Cemetery and buried there: John W. Midkiff (Co. F), and A. D. Stephenson (Co. I), both are listed in Terry Lowry's history of the 26th Battalion. On this particular listing of casualties in Sigel's papers the units are not listed in numerical order, presenting the possibility that the numbers are not matched with the correct unit, i.e. Edgar's and Derrick's casualties are reversed. It seems nearly impossible the 23rd Battalion (Derrick) suffered more than double the losses listed for the 26th Battalion (Edgar).

Wharton's Brigade: Brig. Gen. Gabriel C. Wharton

30th Virginia Battalion: Lt. Col. J. Lyle Clark
306 men: 2 k, 90 w, 0 m = 92[5]

51st Virginia: Lt. Col. John P. Wolfe
680 men: 1 k, 46 w, 0 m = 47[6]

Unattached Commands

VMI Cadet Battalion: Lt. Col. Scott Ship (w), Capt. Henry A. Wise
227 men:[7] 10 k, 47 w, 0 m = 57[8]

3rd Confederate Engineers, Co. E: 1st Lt. M. W. Long
44 men:[9] 0 k, 10 w, 0 m = 10[10]

Rockingham/Augusta Reserves: Col. William Harman
500 men:[11] Not engaged on May 15

5   *Ibid.* See "Casualties in Battle of New Market," undated, Sigel Papers.

6   *Ibid.* Some accounts, Turner included, incorrectly place Col. August Forsberg in command of the 51st. However, Forsberg was in a hospital in Lynchburg and, by his own admission, did not rejoin his regiment until May 20 at Hanover Junction. The regiment was under the command of Lieutenant Colonel Wolfe during his absence. August Forsberg diary, Washington & Lee University.

7   "Strength of Breckinridge's Command," Sigel Papers. This report lists strengths for each infantry brigade, the engineer company, the cadets, Woodson's Missourians, the two artillery batteries and the cadet artillery section, and Imboden's command. Separate figures for each infantry unit or cavalry unit are not included, and the 62nd Virginia is not included. This report gives Breckinridge 4,816 of all arms. The strength of the cadet battalion varies by source. Turner put it at 249. Turner, *New Market Campaign,* 163-4.

8   Couper, *New Market Cadets,* 6, 254. The "killed" tally includes five who were killed outright in battle and five more who died from their wounds. Colonel Ship's official report, dated July 4, 1864, included a list of casualties showing eight killed and 44 wounded. *OR* 37, pt. 1, 91.

9   "Report of Capt. T. Hart's Comp. Engineer Troops, New Market Battle Ground, May 16, 1864," Sigel Papers.

10   *Ibid.* "Casualties in Battle of New Market," undated, Sigel Papers.

11   Davis, *Battle of New Market,* 196.

Cavalry: Brig. Gen. John D. Imboden

18th Virginia Cavalry: Col. George W. Imboden
600 men: 0 k, 1 w, 0 m = 1[12]

23rd Virginia Cavalry: Col. Robert White
315 men.[13] No losses reported

62nd Virginia Mounted Infantry: Col. George H. Smith
510 men:[14] 19 k, 161 w, 0 m = 180[15]

1st Missouri, Co. A: Capt. Charles Woodson
62 men: 8 k, 33 w, 0 m = 41[16]

Davis' Maryland Cavalry: Capt. T. Sturgis Davis
26 men.[17] Losses unknown

12 Delauter, *18th Virginia Cavalry*, 14-16. No muster roll for the 18th during this time period is known to exist. The figure given is from Delauter's history, in which he analyzed the complete compiled service records for the entire unit to determine that total effective strength in the spring of 1864 would have been 575-600 men. Sigel's Papers contains a memo from Imboden's T. B. Berkeley, an adjutant to Breckinridge's chief of staff J. Stoddard Johnston, which gives Imboden's strength—exclusive of the 62nd Virginia—as 930 effectives. Berkeley to Johnston, May 16, 1864, Sigel Papers. For losses, see Berkeley to Johnston, May 16, 1864, Sigel Papers.

13 Kleese, *23rd Virginia Cavalry*, 21; Berkeley to Johnston, May 16, 1864.

14 In a telegraph to Breckinridge dated May 9, 1864, Smith claimed his regiment numbered 510 enlisted men. OR 37, pt. 1, 726. Imboden states the 62nd had "about 550" (Imboden, "Battle of New Market," 484), and Smith "about 500" (Smith, *Battle of New Market*, 8). In his autobiographical sketch, Smith gave his strength at "about or perhaps something over 500" ("Record of George H. Smith," Smith papers, VMI). Isaac White, assistant surgeon of the 62nd, put the unit's strength as "about 500" (White to Jinnie, May 20, 1864, White papers).

15 "Casualties in Battle of New Market," Sigel Papers. The *Staunton Vindicator*, May 23, 1864, states that the regiment "lost about 240 killed, wounded and missing," and gives its source as the regimental adjutant. It also notes that four companies were attached to the 62nd, including Woodson's Missourians, and includes these "extra" companies in the 62nd's total. Though one of the companies states "many lost, not reported," the other two companies with losses named contains many troopers from the 23rd Virginia Cavalry. However, since Imboden reported no losses in the 23rd, these casualties must have been either included in the 62nd's numbers, or possibly not reported at all, with neither regimental adjutant "claiming" the men in question.

16 Scott, *Memorials of E. H. Scott*, 16. Turner, *New Market Campaign*, 113, put the strength at 70. For losses, see the discussion contained in note 15, above.

17 OR 37, pt. 1, 729.

2nd Maryland Battalion: Maj. Harry Gilmor (w)
40 men.[18] Not engaged on May 15

McNeill's Rangers: Capt. John H. McNeill
60 men.[19] Not engaged on May 15

3rd Battalion Virginia Mounted Reserves, Co. A: Capt. George Chrisman
87 men.[20] Losses unknown

Artillery: Maj. William McLaughlin

Chapman's Battery: Capt. George B. Chapman
6 guns, 135 men: 1 k, 4 w, 0 m = 5[21]

Jackson's Battery: 1st Lt. Randolph H. Blain
4 guns, 94 men: 0 k, 1 w, 0 m = 1[22]

McClanahan's Battery: Capt. John McClanahan
6 guns, 93 men: 0 k, 1 w, 0 m = 1[23]

VMI artillery section: Cadet Capt. Collier H. Minge
2 guns, 35 men: 0 k, 2 w, 0 m = 2[24]

---

18 *Ibid.*

19 *Ibid.*, 69.

20 Company strength on original muster (April 3, 1864), and the only figure found for this unit during this campaign. John W. Wayland, *A History of Rockingham County, Virginia*, (Elkton, VA, 1912), 458-459. The company was likely smaller than this at New Market on May 15, 1864.

21 "Report of Artillery Battalion, May 17, 1864," and "Statement of Casualties in Artillery Battalion, May 19, 1864," Sigel Papers. For losses, see William McLaughlin to J. Stoddard Johnston, May 19, 1864, *ibid.*

22 *Ibid.* For losses, see *ibid.*, Sigel Papers.

23 Turner, *New Market Campaign*, 113. According to Lieutenant Carter Berkeley, two of McClanahan's guns were knocked out of action in the May 14 fighting, leaving him with only four guns for the New Market fighting on the 15th. Berkeley also claims that the surviving four guns remained with Imboden during the entire battle at New Market. If true, none of McClanahan's guns were west of Smith's Creek. Driver, *Staunton Artillery*, 88. For losses, see McLaughlin to Johnston, May 19, 1864, and Berkeley to Johnston, May 16, 1864, Sigel Papers.

24 "Strength of Breckinridge's Command," Sigel Papers. For losses, see "Federal Casualties at the Battle of New Market," NMBSHP.

Federal Army: Maj. Gen. Franz Sigel

Infantry Division: Brig. Gen. Jeremiah C. Sullivan

First Brigade: Col. Augustus Moor

18th Connecticut: Maj. Henry Peale
599 men: 1 k, 31 w, 24 m = 56[25]

28th Ohio: Lt. Col. Gottfried Becker
574 men:[26] 0 k, 1 w, 1 m = 2[27]

116th Ohio: Col. James Washburn
766 men. No losses reported[28]

123rd Ohio: Maj. Horace Kellogg (w)
616 men: 5 k, 33 w, 37 m = 75[29]

25 Field Return, Moor's Brigade, May 10, 1864, Moor Papers. However, Peale's official report (*OR* 37, pt. 1, 82) puts his number at roughly 350, but this likely includes the companies that had been detached to guard the Valley Pike and left behind on picket duty, hence Peale's much lower figure. I have used the official return in Moor's Papers for the effective strength of all the regiments of his brigade, even though some of them were not present on the field at New Market in their entirety. For losses, see "Federal Casualties at the Battle of New Market," NMBSHP.

26 *Ibid.*

27 "Field Return of killed, wounded and missing of 28th Ohio during the Campaign up the Shenandoah Valley," undated, Moor Papers. In addition to the two losses recorded for May 15, one man was killed on May 16 at Winchester, and one killed, one wounded, and five missing on May 14 at Strasburg. This last is presumably attributed to some of Mosby's troops, as a memo from Lt. Col. Becker of May 20, also in Moor's Papers, states that several losses "occurred to Veterans [sic] who were to join their Regmt [sic] to escort a train from Martinsburg to Winchester and were attacked by a band of Guerrillas near Strasburg."

28 Field Return, Moor's Brigade, May 10, 1864, Moor Papers; Wildes, *Record of the 116th Ohio*, 82: "Our regiment numbered nearly 800 men and looked like a brigade itself."

29 *Ibid.* For losses, see "Federal Casualties at the Battle of New Market," NMBSHP.

Second Brigade: Col. Joseph Thoburn

1st West Virginia: Lt. Col. Jacob Weddle
387 men: 4 k, 54 w, 18 m = 76[30]

12th West Virginia: Col. William B. Curtis
929 men: 1 k, 27 w, 12 m = 40[31]

34th Massachusetts: Col. George D. Wells (w)
500 men: 30 k, 151 w, 54 m = 215[32]

54th Pennsylvania: Col. Jacob M. Campbell
566 men: 32 k, 100 w, 42 m = 174[33]

Cavalry Division: Maj. Gen. Julius Stahel[34]

First Brigade: Col. William B. Tibbits

1st New York (Lincoln): Lt. Col. Alonzo W. Adams
Losses unknown

30 Rawling, *History of the First West Virginia*, 168. This is roughly one-half the strength that Davis, *Battle of New Market*, 194, attributes to this regiment, but the lower figure seems more likely than 700 given the veteran status of this unit. Rawling claims to have based his figure from a report by either Thoburn or Weddle, which, according to Rawling, has since been lost. For losses, see "Federal Casualties at the Battle of New Market," NMBSHP.

31 Davis, *Battle of New Market*, 194. Although the number of effectives seems high, suggesting a truly green regiment, I have not been able to find any other number than that which Davis uses for the strength of this regiment. For losses, see *ibid.*

32 OR 37, pt. 1, 86. Wells states in his official report that after the detachment of Company C he was left with "about 450 muskets in line." However, a letter to his mother two days after the battle puts the number at "about 250 men in line." The lower figure is all but impossible given the number of casualties (215) the 34th sustained. If Wells' regiment numbered 250 and sustained losses approaching 86%, the 34th Massachusetts would have effectively ceased to exist. I am confident the figure Wells provided in his official report is the correct number. For losses, see "Federal Casualties at the Battle of New Market," NMBSHP.

33 OR 37, pt. 1, 87. For losses, see "Federal Casualties at the Battle of New Market," NMBSHP.

34 *Ibid.*, 87. Determining the strength of Sigel's cavalry division at New Market is all but impossible because of a lack of sources and official reports. The return for the 1st Cavalry Division for May 1864 puts division effective strength at 2,840. *Ibid.*, 571.

1st New York (Veteran): Col. Robert F. Taylor
12 k, 26 w, 9 m = 47[35]

21st New York: Maj. Charles G. Otis
2 k, 12 w, 0 m = 14[36]

1st Maryland, Potomac Home Brigade: Maj. J. T. Daniel
0 k, 0 w, 1 m = 1[37]

14th Pennsylvania: Capt. Ashbel F. Duncan
0 k, 6 w, 2 m = 8[38]

Second Brigade: Col. John E. Wynkoop[39]

15th New York: Maj. H. Roessler
2 k, 3 w, 11 m = 16[40]

20th Pennsylvania: Maj. R. B. Douglas
1 k, 5 w, 15 m = 21[41]

22nd Pennsylvania: Lt. Caleb McNulty
Losses unknown

Artillery: Capt. Alonzo Snow[42]

---

35 "Federal Casualties at the Battle of New Market," NMBSHP.

36 *Ibid.*

37 *Ibid.*

38 *Ibid.*

39 Sources are all but non-existent for Wynkoop's brigade. I used Davis, *Battle of New Market*, for the names of the unit leaders, but have not been able to determine unit strength for any of the brigade's regiments. According to Davis, they were all detachments and not at full strength.

40 For losses, see "Federal Casualties at the Battle of New Market," NMBSHP.

41 *Ibid.*

42 "Field Report of the 1st Infantry Division, Dept of West Va," May 19, 1864, Sigel Papers, lists Snow as "Chief of Artillery." I have arrived at the strength of the artillery batteries—with the exception of Ewing—by adding the recorded losses for each battery as listed in the official casualty report of May 20, 1864, to the figures listed on the "Field Report of the 1st Infantry Division, Dept of West Va," of May 19, 1864, in Sigel's Papers.

Battery B, 1st Maryland: Lt. G. A. C. Gerry
6 guns, 143 men: 0 k, 5 w, 0 m = 5[43]

Battery B, 5th U.S.: Capt. Henry A. DuPont
6 guns, 133 men:[44] No losses reported[45]

30th New York Battery: Capt. Alfred von Kleiser
6 guns, 150 men: 1 k, 4 w, 05 = 5[46]

Battery D, 1st West Virginia: Capt. John Carlin / Lt. Ephraim Chalfant
6 guns, 139 men:[47] 4 k, 3 w = 7

Battery G, 1st West Virginia Light: Capt. Chatham T. Ewing
4 guns, strength unknown: 1 k, 1 w, 1 m = 2[48]

43 For losses, see "Federal Casualties at the Battle of New Market," NMBSHP.

44 A "Muster Roll of DuPont's Battery April 30, 1864 – June 30, 1864," New Market Collection, VMI, provides the entire roster of DuPont's battery and has this note at the end: "There were on detached service two first lieutenants and one corporal. There were one captain, two second lieutenants, seven sergeants, six corporals, one wagoner and 145 enlisted men present for duty." This is a total of 162, which seems high for that time of the war. I have instead used the figures from the report of General Sullivan's 1st Infantry Division of May 19, 1864, in accordance with the other batteries.

45 No losses were recorded for DuPont's battery in the official casualty return ("Federal Casualties at the Battle of New Market," NMBSHP), and DuPont himself made no mention of suffering any losses in either of his accounts of the battle.

46 Von Kleiser's first name appears as "Albert" in most accounts, but it appears to have been "Alfred," as that is what a roster of the unit and documents from what appear to be his pension file in the von Kleiser files at NMBSHP list as his first name. Most contemporary accounts refer simply to "Capt. A. von Kleiser." For losses, see "Federal Casualties at the Battle of New Market," NMBSHP.

47 Carlin was present during the campaign, and presumably the battle, but his battery was under the command of Lt. Ephraim Chalfant during the battle, as per the report of Sullivan's 1st Infantry Division, May 19, 1864, and also in correspondence of von Kleiser concerning his lost cannon. For losses, see "Federal Casualties at the Battle of New Market," NMBSHP.

48 *Ibid.*

Appendix 2

After-Action Battle Reports for
John C. Breckinridge (CSA) and Franz Sigel (USA)

Breckinridge Report

[J. Stoddard Johnston folder, New Market Collection, Virginia Military Institute Archives. Spelling and grammar, including strikeouts, as per original.]

Lt. Col. W.H. Taylor, A.A.G.

I have the honor to submit the following report of the operations of my command from May 5th to June 19th 1864.

Having in the month of March assumed command of the Department of S.W. Virginia with Hd Qrs at Dublin, Pulaski Co. in obedience to the orders of the President I was engaged in disposing my forces to resist a threatened invasion from ~~Kentucky and~~ the Kanawha when on the 4th of May I received a telegram from the President indicating the probable necessity of taking my command to the Valley and directing me to communicate with Gen. Lee and Gen. Imboden, comd'g in the Valley. I accordingly communicated with Gen. Lee informing him of the strength and disposition of my force and the movements of the enemy. On the 5th of May I received a telegram from Gen. Lee directing me to march with all my available force to Staunton, assume command and resist the advance of Sigel then moving upon ~~Staunton~~ the Shenandoah Valley. The situation of affairs in my Department was precarious and nothing but the necessity of preserving Staunton as the left of Gen. Lee's then important line would have justified its temporary abandonment to the occupation of the Enemy. Leaving the cavalry commands of Brig. Gen. W.E. Jones and J.H. Morgan to cover the important interests at the Saltworks and lead mines and a Brigade of infantry (McCausland's) and a portion of a Brigade of cavalry under Brig. Gen. A.G. Jenkins at the Narrows of New River, on the 5th I started for Staunton via Narrows Sweet Springs and Jackson River. On the 6th Echols Brigade (Infantry) which had been in camp at Monroe Draught in Greenbrier County took up its line of march for Jackson's River Depot and on the same day Wharton's Brigade marched from the Narrows. Gen. Imboden having notified me that Sigel was advancing from Winchester I hastened to Staunton and arrived there on the night of the 8th of May in advance of my command to organize such force as I could to assist in repelling the Enemy. The Reserves of Augusta and adjoining Counties were called out and under the efficient exertions of Col. ~~W.M.~~ John H. Harman were promptly on duty. The Corps of Cadets were summoned from Lexington and upon the arrival of my troops on the 11th the Reserves and Cadets were ready for duty. One day, the 12th, was given to resting the commands which had suffered in the heavy march over the mountains occasioned by the heat of the weather and the fact that it was the initial marching of the Season. In this interval I also organized my trains and caused two days rations to be cooked. Being convinced that the Enemy was advancing in comparative confidence, I determined not to await his coming but to march to meet him and give him battle wherever found. In accordance with this design I placed my column in motion at sunrise on the morning of the 13th of May moving upon the Winchester [Valley] Pike. My command consisted of Echols Brigade, Wharton's Brigade, Reserves under Col. Harman, and the Va Military Institute Corps of Cadets, under Lt. Col. Shipp. Of artillery I had three Batteries – Bryan's, Chapman's and Jackson's forming McLaughlin's Battalion together with a section of artillery brought by the Cadets. [Johnston and Breckinridge are mistaken about the presence of Bryan's Battery.] On the night of the 13th I camped near Mt. Crawford and on the 14th I marched to the vicinity of Lacey's Spring 35 miles from Staunton and ordered two days rations to be cooked. ~~Col.~~ General Imboden having been ordered to fall back slowly before the Enemy was at New Market, 9 miles beyond when I camped and reported ~~the Ene~~ Sigel at Mt. Jackson, seven miles beyond him. Having sent for him to join me at Lacey's Springs for conference he met me on the afternoon of the 14th and returned with instructions to keep me fully advised of the progress of the Enemy.

At Nine (9) P.M. Gen. Imboden having notified me of the advance of Sigel to New Market I gave orders for the command to march at 1 ~~PM~~ A.M. with the intention of attacking the Enemy early in the morning. At the appointed hour the Column moved and proceeded to within three miles of New Market where my trains were parked and line of battle formed. My dispositions having been effected shortly after daylight, I directed General Imboden to advance a Skirmish line and feel the Enemy. This movement having demonstrated that there was no enemy in force nearer than New Market, I advanced ~~toward the town~~ and formed Wharton's Brigade upon the heights to the Southwest of the town conducting it under cover of a wood. The Enemy's Skirmishers were deployed along the outskirts of the village his main force occupying the heights to the North West.

The enemy showing no disposition to assume the offensive I made preparation for immediate attack. Col Harman with the Reserves was left as guard to the wagon train. Brig. Gen. Imboden was directed to take position with his cavalry on the extreme right covering that flank and to use every ~~opportunity~~ effort to destroy the bridge across the Shenandoah River in rear of the Enemy with a view to cut off his retreat in case of a reverse to his arms. The topography of the country will ~~in briefly~~ lead to a better understanding of my position. The turnpike running North passes through New Market ~~passing through~~ which lies in a valley, the Eastern boundary of which is at this point the Massanutten range which runs parallel to the Pike two and half miles from it. From the pike to the mountain is a plain or slightly undulating surface sloping Eastward.

West of the pike the land ascends to a range of well defined hills running parallel with thee road, its crest about half a mile distant. The Eastern Slope of this range is gradual and free of timber. The Western is abrupt, wooded and with the river near its base. Upon the crest of this hill I formed my left of Wharton's Brigade. The Corps of Cadets were placed in the Centre and Echols with his right resting upon the turnpike completed ~~the~~ my line of Battle, which it will be seen was a single one without reserves [this too is incorrect, as there were initially three lines].

At nine o'clock having engaged in some skirmishing I opened with one battery of artillery from the crest of the hill to develop the position of the enemy. In a short time ~~the enemy~~ he responded ~~and~~ with several batteries and a general engagement with artillery ensued in which all of my batteries participated. Upon advancing my infantry the Enemy retired with slight skirmishing and thus I continued several hours advancing to successive heights in the undulating ridge of hills the enemy retreating until I had occupied the town of New Market with but few casualties.

Beyond the town the Country ascends by a gradual slope. Upon this elevation at the distance of a mile and a half it was evident that the Enemy had determined to make his final stand. My line not being sufficient to extend across the pike and observing favorable positions for artillery on the East Side, I deployed skirmishers on that side in extension of my regular line and not being able from the conformation of the ground longer to fire over the heads of my troops in advancing to the attack, I advanced six pieces of artillery [actually 8 or 10] on the East side of the pike simultaneously with my line of battle which was now ordered forward to the attack. The enemy with batteries in position and with a line of battle corresponding to my own occupied the crest of the ridge above referred to and as I advanced fired very effectively with his artillery especially when I had come within that range when canister was freely used.

The disposition of my artillery however proved of great advantage. Using my rifle pieces at long range I advanced my Napoleons on my right flank to within very short range and thus obtained an oblique fire upon the enemy my pieces being directed chiefly against the batteries to cause a diversion from the advancing infantry in which I succeeded to my entire satisfaction.

When my line of battle had reached within close range of the enemy a very heavy engagement along the whole line ensued. My troops advanced with great steadiness in the face of a most galling fire. This steadiness together with the well directed fire of the artillery soon showed its effect upon the enemy. His right less favored by the natural advantages than his left was first thrown into confusion. An attempt was made to charge down the turnpike with cavalry upon my right but a few well directed shells dispersed the squadrons after the start was made some fifteen or twenty only reaching my lines as prisoners. With this failure my troops charged with a defiant shout and the enemy fled precipitately leaving his dead and wounded upon the field and four pieces of artillery.

Pursuit was kept up for a mile or two when it was ascertained that the Enemy had made a stand on Rood's Hill a strong position four miles beyond New Market. The exhausted condition of the troops and the length of time they had been in line of battle rendered it necessary to half them for a short rest and replenishing ammunition before advancing to another attack. After readjusting my line and refilling Cartridge boxes I advanced upon Rood's Hill from which the enemy kept up a brisk artillery fire. On a near approach however the fire ceased and on reaching the top of the hill the rear of the Enemy's Column could be seen crossing the bridge at Mt. Jackson, as soon as the passage of which was affected it was fired. My troops pursued to the river when night setting in and it being impossible to cross the river in its swollen condition they were halted on Rudes Hill where wet and weary they bivouacked till morning.

Make appropriate mention of command especially cadets…

Draft of a report of the Battle of New Market May 15 1864 between Gen. Breckinridge and Gen. Sigel written by me

[signed] J Stoddard Johnston

*   *   *

Sigel Report

[Sigel papers, Western Reserve Historical Society. Spelling and grammar, including strikeouts, as per original.]

May 17, 64

General,

I have the honor to report the late operations of the troops in this Department under my immediate command.

After organizing a small column infantry, cavalry and artillery at Martinsburg I learnt that only Imboden's rebel force was in the Shenandoah Valley.

Genl Crook being in the Kanawha Valley operating on the Virginia and East Tennessee Railroad, it was my intention to march my force in the valley towards Staunton in order to relieve Crook by drawing the attention of the enemy in ~~the~~ this ~~Shenandoah Valley~~ direction.

I therefore marched some of my cavalry from Martinsburg ~~on the~~ by two roads avoiding the main road (turnpike) to Woodstock where they captured a number of rebel dispatches. One of these dispatches dated May 5th stated that Breckinridge ~~had~~ would send 4000 men infantry to Staunton and another dated

May 10th stating that Breckinridge had arrived at Staunton. A third dispatch of Imboden to Breckinridge informed the latter that the column marching up the Shenandoah valley would probably turn towards Lee to make a junction with Grant.

All this ~~was evidence~~ information tended to show, that by drawing the enemy into the valley, Genl Crook might be relieved to thereby be enabled to destroy the Virginia and Tennessee Railroad.

This object I think has been attained as shortly after ~~the~~ my force had reached Woodstock and my cavalry with two regiments of infantry had advanced to New Market ~~where~~ information was received that Breckinridge was on ~~his~~ the march down the valley to meet us.

It always appeared to me of importance to occupy New Market not only because it affords a good position but because it places ~~two~~ one important gap (Brocks) on the ~~East~~ West and ~~West in our possession. This road was on through Thorntons Gap via Luray~~ an important road on the East in our hands which leads to Luray and Thorntons Gap. This road would have offered many advantages for a cavalry raid to Charlottesville ~~and the Virginia~~ which [illegible strikethrough] I am confident could have been accomplished by using the road to Port Republic running parallel ~~with~~ to the ~~river~~ Shenandoah River. ~~The gap referred to is Brock's.~~

Brock's Gap in our hands would have facilitated the opening of communications with Crook~~'s command~~ and resulted in a cooperation with the troops under my immediate command.

I therefore marched with my force from Woodstock on the morning of the 15th to if possible gain the position at New Market. On [illegible strikethrough] reaching the advance ~~of the~~ under Col. Moore near New Market in a very fair position, I ordered the entire force to march forward as quickly as possible in order to arrive in time for the attack of the enemy which was just preparing.

The advance severely pressed had to take a second position ~~behind~~ in the rear of which I formed the remainder of the command, my right resting on the Shenandoah River and the left on the turnpike, except two regiments which had not come up to receive [?] the advance guard and to make a stand against the enemy's attack.

The first assault ~~of the enemy~~ was checked by our artillery and infantry so that an attempt was made to return the charge ~~the enemy~~ but the enemy's numbers [illegible strikethrough] so far superior compelled our troops to return to their old position and ~~to~~ gradually to fall back. ~~The~~

In the attack on the advance we had the misfortune to have all the horses of one section of artillery ~~lost~~ shot thereby losing the pieces and in the subsequent assaults three pieces were disabled causing their loss.

I then gave orders to withdraw and to take position ~~to north of~~ behind the Shenandoah River in front of Mt. Jackson. This movement was executed by Brig. Gen. Sullivan with great skill and promptness who under the immediate command of Maj. Gen. Stahel conducted the rear guard.

The enemy followed without ~~showing~~ [illegible] any energy in the pursuit showing that their loss had been so severe that they were obliged to reorganize. It was between 6 to 7 o'clock when the troops crossed the Shenandoah River and took up their new positions ready to withstand the enemy with the advantages of the ground. ~~But we~~ No attack was made [illegible strikethrough] when at 10 P.M. I ordered the retreat towards Woodstock and Cedar Creek after burning the bridge over the Shenandoah near Mt Jackson. On the evening of the 16th I arrived at Cedar Creek having retired very slowly without losing any men or material.

On the morning of the 17th the troops took up their position behind Cedar Creek and are now ready to receive the enemy with new supplies of ammunition [illegible, strikethrough].

Report by Maj. Meysenburg
(New Market 5-17-64)

Appendix 3

The 54th Pennsylvania Infantry at New Market

This article appeared in the June 2006 issue of *Battlefield Journal* and is reprinted here with the kind permission of the publisher.

* * *

Today the small cedar-covered knoll is quiet and peaceful, except for the passing traffic several hundred yards to the west on Interstate 81. The granite soldier stands at rest, his gaze fixed to the east, toward the old Valley Pike, where his comrades in both blue and gray marched almost a century and a half ago. Behind him the ground slowly rises to a hilltop crowned by several artillery pieces. This soldier, who has served as landmark to travelers on the Valley Pike for decades, is a reminder of the slaughter that took place on this ground in May 1864.

In the spring of 1864, the 54th Pennsylvania Infantry Regiment was part of Union Major General Franz Sigel's field army in the Department of West Virginia. Many of its members came from the Johnstown area: Cambria and Somerset counties in the southwestern part of the state. The regiment had been formed in late summer 1861 and trained at Camp Curtin.[1] The 54th had spent the first half of the war stationed along the Baltimore & Ohio Railroad in West

---

1   Charles W. Bennett, Jr., *Four Years with the Fifty-Fourth: The Military History of Franklin Bennett, 54th Pennsylvania Volunteer Regiment, 1861-1865* (Richmond, VA, 1985), 3.

Virginia, guarding the numerous bridges which were favorite targets of Confederate raids. This duty entailed splitting the regiment into individual companies; very seldom was the entire 54th Pennsylvania together. Its original orders in March 1862 had the regiment strung out over 56 miles of track, between Martinsburg, West Virginia, and Cumberland, Maryland.[2]

With the appointment of Lieutenant General U.S. Grant to command of all the Federal armies in early 1864, the outlook for the war in the western part of Virginia changed. Franz Sigel was appointed to command; he was given orders to advance several columns into western Virginia, pinning down Confederate forces there while also depriving the Southern armies valuable supplies—salt and lead mines near Wytheville, food from the Shenandoah Valley—and to cut the vital Virginia & Tennessee railroad which linked Richmond with the Western Confederacy.

Sigel was not Grant's first choice, but rather owed his new position to his political influences. Despite having had little military success in his career, Sigel—born in what is now Germany—was a leader in the large German-American community. Looking to secure German support at the polls, President Abraham Lincoln wanted Sigel given an important and visible role in Grant's spring campaign. Grant recognized Sigel's shortcomings and placed him in what was intended to be largely an administrative position heading up the Department of West Virginia. However, when quarrels with Sigel drove away Grant favorite Maj. Gen. Edward O.C. Ord, who was supposed to lead Sigel's field army, Sigel took command of the field force himself.

The plan was for the Army of the Potomac to advance against Robert E. Lee's Army of Northern Virginia west of Fredericksburg. Another army under Ben Butler was to move against Richmond and Petersburg from the east, threatening Lee's rear as well as the Confederate capital. Sigel meanwhile was to advance two columns out of West Virginia, one under George Crook aimed at the railroad and the lead and salt mines in the southwest corner of Virginia, and another—initially under Ord, but as it played out, under Sigel himself—to move south up the Shenandoah Valley from Martinsburg, to rendezvous with Crook's column at Staunton. From there the combined force was to either move against Lynchburg or operate against Lee's left flank. Grant's plan for

2 Samuel P. Bates, *History of the Pennsylvania Volunteers, 1861-1865* (Harrisburg, PA, 1869-71), 135.

Sigel was perhaps summed up best by Lincoln himself: "If a man can't skin, he must hold a leg while somebody else does."[3]

For his foray into the Shenandoah Valley, Sigel mustered about 10,000 troops. These were organized into one infantry division, consisting of eight infantry regiments, including the 54th Pennsylvania, one cavalry division and five artillery batteries. It was an amalgam of troops, some having seen hard fighting against Lee's troops earlier in the war, while others, like the 54th, had served mostly garrison and railroad guard.

On April 29th, Sigel's army set out from Martinsburg, headed up the Valley [because a geographic quirk, namely the northward flow of the Shenandoah River which has its headwaters south of Staunton and empties into the Potomac at Harper's Ferry, moving south is referred to as "up" the Valley]. Throughout the campaign, the weather was alternately hot and arid one day then rained incessantly for several days.

Opposing Sigel's advance initially was about 1,200 Confederate cavalry under Brigadier General John D. Imboden. Despite being outnumbered nearly 10 to 1, Imboden's troopers and raiders under John McNeill and John Mosby continually harassed Sigel, and forced him to detach large numbers of his cavalry to guard his flanks and supply route. The Federals moved at a glacial pace, with their commander preferring drill and mock battles over any actual military advances. However, when Sigel's advance reached Woodstock on May 11, the Confederates were driven out of town in such haste that they left several telegrams to Imboden from his superior, Major General John C. Breckinridge. These messages revealed that aid was en route to Imboden from southwest Virginia. But instead of spurring Sigel to action, this captured intelligence caused him to take root in Woodstock.[4] During this time, Company C, or at least a portion of it, of the 54th was sent on a raid to destroy nearby Columbia Furnace, one of the local iron furnaces. In addition to burning the furnace, the raid also netted eight boxes of tobacco—a much more popular prize with the men than the destruction of the iron works.[5] But while Sigel delayed, Breckinridge took advantage of the time and drew nearer.

---

3   Ulysses S. Grant, "Preparing for the Campaigns of 1864," 4 vols., *Battles and Leaders*, 4, 112.

4   Davis, *Battle of New Market*, 57.

5   J. F. Klingman to Benjamin A. Colonna, January 26, 1911, NM coll., VMI.

While Sigel set a portion of his army in motion southward again on May 13 and the preliminary skirmishes of the Battle of New Market flared the following day, the 54th Pennsylvania remained in its camp north of Woodstock until Sunday, May 15. The regiment got on the road at 6 a.m. and marched till about midday. Throughout the morning the ominous sound of cannon fire was heard to the south. Lieutenant George Gageby of Company D recorded in his diary, "heavy cannonading was heard at the front [and so] went faster," arriving at Mount Jackson, about eight miles north of New Market at 2 p.m. There was little time for rest, though as things heated up at the front. "Start fires to make coffee, long roll sounds, fall in and start for the front," Gageby recorded.[6]

Things were not going well for the Federals at New Market when the 54th arrived. Sigel's men had already been pushed back from their initial position in and adjacent to the town, and Breckinridge—who had joined forces with Imboden early that morning—with about 4,500 men, had gained possession of the town as well as high ground to the south and west for his artillery. During the initial Confederate advance, the 18th Connecticut and 123rd Ohio had been hit hard and driven in confusion from their position in front of the now-forming main Union line. It had been raining off and on and in the afternoon thunderstorms rolled in, drenching the men and turning the already saturated fields into muck. To make matters worse, Sigel's whole army still was not present—this while a sizeable engagement was taking shape. For behind the 54th, two Ohio regiments and an artillery battery still had yet to reach the field. Thus one Pennsylvanian wrote with considerable understatement, "We came on the field under trying circumstances."[7]

Initially the 54th was in a reserve position behind the 12th West Virginia, about one mile north of New Market, immediately to the west of the Valley Pike. However, the 12th was soon moved to a reserve position on the right and the 54th was moved up into the main line, with the 1st West Virginia to their right, their left resting on the Pike, and an artillery battery and cavalry to their left rear.[8] The Keystoners were on a small ridge, partly covered with small cedar trees. The Federal line ran along this ridge for nearly a mile, from the Shenandoah River to the west, across the Valley Pike and ending near Smith's

6   Gageby to Colonna, May 27, 1911.

7   Bryan to Colonna, March 8, 1911.

8   *OR* 37, pt. 1, 86.

Creek at the foot of Massanutten Mountain to the east. "There we waited for the enemy who were driving some of our cavalry and infantry toward us," remembered one Pennsylvanian.[9] One sergeant remembered how quickly the fight reached the 54th's position. "As soon as we arrived on that ridge . . . we began to fire and I was kept busy pulling our men back out of the line as [they] were killed or wounded . . . the smoke was so thick I could see nothing in front."[10]

What the smoke obscured from view was a solid line of Confederate infantry advancing across the fields toward the Union position. While farther to the west, the massed Union guns and more open terrain were having a more pronounced effect on the advancing Confederates, the 62nd Virginia, possibly some dismounted elements of the 23rd Virginia Cavalry, and the 22nd Virginia kept up a deadly fire on the 54th Pennsylvania. When the Confederate advance stalled and part of the gray line to the west broke, Sigel ordered a counter attack. This attempt to drive Breckinridge back failed, as the breach in the Confederate left and center had been filled by, among others, the Corps of Cadets from Virginia Military Institute, pressed into emergency service as infantrymen. In the confusion of battle, Col. Jacob Campbell, the 54th's commander, apparently never got the order to attack, but "observing the regiment on my right making a charge in the absence of orders, presuming it proper to imitate their example, I ordered the Fifty-fourth to charge."[11]

Simply put, the 54th never had a chance. The cavalry supporting their left was gone, having been decimated in an earlier attempt to break the Confederate right. The 1st West Virginia to the right did not wait for the 54th and thus advanced unsupported and was quickly driven back with loss. Likewise, the 54th was advancing without support on either flank. Also about this time, Confederate units managed to turn the Union right and drive off the guns anchoring that flank. Thus the 54th was advancing against nearly all of Breckinridge's army while all but one other Federal regiment [34th Massachusetts] was abandoning the field. The Pennsylvanians were being flanked on both sides and still facing a galling fire in front. "The order to retreat was sounded," a private in Company C recalled, but "not hearing the sound of

---

9 Gageby to Colonna, May 27, 1911.

10 Bryan to Colonna, March 8, 1911.

11 *OR* 37, pt. 1, 86.

the bugle I stood behind a small tree loading and firing when I looked about me I saw the boys retreating, so I gave one tremendous leap to the rear across a ravine then up the bluff and soon caught up with" his comrades.[12]

The Confederates were close upon the heels of the retreating Federals. Writing to one of the VMI cadets long after war, a sergeant from Company A recalled "I was one of the last men to leave that field. Some of your men called for me to surrender but I kept on running."[13] Lt. George Gageby had a somewhat similar experience as he carried a wounded comrade to shelter in a nearby house. "As the door swung open I saw through a window opposite it a line of Confederates passing along the other side of the house. I turned to go back to my regiment and saw them falling back." Rejoining his command, Gageby "found several of our men, one of whom said Lieut. [sic] we are gone up, I replied not by a d——d sight [sic], I have a brother in Libby Prison now and one of the family at a time is enough for mother to grieve for."[14]

Out of 566 officers and men in the eight companies which entered the fight, in a space of no more than two hours, the 54th Pennsylvania lost 174 men killed, wounded or missing.[15] A report in the New York *Tribune* mistakenly inflated this figure—apparently by a typographical error—by an additional 80 men, for a total of 254 casualties. Because the official casualty report for New Market was lost until just recently, the higher number was the "accepted" casualty total for the 54th, which would give them the highest numerical loss on either side at New Market. However, the original Federal casualty report resurfaced at the National Archives several years ago. With that discovery the highest loss distinction now belongs to the 34th Massachusetts with 215 casualties.[16] Regardless, the 54th Pennsylvania suffered very heavily, losing nearly one-third of their number. One 1921 obituary makes a somewhat suspect statement that Henry Helsel of Company I "was wounded nine times [in] a period of two minutes," carrying one of the bullets in his leg for 20 years.[17]

---

12 Yutzy to Colonna, February 11, 1911.

13 Bryan to Colonna, March 8, 1911.

14 Gageby to Colonna, May 27, 1911.

15 *OR* 37, pt. 1, 87.

16 Gailey, Casualty Report, NMBSHP.

17 Johnstown *Tribune*, March 15, 1921.

Sigel was driven from the field in confusion, the 54th attempting to check the pursuit several times, but it was not before the arrival of the remainder of Sigel's army that the Federals were able to regroup briefly. The army crossed the Shenandoah River, burning the bridge behind them and camped that night at Mount Jackson before retreating toward Winchester the following day. Sigel was relieved of his command several days later.

The 54th Pennsylvania would pass through New Market several more times during the war, certainly evoking memories of that rainy May Sunday. After serving in the Valley for the remainder of 1864, the 54th was transferred to the Petersburg front in late December. During the Appomattox Campaign, the 54th was part of a raiding party dispatched to destroy High Bridge over the Appomattox River and block Lee's line of retreat. However, this force was soundly defeated in the attempt and the 54th was captured almost intact. Thus the Pennsylvanians were present at Appomattox but had the distinction of being Confederate captives. Following Lee's surrender, the 54th was paroled and mustered out in mid-July 1865.[18]

Almost 41 years to the day after the battle, the Pennsylvania legislature approved a bill granting $2,000 to the Association of the Fifty-fourth Regiment Pennsylvania Veteran Volunteer Infantry "for the purpose of erecting a monument on the battlefield of New Market, Virginia." The bill was signed May 11, 1905 by Pennsylvania Governor Samuel Pennypacker.[19]

The following month the Harrisonburg, Virginia, newspaper apprised its readers, many of whom were veterans of New Market, of the plans for a monument. "A Monument will be erected in memory of the 54th Pa. Regiment, U.S. Infantry, who fell there in battle, the location having been determined upon by David Bryan, Robert Parsons, and W.A. Slick, members of the Regiment, during a recent visit to the Battlefield." The point selected was on the cedar-covered knoll just west of the Valley Pike where the 54th had anchored the left flank of the Union infantry. The total cost for the monument was projected to be about $3,000.[20]

The idea was not well received at all by the New Market newspaper that August. "So the Pennsylvanians propose to monument themselves . . . with a

---

18 Bates, *History of the Pennsylvania Volunteers*, 143.

19 Charles R. Knight, *54th Pennsylvania Monument*, NMBSHP.

20 Rockingham *Register*, June 27, 1905.

$2000 or $3000 loftiness," it began. "If they are anxious to do something honorable they can pay something on the barns and mills they burned, the horses and cattle they stole, the grain and property they despoiled this very people of," wrote an embittered J.E. Hopkins, a former Confederate cavalryman. "They had better put the memorial at the bridge," he wrote, in reference to the hasty retreat borne by Sigel's men.[21] Six paragraphs of vitriol in the paper condemned the actions taken, not by the 54th Pennsylvania, but by other troops later in 1864 in destroying the Valley. The idea of the 54th Pennsylvania monument merely served as a convenient outlet for the author to air his bitterness. For after 40 years, most were willing to forgive.

When the unveiling of the monument took place on October 27, 1905, a crowd of about 400 was present. Ironically, rain fell throughout the day, adding a bit of historical authenticity to the affair for the several dozen veterans of the battle who were present. About 100 veterans of the 54th were present, but of these only about 30 had actually been at New Market. Col. Campbell's son C.G. Campbell was one of the leaders of the group. In the audience were numerous Confederate veterans, including David Sites, W.R. Fallis and James Dwyer, all of Charles Woodson's Missouri company, which had fought attached to the 62nd Virginia at New Market. Dwyer and Fallis had only months before erected a small monument to their comrades several hundred yards away from the 54th monument. Also present was Peter W. Roller, of nearby Mount Crawford, who had been in the Cadet Corps in the battle.

About 1 p.m. the Rev. E.L. Wessinger, pastor of Emmanuel Lutheran Church in New Market, delivered an invocation to the crowd assembled in the field alongside the Valley Pike "under a sea of umbrellas." After this Miss Miriam Mosteller, whose father had been in Company B of the 54th, removed the cloth covering the monument, revealing a fine granite sculpture of a soldier standing at "parade rest." The monument stands 17 feet tall, with the soldier standing upon a base of Pennsylvania granite. The front of the base reads "Erected to the Memory / of the Heroic Dead of the / Fifty-Fourth Regiment, P.V.V.I. / Who Lost Their Lives / In Defense of Their Country".[22]

21 *Shenandoah Valley*, August 10, 1905.

22 Rockingham *Register*, October 27, 1905; Knight, *54th Pennsylvania Monument*.

Whether intended or not is not known, the monument stands upon the spot identified by several veterans of the regiment where Capt. Edwin J. Geissinger of Company H was killed.[23]

In August 1911 the 54th Pennsylvania Association held its annual reunion at New Market. One former officer wrote to a former Confederate about the upcoming reunion, "I think it is safe for me to say there is very little, if any, harsh feeling toward those we met there on the 15th of May 1864."[24]

In a ceremony September 16, 1984, title to the monument was passed from the Commonwealth of Pennsylvania to the New Market Battlefield State Historical Park, with Secretary of the Army John O. Marsh, Jr., as keynote speaker.[25]

Today the 54th Pennsylvania monument is one of only two monuments erected by veterans of the battle. When corresponding nearly half a century after the battle, one 54th veteran wrote to a former VMI Cadet some of his recollections about the Battle of New Market, "It has been almost 47 years since that time and as we grow older we forget these things."[26]

The 54th Pennsylvania monument serves as a reminder for generations to come of "these things" which should never be forgotten.

23 Bryan to Colonna, March 8, 1911.

24 Gageby to Colonna, May 27, 1911.

25 Knight, *54th Pennsylvania Monument.*

26   J. F. Klingman to B. A. Colonna, January 26, 1911, NM Coll., VMI.

Appendix 4

The Bushong Family, George Collins, and New Market Battlefield Historical Park

Bushong, originally spelled "Boschong," is among the earliest names to appear in the land records of the central Shenandoah Valley.[1] One history of the Valley states that a John Bushong purchased land between present-day New Market and Luray as early as 1733.[2]

Jacob Bushong's great-grandfather, John Bushong, and his wife Barbara arrived in Philadelphia in September 1731 aboard the *Britannia*. The family settled in the heavily-German Lancaster County in rural Pennsylvania.[3] In the later years of the 18th century, many Germans, the so-called "Pennsylvania Dutch," moved south with many of them eventually settling in the Shenandoah Valley. Several of the Bushongs were included in this immigration.

By 1785, the family had established itself in the central Valley in what is now Shenandoah County. A county census conducted in 1785 records a "John Bushong Sr." living in the area near Strasburg, with a family of seven.[4] Another

---

1 The "Bushong" spelling will be used here simply for continuity.

2 Wayland, *History of Shenandoah County*, 174.

3 Bushong genealogical records, NMBSHP. A good number of Bushongs still inhabit the Lancaster County, Pennsylvania, area.

4 Wayland, *History of Shenandoah County*, 224.

"John Bushong" appears in the same census in the Woodstock vicinity with a family of four.[5]

In June 1791, Henry Bushong purchased 260 acres northwest of New Market—the farm which would be the scene of the heaviest fighting at the Battle of New Market. This land would eventually pass to Henry's son Jacob, born the year before.[6]

In March 1818, Jacob married Sarah "Sallie" Strickler of Page County.[7] Jacob's new bride came from a wealthy family. When Sallie's father died in 1836, his estate was valued at nearly $6,500 and included eleven slaves. The slaves alone were valued at more than $5,300.[8] The earliest known structure built on the property is a two-story log cabin dating to 1818. This is one of two surviving war-time structures on the farm today.[9]

A much larger Federal-style house was constructed adjacent to the cabin in 1825. For unknown reasons, this new home was built facing south, whereas the older cabin faces east. As the family continued to grow, an addition was constructed on the back of the house in 1852, doubling the size of the structure.[10]

When Henry Bushong experienced financial troubles in the early 1820s, Abraham Strickler purchased the farm. Shortly after Strickler's death in December 1836, Jacob Bushong purchased 207 acres of the property from his wife's family for one dollar.[11]

Whatever financial concerns had existed in earlier decades were gone by the eve of the Civil War. Jacob and Sarah had seven children, at least two of whom

---

5   *Ibid.* 230.

6   Bushong genealogy, NMBSHP.

7   *Ibid.*

8   "Inventory and list of the appraisement of the personal estate of Abram Strickler, December 13, 1836," Page County Courthouse, Luray, Virginia.

9   This writer lived for the summer of 1998 on the second floor of this dwelling. As of this writing, the second floor is used as accommodations for the park's "Shaara Scholar," a summer internship sponsored by author Jeff Shaara.

10 Bushong genealogy, NMBSHP. The older front portion of the house has been semi-restored, although it was altered greatly during the 20th century by the addition of a new floor (which has since been removed), several inches higher than the original floor that was sinking, and the installation of electricity and plumbing. The rear addition on the dwelling has been retained as a living quarters for park staff.

11 Shenandoah Country Deed Book QQ, 17-8.

died in childhood. The surviving children helped to run a very large self-supporting farm. In addition to growing wheat, corn, apples, and pears, the family had a considerable amount of livestock including five horses, twenty cows, seven sheep, and nineteen pigs, and also a blacksmith and wheelwright / carpentry shop. According to the 1860 census, the family also had three slaves: a 27-year-old male whose name is not known, a 24-year-old mulatto female named Mary, and a 3-year-old mulatto boy named Israel.[12] It is thought that the slaves occupied either the old 1818 cabin or a loft above the kitchen, but this is not known for certain.

The family's youngest son, Franklin, was a member of the Tenth Legion Artillery, a local militia company. It was sent to Charlestown (in what is today West Virginia) in December 1859 to oversee the execution of John Brown.[13] Despite this pre-war militia service, Franklin did not serve in uniform during the Civil War. His older brother Anderson, however, served briefly as a corporal in Company B, 97th Virginia Militia during the summer of 1861 before going home for a brief furlough from which he did not return. Nothing further is known of his war-time service.[14]

It is not known for certain what religion the family practiced at this time, although they were probably Lutheran because many are buried in the cemetery of St. Matthew's Lutheran Church in New Market (except for Anderson, who was known to be a member of the German Baptist Church and is interred at Cedar Grove Church of the Brethren). Some of the family became members of the Church of the Brethren after the war.[15] Many Valley Brethren as well as Mennonites and Quakers did not support the war and somehow managed to avoid conscription. It is possible that Franklin fell into this category.

Sarah Bushong joined the other women of New Market in doing what they could for the wounded soldiers at the large military hospital established at Mount Jackson during the war's early months. A report of the Soldiers Relief

---

12 Bushong genealogy, NMBSHP.

13 Wayland, *History of Shenandoah County*, 295.

14 Anderson Bushong militia records, NMBSHP.

15 The author owns several books and religious pamphlets that belonged to the Jacob Bushong family, many of which are signed by the family members. Nearly all of the late 19th and early 20th century religious works relate to the Church of the Brethren.

and Aid Association from December 1861 lists "Mrs. Bushong" as contributing two pairs of socks, one "lot" of soap, and various herbs.[16]

Tradition holds that the family was huddled in the basement of the main house as the Battle of New Market raged around them on May 15, 1864.[17] This is confirmed by a recently-discovered account from one of Imboden's men who visited the Bushong House immediately after the battle and spoke with Mrs. Bushong herself.[18] However, the story that as many as seven family members and possibly the three slaves were confined into the basement with all the family's livestock seems far-fetched.[19]

After the battle the house, the barn, and probably all of the out-buildings were used as field hospitals to treat the wounded of both sides. Because the townspeople treated wounded Federals alongside Confederates, the barns on the farms in and around New Market were spared from Federal torches later in 1864.[20]

The farm stayed in the Bushong family into the 20th century. Jacob E. Bushong, grandson of Jacob and Sarah, and his wife Emma capitalized on the historic value of their home by turning it into an inn (aptly named "Battlefield House"). Early advertisements for the inn note that it is an "Historical old

---

16 Good, *Shadowed by the Massanutten*, 463.

17 "Occupants of the Battlefield House on May 15, 1864," S. M. Heflin, August 29, 1972, Bushong genealogical records, NMBSHP.

18 Sager, *Battle of New Market*, 14: "All during the battle, Mrs. Bushong and her family had to confine themselves to the basement of their house as a matter of safety. Still Mrs. Bushong could not control her interest and curiosity. . . . All the pleadings of the family could not keep Mrs. Bushong away from the basement windows. . . . The retreat of the Yankees was a run. Mrs. Bushong at the window, now started clapping her hands. To her family she shouted, 'Now come if you want to see Yankees run.'"

19 It is interesting to note that in his *History of Shenandoah County*, John Wayland makes no mention at all of this story. Given the era in which Wayland wrote and his use of oral traditions as "facts," this omission leads this author to believe that the story is without basis and is retold simply to amuse visitors and school children when taken into the basement of the Bushong House. Also, the three slaves disappear from the family's records before the battle, so it is not known if they ran away or were still with the family in May 1864.

20 Mary Rupp to Frank Bushong, April 23, 1865, NMBSHP, reads: "Providence will still provide for us, we have never suffered for anything in the eating line notwithstanding all the barns were burned last fall and nearly everything else in the eating line destroyed[.] Your father's barn was not burned, the family are all well and getting along very well considering the hard times they still have enough to eat and to wear."

home situated in [the] storm center of New Market Battlefield." It also featured "water and lights" and gave "special attention to week or week-end tourists."[21]

Many of the Bushongs, including Jacob, Sarah, and Franklin, are buried in the cemetery of St. Matthew's Lutheran Church in New Market. Their descendants still live in the area, with others in Florida and Ohio. Also buried in this cemetery is a "D. Bushong," reported to be a member of Company D, 62nd Virginia, killed at New Market. His exact identity is unknown, as there is no official record for someone of that name having served in the 62nd; we do know he was not a direct family member of Jacob Bushong.

In 1942, the farm passed out of the Bushong family with its sale to Everette H. Croxton.[22] Only one year later it was purchased by George R. Collins, of Charleston, West Virginia, a 1911 graduate of VMI.[23] Collins, like all VMI "Rats"—the Institute's nickname for freshmen—had been told the New Market story countless times. Collins had made a small fortune in the West Virginia coal fields and jumped when the opportunity to purchase the Bushong Farm (with its iconic status in the annals of Virginia Military Institute) presented itself. When Collins died not long after the centennial anniversary of the battle in 1964, he left the Bushong Farm and an endowment of $3,000,000 to his alma mater, to operate the farm as a park. His Last Will and Testament reads, in part, that the farm "be used . . . to perpetuate and maintain a Memorial of the Battle of New Market."[24]

Although it was through Collins that today's battlefield park had its genesis, the idea of a "Memorial of the Battle of New Market" took root much earlier. A mere two years after the battle a "Memorial Day" program was held on May 15 to commemorate the battle.[25] The following year, the "Women's Memorial Society of the Lost Cause" was organized and sponsored a memorial program on or close to the anniversary of the battle every year thereafter—one of the first ceremonies of its kind in the South. Notable speakers at the ceremony in the years and decades after the battle included Charles T. O'Ferrall, former

21 Photocopy of advertisement card in author's possession.

22 New Market *Shenandoah Valley*, April 30, 1942.

23 Richmond *News Leader*, December 9, 1964.

24 Keith E. Gibson, "Speaking with Eloquent Voices: A Look at the VMI Museum and the New Market Battlefield Historical Park," January 1987, NMBSHP.

25 Richard Kleese, *Shenandoah County in the Civil War* (Lynchburg, VA, 1992), 117.

lieutenant colonel of the 23rd Virginia Cavalry and later Governor of Virginia; Brigadier General John Echols; and Robert E. Lee, Jr. In the 1898 ceremony, a granite obelisk was dedicated in the graveyard at St. Matthew's, commemorating those killed in the battle who are buried in the churchyard. Former VMI Cadet John S. Wise, one of the more prolific writers of the "New Market Cadets," delivered the address.[26]

In 1905, two more monuments were erected. One, a small stone block with a simple inscription recalling Charles Woodson's Missourians, was erected at the northeast corner of the Bushong orchard. Several months later a much more ornate monument was dedicated to honor the 54th Pennsylvania's participation in the battle. Several hundred people were in attendance for the dedication of the Pennsylvania monument, which sits just off to the west of the Valley Pike.

The Centennial anniversary of the battle in 1964 was a huge event, drawing visitors and reenactors from all across the country. Included in the festivities were several descendants of John C. Breckinridge, at least one Confederate widow, several members of Virginia's Congressional delegation, and the superintendent of VMI.

The construction of Interstate 81 in 1966 greatly altered what, until then, had been a pristine battlefield. The new highway cuts through Shirley's Hill and passes within 100 yards of the Bushong House. A pedestrian tunnel in front of the house now connects the two portions of the battlefield.[27]

In July 1967, Collins' wishes were borne out when the 160-acre New Market Battlefield Park opened to the public. The new park was national news and mentioned in the *New York Times*. Originally the Bushong House was used as the interpretive center, but in 1970 it was replaced by the newly constructed "Hall of Valor Museum."[28] This piece of unique architecture (the original design was rejected and the architect fired for proposing too modern a building) was quite groundbreaking in its day. Park Director James J. Geary had been involved with the Civil War Centennial celebration several years before and was able to secure for the Hall of Valor many exhibits that had been featured at the

---

26 Hildreth, *Brief History of New Market*, 28-32.

27 The skylights for the tunnel in the median of the interstate have given rise to some interesting rumors, one of which is that the portion of the skylights visible above ground are actually coffins of soldiers killed in the battle.

28 Gibson, "Speaking with Eloquent Voices."

Centennial Museum in Richmond, of which he had been Director. The Hall also told the story not just of New Market but of the entire war in Virginia. That same year (1970) the battlefield was declared a Virginia Historic Landmark.

The opening of the new Hall of Valor in 1970 allowed for a portion of the Bushong House to be restored and interpreted as a Civil War-era home. Two rooms on the first floor of the older wing of the house were opened to the public in the summer of 1971.[29]

Of the ten structures comprising the Bushong Farm complex, only two are the original war-time structures—the 1818 house and the "big" house. The original wartime barn survived into the 20th century, only to become a victim of fire in July 1939.[30] The current barn is built on the original foundation. Other outbuildings were moved to the park from other locations (or were rebuilt using timber from 19th century structures) and placed in the known locations of the original structures. The large stone and brick bake oven in the yard dates from about 1870, and was moved to the park in 1967 from a local farm.[31] In late 1968, the orchard was replanted with seven different varieties of apple trees.[32] The construction of the outbuildings was completed in the summer of 1974, having taken two years to construct a blacksmith shop, wheelwright shop, kitchen, hen house, loom house, and stone ice house.[33]

In February 1968, the oak tree that stood behind von Kleiser's battery and had been a landmark on the battlefield for years—and was used by veterans as a reference point in many memoirs—toppled during a storm. Although it had been dead for several years, because of its significance it had been allowed to remain. It had grown to some 70 feet tall and had a diameter of eleven feet.[34] A

29 Harrisonburg *Daily News Record*, August 17, 1971.

30 William Algernon Good, *New Market Volunteer Fire Company, 1791-2000*, records the demise of the barn. "About 1 O'clock on Wednesday July 5, 1939, the barn of Mr. Jacob E. Bushong (at battlefield) was set afire by lightning, the NM fire department responded quickly and were able to save a nearby building by pumping water from a reservoir near the barn. At this time firemen had their new 1937 ford truck equipped with tank and pumper. A new barn built soon after the fire stands today on the old foundation." The current barn was constructed on the old foundation in late July 1941.

31 Harrisonburg *Daily News Record*, September 14, 1967.

32 Strasburg *Northern Virginia Daily*, December 14, 1968. The orchard includes pear trees today as well.

33 *The Shenvaleader*, September 1974.

34 Harrisonburg *Daily News Record*, February 5, 1968.

new tree (which still stands) was planted in July 1968, provided by the Pi Kappa Alpha Fraternity at the University of Virginia, in honor of Cadet Julian E. Wood, a veteran of the battle and founder of the fraternity.[35]

Today the park, now known as New Market Battlefield State Historical Park, has grown to include nearly 300 acres and includes much of the original 200 acres purchased by Jacob Bushong in 1837, as well as portions of Shirley's Hill and Manor's Hill. Interstate 81 bisects the battlefield and the park, but apart from that much of the core area of fighting remains intact. The access road to the park, VA Route 305, is named "George R. Collins Parkway" in honor of the park's benefactor and founder.

In addition to the VMI-owned property, the Shenandoah Valley Battlefields Foundation, which has its headquarters at New Market, has preserved an additional 200 acres. According to the Foundation, the "core area" of New Market battlefield comprises some 2,261 acres, with some 1,527 retaining their wartime appearance. All of the preserved lands are west of the old Valley Pike and do not include (as of the time of this writing) any of the ground traversed by either Echols' Brigade or the Federal cavalry, or the Imboden-Boyd battlefield of May 13.[36]

The park hosts an annual reenactment of the battle every May—one of the few reenactments held on the original battlefield. This reenactment dates back to the early 20th century and perhaps even earlier. In recent years a portion of the Corps of Cadets from VMI has begun making the trek—on foot—from Lexington to New Market, just as their predecessors did in 1864, arriving just in time for the reenactment of their charge.

---

35 Woodstock *Shenandoah Herald*, August 1, 1968.

36 Deborah Fitts, "Three New Market Sites are Preserved," *Civil War News*, January 2006.

Appendix 5

The Role of the
23rd Virginia Cavalry at New Market

There has been some uncertainty and confusion regarding the role that the 23rd Virginia Cavalry played in the fighting on May 15. It is certain that at least a portion of the regiment fought dismounted, attached to the 62nd Virginia Mounted Infantry (which also fought dismounted). What is unclear from previous histories of the battle is whether the entire regiment fought as infantry, or whether part of it remained with Imboden and the 18th Virginia Cavalry. Unfortunately, primary source material on the 23rd Virginia Cavalry is scarce, so one must rely in good measure upon the recollections of the other two regiments (18th Virginia Cavalry and 62nd Virginia Mounted Infantry) in Imboden's Brigade, as well as the commanders themselves. Historians writing after the publication of William C. Davis' *Battle of New Market* have accepted his conclusion that the entire 23rd Virginia Cavalry fought dismounted. However, a close examination of the evidence calls this conclusion into question.

"Our regiment," wrote Isaac White, surgeon of the 62nd Virginia on May 7, 1864, "has been dismounted + all of those belonging to the 23rd + 18th that are without horses have been attached to this regt."[1] According to William C. Davis, the entire 23rd Virginia Cavalry was dismounted and assigned to the 62nd Virginia Mounted Infantry by order of Breckinridge on the morning of

---

1 White to "My Dear Jinnie," May 7, 1864, White Papers.

the 15th.[2] However, neither Imboden nor Charles T. O'Ferrall, the lieutenant colonel of the 23rd Virginia Cavalry, confirm this in their postwar writings. In his prolific postwar recollections, Colonel George Smith of the 62nd Virginia makes no mention of an addition to his command of anything other than Charles Woodson's company of Missourians (see also Appendix 1). If anything, Smith makes an allusion in his postwar book to the 23rd Virginia Cavalry remaining with Imboden.[3] Smith's voluminous postwar correspondence about New Market with Lieutenant Colonel George M. Edgar of the 26th Virginia Battalion, makes no mention of the 23rd Virginia Cavalry being dismounted and attached to (or even near) his command. Nor does such an order appear in Breckinridge's official, but unpublished report. If such an order had been issued, these are the officers who would have been in position to note it.

To the contrary, a letter written the day after the battle by Pvt. John Kiracofe of Company G, 18th Virginia Cavalry, states that "General Breckenridge [sic] with his force & the 62nd done the most of the fighting. Our Regiment & Col White's [23rd Virginia Cavalry] was on the right wing and acted as flankers."[4] In one of George Smith's numerous accounts of the battle, this one in a July 1908 letter to a resident of New Market (and later published in the town's newspaper *The Shenandoah Valley*), the former colonel stated that "Imboden's mounted men, the 18th and 23rd VA regiments, were sent to the right bank of Smith's Creek."[5] He had said the same thing to a former comrade several months earlier: "the 62nd regiment . . . was the only part of Imboden's men in the infantry line."[6] (Admittedly, Smith wrote so many differing versions of the battle that these statements, taken by themselves, should not be accepted as conclusive proof of anything.)

---

2   Davis, *Battle of New Market*, 88-9. However, Davis' earlier Breckinridge biography makes no such claim: "Imboden's command, about 1,400 strong, contributed only some 500 men of the 62nd Virginia to the battle, the rest being as much out of it on the east side of Smith's Creek as if they had not been present at all." Davis, *Breckinridge*, 428.

3   Smith, *Positions and Movements of the Troops*, 32; Smith, *The Battle of New Market*, 12-3. Smith's writings must be used with caution, for no two accounts match. He regularly altered his views on the battle after corresponding with veterans of other commands.

4   Kiracofe to "My Dear Wife & Daughter," May 16, 1864.

5   Wayland, *History of Shenandoah County*, 320.

6   George H. Smith to Thomas H. Neilson, February 13, 1908, Edgar Papers.

Circumstantial evidence from others in Imboden's Brigade also points to the 23rd Virginia Cavalry remaining with Imboden and the 18th Virginia Cavalry. In his description of the role of the mounted arm during the campaign Lieutenant Julian Pratt, Company H, 18th Virginia Cavalry, did not mention the disposition of the 23rd Virginia Cavalry during the battle. Given the level of detail with which he describes other operations, it is reasonable to infer that nothing out of the ordinary occurred for that regiment—like being dismounted and placed in the middle of the infantry line. A brief report by the ordnance officer of Imboden's Brigade the day after the battle states that the 62nd Virginia was detached from the brigade—but he makes no mention of the 23rd Virginia Cavalry being so detached.[7]

One account uses the 23rd Virginia Cavalry's commander as a source, but this does not mesh with either of the other two versions. Writing to one of the cadets almost five decades after the battle, George Edgar, commander of the 26th Virginia Battalion, mentioned that he understood from Colonel White, commander of the 23rd Virginia Cavalry, that the regiment "was dismounted and placed on the right of the turnpike." Edgar does not elaborate, nor does he state where or how he got this information from White. In an accompanying sketch, Edgar placed the 23rd Virginia Cavalry between the 22nd Virginia and 23rd Virginia Battalion.[8] It should be noted that at the time Edgar wrote, he was on a quest to discount almost every account of the battle—including Imboden's—that had found its way into print but did not praise Edgar or his men.

Lieutenant Carter Berkeley, an officer in McClanahan's Battery, wrote that he encountered Breckinridge after Sigel's Bushong Hill line had collapsed, and that the general told the young lieutenant: "I have no cavalry . . . I sent it all with General Imboden to get in the rear of the enemy." This suggests that the 23rd Cavalry was not fighting dismounted with their horses nearby.[9]

Secondary sources on the battle also differ, but most use either Davis' or Imboden's version of events as fact without digging deeper. Edward Turner, citing several different accounts by Imboden, places both the 18th Virginia Cavalry and the 23rd Virginia Cavalry together with Imboden throughout the

7   Griffin T. Ward to Capt. Charles Simple, May 16, 1864, Sigel Papers.

8   Edgar to Colonna, March 25, 1911.

9   Driver, *Staunton Artillery*, 88.

engagement.[10] The short regimental history of the 23rd Virginia Cavalry by Richard Kleese (part of the H. E. Howard's Virginia Regimental History Series) proposes that the entire regiment fought dismounted that day with the 62nd Virginia. Kleese's work does not include individual citations to a specific source, but a careful reading of his book demonstrates that Davis' *New Market* was almost certainly where he got his information.[11] Roger Delauter's volume on the 62nd Virginia, part of the same Howard series, states that "a contingent [of the 23rd] had also been dismounted for the battle."[12] Spencer Tucker's biography of John Imboden also uses Davis' version when addressing the role of the cavalry in the battle, while Harold Woodward's biography of Imboden does not make any mention of the 23rd fighting dismounted.[13] Woodward's account of the battle alludes several times to the 18th and 23rd remaining together (and mounted) with Imboden, and is based on Imboden's postwar article about the battle.[14]

Former U.S. Army historian Colonel Joseph Whitehorne's staff ride for New Market goes back and forth on the issue of the 23rd Virginia Cavalry. The regiment is not mentioned at all in Whitehorne's brief description of the battle. It is placed with Imboden and the 18th Virginia Cavalry in the chronological outline of the action, but it is listed as attached to Gabriel Wharton's Brigade in the order of battle.[15]

Richard Duncan's history of the war west of the Blue Ridge in the spring of 1864 mentions only the 18th Virginia Cavalry's role in the battle at New Market, thereby ignoring the issue completely.[16] Jerry Holsworth's article about the battle in *Blue and Gray* magazine also repeats the "accepted" version of the 23rd

---

10 Turner, *New Market Campaign*, 41. Despite the many shortcomings of Turner's work, it should be remembered that he had the luxury of consulting actual veterans of the battle.

11 Kleese, *23rd Virginia Cavalry*, 21-23.

12 Delauter, *62nd Virginia Infantry*, 30.

13 Spencer C. Tucker, *Brigadier General John D. Imboden: Confederate Commander in the Shenandoah Valley* (Lexington, KY, 2003), 213-220.

14 Harold R. Woodward, Jr., *Pathfinder of the Valley: Brigadier General John David Imboden* (Berryville, VA, 1996), 109-112.

15 Joseph W.A. Whitehorne, *The Battle of New Market* (Washington, DC, 1988), 12, 19, 24-5.

16 Duncan, *Lee's Endangered Left*, 127.

Virginia Cavalry being ordered by Breckinridge to dismount that morning and join the infantry.[17]

So what can we conclude from a careful reading of these often conflicting sources? I believe the confusion over the location of the 23rd Virginia Cavalry during the battle arises from the fact that all of the dismounted men of Imboden's command had been assigned to the 62nd Virginia. Lieutenant Colonel O'Ferrall of the 23rd noted in his memoirs that in April 1864, "I had quite a number of dismounted men."[18] It is likely that they were kept together as a cohesive unit rather than spread among the other companies of the 62nd Virginia. This conclusion is supported by a casualty list for the 62nd published in the Staunton *Vindicator* on May 22 that includes Woodson's Missouri company in addition to the "regular" companies of the 62nd, and also includes three companies (L, M, & N) of troops in the 23rd (and possibly the 18th as well) attached to the 62nd.[19] The heavy casualties reported in these three companies, only two of which actually give names and numbers, clearly indicates that they were in the midst of the fight. In contrast is the official casualty return for Imboden's brigade (minus the 62nd) dated the day following the battle. This lists only one man wounded in the 18th Virginia Cavalry and none at all in the 23rd Virginia Cavalry or McClanahan's Battery.[20]

The members of the 23rd who were listed in the report in the *Vindicator* were not attached to their regiment at the time, or they would have been included in the official brigade return. In light of White's and Kiracofe's accounts, written within days of the battle, the casualty list (incomplete though it is) in the *Vindicator*, and the official brigade casualty return, it seems clear that a portion of the 23rd did indeed fight dismounted with the infantry, but the majority of the regiment remained with Imboden .

*   *   *

Another point of contention, albeit of less consequence, is the "mounted" status of the 62nd Virginia Mounted Infantry. On paper, the regiment was

---

17 Jerry W. Holsworth, "VMI at the Battle of New Market," *Blue and Gray* (Spring 1999), 42.

18 O'Ferrall, *Forty Years Active Service*, 89.

19 Staunton *Vindicator*, May 22, 1864.

20 Casualty report for Imboden's Brigade, May 16, 1864, Sigel Papers.

"mounted infantry." Again, William Davis' version has become widely accepted but may not be completely accurate. Davis states that on the day of the battle, Breckinridge decided to dismount the 62nd and have the men fight as infantry with Wharton's Brigade.[21] While they did indeed augment Wharton's infantry, it was not because of a last-minute decision to deprive them of their horses. This would have weakened the regiment by one-quarter, for when cavalry fought dismounted, every fourth man was detailed to hold the horses of three of his comrades. Using Surgeon White's account of the 62nd, the regiment had been entirely dismounted for at least a week before the battle, and probably longer.[22] The 62nd and the 18th Virginia Cavalry were actually sister units, both having been derived from the First Regiment Virginia Partisan Rangers, Imboden's original command. This unit was raised in early 1862 from companies in what would become West Virginia. When the War Department ordered the Partisan Rangers disbanded in late 1862 and converted into a more conventional army unit, the mounted rangers were mustered into the 18th Virginia Cavalry and the dismounted ones, strangely enough, into the 62nd Virginia Mounted Infantry. Historian Roger Delauter, in his regimental history of the 62nd, claims that it was only after the Jones-Imboden Raid of May 1863 that the 62nd received horses, going on to serve as mounted infantry during the Gettysburg Campaign. Asst. Surgeon White supports that conclusion, writing in mid-September 1863 that the regiment had "been mounted for about 6 weeks."[23] In early May 1864, White wrote that the regiment had been dismounted and all the dismounted men of the 18th and 23rd assigned to it.

Those who subscribe to the theory that the 62nd was dismounted just for the battle of May 15, 1864, do not offer a reason as to why, shortly after the battle when Breckinridge took his command east to join Lee's Army of Northern Virginia, he took the 62nd with him as part of Wharton's Brigade. If the 62nd had indeed been mounted infantry in practice at the time, the move would have complicated the shift of the command east toward the Richmond front. It also would have made little sense: why single out one of three mounted regiments in Imboden's brigade?

---

21 Davis, *Battle of New Market*, 81.

22 White to "Jinnie," May 7, 1864.

23 White to "Jinnie," September 13, 1863.

Clearly, the role envisioned for Imboden after the battle—one of observation—demonstrated little need for a large infantry regiment, whereas the same infantry regiment could be put to much better use with Lee's army. In his autobiographical sketch in his file at VMI, George Smith states that "in this fight, my horses being out to pasture, I was assigned to Wharton's brigade."[24]

24 "Record of George H. Smith," G. H. Smith Papers, VMI.

Appendix 6

Breckinridge, Imboden, and the Confederate Flanking Operation East of Smith's Creek

What John Imboden and his men did during the several hours they were operating east of Smith's Creek, and what they were expected to do there, remains something of a mystery. The known sources for this part of the battle are thin and contradictory.

Almost a decade after New Market, Maj. Peter Otey of the 30th Virginia Battalion wrote, "I haven't spoken of our cavalry as they did nothing."[1] Edward Turner, who had the benefit of interviewing and corresponding with veterans of the battle for his book agreed with Otey: "The Confederate cavalry . . . which had done such brilliant service in resisting the Federal advance before Breckinridge arrived, may be said to have done almost nothing on the day when the battle of New Market was fought."[2]

Never one to shy away from exaggerating his own role in his postwar writings, Imboden's pen remained strangely silent about his sojourn across the creek. In his New Market account that appeared in *Battles and Leaders*, Imboden wrote that after he deployed McClanahan's guns (which worked to great effect against Stahel's horsemen), "my cavalry kept on slowly down the creek *as if*

---

1 Turner, *New Market Campaign*, 43.

2 *Ibid.*

[emphasis added] aiming to get in the enemy's rear."[3] Was Imboden implying that his move was a feint and that he never intended to reach Sigel's rear? The cavalry commander does not mention either his or his cavalry's actions again until he went looking for Breckinridge after the collapse of Sigel's Bushong Hill line. When he found his commander near Rude's Hill, it was "perhaps 5 p.m."[4] Imboden's own time estimate leaves several hours unaccounted for, during which we know little or nothing about what he and his horsemen did. If his men spent two or three hours hunting a ford to cross behind Sigel, Imboden did not think it important enough to mention.

Other sources shed little light on this question. Lt. Col. O'Ferrall of the 23rd Virginia Cavalry left an account of his service during this period but wrote nothing about what his regiment did during the engagement of May 15.[5] John Kiracofe, a private in Company G, 18th Virginia Cavalry, wrote home the day after the battle: "Yesterday morning our Regiment and the battery [McClanahan's] comenced the fight. General Breckenridge [sic] with his force and the 62nd done the most of the fighting. Our regiment and Col White's [23rd Virginia Cavalry] was [sic] on the right wing and acted as flankers."[6] Imboden's personal baggage wagon driver, Allemon Sager, mentions nothing of the actions east of the creek and may have remained on the west bank.[7]

Lt. Julian Pratt (Company H, 18th Virginia Cavalry) wrote a detailed account nearly fifty years later of the actions of Imboden's command during the entire campaign. Pratt was good friends with Imboden's youngest brother Frank, who was Pratt's company commander, and the regiment's commanding officer was another Imboden brother, George. Although Pratt is also largely silent about what transpired east of Smith's Creek, his discussion of the event reads like a defense counsel's brief. Once Pratt's small battalion (which had led the Confederate advance up to New Market the morning of the 15th) was absorbed back into the 18th Virginia Cavalry, he wrote,

3 Imboden, "The Battle of New Market, VA, May 15, 1864," 483.

4 *Ibid.*, 484.

5 O'Ferrall, *Forty Years of Active Service.*

6 Kiracofe to Wife, May 16, 1864.

7 Sager, *The Battle of New Market.*

the command moved across Smith's Creek and north in the direction of Mt. Airy (the Meem Homestead), on the right of the Confederates and separated from them by a stream which was past fording. I [Pratt] was an officer in the same company as the brother of Gen. Imboden and had exceptional advantage in being informed confidentially in reference to our plans and purposes. I know now, I knew then, that Imboden was not expected to cross Smith's Creek or the Shenandoah River to burn the bridge at Mt. Jackson. [Major Harry] Gilmore [sic] says he was told to do it. Imboden did what was expected of him, to exhibit his force on the left and rear of Sigel to hold his cav'y [sic] in check. This was accomplished and contributed as Breckinridge expected. The east side of Smith's Creek would have made the crossing of both streams necessary and both were past fording. This fact was known to the Gen [sic] Commanding and to Imboden.[8]

General Breckinridge's official (unpublished) report, however, says otherwise. In it, Breckinridge wrote that Imboden was "to use every effort to destroy the bridge across the Shenandoah River in rear of the enemy with a view to cut off his retreat in case of a reverse to his arms." Tellingly, this same report says nothing about what the mounted arm actually achieved during its hours spent on the east bank.[9]

J. Stoddard Johnston, Breckinridge's chief of staff and the man who penned his chief's official report on New Market, was critical of Imboden in both of his postwar accounts of the battle. Johnston placed the blame for Sigel's escape squarely at the feet of the cavalry commander. "Had Imboden succeeded in carrying out his instructions," wrote Johnston, "the whole of Siegel's [sic] command would have been captured."[10]

Lieutenant Carter Berkeley of McClanahan's Battery wrote of an encounter with General Breckinridge during the battle, wherein Breckinridge told the young officer, "I have no cavalry, unfortunately. I sent it all with General Imboden to get in the rear of the enemy on the Pike beyond Mount Jackson."

So what did Breckinridge intend for Imboden? Did he expect his cavalry leader to ride north east of Smith's Creek, re-cross to the west side, and get behind Sigel's army to cut off his retreat in case the Federals were driven back, or was Imboden directed to "exhibit his force on the left and rear of Sigel to

8   Pratt to Colonna, November 19, 1910.

9   Breckinridge's Official New Market Report.

10 Johnston, "Battle of New Market," 11.

hold his cav'y [sic] in check," as Lieutenant Pratt claimed and as Imboden implied in his *Battles and Leaders* account?

If Imboden's mission was merely to make a feint beyond Sigel's left flank, why did he take all of his cavalry with him? He knew how little infantry Breckinridge had with him west of Smith's Creek. Imboden's 62nd Virginia Mounted Infantry remained with Breckinridge and fought as foot soldiers with the main army, so perhaps Imboden did not believe he was making the move with his entire command.

It should be remembered that on May 13, just two days before New Market, Imboden engaged in a running fight with Col. William Boyd's 1st New York (Lincoln) Cavalry in the Smith's Creek valley. During that engagement, Imboden witnessed Boyd's inability to get large numbers of men across the swollen creek. More rain fell over the next two days, almost certainly raising the waterway even higher. Imboden knew (or should have known) that fording the stream would be a difficult, and perhaps impossible, proposition. By the time Imboden left to cross Smith's creek, Breckinridge should have known this as well.

Given Breckinridge's claims in his official report, his extensive military experience, his demonstrated field abilities, and his reliance upon Imboden's knowledge of the field at New Market, it seems likely that the Kentuckian intended for his cavalry to cross Smith's Creek with the intention of getting into Sigel's rear.

Until other documents regarding this aspect of the battle surface, however, a definitive conclusion is impossible to reach.

Appendix 7

John C. Breckinridge
and the "Shell-struck Post"

One of the most famous stories about New Market is that Confederate army commander Major General John C. Breckinridge was nearly killed near St. Matthew's Church while observing the Union position. According to the oft-repeated story, Breckinridge and his staff rode along the Valley Pike/Main Street to the high ground at St. Matthew's Church. There, the mounted men attracted the attention of Federal artillery, which sent a shell in their direction. The shell lodged in a fencepost at the corner of Main Street and River Road, "showering [Breckinridge] with splinters, it failed to explode."[1] Did Breckinridge really come this close to death? Maybe not.

While writing his magisterial biography of Breckinridge in the early 1970s, William C. Davis enjoyed access to a vast collection of Breckinridge family papers, including a handwritten note—probably penned by General Breckinridge's son Clifton—with a turn-of-the-century photo of the post. The note repeated the story of Breckinridge's brush with death. However, Clifton Breckinridge (if he is indeed the author, as Davis believes him to be) was not an eyewitness to the event; he was a cadet at the Confederate Naval Academy at the time of the battle. Thus, Clifton was either putting ink to paper about what

1 Davis, *Breckinridge*, 420-1.

he heard from his father, or he was merely repeating the popular story from another source.[2]

The original post stood for decades after the May 1864 battle and attracted much attention. Although it is not known when signage was first installed explaining its significance, an early interpretive sign from 1899 reads: "This post was struck by a 3-inch rifle shell fired from a Federal battery at the Battle of New Market, VA, May 15, 1864, between Gen'l. Breckenridge [sic] & Genl. Seigle [sic]. The Confederates were victorious. J. H. Rupp Aug. 15, 1899."[3] It is interesting to note that there is no mention of the supposed Breckinridge connection.

General John Imboden's headquarters wagon driver, Allmon Sager, seems to have spent a significant portion of the battle riding with Breckinridge and/or Imboden because he recorded conversations between the two generals. In an oral history put to paper by his son years after the battle, Sager dismissed the "shell-struck post" and its connection to Breckinridge: "Another incident in which the public has probably been misinformed happened right on Main Street, or the Pike. An enemy shell, or solid shot, split a gate post open near the top of the post. Then historians, and other writers also, to create interest in their articles had both Gen. Breckinridge and Gen. Imboden mounted on their horses and also some of their staff right there by the post when it was split open. Some even, to add interest to the story placed Breckinridge right up within two or three feet of the post. Father said neither general was even down in that part of town when the post was struck."[4]

Sager's testimony is the only known account by a veteran of the battle to specifically address this issue. John Breckinridge's chief of staff, Major J. Stoddard Johnston, makes no mention of the incident in any of his writings about New Market, and he of all people would have been in a position to know if the story was true. Although it cannot be taken as conclusive proof, Johnston's silence on the matter is a good indication that the story is probably not true.

---

2 Personal correspondence of the author with William C. Davis, November 2009. Complicating matters is the fact that several decades after Davis' *Breckinridge* biography was published, the family gave all of the papers Davis had used to use to the Library of Congress. A recent search of these Breckinridge family papers failed to yield this document.

3 Photo of sign courtesy of John D. Crim, New Market, Virginia.

4 Sager, *Battle of New Market*, 14.

In 2004, what may well be the original "shell-struck post" was discovered in a barn belonging to the Crim family.[5] A replacement post with a replica of the famous shell (actually a wood carving painted black) marks the spot today. Exactly when the original post was replaced with today's replica is not known. A small booklet published by the town of New Market to mark the centennial anniversary of the battle in 1964 includes a photo on the rear inside cover that shows a close-up of what appears to be the original post, but the photo is not clear enough to tell with certainty. It includes this caption: "A three inch rifle shell struck this post unexploded, lodging there at the precise moment that Gen. Breckinridge was making observations of Union troop movements while seated upon his horse in the middle of Congress [Main] Street."[6]

However, early 20th Century Valley historian John Wayland's *History of Shenandoah County* includes a photo of the modern post.[7] James Graves and John Crim (who owns what is probably the original post) show a circa 2004 comparison photo of both the "original" and the modern posts side-by-side in their recent *Around New Market*.[8] However, the same work contains a 1910 view of St. Matthew's Church, which clearly shows the modern post in place.[9]

5   Graves, *Around New Market*, 42.

6   Hildreth, *A Brief History of New Market and Vicinity*, inside rear cover.

7   Wayland, *History of Shenandoah County*, 324.

8   Graves, *Around New Market*, 42.

9   *Ibid.*, 55.

Where Woodson's Heroes Fell:
The 1st Missouri Cavalry at New Market

This article appeared in the April 2006 issue of *Battlefield Journal* and is reprinted here with the kind permission of the publisher.

There was little fanfare, no audience, no elaborate dedication ceremony as the men worked that Saturday morning in the Shenandoah Valley in May 1905. In fact, to anyone traveling along the Valley Pike to the east, they probably would have appeared as though just some farmers repairing a stone wall along the border of the small orchard. However, the four men were erecting the first monument on the battlefield at New Market, scene of one of the most dramatic battles of the Civil War. For that very spot, almost 41 years previous to the day, had been one of the deadliest spots on the battlefield.

The serene surroundings had not been so peaceful in May 1864. Major General Franz Sigel was leading a Federal force of about 10,000 up the Valley toward Staunton, where he was to rendezvous with another Federal column coming across the Alleghenies from West Virginia and deny the Confederates the use of the precious Shenandoah Valley and southwest Virginia. Robert E. Lee and the Army of Northern Virginia were hard-pressed east of the Blue Ridge facing a new opponent in U.S. Grant. Lee could spare no troops to oppose Sigel's advance. Whatever resistance could be mounted would have to come from the somewhat scattered units guarding the Valley and the southwest corner of the state.

Major General John C. Breckinridge, a former U.S. vice president and presidential candidate in 1860, was in command of the Confederate forces in southwest Virginia. When word of Sigel's offensive was received in Richmond, Breckinridge's scope of responsibility was broadened to include the Shenandoah Valley. He had about 5,000 men of all arms in his department, as well as another 1,200 mostly cavalry in the Valley commanded by Brigadier General John D. Imboden. As Sigel slowly moved up the Valley [in somewhat of a geographical quirk, because of the direction of flow of the Shenandoah River, moving southward is referred to as "up" the Valley while conversely moving northward is going "down" the Valley] in early May, Breckinridge charged Imboden with the task of slowing the Federal advance, thus giving Breckinridge time to gather his forces and march to Imboden's aid.

Imboden's Brigade consisted of the 18th and 23rd Virginia cavalry regiments, the 62nd Virginia Mounted Infantry, McClannahan's Battery, and several smaller cavalry commands. Most of Imboden's men were from Virginia [or what is now West Virginia] or Maryland, except for one company of dismounted cavalry from Missouri. This company, officially Company A, 1st Missouri Cavalry, was commanded by a 22-year-old Captain named Charles H. Woodson and was the only unit from Missouri to serve in Virginia.[1]

Woodson and his men had served in various Missouri units earlier in the war and had been captured at Port Gibson, Vicksburg, and other points in the western theater. Woodson himself has somewhat of a murky past, and his actions in the war in Missouri are unclear, but it is known that he was captured in September 1862 in Randolph County, Missouri, possibly while operating as a guerrilla. He and the others were held at a prison compound in Alton, Illinois, and were exchanged in June 1863 at City Point, near Petersburg, Virginia. After their exchange, Woodson and another officer, Edward H. Scott, convinced the authorities in Richmond to let the two of them organize the Missouri troops into a unit to serve in Virginia rather than being sent back to the Trans-Mississippi to rejoin their old units.[2]

In early August 1863, Woodson had gathered about 70 men into his command and he was assigned to Imboden's command in the Shenandoah, with himself as captain and Scott as first lieutenant.[3] The "Missouri exiles," as

---

1   Curran, "Memory, Myth, and Musty Records," 25-6.

2   *Ibid*, 29-31.

3   C. H. Woodson to I.C. Shields, August 10, 1863, Woodson file, NMBSHP.

they styled themselves, were attached to the 62nd Virginia.[4] It should be noted that while technically a cavalry company, Woodson's men had no horses, but neither did the 62nd which was technically a mounted infantry regiment, but in reality usually consisted of the dismounted men of Imboden's command.

During the winter and early spring months of 1864, Woodson's men were camped at Harrisonburg in the central Shenandoah. During this time they endeared themselves to many of the local residents, who gave "a most abundant supply of good, warm, woolen socks," as well as Bibles and religious tracts with which Lt. Scott started a Sunday school class.[5] Just prior to the start of the spring campaign, Woodson's men reenlisted "for 40 years, or the war."[6]

During the first part of May 1864, the Missourians assisted Imboden in slowing Sigel's advance, although the Federal general's personal sloth may have done more to that end than did Imboden's resistance. Before dawn of the 15th, Breckinridge, with about 3,000 infantry and artillery including 257 cadets from the Virginia Military Institute joined forces with Imboden, several miles south of New Market. After dawn, the Confederates advanced to that crossroads village where they met the advance of Sigel's army. In a driving rain, the Confederate advance began in earnest about mid-day, pushing back Sigel's troops to the north of town, to a farm owned by Jacob Bushong.

As the Southern troops advanced, the 62nd held the center, to the left or west of the Valley Pike, with the 1st Missouri as its leftmost company. Capt. Woodson was serving as a field officer, leaving Lt. Scott in tactical command of the company.[7] To the front of the 62nd was a solid line of infantry, consisting of the 54th Pennsylvania with its left anchored on the Pike, the 1st West Virginia, and the 34th Massachusetts supporting three Federal artillery batteries on the far Union right, anchored on high bluffs overlooking the Shenandoah River.

Breckinridge's troops continued their advance up to and just past the Bushong farm house, where they began to falter as they came within canister range of the Federal guns. The troops to the left of the 62nd were particularly hard hit, with part of the line to the immediate left of the Missourians breaking. It was here, in a small apple orchard just north of the Bushong house, where the

4   Price, *Memorials of E.H. Scott,* 13.

5   Rockingham *Register,* February 5, 1864; Price, *Memorials of E.H. Scott,* 13.

6   Rockingham *Register,* April 1, 1864.

7   Price *Memorials of E.H. Scott,* 15.

outcome of the fight seemed in doubt and where the heaviest casualties occurred. "We were now within close pistol shot of the battery," Lt. Scott wrote in his diary, "and just as I had fired the last shot from my revolver at a cannonier [sic], Sergeant Day came up to me pale and staggering with the blood flowing from his breast and back, and said as he gave me his hand, 'Lieutenant I am almost gone, please help me off.'" Casualties mounted rapidly among the Missourians as the artillery to their immediate front, five Napoleons of Captain Alfred von Kleiser's 30th New York Battery, poured canister into their ranks. "Just then I saw Lieutenant Jones . . . fall full length beside me, with the brain oozing from his forehead," Lt. Scott wrote. Others fell, including Scott, wounded in the right arm by a shell fragment, Sgt. William Day and Capt. Woodson. Of the 62 Missourians present when the battle began, by Scott's account only five or six escaped uninjured.[8] [There is some debate over the number of casualties sustained by Woodson's command; the number lies somewhere between 40 and 60.[9]]

It was while the Missourians were being decimated by von Kleiser's guns that the VMI Cadets came into the battle filling the gap to the left of the 62nd. Then, reinforced by the Cadets and others, and with the initiative in their favor after a failed Union counter-attack, Breckinridge's line again swept forward, this time driving Sigel's men from the field, taking several cannon in the process. The pursuit continued for several miles to the Shenandoah River, but ended when Sigel's rear guard burned the bridge across the swollen stream.

When the smoke cleared, almost 1,400 men were killed, wounded or missing at New Market: 841 Federals, 531 Confederates.[10] But no unit on either side had suffered a higher casualty rate than did Woodson's Missourians 64 to 90 percent, depending on the casualty total, with the most likely figure being toward the higher end of that range. When the 62nd left the Valley two days after the battle to reinforce Lee's army, there were only 18 Missourians in the ranks.[11]

After the war, the members of the 1st Missouri Cavalry scattered, some returned home to Missouri, others settled in their adopted home in the Valley.

8   *Ibid.*, 15-16.

9   Curran, "Memory, Myth and Musty Records," 39.

10 Davis, *Battle of New Market,* 200-201.

11 Curran, "Memory, Myth and Musty Records," 39; Price, *Memorials of E.H. Scott,* 16.

Among the latter was James H. Dwyer, who had been wounded four times at New Market. Soon after the war, Dwyer married Ada Sprinkle, who had been his nurse in Harrisonburg while recuperating from his New Market wounds.[12] As many veterans were wont to do, Dwyer felt compelled to visit some of his old battlefields. In October 1903 Dwyer returned to New Market as tour guide for the 3rd U.S. Field Artillery Battery commanded by Captain Charles P. Summerall, who would be one of the prominent US commanders in World War I, showing them around the field, where Dwyer "readily identified" the spot of his wounding in the Bushong orchard. On this visit, he obtained permission from the Bushongs "to erect a stone marker at the point where his company suffered such terrible casualties."[13]

In May 1905, Dwyer again came to New Market, this time accompanied by a former comrade in arms, W.R. Fallis, one of the lucky ones who escaped injury during the battle. On May 20, 1905, Dwyer and Fallis erected, with the help of Major Christian Shirley and Jacob E. Bushong of New Market, the first monument on the field at New Market. It was a simple limestone block on which was carved "This rustic pile / The simple tale will tell: / It marks the spot / Where Woodson's Heroes fell."[14]

This marker still stands today at the northeast corner of the Bushong orchard; one of two monuments erected at New Market by veterans of the battle. Simple in appearance and subtle in its message, the monument serves as a visible reminder of the sacrifices and devotion of several dozen Missourians who found themselves hundreds of miles from their homes yet fought as bravely as if defending their own lands. Col. George H. Smith, commander of the 62nd Virginia at New Market, long after the war wrote of Woodson's command, "the monument erected by [Dwyer] on the field is a touching and well deserved memorial of his comrades whose gallantry was not surpassed by that of any on the field. Nor could the inscription on it be well improved."[15]

12 John W. Wayland, *Men of Mark and Representative Citizens of Harrisonburg and Rockingham County, Virginia*, (Staunton, VA, 1943), 297.

13 *Shenandoah Valley*, October 15, 1903.

14 "Where Woodson's Missourians Fell," *Shenandoah Valley*, May 25, 1905.

15 George H. Smith, *Positions and Movements of the Troops at the Battle of New Market* (Los Angeles, CA, 1913), 54-55.

Bibliography

Manuscripts

Auburn University, R.B. Draughon Library, Auburn, AL
  Arthur M. Stone Papers

Bowling Green State University, Center for Archival Collections, Bowling Green, KY
  Leander Coe diary, (MS # 45), Dorothy Ringle collection

Duke University, William R. Perkins Library, Durham, NC
  John F. Houser Papers

East Carolina University, J.Y. Joyner Library, Greenville, NC
  George D. Wells letterbook (Collection #241)

Hagley Museum & Library, Wilmington, DE
  Jessie Rupert Papers

Handley Library, Winchester, VA
  Mrs. Hugh Holmes Lee diary

Illinois Historical Survey, University of Illinois, Champaign-Urbana, IL
  Augustus Moor Papers, Heinrich A. Rattermann collection

Library of Virginia, Richmond, VA
  Charles J. Anderson recollections, (Accession # 40085)
  George W. Chappelear Papers, Rockingham County notes, (Accession # 23772)
  John H. Kiracofe letter, May 16, 1864 (Accession # 39194)
  George W. Thompson diary (Accession # 38715)
  Anna Kagey Wayland journal (Accession # 24649b)

Maryland Historical Society, Baltimore, MD
  Harry Gilmor Papers

Massachusetts Historical Society, Boston, MA
  J. Chapin Warner Papers

Morrisville State College, Morrisville, NY
  Alfred H. Voorhees diary

Museum of the Confederacy, Richmond, VA
    J. Stoddard Johnston Papers

New Market Battlefield State Historical Park, New Market, VA
    54th Pennsylvania file
    L.J. Alleman diary
    Bushong family genealogical records
    "Federal Casualties at the Battle of New Market," ed. by Charles K. Gailey III
    Alfred von Kleiser file
    Charles Woodson file

New York State Library, Albany, NY
    William Tibbits diary (#SC13256)

Page County Courthouse, Luray, VA
    Estate of Abram Strickler, December 13, 1836

Private Collections
    Nancy Armstrong, Endwell, NY
        Autobiography of Jacob Lester, privately published 1931
    Richard Bazelow, Wolden, NY
        Jessie Rupert Papers
    John Crim, New Market, VA
        "Shell-struck post" collection
    Mark Dudrow, Winchester, VA
        William A. McIlhenny diary
    Dianne McGinley Gardner, Lost River, WV
        Thomas Winton Fisher Papers
    Janet Greentree, Burke, VA
        George W. Baker family history
    Charles Harris, Ooltewah, TN
        Jacob Cohn diary
    Wilda Hogbin, Petersburg, WV
        James C. Hogbin diary
    Charles Knight, Norfolk, VA
        Bushong family records
        Arthur Stone letter, April 29, 1864
        William Tibbits letters, May 12 & 28, 1864
    Don Polly, Leesburg, FL
        Corporal Ensign Marshal Smith's Story

Rice University, Fondren Library, Houston, TX
    Cyrus B. Smith Papers (MS #411)

Shenandoah County Courthouse, Woodstock, VA
    Shenandoah County land records

Stanford University libraries, Palo Alto, CA
    E.O.C. Ord Papers

United States Army Military History Institute, Carlisle, PA
    Albert A. Wright diary

University of Kentucky, Margaret I. King Library, Lexington, KY
    John D. Imboden Papers

University of North Carolina, Chapel Hill, NC
    George M. Edgar Papers (Collection # 3633)

University of Virginia, Albert & Shirley Small Special Collections Library, Charlottesville, VA
    Joseph Addison Waddell diary (Accession # 38-258)

Virginia Historical Society, Richmond, VA
    Kellian Van Rensalear Whaley Papers
    Rufus J. Woolwine memoirs

Virginia Military Institute Archives, Lexington, VA
    Henkel Papers
    New Market Collection
    Peter J. Otey Alumni file
    Scott Ship[p] Alumni file
    Francis H. Smith Papers
    George H. Smith Alumni file

Virginia Tech University, Blacksburg, VA
    Henry C. Carpenter Papers
    Jane Wade Papers
    Isaac White Papers

Washington & Lee University, James G. Leyburn Library, Lexington, VA
    August Forsberg diary
    Frank Smith Reader diary

West Virginia University, West Virginia Regional History Collection, Morgantown, WV
    Jacob M. Campbell diary

Western Reserve Historical Society, Cleveland, OH
    Franz Sigel Papers

Official Records

The War of the Rebellion: A Compilation of the Official Records of the Union and Confederate Armies.
Washington, D.C.: Government Printing Office, 1881-9.
Supplement to the Official Records of the Union and Confederate Armies. Wilmington, NC: Broadfoot,
1996.

Newspapers

Boston (MA) *Herald*
Harrisonburg (VA) *Daily News Record*
Ironton (OH) *Register*
Johnstown (PA) *Tribune*
Lexington (VA) *Gazette*
Lynchburg (VA) *News*
New Market (VA) *Shenandoah Valley*
Richmond (VA) *Daily Whig*
Richmond (VA) *Examiner*
Richmond (VA) *News Leader*
Richmond (VA) *Sentinel*
Richmond (VA) *Times-Dispatch*
Rockingham (Harrisonburg, VA) *Register*
Springfield (MA) *Daily Republican*
Staunton (VA) *Spectator*
Staunton (VA) *Spectator & Vindicator*
Staunton (VA) *Vindicator*
Strasburg(VA) *Northern Virginia Daily*
Washington (DC) *Times*
Wheeling (WV) *Intelligencer*
Wheeling (WV) *Register*
Woodstock (VA) *Shenandoah Herald*
Worcester (MA) *Aegis and Transcript*

Published Sources

Primary Works

Barrett, John G. and Robert K. Turner, Jr., eds., *Letters of a New Market Cadet: Beverly Stanard.*
Bay Shore, NY: Evergreen Press, 1961.
Beach, William H., *The First New York (Lincoln) Cavalry From April 19, 1861 to July 7, 1865.* New
York: Lincoln Cavalry Association, 1902.
Buck, William P., *Sad Earth, Sweet Heaven: The Diary of Lucy Rebecca Buck During the War Between
the States.* Birmingham, AL: Buck Publishing, 1992.
Cocke, Preston, *The Battle of New Market and the Cadets of the Virginia Military Institute.* Richmond,
VA, 1914.

Colonna, Benjamin A., "Battle of New Market," *Journal of the Military Service Institution of the United States*, vol. LI, 1912, pp. 344-351.

Cozzens, Peter and Robert I. Girardi, eds., *The Military Memoirs of General John Pope*. Chapel Hill, NC: University of North Carolina Press, 1998.

Crim, Eliza C., "Tender Memories of the VMI Cadets," *Confederate Veteran*, June 1926, pp. 212-213.

Dowdey, Clifford and Louis Manarin, eds., *The Wartime Papers of R.E. Lee*. Boston: Little, Brown & Co., 1961.

Drickamer, Lee C. and Karen D., eds., *Fort Lyon to Harpers Ferry: On the Border of North and South with "Rambling Jour": The Civil War Letters and Newspaper Dispatches of Charles H. Moulton, 34th Massachusetts Volunteer Infantry*. Shippensburg, PA: White Mane Publishing, 1987.

Duncan, Richard R., ed., *Alexander Neil and the Last Shenandoah Valley Campaign*. Shippensburg, PA: White Mane Publishing, 1996.

DuPont, Henry, *The Battle of New Market, Virginia, May 15, 1864*. Winterthur, DE: Privately published, 1923.

Early, Jubal A., *Jubal Early's Memoirs: Autobiographical Sketch and Narrative of the War Between the States*. Baltimore, MD: Nautical & Aviation Publishing, 1989.

Eby, Cecil D., Jr., ed., *A Virginia Yankee in the Civil War: The Diaries of David Hunter Strother*. Chapel Hill, NC: University of North Carolina Press, 1961.

Echols, John, *Address on the Life and Character of Gen. John C. Breckinridge*. New Market, VA: New Market Memorial Association, 1877.

Farrar, Samuel C., *The Twenty-Second Pennsylvania Cavalry and the Ringgold Battalion, 1861 – 1865*. Pittsburgh, PA: 22nd Pennsylvania Cavalry Association, 1911.

Fitz-Simmons, Charles, "Sigel's Fight at New Market," *Military Order of the Loyal Legion of the United States, Illinois* (Chicago, no date), III.

Fluharty, Linda C., ed., *Civil War Letters of Lt. Milton B. Campbell*. Baton Rouge, LA: self-published, 2004.

Foster, Catherine, "VMI Cadets at New Market," *United Daughters of the Confederacy Magazine*, Vol. XX, No. 7, July 1957. Typescript at NMBSHP.

Gailey, Charles K., III, ed., *Federal Casualties at the Battle of New Market, May 15, 1864*. April 2003. Copy at New Market Battlefield State Historical Park.

Gilmor, Harry, *Four Years in the Saddle*. New York: Harper & Brothers, 1866.

Grant, Ulysses S., *Personal Memoirs of U.S. Grant*. 2 vols. New York: Charles L. Webster & Co., 1886.

———, "Preparing for the Campaigns of 1864," *Battles and Leaders of the Civil War*, vol. IV, Secaucus, NJ: Castle, no date, pp. 97-117.

Halpine, Charles G., *Baked Meats of the Funeral*. New York: Carleton, 1866.

Harris, Jasper W., "Sixty-Second Virginia at New Market," *Confederate Veteran*, Vol. XVI, 1908, pp. 461-2.

Hewitt, William, *History of the Twelfth Regiment West Virginia Volunteer Infantry*. Steubenville, OH: Twelfth West Virginia Infantry Association, 1892.

Hildebrand, John R., ed., *A Mennonite Journal, 1862-1865: A Father's Account of the Civil War in the Shenandoah Valley*. Shippensburg, PA: Burd Street Press, 1996.

Howard, John C., "Recollections of New Market," *Confederate Veteran*, February 1926, pp. 57-59.

Imboden, John D., "The Battle of New Market, VA., May 15th, 1864," *Battles and Leaders of the Civil War*, vol. IV, Secaucus, NJ: Castle, no date, pp. 480-486.

Johnston, A. S., *Captain Beirne Chapman and Chapman's Battery*. Union, WV: Privately printed, 1903.

Johnston, J. Stoddard, "Sketches of Operations of General John C. Breckinridge," *Southern Historical Society Papers*. June 1879, pp. 257-62.

Keyes, C. M., *The Military History of the 123rd Ohio Volunteer Infantry*. Sandusky, OH: Register Press, 1874.

Lang, Theodore F., *Loyal West Virginia From 1861 to 1865*. Baltimore, MD: Deutsch Publishing Co., 1895.

Lincoln, William S., *Life with the 34th Massachusetts Infantry in the War of the Rebellion*. Worcester, MA.: Noyes, Snow & Co., 1879.

Lynch, Charles H., *The Civil War Diary 1862-1865 of Charles H. Lynch, 18th Connecticut Volunteers*. Hartford, CT: Case, Lockwood & Brainard, 1915.

Mahon, Michael G., ed., *Winchester Divided: The Civil War Diaries of Julia Chase and Laura Lee*. Mechanicsburg, PA: Stackpole, 2002.

McDonald, Cornelia, *A Diary with Reminiscences of the War and Refugee Life in the Shenandoah Valley, 1860-1865*. Annotated by Hunter McDonald. Nashville, TN.: Cullom & Ghertner, 1934.

Miller, James N., *The Story of Andersonville and Florence*. Des Moines: Welch, 1900.

Moore, Frank, comp. *The Rebellion Record*. 12 vols. New York: G.P. Putnum, 1862-1868.

Newcomer, C. Armour, *Cole's Cavalry: Three Years in the Saddle in the Shenandoah Valley*. Baltimore, MD: Cushing & Co., 1895.

O'Ferrall, Charles T., *Forty Years of Active Service*. New York: Neale, 1904.

Porter, Horace, *Campaigning with Grant*. New York: Mallard Press, 1991.

Price, William T., *Memorials of Edward Herndon Scott, M.D.* Wytheville, VA: Jim Presgraves, 1974.

Rawling, Charles J., *History of the First Regiment West Virginia Infantry*. Philadelphia: Lippincott, 1887.

Schmitt, Martin F., ed., *General George Crook: His Autobiography*. Norman, OK: University of Oklahoma Press, 1960.

Senseny, Charles H., *Address Delivered by C.H. Senseny to his Comrades at the Fiftieth Anniversary of the Enlistment of Battery D, 1st W.Va. Light Artillery*. Wheeling, WV, 1912.

Sigel, Franz, "Sigel in the Shenandoah Valley in 1864," *Battles and Leaders of the Civil War*, vol. IV, Secaucus, NJ: Castle, no date, pp. 487-491.

Smith, George H., "More of the Battle of New Market," *Confederate Veteran*, November 1908, pp. 569-572.

———. *The Battle of New Market*. Los Angeles: self-published, 1908.

———. *The Positions and Movements of the Troops in the Battle of New Market*. Los Angeles: self-published, 1913.

Snyder, Edmund P., *Autobiography of a Soldier of the Civil War*. Ohio: Privately-printed, 1915.

Snyder, Edwin, *Adventures and Misadventures of a Union Veteran of the Civil War*. Topeka, KS: Cavanaugh Printing, 1909.

Stevenson, James H., *Boots and Saddles: A History of the First Volunteer Cavalry of the War Known as the First New York (Lincoln) Cavalry*. Harrisburg, PA: Patriot Publishing, 1879.

Swiger, Elizabeth D., ed., *Civil War Letters and Diary of Joshua Winters: A Private in the Union Army, Company G, First Western Virginia Volunteer Infantry*. Parsons, WV: McClain, 1991.

Tower, R. Lockwood, ed. *Lee's Adjutant: The Wartime Letters of Colonel Walter Herron Taylor, 1862-1865*. Columbia, SC: University of South Carolina Press, 1995.

Town, Franklin E., "Valor at New Market," *Southern Historical Society Papers*, vol. 41, 1916, pp. 179-184.

Walker, William C., *History of the 18th Regiment Connecticut Volunteers in the War for the Union*. Norwich, CT: (no name given), 1885.

Wildes, Thomas F., *Record of the One Hundred and Sixteenth Regiment Ohio Infantry Volunteers in the War of the Rebellion*. Sandusky, OH: I.F. Mack & Brother Printers, 1884.

Williamson, James J., *Mosby's Rangers*. New York: Ralph B. Kenyon, 1896.

Wise, Henry A., "The Cadets at New Market, VA," *Confederate Veteran*, August 1912, pp. 361-2.

Wise, John S., *The End of an Era*. New York: Houghton Mifflin, 1901.

———. "The West Point of the Confederacy," *Century Magazine*, vol. XXXVII, January 1889, pp. 461-471.

Secondary Works

Alphin, Elaine M., *Ghost Cadet*. New York, Holt, 1991.

Bates, Samuel P., *History of the Pennsylvania Volunteers, 1861-1865*. Harrisburg, PA: State Printer, 1869-1871.

Bennett, Charles W., Jr., *Four Years with the Fifty-Fourth: The Military History of Franklin Bennett, 54th Pennsylvania Volunteer Regiment, 1861-1865*. Richmond, VA: self-published, 1985.

Bonnell, John C., Jr., *Sabres in the Shenandoah: The 21st New York Cavalry, 1863-1866*, Shippensburg, PA: Burd Street Press, 1996.

Cohen, Stan and Keith Gibson, *Moses Ezekiel: Civil War Soldier, Renowned Sculptor*. Charleston, WV: Pictorial Histories, 2007.

Conrad, James L., *The Young Lions: Confederate Cadets at War*. Mechanicsburg, PA: Stackpole, 1997.

Couper, William, *Virginia Military Institute and the Battle of New Market*. No place or date.

———. *The V.M.I. New Market Cadets*. Charlottesville, VA: Michie, 1933.

Curran, Thomas F., "Memory, Myth, and Musty Records: Charles Woodson's Missouri Cavalry in the Army of Northern Virginia." *Missouri Historical Review*, October 1999, Vol. XCIV, No. 1, pp. 25-41.

Davis, James A., *51st Virginia Infantry*. Lynchburg, VA: H.E. Howard, 1984.

Davis, William C., *Breckinridge: Statesman, Soldier, Symbol*. Baton Rouge, LA: Louisiana State University Press, 1992.

———. *The Battle of New Market*. Baton Rouge, LA: Louisiana State University Press, 1975.

Delauter, Roger U., Jr., *18th Virginia Cavalry*. Lynchburg, VA: H.E. Howard, 1985.

———. *62nd Virginia Infantry*. Lynchburg, VA: H.E. Howard, 1988.

———. *Winchester in the Civil War*. Lynchburg, VA: H.E. Howard, 1992.

Dickinson, Jack L., *Diary of a Confederate Sharpshooter: The Life of James Conrad Peters*. Charleston, WV: Pictorial Histories Publishing, 1997.

———. *Jenkins of Greenbottom: A Civil War Saga*. Charleston, WV: Pictorial Histories Publishing, 1988.

Driver, Robert J., *The Staunton Artillery: McClanahan's Battery*. Lynchburg, VA: H.E. Howard, 1988.

Duncan, Richard R., *Beleaguered Winchester: A Virginia Community at War, 1861-1865*. Baton Rouge, LA: Louisiana State University Press, 2007.

————. *Lee's Endangered Left: The Civil War in Western Virginia, Spring of 1864*. Baton Rouge, LA: Louisiana State University Press, 1998.

————. "The Raid on Piedmont and the Crippling of Franz Sigel in the Shenandoah Valley," *West Virginia History*, vol. 55, 1996, pp. 25-40.

Duppler, Jorg, ed., *Evolution of a Friendship: Selected Documents on the German-American Relations*. Potsdam, Germany: Military History Research Institute, 2002.

Earley, Gerald L., *I Belonged to the 116th*. Bowie, MD: Heritage Books, 2004.

Engle, Stephen D., *Yankee Dutchman: The Life of Franz Sigel*. Fayetteville, AK: University of Arkansas Press, 1993.

Fitts, Deborah, "Three New Market Sites are Preserved." *Civil War News*, January 2006.

Fluharty, Linda C., and Edward L. Phillips, *Carlin's Wheeling Battery: A History of Battery D, First West Virginia Light Artillery*. Baton Rouge, LA: self-published, 2005.

Gabriel, H. William, "William P. Hickman in the New River Valley, 1852-64," *The Smithfield Review*, Vol. III, 1999, pp. 53-82.

Gallagher, Gary W., *Struggle for the Shenandoah: Essays on the 1864 Valley Campaign*. Kent, OH: Kent State University Press, 1991.

Gibson, Keith E., "Speaking with Eloquent Voices: A Look at the VMI Museum and the New Market Battlefield Historical Park," January 1987, NMBSHP.

Good, William A., *Grantees of Early New Market Lots: Indian Trails & Waggon Roads, 1740-1830*. Broadway, VA: self-published, 1997.

————. *Shadowed by the Massanutten: A History of Life Along Smith Creek*. Broadway, VA: self-published, 1992.

Graves, James R. and John D. Crim, *Around New Market*. Charleston, SC: Arcadia, 2007.

Hearn, Chester G., *Six Years of Hell: Harpers Ferry During the Civil War*. Baton Rouge, LA: Louisiana State University Press, 1996.

Heatwole, John L., *Remember Me is All I Ask: Chrisman's Boy Company: A History of the Civil War Service of Company A, 3rd Battalion, Virginia Mounted Reserves*. Bridgewater, VA: Mountain & Valley Publishing, 2000.

Hildreth, Arthur, *A Brief History of New Market and Vicinity*. New Market, VA: Henkel Press, 1964.

Holsworth, Jerry W., "VMI at the Battle of New Market," *Blue and Gray*, Spring 1999, pp. 6-24, 40-52.

Jones, Virgil C., *Gray Ghosts and Rebel Raiders*. McLean, VA: EPM Publications, 1984.

Kercheval, Samuel, *A History of the Valley of Virginia*. Strasburg, VA: Shenandoah Publishing House, 1925.

Kleese, Richard B., *23rd Virginia Cavalry*. Lynchburg, VA.: H.E. Howard, 1996.

————. *Shenandoah County in the Civil War*. Lynchburg, VA: H.E. Howard, 1992.

Krick, Robert K., *Lee's Colonels: A Biographical Register of the Field Officers of the Army of Northern Virginia*. Dayton, OH: Morningside, 1996.

Lewis, Thomas A., *The Shenandoah in Flames*. Alexandria, VA: Time-Life, 1987.

Lowry, Terry D., *22nd Virginia Infantry*. Lynchburg, VA: H.E. Howard, 1988.

————. *26th Battalion Virginia Infantry*. Lynchburg, VA: H.E. Howard, 1991.

Loth, Calder, ed., *The Virginia Landmarks Register*. Charlottesville, VA: University Press of Virginia, 1986.

McManus, Howard R., *The Battle of Cloyds Mountain: The Virginia and Tennessee Railroad Raid, April 29-May 19, 1864.* Lynchburg, VA: H.E. Howard, 1989.

Maddy, W. T., *History of Marie Community, Summers and Monroe Counties, West Virginia.* Morgantown, WV: Agricultural Extension Division, 1925.

Monacello, Anthony, "Strange Odyssey of the 1st Missouri," *America's Civil War*, March 1999, pp. 26-33.

Moore, Robert H., II, *Graham's Petersburg, Jackson's Kanawha, and Lurty's Roanoke Horse Artillery.* Lynchburg, VA: H.E. Howard, 1996.

Pond, George E., *The Shenandoah Valley in 1864.* Wilmington, NC: Broadfoot Publishing, 1989.

Quarles, Garland R., *Occupied Winchester 1861-1865.* Winchester, VA: Winchester-Frederick County Historical Society, 1991.

Quesenbery, Erika L., *A Snowball's Chance: Battery B, Maryland Light Artillery 1st, Snow's.* Port Deposit, MD: Port Deposit Heritage Corporation, 2003.

Reed, Thomas J., *Tibbits' Boys: A History of the 21st New York Cavalry.* New York: University Press of America, 1997.

Roe, Alfred S., *An Angel of the Shenandoah: A Life Sketch of Mrs. Jessie Hainning Rupert.* New Market, Virginia, Worcester, MA: Commonwealth Press, 1913.

Sager, Robert A. W., *The Battle of New Market, May 15, 1864.* Petersburg, WV, copy at NMBSHP.

Scott, J. L., *23rd Battalion Virginia Infantry.* Lynchburg, VA: H.E. Howard, 1991.

————. *Lowry's, Bryan's, and Chapman's Batteries of Virginia Artillery.* Lynchburg, VA: H.E. Howard, 1988.

Smith, James Power, "The Battle of New Market," *Southern Historical Society Papers*, vol. 41, 1916, pp. 152-157.

Stewart, Nancy B., *Rough Winds: The Battle of New Market.* Broadway, VA: self-published, 1994.

Tucker, Spencer C., *Brigadier General John D. Imboden: Confederate Commander in the Shenandoah.* Lexington, KY: University Press of Kentucky, 2003.

Turner, Edward R., *The New Market Campaign.* Richmond, VA: Whittet & Sheperson, 1912.

Wayland, John W., *A History of Rockingham County, Virginia.* Dayton, VA: Ruebush-Elkins, 1912.

————. *A History of Shenandoah County, Virginia.* Baltimore, MD: Regional Publishing, 1998.

————. *Battle of New Market: Memorial Address, 62nd Anniversary of the Battle of New Market, VA.* New Market, VA: Henkel Press, 1926.

————. *Men of Mark and Representative Citizens of Harrisonburg and Rockingham County, Virginia.* Staunton, VA: McClure Co., 1943.

Wert, Jeffry D., *Mosby's Rangers.* New York: Simon and Schuster, 1990.

West, Michael, *30th Battalion Virginia Sharpshooters.* Lynchburg, VA: H.E. Howard, 1995.

Whitehorne, Joseph W. A., *The Battle of New Market.* Washington, DC: U.S. Army Center of Military History, 1988.

Wise, Jennings C., "A Letter Concerning a Noble Tradition," February 8, 1912, *A Scrap Book of Papers*, Richmond, VA: privately printed, 1912.

————. *Virginia Military Institute: Military History.* Lynchburg, VA: J.P Bell, 1915.

Woodward, Harold R., *Defender of the Valley.* Berryville, VA: Rockbridge Publishing, 1996.

Index

About the Author: Charles R. Knight is a native of Richmond, Virginia. He is a former Historical Interpreter at New Market Battlefield State Historical Park, and currently serves as the curator of the Douglas MacArthur Memorial. Charlie has written articles for various Civil War and railroad publications, including *Blue & Gray Magazine, Classic Trains*, and *NRHS Bulletin*. He lives in Norfolk, Virginia, with his wife and son.